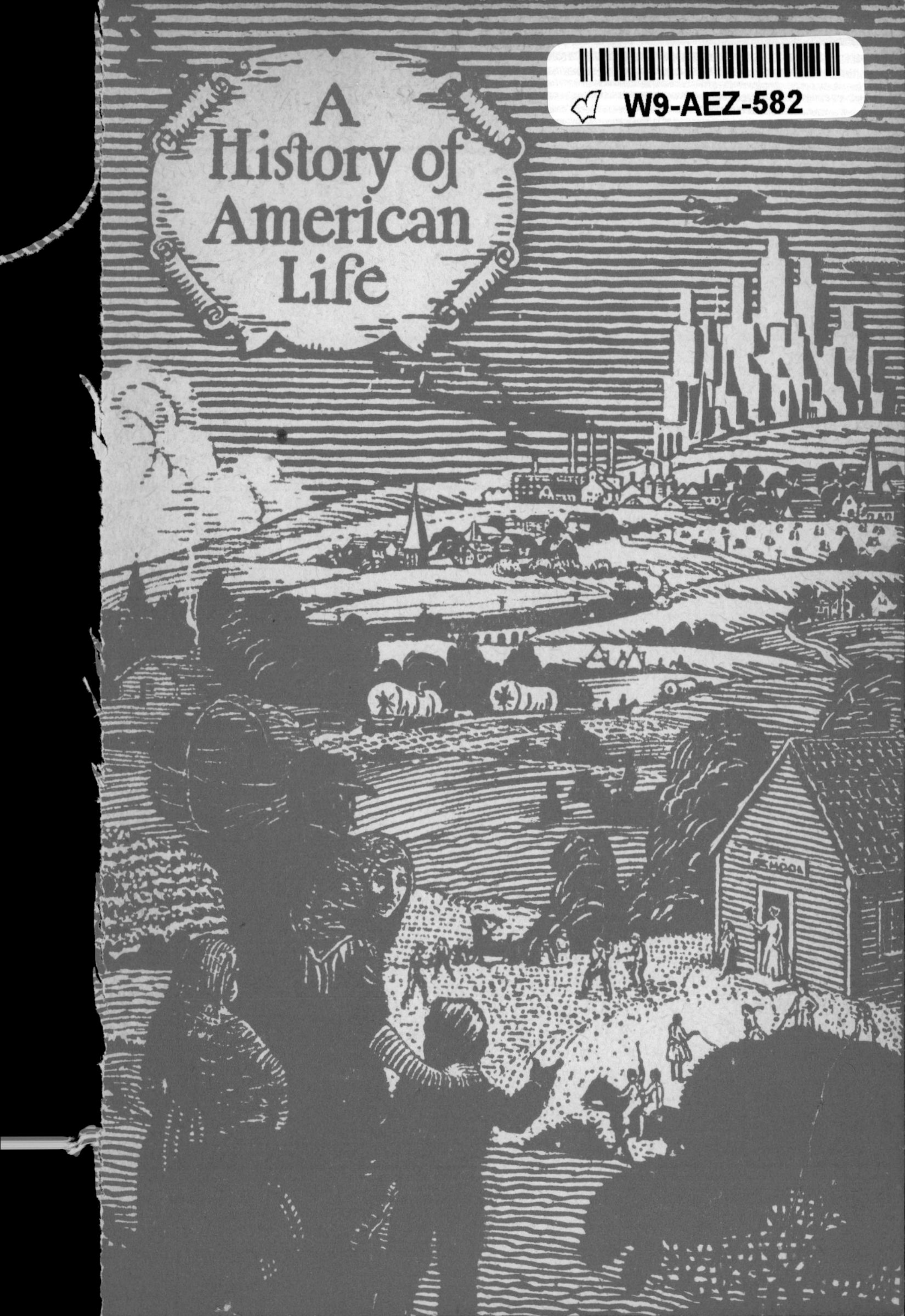
A
History of
American
Life

A HISTORY OF AMERICAN LIFE

IN

TWELVE VOLUMES

ARTHUR M. SCHLESINGER
DIXON RYAN FOX
Editors

ASHLEY H. THORNDIKE CARL BECKER
Consulting Editors

A HISTORY OF AMERICAN LIFE

VOL. I. THE COMING OF THE WHITE MAN, 1492-1848
By Herbert I. Priestley

VOL. II. THE FIRST AMERICANS, 1607-1690
By Thomas J. Wertenbaker

VOL. III. PROVINCIAL SOCIETY, 1690-1763
By James Truslow Adams

VOL. IV. THE REVOLUTIONARY GENERATION, 1763-1790
By Evarts B. Greene

VOL. V. THE COMPLETION OF INDEPENDENCE, 1790-1830
By John Allen Krout and Dixon Ryan Fox

VOL. VI. THE RISE OF THE COMMON MAN, 1830-1850
By Carl Russell Fish

VOL. VII. THE IRREPRESSIBLE CONFLICT, 1850-1865
By Arthur Charles Cole

VOL. VIII. THE EMERGENCE OF MODERN AMERICA, 1865-78
By Allan Nevins

VOL. IX. THE NATIONALIZING OF BUSINESS, 1878-1898
By Ida M. Tarbell

VOL. X. THE RISE OF THE CITY, 1878-1898
By Arthur Meier Schlesinger

VOL. XI. THE QUEST FOR SOCIAL JUSTICE, 1898-1914
By Harold U. Faulkner

VOL. XII. THE GREAT CRUSADE AND AFTER, 1914-1928
By Preston W. Slosson

A HISTORY OF AMERICAN LIFE
Volume XI

THE QUEST FOR SOCIAL JUSTICE
1898-1914

BY

HAROLD UNDERWOOD FAULKNER
ASSOCIATE PROFESSOR OF HISTORY, SMITH COLLEGE

New York
THE MACMILLAN COMPANY

Printed in the United States of America

The conscious recognition of grave national abuses casts a deep shadow across the traditional American patriotic vision. The sincere and candid reformer can no longer consider the national Promise as destined to automatic fulfillment. The reformers themselves are, no doubt, far from believing that whatever peril there is cannot be successfully averted. . . . They proclaim . . . their conviction of an indubitable and a beneficent national future. But they do not and cannot believe that this future will take care of itself. As reformers they are bound to assert that the national body requires for the time being a good deal of medical attendance, and many of them anticipate that even after the doctors have discontinued their daily visits the patient will still need the supervision of a sanitary specialist. He must be persuaded to behave so that he will not easily fall ill again. . . . Consequently, just in so far as reformers are reformers they are obliged to abandon the traditional American patriotic fatalism. The national Promise has been transformed into a closer equivalent of a national purpose, the fulfillment of which is a matter of conscious work.

HERBERT CROLY, *The Promise of American Life* (New York, 1909), 20-21.

CONTENTS

ILLUSTRATIONS

(By the Editors)

PLATE

I. From the Depths

A somewhat melodramatic suggestion of the quest for social justice so strongly urged during the early years of the twentieth century. This wash drawing first appeared as an illustration in *Life* and then in its editor John Ames Mitchell's sociological novel, *The Silent War* (N. Y., 1906), facing page 200. The artist was William Balfour Ker, long on the staff of *Life*, by permission of whose editors it is here reproduced.

II. They See the Promised Land

From an illustration by Corwin Knapp Linson in *McClure's Magazine*, XX, no. 1 (November, 1902), 72. The immigration of that year, about 650,000, had been surpassed only in 1881, but it was to pass the million mark in six different years before the end of 1914 and then, by reason of the war and adverse legislation, continue at a much lower rate.

III. Big Business at Home and Abroad

(a) The Invasion of Europe by Our Trusts, a cartoon by "Zim" (Eugene Zimmerman, 1862-), who for thirty years contributed much to the power of *Judge* as a Republican journal. The artist, apparently with much satisfaction, sees the purpose of big business as the conquest of the world's markets. The figures on the European side indicate that an apprehension of "Americanization" developed much earlier than some have supposed. The cartoon was reproduced in the supplementary advertising pages of the *Cosmopolitan*, XXXIII (1902).

(b) J. Pierpont Morgan (1837-1913) in his banking office at the corner of Broad and Wall streets, New York. From an illustration in *McClure's Magazine*, XVII, no. 6 (October, 1901), frontispiece, drawn from life by William Robinson Leigh, an artist eminent as a figure and portrait painter as well as an illustrator.

IV. The Wars of Labor

(a) Two stickers (each three inches long) circulated by the Industrial Workers of the World about 1913. There were a number of designs, most of them exhorting workers to slow down in production and to annoy their employers as much as possible, especially by sabotage, as a means of im-

PLATE

mediately coercing them into raising wages, though the I. W. W. expected and desired the ultimate abolition of the wage system.

(b) Eviction during the Coal Strike of 1902. These houses rented by the day and tenants might be evicted at any moment. This was one of many ways in which the liberty of wage bargaining was limited. From John Mitchell (1870-1919), *Organized Labor* (Phila., 1903), facing page 260.

V. SOCIAL POLITICS

(a) A cartoon by Edward Windsor Kemble, from *Harper's Weekly*, LVI, whole number 2909 (September 21, 1912), 9. It is entitled "W. J. B.—'Say, Debs, he's hooked everything that belonged to me, and now he's gone off with yours.' " The reference is, of course, to the historic sources of Roosevelt's progressivism. Another marooned swimmer, Robert M. La Follette, might have been included in the cartoon along with Bryan and Debs, for his political wardrobe had also been stolen. During the nineties E. W. Kemble had made a wide reputation for his comic pictures of Southern Negroes. He was considered a master of the fine pen line. In 1903 he turned to political controversy, first for *Collier's* and then for *Harper's Weekly*. He is pictured before his easel in the *Independent*, LIX, 1407 (December 14, 1905).

(b) Liberalism in Cleveland. From Tom L. Johnson, *My Story* (N. Y., 1913), 84. In 1894, while he was still an "unconverted monopolist," he hired a showman's tent in lieu of a hall. Always picturesque, he found this went well with his character and his message and in the early years of the twentieth century he campaigned through the wards of Cleveland again and again under canvas.

VI. JOURNALIST CRUSADERS

(a) Ida M. Tarbell. From a photograph by Gertrude Käsebier which appeared in the *Craftsman*, XIV, no. 1 (April, 1908), facing page 3. Miss Tarbell's *History of the Standard Oil Company*, which was published in *McClure's Magazine* and then as a two-volume book in 1904, and her later articles on the protective tariff and its effect on business, revealed her to be one of the most scholarly writers in the "literature of exposure."

(b) Lincoln Steffens. From a photograph by Hollinger reproduced in *McClure's Magazine*, XXIV, no. 1 (November, 1904), 111. Educated in the state university of his native California and in several European universities he had well learned what politics should be; his experience as a New York City newspaper man during the decade following 1892 suggested some shortcomings in political practice; his investigations early in the twentieth century and the resulting

PLATE

articles made him the leading Muckraker exposing political graft.

VII. MAN FLIES

The Wright brothers' first flight at Kill Devil Hill near Kitty Hawk, North Carolina, December 17, 1903. From an illustration in the *Century Magazine,* LXXVI, no. 5 (September, 1908), 644. The machine, piloted by Orville Wright, has just left the monorail on which it gathered flying speed under the combined thrust of its propellers and of a launching catapult, and now flies for twelve seconds against a twenty-four mile wind. The figure beside it is that of Wilbur Wright. It was the first flight "in the history of the world in which a machine carrying a man had raised itself by its own power into the air in free flight, had sailed forward on a level course without reduction of speed, and had finally landed without being wrecked."

VIII. HOMES

(a) Tenements. An air shaft of the size permitted by the New York law prior to 1901, twenty-eight inches wide, with twenty-five rooms opening solely upon it. The fifty-six-inch shaft when such buildings came together marked the "dumb-bell type," almost the only kind of tenement erected in Manhattan during the previous twenty years. From the *First Report of the Tenement House Department in the City of New York* (N. Y., 1903), I, 134.

(b) A new-law tenement, the shaft twelve and a half feet wide and twenty-five feet long, erected after 1901. From the same, page 136.

(c) An interior in the home of a well-to-do Ohio business man. The cluttered stuffiness of the preceding decades gave way in many places before the onslaught of "mission" furniture, distinguished for clean, square lines but tending to become oversized and clumsy. It was succeeded by the "craftsman" type here represented, which owed much to the tradition of Ruskin, Morris and the neomedievalists, a style appreciated by a generation which had had manual training in school. A generous use of fumed oak, leather, brass studding, open beams, leaded glass and American Indian rugs gave an atmosphere of wholesome and honest sturdiness. Gustav Stickley was its leading exponent. Our illustration is taken from his *What Is Wrought in the Craftsman Shop* (Syracuse, 1904), 57.

IX. THE QUEEN

(a) The frontispiece of Howard Chandler Christy's *The American Girl* (N. Y., 1906). Christy, whose great popularity began with his drawings of the Spanish War done on the battle front, shortly afterward turned all his attention

PLATE

to the American girl, whom he depicted hundreds of times without varying far from the favorite elegant and statuesque type. He regarded her, as he says in his foreword to the book cited above, as a blend of Teutonic sobriety and dignity (mentioned first), English love of home, French smartness (acquired by imitation), and Celtic romanticism and humor.

(b) From an illustration in *Harper's Weekly*, LV, whole number 2851 (August 12, 1911), 18.

X. CHILDREN

(a) "The Night Shift." From a photograph taken in a Pennsylvania glass works and reproduced in *Charities and the Commons*, XV, no. 18 (February 3, 1906), 603. The caption under the picture, which illustrates an article by Scott Nearing, reads, "One week the boys work all day, the next week all night. But night work has its drawbacks. As one Hungarian boy of 14 said after trying it for a year, 'You get too much sleepy and then you get burn.'" Children beginning to work at eleven or twelve of course had little or no school opportunities thereafter.

(b) Girls' section of the Guldlin Playground, Fort Wayne, Indiana. From the *American City*, VI, no. 5 (May, 1912), 716. Typical of recreation centers, largely introduced during this period, this was, like many others, paid for partly by private subscription and partly by a city appropriation.

XI. JOHN DEWEY

The country's leading educational philosopher in the first years of the twentieth century. From a painting by Edwin B. Child, owned by Columbia University.

XII. RELIGIOUS FORCES

(a) The Reverend "Billy" Sunday in a characteristic pose. From a lithograph by George W. Bellows, N. A. (1882-1925), here reproduced by permission of Frederick Keppel and Company. Though chiefly famous for his paintings, especially of athletes and genre groups, represented in nearly every American museum, Bellows made an enviable name also in lithography. See Thomas Beer and others, *George W. Bellows, His Lithographs* (N. Y., 1927).

(b) The First Church of Christ Scientist, Boston, Massachusetts, known as the "Mother Church." The towered edifice on the right is the original church built in 1894 as "a testimonial to our beloved teacher the Reverend Mary Baker Eddy" (1821-1910); but the huge "temple extension" which occupies the foreground was completed and dedicated in 1906, thirty thousand Christian Scientists being present. The ceremonies opened with a testimonial meeting and, says one biographer, "not only of the vanquishment of cancers,

PLATE

consumption, broken limbs, malignant diseases, and paralysis did these votaries of Christian Science testify, but of poverty overcome, victory gained over drunkenness, morphine, and immoral lives." See Sybil Wilbur, *The Life of Mary Baker Eddy* (N. Y., 1908), 355-356. Our picture is from a post card, published by the Christian Science Publishing Society of Boston.

XIII. A HEALING MISSION

A poster used by medical officers supported in large part by a Rockefeller gift, announcing both a warning and an invitation to the people in three towns in Bertie County, near Albemarle Sound, North Carolina. From an article by Walter H. Page in the *World's Work*, XXIV, no. 5 (September, 1912), 506. The article begins as follows: "The discovery by Dr. Charles W. Stiles of the hookworm disease in the United States is the most helpful event in the history of our Southern states."

XIV. VIGOROUS ROMANTICISM IN ART

(a) A portrait of William Merritt Chase (1849-1916) by John Singer Sargent (1856-1925). Chase was the greatest American teacher of art in the early years of the twentieth century. His many students raised a fund for a portrait by Sargent and in 1902 the subject went to London for six sittings with the painter; in 1905 the painting (62 x 41 inches) was presented to the Metropolitan Museum of Art. The painter said it was "more like Chase than Chase himself." Sargent, who always considered himself an American though the son of a New England physician in Florence and spending much of his life in Europe, was thought by many critics the greatest portrait painter of his time, always interested in character, in the "inner face."

(b) "The Mares of Diomedes," by [John] Gutzon [de la Mothe] Borglum. This huge group was certainly the sculptor's masterpiece when it was purchased by James Stillman, the banker, and given by him to the Metropolitan Museum. See *Current Literature*, XL, no. 5 (May, 1906), 501. His later statues of Lincoln became more famous. Borglum was born in Utah and as a youth formed a strong attachment for horses, as one might guess from this group. Combining virility with a fine idealism he well illustrates the conquering spirit of American sculptors at the beginning of the twentieth century.

XV. HISTORICAL ROMANCE ON THE STAGE

"Put up your swords or draw them on Mary Tudor, the sister of your King,"—a scene from Act III of "When Knighthood was in Flower," based on Charles Major's novel by the same name (1898); this illustration is reproduced

PLATE

from the "Theatre Edition" of the book (N. Y., 1907). It was immensely popular in both forms and may well stand for the favorite mode of drama as well as fiction at the turning of the century.

XVI. TWO ASPECTS OF IMPERIALISM

(a) An anti-imperialist cartoon by William H. Walker. For many years following 1898 he contributed social and political cartoons to *Life*, upon whose cover this appeared, LXXXIII, whole number 863 (June 8, 1899), and by permission of whose editors it is herewith reproduced. Competent, accurate line drawing was a feature of that periodical.

(b) The J. Fenimore Cooper School, Sabana Grande, Porto Rico, a sample of the schools built by the United States government in the new insular possessions. From [Samuel McCune Lindsay], *Report of the Commissioner of Education for Porto Rico for 1904* (Washington, 1904). In his article on "The Inauguration of the American Public School System in Porto Rico," in the *Report of the [U. S.] Commissioner of Education for the Year Ending June 30, 1905* (Washington, 1907), I, Professor Lindsay says that under the Spanish régime, "No buildings had been constructed for school purposes. Most of the schools were held in private houses occupied by the teacher, who devoted one room, of such space as he deemed necessary for the purpose, to holding his school or class." 18,243 children were said to be regularly attending school in 1898; 41,798 were reported in 1904. The number of schools was more than doubled and virtually every town of considerable size had a new well-constructed school building. See pp. 297, 307, 342. These schoolhouses bore such names as "J. Fenimore Cooper," "Whittier," "Longfellow," "Washington," "McKinley," etc.

EDITORS' FOREWORD

Less than three score years after the common man won enlarged rights in government and society in the tumultuous days of Andrew Jackson, the democratic principle in America faced another grave crisis. The profound social changes resulting from the growth of giant industry, the dislocations wrought by rapid urbanization, the decline of rural opportunity as the free lands were exhausted, the increasing rapacity of "malefactors of great wealth" and their subservient allies, the political bosses of city, state and nation, the menacing growth of class feeling—all these helped to create a condition of affairs in which the vaunted "unalienable rights" of "life, liberty and the pursuit of happiness" had become the despair of an ever larger proportion of average humanity. As Professor Faulkner says, "To many thoughtful men in the opening years of the twentieth century it seemed that America in making her fortune was in peril of losing her soul."

Against this background of cynical self-seeking and social disorganization the author pictures the tremendous revolution in public opinion and community effort which centered in a new "quest for social justice." The old doctrines of extreme individualism and a purely competitive industrial system, relics of a rural civilization, were breaking down before the new complexities of American life; a Hamiltonian exertion of governmental power had become necessary in order to restore Jeffersonian conditions of equal opportunity. The battle was waged on many fronts. To the traditional Western advocacy of popular rights was now added the aggressive championship of the reform parties in the great urban centers. Half-forgotten leaders flash across Professor Faulkner's pages, winning skirmishes or suffering defeats whose outcome held the public in breathless suspense. Roosevelt and Wilson are seen, not as the makers of an era, but rather as the beneficiaries of an awakening sentiment which reached back to every village and community of the land. The reader is made aware of the tense emotion which stirred the actors and of the dramatic quality which characterized many of their steps and decisions. Yet Professor Faulkner's sympathetic portrayal is tempered by the historian's obligation to appraise as well as to narrate, to set down failures and inconsistencies as well as to record lofty aspirations.

Although American politics had never before been so preoccupied with the vital concerns of the plain people, the social note was as strongly sounded in nearly every other phase of human activity. Under the hammering blows of the Muckrakers captains of business discovered the wisdom of conciliating the consuming public upon whose good will their prosperity rested. Organized labor consolidated its position and, sobered by power, advanced more swiftly the cause of better conditions for the wage-earners. Resolute drives were launched against the squandering of the nation's natural wealth, against the waste of life in industry, against food adulteration and the liquor evil. While women continued their march toward economic and political equality, the generation made perhaps its greatest humanitarian contribution in an energetic concern for the long-neglected rights of childhood.

Organized religion caught the new spirit and, heedless of denominational barriers, gave earnest attention to the exigent problems created by man's inhumanity to man. Novelists and playwrights, after a brief dalliance with the romantic past, turned almost fiercely to the stern realities of the present. Scientists and scholars likewise made their contributions to human welfare; and the expanding interest in sport, along with the growing vogue of the automobile, restored outdoor life to increasing numbers of city-dwelling folk. Even the adventure in overseas imperialism, which was bitterly contested by some as a fateful departure from time-honored American doctrine, was not without its beneficent social aspects, for it led to epoch-making medical discoveries and introduced into the tropics educational and sanitary improvements of incalculable human value.

Basing his conclusions on a wide examination of contemporary accounts and official investigations, Professor Faulkner has brought the multifarious movements and events of the period into a synthesis and has related them to older trends in national development. Many of the achievements reflected similar measures in other lands; America was not living aloof from the world. Yet in the energy, the optimism and sometimes the precipitancy with which the new ideas were put into effect they evidence their authentic American character. The great task of the generation was to put the national house in order. They wrought unmindful of the storm clouds of international strife which loomed just ahead.

A. M. S.
D. R. F.

THE QUEST FOR SOCIAL JUSTICE 1898-1914

THE QUEST FOR SOCIAL JUSTICE

CHAPTER I

THE TURN OF THE CENTURY

To the American people wearied by a quarter-century of economic strife the Spanish-American War came as a welcome relief. If in retrospect the bizarre aspects of the 1890's lend an appearance of "mauve," [1] to the people then living the decade seemed deeply tinged with red, with the dread menace of social upheaval and revolution. The Panic of 1893, the lengthening bread lines, the pitched battles between capital and labor, the threatening growth of Populism, the class war preached by the Bryanites in 1896—all these made the dying years of the century a time of sober thought and grim endeavor. Little wonder, then, that with the mysterious destruction of the battleship *Maine* in Havana Harbor the nation plunged into a great emotional debauch which enabled it, for the moment, to forget its more serious tasks. The war had its Santiago, its Manila Bay and its heroes—Hobson, Roosevelt, Dewey; but it also had its inefficient war department, its Sampson-Schley controversy and its "embalmed-beef" scandal. The conflict at best offered but temporary relief, and as the decade drew to a close the more thoughtful realized that not only were the old problems still before the nation, but new ones had been added, notably the exigent one of imperialism.

As a further complicating factor, America awakened to find herself somewhat in the position of a man who

[1] Thomas Beer, *The Mauve Decade* (N. Y., 1926).

had unexpectedly lost most of his fortune. For three centuries the national social, economic and political life had been dominated by one outstanding influence: an abundance of unoccupied and fertile land. The free land to the west had afforded opportunities for the energetic and an outlet for the discontented. It had absorbed millions of immigrants from Europe and had, by its plentiful eastward shipment of agricultural products, kept the cost of living low. To be sure, the boundless natural resources which were opened up as each succeeding wave of frontiersmen pushed farther westward were exploited in a most wasteful manner, but the incurable optimism and strong individualism which this wealth engendered became a part of the national habit of mind. The mark of the rapidly moving frontier had been strong upon the content and direction of foreign trade, upon the manufacturing, banking and transportation systems; in fact, upon all phases of our economic life.[1] Already in 1890 the unsettled area was so broken into that the frontier line had ceased to exist, and by the close of the decade the nation faced a situation unlike any that had gone before.[2]

The rapidly diminishing supply of good free land, while only one of the forces destined to mold social growth in the new century, was probably the most important. It gave an impetus to intensive and scientific farming and to a more serious consideration of conservation. It portended a type of manufacturing less likely to be a simple supplement to extractive industry, but rather, by the greater use of skilled labor and improved machinery, to carry its processes much farther. As domestic needs caught up with the agricultural products,

[1] F. J. Turner, *The Frontier in American History* (N. Y., 1921); F. L. Paxson, *History of the American Frontier* (Boston, 1924).

[2] C. W. Wright, "The Significance of the Disappearance of Free Land in Our Economic Development," *Am. Econ. Rev.*, XVI, sup., 264-271.

commerce, which had been chiefly concerned with the exportation of raw or semimanufactured materials and the importation of manufactured products, rapidly changed to provide for the importation of raw products and the exportation of manufactured goods, thus laying the foundations for an economic imperialism, of great consequence in the years to come.[1]

With the end of the era of free land, also, the opportunities for the less fortunate to escape from intolerable conditions became more limited; there were evidences of the development of class consciousness and a tightening of the lines of battle in the conflict between capital and labor. With reason many people feared that American conditions were tending to approximate more closely those of the economically advanced nations of Europe.

Fortunately, certain counteracting influences were at work. Though very little good agricultural land in 1898 remained open to settlement,[2] there were nevertheless over five hundred and seventy million acres yet unclaimed, a goodly portion of which might be used for dry farming or be brought into use by irrigation. That this land was rapidly taken up, particularly after the homestead requirement was reduced from five to three years in 1912, is evidenced by the fact that the entries for the twenty-year period following 1898 were much larger than those for the preceding two decades.[3] The good free land might be gone, but cheap land in abundance remained, and for those who still desired free land for general agriculture it was possible, as thousands did, to emigrate to Canada. The twentieth-century immi-

[1] H. U. Faulkner, *American Economic History* (N. Y., 1924), chap. xxv.

[2] Max West, "The Public Domain of the United States," Dept. of Agr., *Yearbook for 1898*, 327.

[3] B. H. Hibbard, *A History of the Public Land Policies* (N. Y., 1924), 396-398.

grant might have to pay for his land, but he might also escape many of the hardships of the first settlers.[1]

The tendency of the federal government to liberalize the land acts, as exemplified by the three-year homestead act of 1912, distinctly benefited the Western farmer.[2] He also profited, directly and indirectly, from the interest of the federal government in conservation and reclamation which developed during the Roosevelt administration, chiefly through the work of such men as Frederick Haynes Newell of the United States geological survey and Gifford Pinchot, head of the bureau of forestry.[3] Of immediate aid to the West was the Newlands act of 1902 which set aside the proceeds from the sale of public lands in sixteen states for use as a fund for the development of irrigation. With the money so obtained contracts were awarded for irrigation purposes, the cost to be defrayed, usually in annual payments, by the beneficiaries, thus making the fund self-perpetuating. By the end of 1914 over a million acres had in this way been added to cultivation, and remarkable engineering projects were under way or completed, including the Shoshone Dam in Wyoming, the Elephant Butte Dam in New Mexico, the Gunnison Tunnel in Colorado, the Arrowrock Dam in Idaho—the highest dam completed up to 1915 in any part of the world—and the Roosevelt Dam in Arizona, the greatest irrigation enterprise yet attempted.[4]

The interest of the federal government in irrigation was but one indication of a new and better day for the West. Although homesteading went on continually, the

[1] C. M. Harger, "Today's Chance for the Western Settler," *Independent*, LXXVIII, 980-982 (Dec. 17, 1904).

[2] *U. S. Statutes at Large*, XXXVII, pt. i, 123. See also Hibbard, *Public Land Policies*, 391 ff.

[3] See F. H. Newell, "Irrigation," Smithsonian Institution, *Ann. Rep. for 1902*, 407-423; Gifford Pinchot, *The Fight for Conservation* (N. Y., 1910).

[4] G. W. James, *Reclaiming the Arid West* (N. Y., 1917), *passim*.

pioneering days for the greater part of the Middle and Far West were over. The hard years of the 1880's and 1890's had temporarily passed and a succession of good harvests after 1897 enabled the farmer to pay his debts, enlarge his operations and improve his facilities. The farmer, who had lived since the Panic of 1893 on the ragged edge of financial solvency, looked forward with renewed hope; between 1900 and 1910 the prices of agricultural products increased by nearly half while the value of farm property doubled.[1] Occasional sod houses were still to be seen on the prairies of Nebraska or the Dakotas, but the typical farm now had its frame house and commodious barns,[2] and the agricultural West, which for three decades had seethed with unrest, showed by its well-kept buildings, its new equipment and improved roads that a new era had come.[3]

There were few well-established farmers who could not afford spring buggies, upholstered furniture, a telephone and even a piano. Though the thousands of villages strung along the railroads might each contain but a single general store, a post office, a schoolhouse, a church and the inevitable "Palace Hotel," all facing the single street like soldiers on dress parade,[4] the near-by farmer was no longer cut off from the world. Better roads, better train service, the spreading routes of rural free delivery and, later, the automobile increased his mobility and his contacts. The women found time for sewing circles and even literary societies, while many of the second generation had college diplomas to hang on

[1] *U. S. Thirteenth Census* (1910), V, 42; *U. S. Fourteenth Census* (1920), VI, 18.

[2] C. M. Harger, "Era of Thrift in the Middle West," *World's Work*, V (1903), 3090-3093.

[3] R. S. Baker, "The New Prosperity," *McClure's*, XV (1900), 86-94.

[4] S. M. Dale, "The West through Eastern Eyes," *Independent*, LVII, 903-909 (Oct. 20, 1904).

the wall.[1] But above all there was a new spirit of optimism and confidence in the future far different from the years of Populism.

The ample prosperity enjoyed by the agricultural regions of the trans-Mississippi West was not universal. Two geographic sections, New England and the East North Central states, showed an absolute decrease in rural population between 1900 and 1910, and in the decade from 1910 to 1920 the same was also true of the Middle Atlantic group.[2] There was, indeed, a "back-to-the-country" movement on the part of a few from the larger cities, but it seldom reached far beyond the fringe of suburbs. Although a majority of the states showed an actual increase in rural population, there was, as compared with urban population, a relative decline during these decades. Of the increase between 1900 and 1910 (nearly 16,000,000) seven tenths was urban, that is, in towns of twenty-five hundred or more. The urban increase, particularly in the larger centers, was chiefly due to foreign immigration, but careful estimates indicate that over three million people moved from rural to urban districts during the first decade of the century.[3] This cityward movement of population, of course, was but the continuation of a trend already well marked in the last decades of the nineteenth century.[4] On the one hand, with the introduction of new agricultural machinery, fewer people were needed in the rural districts;

[1] C. M. Harger, "The Prairie Woman: Yesterday and Today," *Outlook*, LXX, 1008-1012 (April 26, 1902); T. N. Carver, "Life in the Corn Belt," *World's Work*, VII (1903), 4232-4237.

[2] Bureau of the Census, *Abstract of the Thirteenth Census, 1910*, 54 ff.; *U. S. Fourteenth Census* (1920), I, 43 ff.

[3] J. M. Gillette and G. R. Davis, "Measure of Rural Migration and Other Factors of Urban Increase in the United States," Am. Statistical Assoc., *Quar. Publs.*, XIV, 642-652.

[4] See A. M. Schlesinger, *The Rise of the City* (*A History of American Life*, X), chap. iii.

on the other, the city acted like a magnet to draw the more restless and ambitious. The larger group went for better economic opportunities, but the desire for greater educational and social advantages was almost equally potent.[1] Whatever the causes, sociologists saw in the situation not alone a numerical depletion, but a physical and moral decline which boded ill for the future of the countryside as the better stock moved out.[2] Patriots who had been reared on the tradition of the superiority of rural environment were profoundly disturbed. President Roosevelt in 1908 appointed a commission on country life to study the problem, whose work kept interest in the subject alive, if it accomplished little of immediate importance.[3]

While large portions of the nation saw an actual decline in rural population, the urban districts were advancing. Every state in the Union during the first decade of the century showed such a gain and in all but two commonwealths, Montana and Wyoming, the towns grew more rapidly than the country districts. The tendency was evident even in distinctly rural states; in Iowa seventy-seven counties out of ninety-nine showed an aggregate loss of 108,000, while her cities increased.[4] Especially noticeable was the development of such California cities as Berkeley, Los Angeles, Oakland and Pasadena, and the Florida cities of Jacksonville and Tampa, which were profiting by migration from other sections; the New Jersey cities which had caught large numbers of

[1] C. C. Taylor, "Our Rural Population Decline," *Am. Econ. Rev.*, XVI, sup., 158.

[2] E. A. Ross, "Folk Depletion as a Cause of Rural Decline," Am. Sociological Soc., *Publs.*, XI, 21-30.

[3] Theodore Roosevelt, *Autobiography* (N. Y., 1913), 452-456.

[4] Nineteen states reported an urban gain of fifty per cent or more, and twelve states of from thirty to fifty per cent; of the 225 cities having a population of 25,000 in 1910, all but three reported growth. Bureau of the Census, *Abstract of Thirteenth Census*, 58-59, 63-65.

European immigrants and the overflow from New York; and many towns which had grown from the development of industries old and new—Birmingham, Alabama, from iron, Detroit, Flint and Lansing, Michigan, and Akron, Ohio, from automobiles, and Schenectady, New York, from electricity.

In spite of the fact that the frontier line as conceived by the census bureau had disappeared, the population continued to be extremely mobile. In 1910 over one fifth of the people were living in states other than those in which they were born, a mobility slightly higher than in the two previous decades. Although the movement was in all directions, the primary trend was still from east to west, a circumstance which may in part explain the continued rural depletion of the East. The country east of the Mississippi lost more than it gained by this population movement while the trans-Mississippi West benefited. Indeed, over fifty per cent of the population of ten Western states were born elsewhere.[1] Notwithstanding the large migration to the Pacific Coast in the years following the discovery of gold, the proportion of native population born outside was greater in 1910 than in any preceding census back to and including 1870. California, for instance, contained people from every state, mainly agriculturists who had sold out to begin life anew. East of the Mississippi the heaviest migrations of native stock were to New Jersey and Florida, the former because of the rapid suburban and manufacturing development, and the latter because of agricultural extension and its mounting popularity as a winter resort. The Negro migration, which was to reach its height in the war years 1916-1917, was also in evidence.[2] The move-

[1] Bureau of the Census, *Abstract of Thirteenth Census*, 170, 172 ff.

[2] See P. W. Slosson, *The Great Crusade and After* (*A History of American Life*, XII), 253-255.

ment was both north and west and was participated in not only by the manual workers of the race but also by the "talented tenth." [1] The most intelligent of the race gravitated chiefly to the colored districts of the great Northern cities where their separation from the whites was even more complete than in the South.

In spite of a population movement similar to that affecting other sections of the country, the South by 1898 had achieved a degree of stabilization unknown since *ante-bellum* days. Economically the section had definitely turned its eyes toward manufacturing. Although the production of iron remained about stationary, the South doubled her output of steel between the years 1903 and 1914 and absorbed most of the tremendous growth of cotton spinning during the period.[2] Charlotte, North Carolina, by the close of the century was already the hub of a spinning district containing within a radius of a hundred miles over two million spindles. Columbia, South Carolina, was another important center, while Greenville, which two decades earlier had been an unimportant country market town, commanded within a twenty-mile radius more than half a million spindles employing nearly twelve thousand operatives.[3] Birmingham in 1898 was said to be the third largest iron-shipping point in the world.[4]

The rapid economic development of the South afforded new opportunities for the middle class and profoundly affected the life of the poorer whites. Though the cotton mills, manned almost entirely by whites, in-

[1] C. G. Woodson, *A Century of Negro Migration* (Wash., 1918), chap. viii; U. S. Department of Labor, *Negro Migration in 1916-1917* (Wash., 1919); Bureau of the Census, *Abstract of Thirteenth Census*, 174.

[2] V. S. Clark, *History of Manufactures in the United States* (Carnegie Inst., *Contribs. to Am. Econ. History*, N. Y., 1929), III, 26, 172.

[3] Clark, *History of Manufactures*, III, 175.

[4] Clark, *History of Manufactures*, III, 25.

volved child labor and ruthless exploitation, they also enabled the poor white to escape from the hillside farm and opened his eyes to a new world. His political gains, however, were more immediate than his economic or social. To keep the Negro in subserviency, it was necessary to consolidate poor and middle-class whites and these groups found themselves endowed with new political importance.[1] While the abler Southerners threw their energies into economic development, an inferior type seized the reins of political power. "Rabble-rousing" politicians of the stamp of J. K. Vardaman of Mississippi, Jeff Davis of Arkansas, Hoke Smith of Georgia and Cole Blease of South Carolina looked to the poor and middle class for support and found it a successful vote-getting device to perpetuate the Negro question as a political issue and deprecate movements for the uplift of the race.[2]

Though the white society of the South was in a better position than it had been in many years, the Negro race, comprising approximately one third of the population, entered the most discouraging period since its emancipation in 1865. By such devices as intimidation, literacy and character tests, taxation requirements and the grandfather clause, it was being effectively disfranchised in most Southern states. It was estimated that of 181,471 Negro males of voting age in Alabama in 1900 only 3000 were registered.[3] Through the tenant and credit systems, which had developed with the break-up of the old plantations, and the widespread custom of allowing fines for petty crimes to be worked out for the person who paid them, many Negroes had become reduced to a

[1] E. G. Murphy, *The Problems of the Present South* (N. Y., 1904), chap. i.

[2] R. S. Baker, *Following the Color Line* (N. Y., 1908), chap. xi.

[3] C. W. Chesnutt, "The Disfranchisement of the Negro," B. T. Washington and others, *The Negro Problem* (N. Y., 1903), 86.

state of virtual peonage.[1] Segregation in conveyances and public places, which had been common since the eighties, was followed in the years 1911-1913 by ordinances in many cities legally establishing white and colored districts in the professed hope that such a policy might promote racial harmony and purity.[2] Negro-baiting politicians were emulated by Southern authors like the Reverend Thomas Dixon who in *The Leopard's Spots* (1902) and other novels intentionally fanned the fires of racial animosity. Reminiscent of the polemics of the slavery struggle, a religious publishing house in St. Louis lent its imprint to a book which maintained that the Negro, though endowed with articulate speech and hands, was in reality a beast without a soul.[3] Many respectable churchmen condoned the extralegal methods of dealing with Negro crime, while organized labor, sympathetic in its earlier years toward the race, cooled perceptibly.[4] The animosity which burst forth following Roosevelt's invitation to Booker T. Washington to lunch with him at the White House in 1901 astonished many, including the principals,[5] but the holocaust of lynchings which characterized the years 1900 and 1901,[6] as well as the growing frequency of race riots, should have been indicative of the increasing tension.

Despite these and other less spectacular methods of

[1] Baker, *Following the Color Line*, 97-98.

[2] G. T. Stephenson, "The Segregation of the White and Negro Races in Cities by Legislation," *Natl. Municipal Rev.*, III, 496-504.

[3] Charles Carroll, *The Negro a Beast or in the Image of God*, published by the American Book and Bible House, St. Louis, in 1901.

[4] C. H. Wesley, *Negro Labor in the United States* (N. Y., 1927), chap. ix.

[5] B. F. Riley, *The Life and Times of Booker T. Washington* (N. Y., 1916), 167-168.

[6] Two hundred and fourteen were lynched in these two years. *World Almanac for 1928*, 327. On lynching, see also Walter White, *Rope and Faggot* (N. Y., 1929), and Scott Nearing, *Black America*. (N. Y., 1929). 197 ff.

"keeping the Negro in his place," these years, which marked the nadir for the black man, were not without hope of a brighter future. The race itself was steadily advancing. The proportion of illiterates declined from 44.5 per cent in 1900 to 30.4 in 1910. The number operating farms in the South grew by a fifth between 1910 and 1920 and the number of owners by almost as much, a rate four times as great as the increase of Negro population in the rural districts. The proportion engaged in skilled labor also showed a notable advance, and the race could now boast of individuals of outstanding talent in many fields of endeavor.[1] Even the number of lynchings showed a tendency to decline though no year yielded fewer than forty-nine such crimes.

Within its own ranks, moreover, the race had able leaders, although leaders who differed sharply as to methods. On the one hand was Booker T. Washington who, as in earlier years, preached Negro salvation through education and hard work. "The race, like the individual, that makes itself indispensable," said he, "has solved most of its problems." [2] On the other hand was the younger group who chafed at the ostracism and persecution of their race by the whites and demanded equality of opportunity and equality before the law. The revolt of the younger intellectuals against the conservative policies of Washington found expression in July, 1905, at a Niagara Falls conference when a "statement, complaint and prayer" was issued to the country and an organization formed to carry on the agitation for Negro rights. Though the need was great, the time was not yet ripe, and the Niagara Movement, as such, died within

[1] Booker T. Washington, educator; W. E. B. Du Bois, sociologist; Charles W. Chesnutt, novelist; Paul L. Dunbar, poet; H. O. Tanner, artist.

[2] Speech before the National Education Association in St. Louis, June 30, 1904.

three or four years.[1] It did, however, bring to the front a new leader in W. E. Burghardt Du Bois, a mulatto of fine intelligence and an unusual gift of literary expression. Born in 1868 at Great Barrington, Massachusetts, Du Bois had been educated at Fisk, Harvard and Berlin. After winning in 1895 the degree of Doctor of Philosophy from Harvard, for which he presented a notable thesis on the *Suppression of the African Slave-Trade* (N. Y. 1896), he spent the next fifteen years as professor of history and economics at Atlanta University, engaging in various sociological studies and contributing frequently to leading magazines. When the Niagara Movement disintegrated, he allied himself with the National Association for the Advancement of Colored People (organized 1909-1911) as director of publications and research, where he speedily became the chief source of strength to the left wing, an element which had gathered to itself a large majority of the "talented tenth." Its organ, the *Crisis,* carried on the policy, laid down years earlier by Du Bois, that "persistent manly agitation is the way to liberty." [2]

Of less significance than the Negroes were the representatives of the other nonwhite races in the nation. Although the Indian population in 1898 was perhaps as large as it had been when the continent was discovered, the problem of the red man interested the nation but little. In Oklahoma the members of the Five Civilized Tribes were tasting the delights of political self-government along with their white fellow citizens and were helping to prepare the territory for the boon of statehood. Elsewhere the government, under the policy

[1] *Outlook,* LXXX, 795 (July 29, 1905); Benjamin Brawley, *A Short History of the American Negro* (rev. edn., N. Y., 1919), 167-168.

[2] Baker, *Following the Color Line,* chap. x; National Association for the Advancement of Colored People, *Tenth Annual Report* (1919).

embodied in the Dawes act of 1887, sought gradually to break down the reservation system of communal living and make the Indian economically independent.[1] Many of the individuals who were thus granted citizenship abused their new-found liberty by drinking to excess and selling their votes to unscrupulous white politicians. To others, more capable and ambitious, the twenty-five-year period necessary for final ownership of the land allotments proved a discouragement. In 1906 the Dawes law was modified by the Burke act which authorized the bestowal of full property title upon deserving individuals without awaiting the specified period. By withholding citizenship until full ownership was granted the new law also rendered illegal the sale of intoxicants to Indians during the period of probation.[2]

Despite the well-intentioned efforts of Congress and the opportunities for education extended by the government, the red man did not assimilate the white man's civilization as rapidly as his friends had expected. The blame did not lie wholly with the Indians, but must be shared by the officials on whom the government relied for the execution of its Indian policy. The conditions, of course, were worst among the tribes which persisted in clinging to reservation life. Desperately poor, scourged by tuberculosis and trachoma, the descendants of the once proud race continued to be exploited by the white man and but inadequately protected by the government.[3]

Owing to the national policy of exclusion adopted in the eighties the question of Chinese immigration had

[1] Schlesinger, *Rise of the City*, chap. xii.

[2] *U. S. Statutes at Large*, XXXIV, 182. Not until 1924 did the United States grant citizenship to all Indians. *U. S. Statutes at Large*, XLIII, 253.

[3] Lewis Meriam and others, *The Problem of Indian Administration* (Institute for Government Research, *Studies in Administration*, Balt., 1928), summarizes the situation at the time of publication.

ceased to agitate the people. Chinese, of course, continued to slip in after 1898, but their number was negligible. If, however, the problem of one Oriental people was solved, that of another, the Japanese, was just beginning. Comprising but a bare two thousand in 1890, they already numbered twenty-four thousand in 1900 and had increased to seventy-two thousand by 1910.[1] They formed, to be sure, but a tiny part of the population of even the Pacific Coast, where they were chiefly to be found, but wherever they went their lower standard of living and superior industry brought them into deadly competition with the white wage-earner and small farmer. Just as the earlier agitation against the Chinese had emanated chiefly from organized labor, so now it was the same group which gave strength to the Asiatic Exclusion League, formed in 1905, and made it possible for the labor government of San Francisco to segregate the Chinese and Japanese children in a separate school. The famous order of the San Francisco board of education of October, 1906, affected only ninety-eight Japanese children, but it brought vigorous protests from the Japanese government. President Roosevelt exercised pressure upon the school committee to revoke the order, and in the next year a temporary quietus was put to the matter by an executive arrangement between the two governments negotiated by Secretary of State Root and Ambassador Takahira, in which the Japanese government agreed not to issue passports to skilled and unskilled laborers desiring to go to the continental United States.

The "Gentlemen's Agreement" offered a *modus operandi,* if it did not provide a solution. On its part the Japanese government acted in good faith, refusing to issue, after 1920, passports to women married *in absentia*

[1] U. S. Department of Commerce, *Statistical Abstract for 1920,* 41.

who desired to join their husbands, the "picture brides" whose coming the Californians so bitterly opposed. The anti-Japanese agitation in California, however, did not subside; the legislature at various times urged the extension of the Chinese exclusion laws to the Japanese and, by acts of 1913 and 1920, the Japanese were effectively debarred from acquiring either by ownership or lease agricultural and other real property. The whole matter was to reach its climax later during the Coolidge administration.[1]

The anti-Japanese furor on the Pacific Coast was but the most spectacular aspect of a growing demand for immigration restriction. The American Federation of Labor more than once offered suggestions as to how the "present stimulated influx of cheap labor so ruinous to the workers here" [2] might be prevented; farmers' organizations also protested against the rapid inflow, while patriotic societies viewed with alarm the increasing inundation of people so different in racial and intellectual background.[3] From 1820, when the first immigration records were kept, until 1898, over seventeen million aliens had come to America and this tide, stemmed by the Panic of 1893, again flowed freely in the prosperous years which followed the Spanish-American War. From 1903 until 1914 there were but two years in which the migration fell below seven hundred thousand, and in 1905, 1906, 1907, 1910, 1913 and 1914 it rose beyond the million mark. There were no less than 13,500,000 inhabitants of the United States in 1910 born in other countries, about one seventh of the whole, while an

[1] R. L. Garis, *Immigration Restriction* (N. Y., 1927), chap. x; G. M. Stephenson, *A History of American Immigration, 1820-1924* (N. Y., 1926), chap. xxi; Slosson, *Great Crusade and After,* 300-301.

[2] American Federation of Labor, *Report of the Proceedings of the Twenty-Ninth Annual Convention* (1909), 183.

[3] F. J. Warne, *The Tide of Immigration* (N. Y., 1916), 258 ff.

equal number were native whites of foreign parentage. An additional 6.5 per cent were of mixed native and foreign parentage.[1] In two sections of the country, New England and the Middle Atlantic states, the foreign-born white and the native white of foreign or mixed parentage comprised a majority of the population.

While the accession of almost a million newcomers a year did not materially change the ratio of the foreign-born population to the rest, it was accompanied by a significant shift in source that portended a racially new America. For a decade or more an increasing number of immigrants had been coming from eastern and southeastern Europe, especially Austria-Hungary, Italy and Russian Poland, but it was not until 1896 that the "new immigration" first outnumbered the old. So quickly did it develop that it already provided over half the foreign arrivals in the 1890's. During the first decade of the new century only about one in twenty-five was furnished respectively by the German Empire, England and Ireland, while in the year 1907, which marked the greatest alien influx in our history, the new immigration contributed over four fifths of the total. To the poverty-stricken Italian peasant, the subject Slav of Austria-Hungary and the relentlessly persecuted Jew of Russia, the New World held out hope, while the improvement of transportation facilities speeded the movement. In America the unexampled industrial expansion and the attendant prosperity after 1898 formed the chief magnet, but, as earlier, the desire of the oppressed people was greatly whetted by the immigration agents of steamship companies, land-grant railroads and the illegal activities of labor contractors.

Unwilling to lower his standard of living to that of the south European, the peasant and workman of north-

[1] Bureau of the Census, *Abstract of Thirteenth Census*, 187 ff.

ern and western Europe—formerly the backbone of American immigration—tended to stay at home. Moreover, the remarkable industrial expansion of Germany accompanied with wise social legislation, the improvement of conditions in England, and the agrarian policy of the British government in Ireland helped to ease the situation in northwestern Europe at the time when the reservoir of free land was giving out in America. That the new immigration would modify the structure and complicate the social problems of twentieth-century America was quickly evident. The economic and educational strata of the new immigrant on the whole were much lower than that which characterized earlier accessions. The illiteracy of those over fourteen who arrived in the decade 1899-1909 was nearly twenty-seven per cent, more than half of the largest single group, the south Italians, being illiterate.[1] Since only a small proportion of the new arrivals could speak English, the great majority of them—nearly two thirds—crowded into the cities among their own kind where they lived in compact colonies isolated from American influences.[2] Assimilation was further retarded by the fact that at least one third of them planned to return to their home country.

Yet in spite of what appeared to be almost insuperable obstacles Americanization went on rapidly. The more ambitious immigrants were anxious to make a place for themselves in the new country and give their children a larger chance. The federal immigration commission found that over half of the school children in thirty leading cities had foreign-born fathers,[3] and there seemed to be some basis for the belief that American environment affected even the physical characteristics of

[1] J. W. Jenks and W. J. Lauck, *The Immigration Problem* (N. Y., 1911), 35.

[2] Immigration Commission, *Reports* (Wash., 1911), III, 421.

[3] Immigration Commission, *Reports*, I, 43.

the second generation.[1] But the assimilation of the foreigner was biological as well as cultural. Although there was some difference in the rapidity with which the native American stock mixed its blood with the new immigrant, what Professor E. A. Ross has called the "Great Dilution" was going on.[2] The United States of the twentieth century was destined racially to be a mixture of all Europe, not merely of its western fringe, including, of course, a strong infusion of African blood. The future American, it was predicted, would be shorter in stature, swarthier of skin and more "temperamental" in disposition.

This racial change was hastened by the declining birth rate of the American family. Psychological, sociological and economic explanations were advanced for this,[3] but the fact remained that in the higher ranks of native stock the size of the family was becoming smaller. The end of the era of free land, the higher standard of living, the increasing bitterness of economic competition, the development of urban life, played their parts as well as the fact that the large immigration tended to fill any existing population vacuum. In most parts of the country large families were no longer economically profitable, and as they became undesirable they became unfashionable. That a growing number of city apartments found it possible to cater exclusively to childless couples was a significant sign of the times, and many were horrified to discover that the "best" of the native American stock was not perpetuating itself. The interest which scientists had in the matter was broadened to the common man by

[1] Immigration Commission, *Reports*, I, 44.

[2] E. A. Ross, "The Value Rank of the American People," *Independent*, LVII, 1063 (Nov. 10, 1904).

[3] "Birth-Rates," W. D. P. Bliss, ed., *The New Encyclopedia of Social Reform* (N. Y., 1908), 116-118; Lydia K. Commander, *The American Ideal* (N. Y., 1907); E. L. Thorndike, "The Decrease in the Size of American Families," *Pop. Sci. Mo.*, LXIII (1903), 64-70.

Roosevelt's denunciation of "race suicide,"[1] but the latter's exhortations could hardly stay the tendency. Studies of the census of 1910 showed not only that the fecundity of immigrant women was higher than that of native Americans, but in general that the birth rate among immigrants from southern and eastern Europe was higher than among those coming from northwestern Europe. At the same time it appeared that immigrant women of the second generation in the cities followed the example of their native sisters in curtailing the number of children, thus ever passing on to the newer arrivals the burden of race propagation.[2]

In spite of continuous agitation no radical departure in immigration policy took place up to the opening of the World War, but there was a steady movement toward increased restriction. A general revision of the immigration law in 1903 was characterized by an increase in the number of excluded persons—with especial attention to prostitutes and, because of the circumstances of President McKinley's assassination, to anarchists—by more stringent regulations for the return of aliens who entered illegally, and by provisions for better inspection.[3] In 1907 the excluded list was extended to include imbeciles, feeble-minded, persons afflicted with tuberculosis and other groups, including those whose passage was paid for by some corporation, association or government.[4] These laws, however, did not noticeably affect the incoming stream, and the groups who opposed, as they put it, making the United States "the world's dumping ground" concentrated upon a demand for a literacy test. Both parties indorsed this test in their platforms, but

[1] Roosevelt, *Autobiography*, 176 ff.

[2] Jenks and Lauck, *Immigration Problem*, 60 ff., summarizes vol. xxviii of the *Reports* of the Immigration Commission.

[3] *U. S. Statutes at Large*, XXXII, pt. i, 1213 ff.

[4] *U. S. Statutes at Large*, XXXVI, 1363, 1442.

laws providing for it were vetoed by Cleveland in 1897, by Taft in 1913 and by Wilson in 1915. In the meantime the nation had been supplied with an immense amount of data on the subject in a forty-one-volume report by the immigration commission, a report which was to have an important influence in later years.

Any effort to understand the economic and social realities of American life at the opening of the century would be incomplete without a knowledge of the distribution of wealth and material well-being. The census of 1900 placed the total wealth of the nation at approximately eighty-eight and one-half billions, but statistics purporting to show the distribution are exceedingly meager. According to a study made in 1890, seven eighths of the families held but one eighth of the wealth, while one per cent of the people owned more than the remaining ninety-nine; [1] and a decade later there appeared to be little change. A study made of estates probated in five Wisconsin counties during the year 1900 revealed the fact that the poorest two thirds of the population owned only five or six per cent of the wealth and the poorest four fifths scarcely ten per cent, while the richest one per cent owned about half of the property probated.[2] As these Wisconsin counties comprised both rural communities and cities, including Milwaukee, and as the findings agree with similar studies made at different periods in Massachusetts, they may be taken as typical. They point inevitably to the fact that fully eighty per cent of the people lived on the margin of existence while the wealth of the nation was owned by the remaining twenty per cent.

Measured by the standards of today the wages of the

[1] C. B. Spahr, *The Present Distribution of Wealth in the United States* (N. Y., 1896), 65.

[2] W. I. King, *The Wealth and Income of the People of the United States* (N. Y., 1915), 72-87, 90-105.

average worker at the conclusion of the last century seem small indeed. According to the carefully tabulated returns of the census of 1900, only occasional groups of workers were paid as much as $18 a week, two thirds of the male workers over sixteen years of age receiving less than $12.50.[1] The interstate commerce commission reported that eighty-two per cent of the million persons, exclusive of officers, employed on railroads received less than $2.05 per day.[2] Throughout the nation the average wage was less than two dollars a day, and only the most highly paid skilled worker was able to obtain three. Specialists studying wage scales in 1904 and 1905 agreed that at least two thirds of the adult male workers failed to obtain $600 a year,[3] and their findings were in part verified by the census of manufactures of 1905.[4]

In checking the wage statistics against prices to determine the standard of living the student finds himself in a different world. Those were the days when beef sold for 17½ cents a pound, fresh pork for 14, eggs for 21½ cents a dozen, potatoes at $1.14 a bushel, flour at $4.69 a barrel and hard coal at $6.65 a ton. A good pair of shoes could be bought for two dollars and an excellent suit of clothes for twenty.[5] Low as these prices seem, the income of the average wage-earner failed to meet them. Dr. Ryan in 1906 named $600 as the absolute yearly minimum; Chapin in 1909 placed it at $900 for New York City, and Streightoff in 1911 put $600 as the low-

[1] Bureau of the Census, *Employees and Wages* (*Special Rep. for 1900*), ci-civ.

[2] Interstate Commerce Commission, *Thirteenth Annual Report* (1899), 34, 40.

[3] J. A. Ryan, *A Living Wage* (N. Y., 1906), 162; W. E. Walling, "The New Unionism the Problem of the Unskilled Worker," Am. Acad. of Polit. and Social Sci., *Annals*, XXIV, 300.

[4] Bureau of the Census, *Census of Manufactures for 1905*, pt. iv, 645.

[5] These figures are for Massachusetts for 1902, a state in which foodstuffs and coal are comparatively high, and represent the annual average prices. Commission on the Cost of Living, *Report* (Boston, 1910), 64.

est in the South and $650 as the "extreme low limit" in the cities of the rest of the country.[1] Yet these minima were achieved by a comparatively few wage-earners. After an exhaustive analysis of the available data Robert Hunter went so far as to conclude in 1904 that not less than ten million persons in the United States lived in poverty.[2] Hunter's estimates may have been a little high,[3] but they reveal a situation far different from the roseate picture of the land of promise which immigrant agents had conjured in the minds of the workers of Europe. The oft-repeated statement that the American laborer was better off than his fellow workman in Europe was undoubtedly true for the country as a whole, but the descriptions by Jacob Riis of poverty in New York equaled, if they did not surpass, the statistics collected by Booth and Rowntree for London.[4]

Low as were real wages in 1900 they were destined to decline during the next decade. The years from the Panic of 1873 to the close of the century had seen a fall in the cost of living and a rise in the purchasing power of wages. Postwar deflation, combined with currency contraction and rapid exploitation of natural resources as the frontier moved onward, had been primarily responsible, but as these conditions were modified the cost of living began to mount. Population and demand were catching up with production, and at the same time the discovery of gold in 1897 in the Klondike region of Alaska and the introduction of improved methods of extracting gold from inferior ores tended to inflate the cur-

[1] Ryan, *Living Wage*, chap. vii; R. C. Chapin, *The Standard of Living in New York City* (N. Y., 1909), 246; F. H. Streightoff, *The Standard of Living among the Industrial People of America* (Boston, 1911), 162. See also the *Monthly Labor Review*, I, no. 4, 18-21.

[2] Robert Hunter, *Poverty* (N. Y., 1904), 60 ff.

[3] J. L. Gillin, *Poverty and Dependency* (N. Y., 1921), 36.

[4] J. A. Riis, *A Ten Years' War* (Boston, 1900), chap. ii; Hunter, *Poverty*, 73 ff.

rency.[1] To these primary causes economists suggested contributory influences, such as the rising standard of living, the exhaustion of natural resources, the relative decline of agriculture and the urban trend, uneconomical and wasteful production and distribution, the increasing burden upon society of accident, disease, pauperism, crime and militarism, the high tariffs and the arbitrary raising of prices by trusts and of wages by labor unions.[2] If the last three items are discarded as controversial, there still remain sufficient forces to explain an era of rising prices. The federal commission on industrial relations reported that, while the nation's wealth between 1890 and 1912 had increased from sixty-five to one hundred and eighty-seven billions, or one hundred and eighty-eight per cent, the aggregate income of wage-earners in manufacturing, mining and transportation had risen only ninety-five per cent.[3] Rubinow believed in 1914 that real wages "were rapidly falling," [4] but a more conservative conclusion is that of Professor Woods when he said that, despite higher pay, "the American worker found himself at the outbreak of the World War handicapped by a slight but unmistakable decline in the purchasing power of his wages. They sufficed to buy somewhat less than had the wages of the year 1900." [5] The phrase "high cost of living" was used so universally that it even found its way into popular songs.

The decline in real wages, however, did not necessar-

[1] Mark Sullivan, *Our Times* (N. Y., 1926-), I, 299.

[2] Massachusetts Commission on the Cost of Living, *Report* (Boston, 1910), 194 ff.

[3] The commission also pointed out that the wage-earners' share of the net product of industry in the case of manufactures had declined from 44.9 per cent in 1889 to 40.2 in 1909. Commission on Industrial Relations, *Final Report* (Wash., 1916), I, 21.

[4] I. M. Rubinow, "The Recent Trend of Real Wages," *Am. Econ. Rev.*, IV, 194 ff.

[5] E. B. Woods, "Have Wages Kept Pace with the Cost of Living?," Am. Acad. of Polit. and Social Sci., *Annals*, LXXXIX, 135-147.

ily mean a lowering of the standard of living. Improved machinery and large-scale manufacturing decreased the cost of production and helped to overcome the rising prices of raw materials. The nation's wealth was advancing by leaps and bounds, and some portion of it in addition to mere wages benefited the average man. Those common enterprises in which the whole people participated, such as the public schools, roads, water supply and sewage disposal, showed improvement during the period and helped to diffuse the benefits of the rapid production of wealth. The same was true of the large contributions which the new millionaires were making to higher education, medical research and other endowments. The ethics of a civilization which allowed comparatively few men to accumulate most of the wealth and then dole part of it back in charity might well be questioned, as indeed it was, but the fact remained that some portion of it found its way back to the mass of the people.

As important in raising the standard of living as the mere multiplication of wealth were the new inventions which were making life more comfortable. These had to do particularly with time and labor-saving devices and providentially were of benefit to the housewife and farmer as well as to the factory mechanic. In the home the gas stove was rapidly driving out the coal range, and electricity was eliminating both the oil lamp and gas illumination, while electric power and the gasoline engine were destined ere long to modify farm life. That great giant, electric power, whose diverse applications were to feature the early decades of the new century, had already speeded city and interurban transportation, pointing unmistakably to a civilization of ever greater mobility. As American life became more complex and economic competition keener, a certain compensation was afforded by myriad inventions which were making easier and more pleasant the art of living.

To a thoughtful visitor America at the turn of the century must have appeared a land of curious contradictions. Blessed as it was with unparalleled economic resources and opportunities, its wealth, nevertheless, was almost as unevenly distributed as that of Europe and its slums nearly as desperate. In spite of the belief cherished by those who sought our shores that America was inhabited by a prosperous and happy people, the nation was just recovering from a long period of economic unrest which had but recently culminated in the campaign of 1896. In a nation boasting the most widespread system of free education in the world, the census of 1900 found over six million illiterates.[1] On the one hand was an idealism and humanitarianism which led millionaires to lavish endowment upon educational and charitable institutions; on the other, a carelessness of life which put America behind all civilized nations in the number of unnecessary industrial accidents. In no nation was the status of the women higher or the lot of the child better, yet social legislation respecting women was far behind that of other progressive nations and child labor existed under conditions too horrible to believe.[2] Yet, at a time when the successful business man represented the American ideal and the people seemed lost in a scramble for wealth, the nation was girding itself for a mighty drive against special privilege and for an attempt to achieve some degree of social justice. Crude and chaotic as was this civilization in many respects, its essential soundness became manifest in the next decade and a half as the rising social consciousness of the people directed the national energy into fresh and nobler channels.

[1] Bureau of the Census, *Abstract of the Thirteenth Census*, 239.
[2] Hunter, *Poverty*, 244, 356-357.

CHAPTER II

BIG BUSINESS GROWS BIGGER

As the nation recovered from the Panic of 1893 and swung buoyantly on the upgrade of a new business cycle, an unprecedented era of prosperity and industrial expansion burst on the country. McKinley, trumpeted before the election as the "advance agent of prosperity," was scarcely inaugurated before he issued a call for a special session of Congress to revise the tariff. The Wilson-Gorman act of 1894 was speedily wiped from the statute books and for it was substituted the high Dingley tariff, destined to a longer life than any tariff law to date.[1] The bitterness of the free-silver campaign of 1896 delayed for a short time the formal establishment of the gold standard, but this came in the currency act of 1900.[2] An administration so receptive to the wishes of "big business" was not likely to enforce either the Sherman anti-trust law or the equally feeble interstate commerce act. With the nation ready for another period of economic advance and the political machinery in the hands of a party committed to *laissez faire* and the Dingley tariff, the way was cleared for an epoch of gigantic industrial development.

Though the prosperity of the new era, as we have seen, was shared by the farmer, its richest rewards fell to

[1] The Dingley tariff of 1897 raised the average level to 57 per cent, the highest up to that time since the Civil War. It maintained in general the lower rates of 1894 on metals, but high duties were reimposed on raw wool and hides, while the rates on linens, silks, woolens, pottery and sugar were raised.

[2] *U. S. Statutes at Large*, XXXI, 45.

the industrialist. By 1898 the United States had become preëminently a manufacturing nation, the greatest in the world. Tendencies long evident were now culminating. From 1850 to 1900, while the population trebled and the value of agricultural products kept close pace, manufactures had increased elevenfold in value. A variety of factors had made this possible—cheap foodstuffs, cheap raw materials, cheap immigrant labor, an expanding market and a high protective tariff. Financial power shifted steadily from agriculture to industry and from the country to the city, and with the shift in wealth went that of political power.

Industrialization was accompanied by a pronounced movement toward concentration of ownership. After the "trust"—in the technical sense of the term—had been outlawed by the courts in the 1880's, the form usually taken was that of the holding company, a corporate organization set up for the purpose of holding stock in various branches of the same business and, by this means, controlling them. But under whatever form consolidation took place, the process went on with little interruption, and was the outstanding feature of American economic life at the opening of the new century. In 1904 John Moody listed 318 "greater" or "lesser" industrial trusts representing mergers of nearly 5300 distinct plants and a capitalization of over seven billions.[1] Seven of the greater trusts—the Amalgamated Copper Company (formed in 1899), the American Smelting and Refining Company (1899), the American Sugar

[1] Of these 318 industrial trusts, 236 had been incorporated since January 1, 1898 (170 of them organized under New Jersey laws), five sixths of the capital being held by those dating since the beginning of 1898. John Moody, *The Truth about the Trusts* (N. Y., 1904), 486. For another contemporary tabulation of combinations, see Luther Conant, jr., "Industrial Consolidations in the United States," Am. Statistical Assoc., *Publs.*, VII, 208-217.

Refining Company (1891), the Consolidated Tobacco Company (1901), the International Mercantile Company (1902), the Standard Oil Company (1899) and the United States Steel Corporation (1901)—boasted a total capitalization of over two and one half billions and, with a single exception, all were formed after 1898 and all incorporated under New Jersey laws.[1] Though by 1914 establishments doing an annual business of over one hundred thousand dollars numbered less than one eighth of the total, they employed over three fourths of the wage-earners and turned out more than four fifths of the products in value. Indeed, nearly half the products came from the 1.4 per cent of concerns which had an annual output of over a million dollars each.[2]

It was of especial significance that in the years 1898-1900 some twenty-one important combinations took place in the iron and steel business, for these prepared the way for the greatest of all consolidations, the United States Steel Corporation, formed in 1901.[3] Competition had always been exceedingly stiff in the manufacture of iron and steel and their primary products, and the business had suffered severely in the years from 1893 to 1897. As the industry picked up thereafter, and the leading units began to reach back to assure themselves of raw materials and forward to make certain of a market, the stage was set for a titanic struggle, with the financial giants, Morgan, Carnegie and Rockefeller, as the leading

[1] This list, it will be noted, does not include transportation companies or other public utilities where the same movement toward consolidation was evident.

[2] Bureau of the Census, *Abstract of the Census of Manufactures for 1919*, 354.

[3] These included the Federal Steel Company, which operated a belt of factories around Chicago, the American Steel and Wire Company, the American Tin Plate Company, the American Steel Hoop Company, the National Steel Company and two consolidations earlier effected by the Morgan interests: the National Tube Company and the American Bridge Company.

figures. The formation of the United States Steel Corporation involved two of them: Andrew Carnegie, the colossus of the steel industry, and J. Pierpont Morgan, head of the leading banking firm of the country. Carnegie was a strong individualist and a ruthless competitor. By 1900 the recently organized Carnegie Steel Company dominated the production of crude and semi-finished steel and commanded large reserves of ore and coke as well as a number of transportation companies and steel mills. Restless and active minded, Carnegie had become tired of business and was anxious to devote himself to literary ventures and schemes of philanthropy. His holdings, however, were so large that, in order to dispose of them to best advantage, it was necessary for him to interest Morgan in forming a superconsolidation in the steel field.[1]

To this Morgan was not averse, although he intended to act, if at all, in his own way and on his own terms. Brusque, taciturn, imperious, Morgan stood at the height of his career with three decades of successful financial operations behind him. Unlike Carnegie he had entered his life work with all the advantages of a superior education and the backing of his father's fortune, and for many years had been head of the leading financial house in America.[2] Among his far-flung business enterprises Morgan had recognized the pivotal importance of the steel industry by organizing the Federal Steel Company and investing heavily in the National Tube Company and the American Bridge Company.

[1] Andrew Carnegie, *Autobiography* (Boston, 1920), 255-256; Mark Sullivan, *Our Times* (N. Y., 1926-), II, chap. xviii; John Moody, *Masters of Capital* (Allen Johnson, ed., *Chronicles of America Series*, New Haven, 1918-1921, XLI), chaps. iii-iv; J. H. Bridge, *The Inside History of the Carnegie Steel Company* (N. Y., 1903), chaps. xvii-xxiii.

[2] Carl Hovey, *Life Story of J. P. Morgan* (N. Y., 1911), chap. x; Moody, *Masters of Capital*, chaps. i-ii, v; B. J. Hendrick, *The Age of Big Business* (Johnson, ed., *Chronicles of America*, XXXIX), chap. iii.

When Carnegie thought the psychological moment had arrived, he boldly announced plans which, if carried through, would inflict ruinous competition and perhaps destruction upon the steel interests of Morgan and other great capitalists. He purchased a huge tract at Conneaut and began building an enormous plant for the manufacture of steel tubes, a business in which he had not hitherto engaged. He started a monster rod mill in Pittsburgh to compete with John W. Gates's American Steel and Wire Company. At the same time he showed an active interest in the building of a new ore-carrying railroad from Pittsburgh to the seaboard, and equipped a great fleet of ore ships to fight Rockefeller in that very profitable field. The canny Scot was completely justified by the outcome. The panic-stricken millionaires quickly decided that to save their skins Carnegie must be bought out and, in order to stabilize conditions for the future, Morgan agreed to use the occasion for a consolidation of the industry.[1]

The task was no simple one. Not only was it necessary to pay Carnegie his price of approximately $447,000,000, but also to reconcile the interests of other steel magnates whose companies carried a large amount of "water" and desired to come in at an inflated figure. In the devious negotiations which followed Morgan depended chiefly on the experience and legal acumen of Judge Elbert H. Gary, president of the Federal Steel Company, and in the end success was achieved.[2] The actual value of the tangible property of the merger was estimated by the commissioner of corporations at $682,000,000, yet it was capitalized at $1,402,847,000 of which $510,206,000 represented preferred stock and

[1] U. S. Steel Corporation, *Hearings before the Committee on Investigation* (Wash., 1911-1912), I, 30-44; II, 2377 ff.

[2] Ida M. Tarbell, *The Life of Elbert H. Gary* (N. Y., 1925), chap. v.

$508,227,000 common.[1] Obviously all of the common stock and from one to two fifths of the preferred stock represented "water." The concern, however, at its organization controlled over half of the iron and steel business; it was not only a horizontal trust but a vertical one, its operations extending from the mine to the finished product. Its power was so great, and its profits so large, that it eventually absorbed the water and, with the exception of two years, regularly paid dividends on its common stock.

The immensity of the deal struck some with awe and many more with apprehension. Yet it was merely symptomatic of what was being done in a smaller way by scores of other business groups. Henry Demarest Lloyd's complaint in 1894 that most of the necessities of life were already in the hands of a comparatively small group of men was fully justified by the conditions of American life a decade later.[2] By 1904 it was difficult to discover any primary product which did not bear the label of a great corporation. Consolidation, moreover, had progressed steadily not only in "industrials" but in public utilities of various kinds, including anthracite coal and railroads. By the opening of the century ninety-five per cent of the higher-grade mileage was in the hands of six powerful groups: the Vanderbilt interests, dominating the Northeast (except New England); the Pennsylvania interests, serving the Middle Atlantic region and west to the Mississippi River; the Morgan-Hill alliance, controlling the far Northwest, with connections to the seaboard through the Erie and Lehigh Valley and other holdings in the South; the Gould-Rockefeller

[1] The remainder consisted of bonds, mortgages and similar obligations. U. S. Commissioner of Corporations, *Report on the Steel Industry* (Wash., 1911), pt. i, xvii ff., 242.

[2] H. D. Lloyd, *Wealth against Commonwealth* (N. Y., 1894), chap. ii.

group, controlling the far Southwest with connections to the Eastern seaboard; the Harriman and the Kuhn, Loeb interests, in control of the Union Pacific, Southern Pacific, Illinois Central and other roads; and the Moore group operating the Rock Island and other lines radiating from Chicago. Each of these groups represented a capitalization of over a billion dollars, and combined they controlled 164,500 out of the total mileage of 204,000. Most of the remaining mileage was largely worn out or profitless, but wherever there existed a road, such as the New Haven or the Delaware and Hudson, which seemed to have possibilities, large blocks of their stock were in the hands of some one of the major interests. Thus the Rockefeller, the Morgan and the Pennsylvania groups were all interested in the New Haven, and both the Vanderbilt and the Rockefeller groups in the Delaware and Hudson.[1]

Not content with this degree of concentration, the railroads were tending to draw even closer together. Before this was consummated, however, Wall Street was rocked to its foundations in a last great struggle between the two great masters of the rail empire west of the Mississippi: James J. Hill, who with Morgan's aid controlled the Great Northern and the Northern Pacific; and Edward H. Harriman, a comparative newcomer in the world of railroad finance, who with the help of the banking house of Kuhn, Loeb and Company had recently gained control of the Union Pacific and the Southern Pacific.[2] Both men were anxious to acquire the Chicago, Burlington and Quincy road in order to command an entrance to Chicago; its control by Hill would, in addition, make the Hill-Morgan lines a competitor of the

[1] Moody, *Truth about the Trusts*, 431 ff.

[2] Joseph Pyle, *Life of James J. Hill* (Garden City, 1917), chaps. xx, xxii.

Harriman-Kuhn, Loeb roads for a third of the distance between the Pacific and the Mississippi.

Victory seemed to rest with the Hill-Morgan group when, in 1901, directors of the Burlington sold about ninety-seven per cent of its stock to the Northern Pacific and Great Northern. Harriman promptly struck back by an active drive to purchase control of the Northern Pacific. The moment was well chosen, for Hill was in the West on an inspection trip and Morgan in Germany recuperating from the strain of his steel-trust operations. When Hill first learned from the scant reports in the Western papers that Northern Pacific was being heavily bought, he suspected the hand of his rival and, ordering the rails to be cleared, dashed for New York in his private car. Fearful lest he be too late, he communicated with Morgan, who immediately cabled his firm to buy 150,-000 shares. Northern Pacific common which had been selling in April around $110 a share rose on May 9 to $1000. Actually 78,000 more shares of stock had been sold than were in existence; both interests had purchased far more than a majority of the stock. The market was cornered and the "shorts" were caught. Stocks of all kinds were tumbling rapidly when the giants called a truce to save the financial world from a severe panic.

The outcome was the formation of an immense holding company, the Northern Securities Company, with a capital of four hundred million dollars, nearly all of which was issued to acquire the stock of the Great Northern and Northern Pacific and thus control the Chicago, Burlington and Quincy. Since the Harriman-Kuhn, Loeb interests owned substantially half of the Northern Pacific stock, this meant an equal representation on the board of the new company, and as the same group already owned the Union Pacific and Southern Pacific, railroad competition in the vast region west of the Mississippi was virtually eliminated.[1] The company itself was short-lived. Scarcely three months after its organization the reviving storm of antitrust agitation broke upon it when the federal government instituted suit under the Sherman act, and in 1904 the Supreme Court ordered its dissolution.[2]

Undeterred by government opposition to the Northern Securities Company, Morgan pressed on his work of consolidation. In 1902 the International Harvester Company had been successfully launched. His next venture, however, did not turn out so well. This was the great shipping combination, the International Mercantile Marine Company, organized in the same year. With reckless disregard of values Morgan attempted to buy in the leading transatlantic lines. The White Star, the Leland, the Red Star and the American lines, unable to resist the absurdly extravagant valuations, succumbed, but the Cunard and the German lines, more sensitive to public opinion, refused to join. In spite of even the Morgan prestige the stock of this new combination was eyed dubiously by investors. Their suspicion was completely vindicated. Since 1897 stock issues of the new mergers had been dumped into the eager hands of speculators until the buying capacity of the public seemed finally to have been exceeded and the market crammed with what Morgan called "undigested securities." [3]

The overexpansion and speculation which accompanied the great period of trust making brought the inevi-

[1] The Northern Securities Company was chartered by New Jersey in November, 1901. See Pyle, *Life of James J. Hill,* chaps. xxvii-xxix; George Kennan, *E. H. Harriman* (Boston, 1922), chaps. xi-xii; Moody, *Masters of Capital,* 97 ff.; Balthasar Meyer, *A History of the Northern Securities Case* (Madison, 1906).

[2] 193 U. S., 197.

[3] *N. Y. Times,* March 31, 1903. James J. Hill called them "indigestible securities."

table reaction in the depression of 1903.[1] With most of the major industries at least partly integrated, investors had come to learn that neither great size nor virtual monopoly necessarily meant big profits. At the same time the critical attitude of the Roosevelt administration, as revealed in the creation of the bureau of corporations in 1903, in the decision against the Northern Securities Company in 1904 and in other antitrust suits, was not encouraging to those anxious to create monopolies. From the point of view of the investor, however, there was nothing more sobering than the slippery methods employed even by eminently respectable financiers to achieve their objects.

No better example of this and of the absurd length to which the fever for consolidation ran can be found than in the history of the ill-fated "Shipbuilding Trust." In June, 1902, three "dummy" incorporators organized the United States Shipbuilding Company with $3000 and a few days later three "dummy" directors, poor clerks in a Jersey City trust company without ownership of a single share of stock or even knowledge of the whereabouts of the plants which the new company expected to control, coolly voted to authorize the issue of $71,000,000 to purchase some eight shipbuilding or manufacturing companies. The real principals were John W. Young, a son of the Mormon prophet, who undertook to market the securities; D. Leroy Dresser, an amateur financier who, as president of a newly formed bank, underwrote a ten-million-dollar bond issue; and Lewis Nixon, a practical shipbuilder but, in matters of finance, a veritable "babe in the woods." One of their first moves was the purchase of the Bethlehem Steel Company from Charles M. Schwab, a concern which had more tangible

[1] A. D. Noyes, *Forty Years of American Finance* (N. Y., 1909). 309 ff.

value than the whole outfit of shipbuilding plants. According to the ethics of the time Schwab knew what he was about, for he obtained terms which left him not only in control of his own company but of the other properties as well. In their eagerness the promoters had exchanged some sixty-eight million dollars in stocks and bonds for properties worth at the most twelve million dollars, though they had not failed to distribute among themselves bonuses of million-dollar blocks of stocks. Once in control of the enterprise, Schwab forced it into bankruptcy, lopped off the worthless properties and attached the better ones to his Bethlehem company as subsidiaries.

Enraged at what appeared a "deliberate attempt to wreck" the undertaking, certain of the bona-fide bondholders sued for a permanent receivership. The receiver, James Smith, jr., described the principals as men "who while thoroughly understanding 'the intricacies of higher finance' seemed to have overlooked the requirements of fairness," and characterized the whole procedure as an "artistic swindle." The deliberate gutting of the shipbuilding trust, involving losses to hundreds of investors, called down the severest denunciation from even the most conservative newspapers, but so low was the business morality of the period that the man who profited most by the transaction was rather admired for his cleverness than condemned for his ruthlessness.[1] And there were many who still sympathized with the famous remark of Henry O. Havemeyer: "You cannot wet nurse people from the time they are born until the time they

[1] H. W. Lanier, "One Trust and What Became of It," *World's Work*, VII (1904), 4445-4457; *Literary Digest*, XXVII, 533, 654 (Oct. 24, Nov. 14, 1903); W. Z. Ripley, ed., *Trust Pools and Corporations* (rev. edn., Boston, 1916), chap. xii; A. S. Dewing, *Corporate Promotions and Reorganizations* (*Harvard Econ. Studies*, X), chaps. xvii-xviii; H. R. Seager and C. A. Gulick, jr., *Trust and Corporation Problems* (N. Y., 1929), chap. xii; Moody, *Truth about the Trusts*, 336-368.

die. They have got to wade in and get stuck, and that is the way men are educated and cultivated." [1]

The setback of 1903 was but temporary. Record-breaking crops of wheat, corn and cotton in 1905 and 1906 combined with rising prices brought a real prosperity to the farmer which was in part responsible for the revived industrial boom. Although the consolidation movement slowed up, there quickly developed a renewed frenzy for speculation. One of the most abundant sources of capital for financing new enterprises consisted of the funds of the insurance companies. American insurance in its earlier stages had been conservatively conducted for the benefit of the policy holder whose interests, it was believed, were reasonably safeguarded by the state laws. The assets of insurance companies had not generally been regarded by Wall Street as available for speculation and industrial financing; but by the middle nineties their business had become so great that the financial magnates began to cast longing eyes at their overflowing treasuries. It was not long before a method to tap them was found. Insurance companies were allowed to invest in trust companies, and under the law such institutions could not only conduct a regular banking business but also engage in many other operations, including the underwriting of new financial schemes. As the new type of life-insurance official became infected with the reckless and unscrupulous spirit of the period, the savings of millions of policy holders began to flow toward Wall Street through this channel. Just as the Rockefellers and Morgans had their own banks through which they worked, so the insurance companies, particularly the big three—the Equitable, the Mutual and the New York Life—had their trust companies. The outstanding examples were the Guaranty Trust Company

[1] Industrial Commission, *Report* (Wash., 1900-1902), I, pt. ii, 123.

and the United States Mortgage and Trust Company acquired by the Mutual Life.

By means of these satellite banks the accumulated savings of small policy holders found their way into highly speculative enterprises forbidden to the companies themselves, and even into the hands of insurance officials for private speculation and enrichment. Not only did representatives of the Rockefellers, the Morgans and other Wall Street interests sit on the boards of the trust companies alongside representatives of the insurance companies, but presently they began to penetrate even to the directorships of insurance companies. The prostitution of life insurance to the needs of big business grew with the venality of the officials and the stringency of the money market until in 1905 the New York legislature investigated the situation and passed remedial laws.[1]

In spite of the cooling effect of the insurance investigation, the orgy of speculation with its overexpanded bank credits continued until it was world-wide in 1906. In that year Harriman raised the dividends of the Union Pacific from six to ten per cent and was using the funds released by the dissolution of the Northern Securities Company to purchase new branch lines and large blocks of New York Central and Baltimore and Ohio stock. Morgan and Hill were lavishing money on the improvement of their properties, while lesser speculators were promoting dubious ventures on a vanishing margin of capital. Thousands, owing to the discovery of silver in the Cobalt region of Nevada, were seized with a craze for mining stock. In imitation of the Morgans and Rockefellers, Charles W. Morse obtained control of the Bank of North America and then of other banks, using

[1] *Testimony Taken before the Joint Committee of the Senate and Assembly of the State of New York* (Albany, 1906); W. H. Price, *Life Insurance Reform in New York* (Cambridge, Mass., 1909); B. J. Hendrick, *The Story of Life Insurance* (N. Y., 1907).

the resources of these "chain banks" to float a coastwise steamship consolidation and other large schemes; and he in turn was copied on a lesser scale by such speculators as Charles T. Barney of the Knickerbocker Trust Company and F. Augustus Heinze of the Mercantile National Bank.

Overexpansion and reckless speculation brought the day of reckoning when in March, 1907, the stock market suddenly crashed, bringing ruin to the small-margin speculator and heavy losses to the wealthy. Help from the federal treasury, European gold drawn hither by high money rates and the natural gravitation of money to New York as the crop-moving period ended, stayed for a time the panic, but relief was merely temporary. Money became so tight during the summer that even the city of New York failed twice to sell a bond issue.[1] The New York street-railway combination went into receivers' hands, Morse's grand scheme of a coastwise shipping monopoly collapsed like a house of cards, while railroads and other industries reported declining earnings.[2]

The "silent panic" of March was followed by the "bankers' panic" of October. The second crash was precipitated by the failure of a group of copper speculators, headed by the Heinze brothers, to corner United Copper, and the subsequent appeal by the Heinze banks, the most important of which was the Mercantile National, to the clearing house for aid. Anxious to eliminate the more notorious speculators, the conservative bankers of the clearing-house committee promised help upon receipt of the resignation of the officers and directors of these banks.

[1] *Commercial and Financial Chronicle,* LXXXIV, 1514 (June 29, 1907); LXXXV, 371 (Aug. 17, 1907).

[2] "Solving a Great City's Transportation Problem," *World's Work,* XV (1907), 9594-9597; Moody, *Masters of Capital,* 42 ff.

Meanwhile the National Bank of Commerce (October 21) refused longer to honor checks of the Knickerbocker Trust Company, the third largest trust company in the city, and the next morning a run began on this bank which quickly forced it to close its doors. Before night Morse's National Bank of North America had failed and nearly every trust company in New York was besieged by long lines of depositors eager to withdraw their money. Currency went to a premium of 4½ per cent, and call money was practically unobtainable. As a measure of relief Secretary of the Treasury George B. Cortelyou deposited $35,000,000 with the New York national banks to be loaned to the trust companies and hastened to New York to urge the masters of finance to exert a quieting influence. Men of the type of Morgan, Stillman, Harriman and Frick were quite willing to use the situation to strengthen their own interests and at the same time get rid of such competitors as Heinze, Morse and Barney. Morgan bestirred himself to save the Trust Company of America and the Lincoln Trust Company. With Rockefeller he coöperated in loaning bonds and in forcing gold shipments from Europe by buying bills of exchange. The situation was further helped by the action of the government in permitting the banks to issue clearing-house loan certificates on approved securities, while outside of New York state governors lent their aid by declaring "bank holidays" and financiers by closing stock exchanges.[1]

Although in New York City the Panic of 1907 was more severe than that of 1893, its results were not widespread owing to the fundamental prosperity of the nation. By February of the next year confidence was re-

[1] The best general account is O. M. W. Sprague, *History of Crises under the National Banking System* (Wash., 1910), 236 ff. See also Noyes, *Forty Years of American Finance*, chap. xv; *Commercial and Financial Chronicle*, LXXXV, Oct. 26 and Nov. 2, 1907.

stored even in the metropolis. To account for the panic many explanations were offered. Business men were prone to attribute it to the meddlesome activities of the Roosevelt administration. "Hail Caesar," cried the *New York Sun*, "we who are about to bust salute thee." [1] But the shallowness of this charge is proved by the fact that the government's antitrust suits had practically no effect upon the earning power of the corporations, while the railroad legislation of 1906 actually helped the transportation companies. The passing of the Hepburn act, indeed, aroused such confidence on the part of Europeans that millions of dollars poured in for investment. Instead of curtailment, Hill and Morgan were excited to new and vaster schemes for the improvement, consolidation and extension of railroads.

On the other hand, some of the more radical critics asserted that the panic was simply part of a scheme of the great interests to force out the little fellows, or that it had been caused by the great chieftains warring upon one another.[2] Roosevelt in his annual message of December, 1907, denounced as dangerous criminals those capitalists responsible for "swindling in stocks, corrupting legislatures, making fortunes by the inflation of securities, by wrecking railroads, by destroying competitors through rebates," [3] and it was a ready inference that he believed this to be the sort of thing that had hastened the panic. These practices, however, were merely the worst indications of the overspeculation and overbuying which ordinarily mark the end of a business cycle.

If the Panic of 1907 exerted slight influence upon the general economic trend, it did, as is usual with panics,

[1] *Literary Digest*, XXXV, 671 (Nov. 9, 1907).

[2] H. L. Loucks, *The Great Conspiracy of the House of Morgan Exposed* (Watertown, S. D., 1913), 96 ff.

[3] J. D. Richardson, comp., *Messages and Papers of the Presidents* (Wash., 1910), X, 7471.

increase the speed with which wealth and power were concentrated. Many of the smaller speculators and capitalists, unable to weather the storm, saw their holdings quickly taken over by the larger interests. The Morgans gathered in the Morse shipping interests (competitors to the New Haven railroad) and the Rockefellers the Heinze holdings, but the outstanding example was the purchase of the Tennessee Coal, Iron and Railroad Company by the United States Steel Corporation. This came at a critical moment of the panic. The prominent Wall Street brokerage firm of Moore and Schley had pledged six million of the stock of the Tennessee Company for loans at the banks. The banks were now calling the loans and Moore and Schley were unable to meet them. Since the collapse of this firm would probably have caused an epidemic of brokerage failures, the Morgan interests considered the purchase of the Tennessee Coal and Iron stock. In order to play safe, however, Henry C. Frick and Elbert H. Gary were sent to Washington to ascertain the attitude of the government. Roosevelt, having heard their story, answered that while he "could not advise them to take the action proposed," he "felt it no public duty . . . to interpose objections." [1] This was enough. The United States Steel paid thirty million dollars in bonds for the stock, Moore and Schley were saved, and the Steel Corporation found itself stronger than ever.

The results of the mad scramble for the nation's wealth were appearing in the formation of two powerful financial groups: the Standard Oil and the Morgan. The enormous and steady profits which the able management of Rockefeller and his associates had dumped into the pockets of the oil speculators became too great for even the expanding oil industry. Taking over the City Bank

[1] Theodore Roosevelt, *Autobiography* (N. Y., 1913), 479; Tarbell, *Life of Elbert H. Gary*, 196 ff.

of New York, the Standard Oil financiers began to invest in many fields. Already possessing substantial interests in the Lake Superior ore lands and in railway transportation, John D. Rockefeller and his brother William proceeded to invade the copper industry by their formation of the Amalgamated Copper Company and to acquire rail properties in almost every section of the nation.[1] Others of the Standard Oil group went into public utilities. Beginning in 1899, when the lighting companies of New York were brought under single control, the Standard interests formed powerful connections with the United Gas Improvement Company of Philadelphia, with the Public Service Corporation of New Jersey (short electric railroads) and with the telephone and telegraph company groups. They also became dominant in the "Smelter Trust," the "Ice Trust" and the "Tobacco Trust." Commanding vast financial resources through the City Bank (afterward called the National City Bank) and its string of banks, the Standard magnates and their satellites were in a position of extraordinary power in the American business world.[2]

The suzerainty of the oil barons was threatened only by the pretensions of the House of Morgan, which now dominated the transportation systems of the Northwest and South and controlled the Erie, the Chesapeake and Ohio, and the Hocking Valley. The Morgans not only operated through their own bond house, but like the Rockefellers they controlled a powerful banking chain led by the National Bank of Commerce, the First National Bank and the Chase National Bank. The Electrical Supply Trust, the "Shipping Trust," the "Rubber Trust," were all appanages of the House of Morgan,

[1] Their interests included not only the 28,000 miles generally classified as the "Gould-Rockefeller System" but they were also heavy owners in the railroads managed by Harriman and Kuhn, Loeb.

[2] Moody, *Truth about the Trusts*, 490-492.

with the United States Steel Corporation as its crowning achievement.

The Rockefeller and Morgan groups were by no means relentless rivals, for as time went on they worked more and more harmoniously together as they became involved in an infinite number of cross investments and interlocking directorates. "Around these two groups," said Moody in 1904, "or what must ultimately become one greater group, all the smaller groups of capitalists congregate. They are all allied and intertwined by their various mutual interests." [1] The Pennsylvania Railroad interests, he pointed out, were on the one hand allied with the Vanderbilts and on the other with the Rockefellers, while the Vanderbilts in turn were closely associated with the Morgan group, and both the Vanderbilt and the Pennsylvania interests had recently become the dominating factors in the Reading system, which for years had been controlled by the Morgans. Whenever battle was joined between the giants, after the smoke cleared away the tendency toward closer alliances seems to have been hastened. Thus, as we have seen, the struggle for the Burlington system ended in an alliance through the agency of the Northern Securities Company.

With the end of the "bankers' panic" concentration of the nation's industrial and financial life continued, but more slowly and more quietly than in the hectic days between 1899 and 1904. The panic itself removed many of the lesser speculators from the scene, and the watchful attitude of the Roosevelt administration put a damper on some of the greater plungers. Moreover younger captains were forging to the front who were primarily occupied with the staggering task of keeping in operation the immense machinery which their predecessors had

[1] Moody, *Truth about the Trusts,* 493; S. S. Pratt, "Who Owns the United States," *World's Work,* VII (1903), 4259-4266.

thrown together. Consolidation nevertheless proceeded. The death in 1909 of Harriman, one of the ablest and most daring of the railroad manipulators, enabled the Morgan group to acquire his stock in the Guaranty Trust Company and with it large power in the Mutual Life. Soon after, Morgan obtained from Thomas F. Ryan control of the Equitable Life Assurance Society. Since he already controlled the New York Life, he now dominated the "Big Three" in the insurance world and through them was the chief factor in the trust companies of New York City.

Although the operations of high finance were but vaguely understood by the public at large, suspicion was widespread that the economic power of the nation was rapidly centering in the hands of a small group of New York financiers. The situation was thoroughly ventilated by a congressional committee in 1913,[1] which had no hesitancy in asserting that an increased concentration of money and credit had been effected, largely through the activities of J. P. Morgan and Company, the First National Bank and the National City Bank of New York, and the three bond houses of Lee, Higginson & Co., Kidder, Peabody & Co. and Kuhn, Loeb & Company.[2] How far this had gone was suggested by the fact that four allied financial institutions in New York City held 341 directorships in bank, transportation, public-utility and insurance companies, whose aggregate resources were $22,245,000,000. "If by a 'money trust,'" said the committee,

> is meant an established and well-defined identity and community of interest between a few leaders of finance,

[1] Committee on Banking and Currency of the House of Representatives, *Money Trust Investigation* (3 vols., Wash., 1913).

[2] Committee to Investigate Concentration of Control of Money and Credit, *Report* (62 Cong., 3 sess., *House Rep.*, no. 1593), 131.

> which has been created and is held together through stock holdings, interlocking directorates and other forms of domination over banks, trust companies, railroads, public-service and industrial corporations, and which has resulted in a vast and growing concentration of control of money and credit in the hands of a comparatively few men—your committee, as before stated, has no hesitation in asserting as a result of its investigation up to this time that the condition thus described exists in this country to-day.[1]

During the course of the investigation George F. Baker, second only to Morgan as a factor in the concentration of banking control, admitted on the stand that the financial welfare of the nation was now dependent largely on the type of men who held the reins of power. When asked, "Do you think that it is a comfortable situation for a great country to be in?" he answered, "Not entirely." [2]

That the situation was not "comfortable" was soon to be proved by the interstate commerce commission, even then unearthing "one of the most glaring instances of maladministration revealed in all the history of American railroading." [3] In 1903 the New York, New Haven and Hartford Railroad Company, upon whose board sat J. P. Morgan, William Rockefeller and representatives of leading Connecticut enterprises, called to the presidency of the road Charles S. Mellon, a man with long experience and wide knowledge of New England transportation. Under the "Mellon-Morgan-Rockefeller management" the railroad in the next decade left no stone unturned in its purpose to effect a monopoly of

[1] Committee to Investigate Money and Credit, *Report*, 130.

[2] Committee on Banking and Currency, *Money Trust Investigation*, II, 1568.

[3] Interstate Commerce Commission, *Reports*, XXXI (1914), 38; XXVII (1913), 560-617.

New England transportation. Acquiring the New York, Ontario and Western in 1904, which gave it access to the coal fields, the New Haven obtained control of the Boston and Maine three years later and in 1911 purchased the Rutland Railroad. In the same year, by an arrangement with the New York Central, the Boston and Albany was brought into the combination.[1] Not content with railroad monopoly, the New Haven rapidly bought up competing electric-trolley lines in Connecticut, Rhode Island and Massachusetts and eventually gained absolute mastery of ninety per cent of the water transportation to and from New England.

The methods employed in building this enormous edifice not only involved, in the words of the interstate commerce commission, "a loose, extravagant and improvident management," but were accompanied by the corruption of legislators, the subsidizing of the press, fictitious sales of stock to boost market prices, the habitual payment of unitemized vouchers for purposes not clearly specified, and the creation of a web of entangling alliances which were "seemingly planned, created, and manipulated by lawyers expressly retained for the purpose of concealment or deception"—and all this done for a purpose which under the Sherman act was patently illegal.[2] The capitalization of the New Haven Company in the nine years 1903-1912 increased from $93,000,000 to $417,000,000, of which only $120,000,000 was expended for improvements and equipment.[3]

Typical of many transactions was that which resulted in the building of the New York, Westchester and Boston, a short electric line running from New York City into Westchester County. Two charters were in existence,

[1] W. Z. Ripley, *Railroads; Finance and Organization* (N. Y., 1915), 468 ff.

[2] Interstate Commerce Commission, *Reports*, XXXI, 34.

[3] Interstate Commerce Commission, *Reports*, XXXI, 33.

one allowing the construction of a line from White Plains to New York and the other from Port Chester. Just enough construction had been done to hold the charters when the New Haven Railroad, apparently to throttle potential competition, appointed a committee of its directors consisting of Mellon, Morgan, Rockefeller and George M. Miller to look into the matter. This committee—or rather Morgan, for Mellon himself did not always know what was going on—paid approximately $36,000,000 for the franchises and property of a road eighteen miles long without an adequate city terminal, worth in all about $5,000,000, and not only duplicating the main line of the New Haven but of necessity operated at a loss on the investment of $1,250,000 annually. All this was done without either the board or the stockholders being informed as to the details of the purchase. The transactions were carried on with great secrecy through two bankers who operated with New Haven money carried on the books of J. P. Morgan and Company as "Special Account No. 2" and under circumstances which suggested that a million and a half had been illegally spent for political corruption in clearing away franchise difficulties.[1] Even more astounding were the devious transactions by which the New Haven circumvented the Massachusetts law in acquiring control of the Boston and Maine by stock manipulations which gave one of the New Haven directors, John L. Billard, without the investment of a dollar, profits of $2,748,700 at the expense of the stockholders.

This sort of recklessness and improvidence could have but one result. Dividends were passed in 1913, bringing embarrassment to thousands of stockholders, and for a decade the road hung on the verge of bankruptcy. Suit

[1] Interstate Commerce Commission, *Reports*, XXVII, 580-582; XXXI, 35-41, 66-67.

under the Sherman act quickly brought a dissolution of the monopoly [1] and the criminal indictment of the directors in 1914 served to keep the sorry story before the public for many months.[2] If any advance in business ethics had been made since the sordid days of the 1860's and 1870's, certainly there was little to show it in the record of the New Haven. The fate of this great railroad under Rockefeller and Morgan was little better than that of the Erie under Fisk and Gould.[3]

Such ugly incidents only served to throw into sharper relief certain hopeful, though less spectacular, features in the general business situation. Evidences were multiplying that, slowly but surely, big business was passing from a state of brigandage to the beginnings of responsibility, a metamorphosis undoubtedly hastened by the critical attitude of the government at Washington as well as by a rising social consciousness. American civilization had become too complicated for the unbridled individualism of earlier days, and the people less tolerant of an ethical code subversive of the public interest. Even Morgan and his associates in the New Haven deals undoubtedly believed that in building a transportation monopoly they were working for the ultimate benefit of the community.

Whatever the methods by which the colossal economic power of America became concentrated in the hands of a few capitalists, the result was fraught with important economic and social consequences. Much time was spent by economists in studying its effects upon the quality and prices of products, but little or none in appraising its

[1] *Poor's Manual of Railroads for 1924*, 1445 ff.

[2] *Literary Digest*, XLVIII, 141-143, 606 (Jan. 24, March 21, 1914); XLIX, 136 (July 25, 1914); *Independent*, LXXXV, 115 (Jan. 24, 1916).

[3] See Allan Nevins, *The Emergence of Modern America* (*A History of American Life*, VIII), 194-199.

far-reaching social implications. The small industry, conducted by the man who had built it up and hence entailing an intimate relationship between employer and employee, was rapidly passing. In its place had come the mighty corporation with its thousands of stockholders, dominated by financiers who knew little or nothing of the business, and conducted by delegated managers for the primary purpose of producing dividends. The centripetal movement which culminated in the first decade of the century produced two results of outstanding importance to American civilization. In the first place, it shifted a large portion of the operation and ownership of the common industries from the actual producer to the banker and nonresident stockholder. In the second place, it speeded the concentration of wealth in the hands of the few, thus creating a class more powerful than the people and, indeed, more powerful than the government—a compact group which, often with utter unscrupulousness and disregard of the public welfare, played fast and loose with the nation's wealth. Whether this power could be adequately curbed was one of America's gravest problems.

CHAPTER III

THE LABOR WORLD

LABOR faced a new era as the nineteenth century hurried to a close. In earlier years business consolidation had been achieved at the cost of labor disorganization, but now the right of the wage-earner to organize was no longer seriously challenged either by the courts or the employing class. The bitter industrial struggles of the 1880's and 1890's had been a rough school of experience, but from it the American workers learned lessons in organization and tactics that were to give them a new confidence and steadiness of purpose in the years of prosperity and confusion which now lay ahead. Diversity, however, rather than uniformity marked the labor movement.

Of the various national labor bodies which had sprung up in the earlier period, the American Federation of Labor under the leadership of Samuel Gompers had far outstripped all competitors. Its ranks included nearly three fifths of the total trade-union membership, which in 1898 numbered approximately a half million.[1] The strongholds of the Federation were to be found in the urban districts and among the intelligent skilled workers in the mining industry, the building trades, the machine shops and the trades engaged in the preparation of food, liquor and tobacco. Of the unions unaffiliated with the American Federation of Labor the most important were the Railway Brotherhoods, whose well-stocked treasur-

[1] Selig Perlman, *Growth of American Trade Unionism* (N. Y., 1924), 33.

ies and long-established benevolences and traditions made them unwilling to endanger their freedom by any alliances. Notwithstanding the progress which had been made, only a small fraction—less than four per cent—of the wage-earners were organized, but it was the unskilled, ill-paid, migratory or casual worker, the woman and the newly arrived immigrant, for the most part, who remained outside the ranks.[1]

Whatever had been the internal divergences of opinion in earlier years, by 1898 the policies of the dominant leadership in the American Federation of Labor were firmly established. Its leaders were agreed that, for the moment at least, most would be gained by following the lines of the old-fashioned trade unionism, eschewing party politics and avoiding radical prophets and programs. This policy of old-line unionism was amply vindicated by a rapid growth in numerical strength and public favor. In many respects the years from 1898 to 1905 were the most successful which the Federation had experienced.[2] The membership increased from 278,000 to 1,676,000.[3] At the same time the cause of the workingman received unexpected recognition from responsible leaders outside of labor's ranks. The most notable example of this was the formation in 1901 of the National Civic Federation with Marcus A. Hanna as president and Gompers vice-president. Frankly recognizing unionization and the trade agreement as fundamental in the relations of capital and labor, this body sought to bring employer, employee and the general public together in the solution of national industrial problems. "It was the

[1] G. E. Barnett, "Growth of Labor Organizations," *Quar. Journ. of Econ.*, XXX, 780.

[2] J. R. Commons and others, *History of Labour in the United States* (N. Y., 1918), II, 521 ff.

[3] *American Labor Yearbook for 1916*, 20. See also Selig Perlman, *A History of Trade Unionism in the United States* (N. Y., 1922), 163 ff.

harvest," as Gompers put it, "of the years of organizing work which were beginning to bear fruit." [1]

So far did the *rapprochement* progress that one labor historian has called the years from 1898 to 1904 "a honeymoon period of capital and labour." [2] Never before had organized labor attained so favorable a position in American society, and never before was the employing class so well disposed toward what John Mitchell called "the hope of future peace in the industrial world"—the trade agreement.[3] The period opened auspiciously in the machinery and metal trades by an arbitration agreement between the National Founders' Association (organized in 1898) and the International Molders' Union of North America. This was followed the next year by a similar pact between the National Metal Trades' Association and the International Association of Machinists. Unfortunately neither agreement lasted long, and in the succeeding years the metal trades returned to a condition of warfare and chaos. A happier fate befell the efforts of the Newspaper Publishers' Association and the International Typographical Union, which commenced in 1900 a series of one-year trade agreements that brought comparative peace in this important branch of the printing trade. The four Railway Brotherhoods had for many years received recognition and, until the high cost of living began to press them closely in the years 1912-1914, dwelt in relatively amicable relations with their employers.

[1] Samuel Gompers, *Seventy Years of Life and Labor* (N. Y., 1925), II, 104 ff. Help came also from the National Consumers' League, organized in 1898, an effective agency in combating the sweatshop evil; from the National Child Labor Committee, formed in 1904 to agitate for the abolition of child labor; and from the American Association of Labor Legislation (1906), which was interested in both better labor legislation and the stricter enforcement of existing laws.

[2] Commons and others, *History of Labour*, II, 524.

[3] John Mitchell, *Organized Labor* (Phila., 1903), 347.

In the tempestuous history of the mining industry is illustrated both the increasing strength of the labor movement and the development of the trade agreement as a lever to secure better conditions. The United Mine Workers of America, with ten thousand members in 1897, mostly in Ohio, represented but a handful of the entire number. Nevertheless, believing the time ripe for action, the leaders called a strike in the central bituminous field. At least one hundred thousand miners dropped their tools and, after a twelve weeks' struggle, won an unqualified victory, including a twenty-per-cent wage increase, the eight-hour day, the abolition of company stores, recognition of the union and a provision for annual joint conferences with the operators. Although the United Mine Workers made little headway among the Negroes and mountain whites in West Virginia, their firm adherence to trade agreements did much to stabilize the more or less chaotic conditions in the central bituminous region.

In organizing the anthracite regions of northeastern Pennsylvania they faced a more difficult task. There the miners were chiefly foreign, and the operators were so closely joined by a community of interest that the industry was virtually controlled by a trust. Eight railroads—the Pennsylvania, the Lehigh Valley, the Reading, the Central Railroad of New Jersey, the Delaware, Lackawanna and Western, the Delaware and Hudson, the Erie, and the New York, Ontario and Western—not only monopolized the transportation facilities to the tidewater, but also, through their subsidiary companies, mined approximately two thirds of the coal. Through the purchase and interchange of stocks these railroads were themselves controlled by a few large capitalists [1] and the independent operators were quite at their beck

[1] Industrial Commission, *Report* (Wash., 1900-1902), IX, xxiv-xxvi.

and call. It was against this powerful financial group that the United Mine Workers, comprising but eight thousand in the anthracite regions, decided in 1900 to strike.

The call was obeyed by over one hundred thousand miners and the walkout became general. Fearing its effect upon McKinley's candidacy in the impending presidential campaign, Senator Hanna induced the operators to give way. They agreed to abolish the sliding scale of wage payments, increase the rates ten per cent and meet committees of miners for the adjustment of grievances. This, however, did not carry a formal recognition of the union, nor was a trade agreement provided for, but only an unwritten understanding. In two years' time matters were as bad as before. When the miners demanded a reduction of hours from ten to nine, a twenty-per-cent increase in wages, payment according to the weight of coal mined and recognition of the union, there ensued the famous strike of 1902, one of the most significant episodes in trade-union history. For the workers this was a fight not only for recognition, but also for tolerable conditions of work.

So certain was John Mitchell, who directed the strike with extraordinary ability, that his cause was just that he offered to submit the miners' demands either to a committee selected by the National Civic Federation or to one composed of Archbishop Ireland, Bishop Potter and any third person whom they might select.

> If they [the committee of three] decide that the average annual wages received by anthracite mine workers are sufficient to enable them to live, maintain and educate their families in a manner conformable to established American standards and consistent with American citizenship, we agree to withdraw our claims for higher wages and more equitable conditions of employment,

> providing that the anthracite mine operators agree to comply with any recommendations the above committee may make affecting the earnings and conditions of labor of their employees.[1]

In his reply to Mitchell, George F. Baer, a leading operator, tersely expressed the attitude of his colleagues. "Anthracite mining is a business," he said, "and not a religious, sentimental or academic proposition." [2] The operators prepared to fight to the last ditch. On their side the employees, skillfully led, and enjoying the sympathy of the general public, received large contributions from labor and outside sources and managed to maintain a united front from May to October. As winter approached, the East faced a terrible coal famine, and President Roosevelt decided to intervene. Acting on the widest conception of the executive function, he sent, as his emissary to Wall Street, Mark Hanna, but the latter could do nothing against the firm determination of Baer.[3] There followed a stormy but futile conference in Washington on October 3, after which Roosevelt, as a last resort, sent Secretary of State Elihu Root to New York in an effort to bring peace. With the president resolved, if necessary, to operate the mines with troops during the emergency, Root was successful in winning over Morgan and exerting sufficient pressure on the operators to force their capitulation. The strike ended on October 23 with an agreement that the differences should be arbitrated by a commission appointed by the president.

[1] Letter of May 8, 1902, to operators. Anthracite Coal Strike Commission, *Report to the President on the Anthracite Coal Strike of May-October, 1902* (Wash., 1903), 34.

[2] Anthracite Coal Strike Commission, *Report*, 35.

[3] Hanna's letter of September 29 to Roosevelt, given in Herbert Croly, *Marcus Alonzo Hanna* (N. Y., 1912), 398.

The arbitral award, made five months later, conceded a ten-per-cent increase in wages, a shorter work day and the privilege of having a union check-weighman at the scale.[1] Though formal recognition was not accorded the union, provision was made for the adjustment of future difficulties by a board of conciliation, and a decade of comparative peace ensued. At the end of that time, however, trouble broke out anew. A one month's strike in 1912 resulted in partial success for the miners and a new four-year contract involving higher pay. The years from 1912 to 1916 were used by the union in building up its membership and, when the agreement was renewed in the latter year, the anthracite miners obtained the eight-hour day, increased pay and the coveted recognition of the union.[2]

Quite as remarkable was the new position won by labor in the New York clothing industry. Here the workers were chiefly immigrants and women, largely unorganized, and sweated by long hours, low wages and unsanitary conditions. In the fall of 1909 the Ladies' Waist Makers' Union, Local 25 of the International Ladies' Garment Workers' Union, called a strike in two shops in protest against the system of subcontracting, then prevalent in the industry, and at a subsequent mass meeting it was voted to make the walkout general. Twenty thousand women were soon on strike, and New York was treated to the sight of dozens of women picketers dragged daily to the police stations to be fined by the magistrates.[3] So general was the belief that the

[1] Eight hours for certain groups and nine hours for others. Anthracite Coal Strike Commission, *Report*, 80.

[2] On the coal strike of 1902, see Anthracite Coal Strike Commission, *Report;* J. F. Rhodes, *The McKinley and Roosevelt Administrations* (N. Y., 1922), 236-247; Theodore Roosevelt, *Autobiography* (N. Y., 1913), 464-478; Mark Sullivan, *Our Times* (N. Y., 1926-), II, chap. xxiv.

[3] Louis Levine, *The Women's Garment Workers* (N. Y., 1924), 158.

police authorities favored the employers, and so widespread the sympathy with the strikers, that society women became interested and help came from the most conservative quarters. Eventually the New York employers were willing to make peace, and the strikers, whose interests were represented in the conferences by John Mitchell and Morris Hillquit, won substantially all their demands but the closed shop. It was a remarkable testimonial to the value of organized effort.

The "uprising of the twenty thousand" demonstrated, as Gompers pointed out, "the extent to which women are taking up industrial life, their consequent tendency to stand together in the struggle and the capacity of women as strikers to suffer, to do, and to dare in support of their rights." [1] But its immediate significance was more portentous, for it served as the preliminary to an even greater struggle. On July 6, 1910, the New York cloak and suit makers, an unorganized mass of sweated workers, went out on a strike to secure the abolition of subcontracting and obtain higher wages and better working conditions, to which was later added a demand for the closed shop.[2] The International Ladies' Garment Workers' Union took charge, its membership jumping in two weeks from twenty thousand to seventy thousand. In a series of conferences, the prime mover of which was Louis D. Brandeis, the strikers won all their demands but the closed shop. What was more important for the industry, a machinery of arbitration was set up to take care of future disputes. Thus two relatively short strikes changed the manufacture of women's clothing from an oppressively sweated trade characterized by

[1] American Federation of Labor, *Report of the Proceedings of the Thirtieth Annual Convention* (1910), 23.

[2] *American Year Book for 1910*, 426-428.

chaotic conditions to one strongly organized and possessing effective methods of self-control.[1]

According to an exhaustive study of strikes during the period 1881-1905, three fifths of those called in 1881 were for increased wages and but one sixteenth for recognition of the union, while in 1905 less than one third were for higher pay and about an equal proportion for recognition of the union. Furthermore, while the unions were responsible for less than half the strikes in the earlier year, they instigated directly or indirectly three fourths of those in 1905.[2] Between 1898 and 1905 the number of strikes doubled, and the conflicts were often accompanied by violence and bloodshed.[3] This increasing industrial strife and the waxing strength of labor inevitably brought counterattacks from the employing class. To a man, who after great effort over a long period of years had established a business and developed friendly relations with his workingmen, it was highly irritating to have a labor organizer or "walking delegate" suddenly appear to tell him how to run his affairs. The more conciliatory employers might join the National Civic Federation and accede to trade agreements with their workmen, but the more conservative stiffened their backs. The leadership in the fight was taken by the National Association of Manufacturers, founded in 1895 chiefly to promote export trade, but now boldly declar-

[1] Levine, *Women's Garment Workers*, chap. xxii; Samuel Gompers, "The Struggles in the Garment Trades," *Am. Federationist*, XX (1913), 185-202.

[2] U. S. Commissioner of Labor, *Twenty-First Annual Report* (1907), 32.

[3] U. S. Comr. of Labor, *Twenty-First Ann. Rep.*, 15; and analysis in G. G. Groat, *Organized Labor in America* (N. Y., 1919), chap. x. The number of strikes had increased from 471 in 1881 to 1056 in 1898, 3494 in 1903 and 2077 in 1905. Of the 36,757 strikes taking place in the quarter-century 1881-1905 over half (18,596) had occurred in the last eight years.

ing war against organized labor.[1] Whatever the cause, the American Federation of Labor entered again on a period of lean years. Not only was its membership less in 1910 than in 1905,[2] but it had seen its status before the law continually whittled away by the judiciary.

The lead in the opposition to labor in the courts was taken by the American Anti-Boycott Association, organized in 1902.[3] Of the various legal battles which it financed, that involving the Danbury Hatters' boycott is the most famous. In 1902 the Hatters' Union attempted to force D. E. Loewe and Company of Danbury, Connecticut, to adopt the closed shop and, when Loewe refused, instituted a nation-wide boycott against the products of his concern. Suit was promptly brought in the federal courts charging the unions with violating the Sherman antitrust act. The case dragged along for fourteen years, reaching the Supreme Court three times, but in the end the plaintiff won a verdict for $80,000, which, trebled under the law and with costs added, amounted to $252,000.[4] The company proceeded to attach the bank accounts and institute foreclosure proceedings against one hundred and forty homes belonging to union men, but before they were sold the unions settled for $235,000. The greatest blow, however, was the decision of the court that an interstate boycott fell under the Sherman law. To counteract this, labor succeeded in introducing

[1] In 1903 it founded the Citizens' Industrial Association to oppose the demands of labor, and four years later fathered the National Council for Industrial Defense in order to lobby against labor bills in the state and federal legislatures.

[2] 1,676,000 in 1904, and 1,562,000 in 1910.

[3] Later called the League for Industrial Rights.

[4] Loewe *v.* Lawlor, 208 U. S., 274 (1908); Lawlor *v.* Loewe, 235 U. S., 522 (1915). See also H. W. Laidler, *Boycotts and the Labor Struggle* (N. Y., 1913), chap. ix; Leo Wolman, *The Boycott in American Trade Unions* (Balt., 1916); American Federation of Labor, *Rep. of the Proceeds. of the Thirty-Fifth Ann. Conv.* (1915), 73-77; and the files of the *American Federationist*, XV (1908).

in the Clayton act of 1914 a clause which was intended to exempt labor unions from prosecution under the anti-trust laws, an exemption which, however, was speedily nullified by the Supreme Court.[1]

While the Danbury Hatters' case was still pending, the Federation as a whole became involved in another boycott suit. In 1906 the metal polishers in the works of the Buck Stove and Range Company of St. Louis struck for a nine-hour day and appealed to the central organization for aid. The Federation, after investigation, added the name of this company to the "We Don't Patronize" list in the *American Federationist* and members were admonished to boycott the concern. So effective was the boycott that J. W. Van Cleave, president of the company, widely known as a bitter foe of organized labor, obtained an injunction from the supreme court of the District of Columbia forbidding the officers and members of the American Federation of Labor not only to include the plaintiff's name in their unfair list but also to refer to the dispute in print or by word of mouth. This injunction, accurately characterized as "one of the most sweeping orders given in American jurisprudence," [2] was obeyed in so far as the unfair list was concerned, but otherwise ignored, and Gompers continued to discuss the case and to denounce the injunction in the labor press and on the platform.

On March 11, 1909, the original injunction was so narrowed by the court of appeals as to make such acts legal; but in the interval Judge Daniel W. Wright sentenced Gompers, Mitchell and Frank Morrison to one

[1] Samuel Gompers, "The Charter of Industrial Freedom," *Am. Federationist*, XXI (1914), 957-974. For the court proceedings, see Duplex Printing Press Co. *v.* Deering, 254 U. S., 443, and Truex *v.* Corrigan, 257 U. S., 312; also J. A. Fitch, *The Causes of Industrial Unrest* (N. Y., 1924), 308 ff.

[2] Laidler, *Boycotts and the Labor Struggle*, 143.

year, nine and six months in prison respectively for contempt of court in an astonishing scene in which for two hours the judge excoriated the defendants as leaders of "the rabble" and as public enemies who would "smite the foundations of civil government" and subordinate law to "anarchy and riot." [1] While these contempt decisions were pending in the United States Supreme Court, Van Cleave died and his company made peace with the unions and requested the dismissal of the injunction. The court thereupon dismissed the injunction and the contempt proceedings dependent upon it, but without prejudice to the power of the supreme court of the District of Columbia to punish any contempt against it; whereupon Judge Wright appointed a committee of three lawyers, all of whom had been conspicuous as attorneys for the Anti-Boycott and National Manufacturers' associations, to recommend prosecution or dismissal.[2] This committee, of course, recommended prosecution, and the case dragged on until 1914 when it was dismissed by the United States Supreme Court as outlawed by the statute of limitations.[3] Again the judiciary had seemed reluctant to show favor to labor.

Organized labor had tried to make a test case of the Buck Stove injunction, but the United States Supreme Court avoided a discussion of the fundamental issues. As conceived by labor these issues involved the power of a court to issue an order restraining citizens in an industrial dispute from exercising their constitutional guarantees of

[1] Wright's decision and Gompers' description of the scene, as well as the reply of himself, Mitchell and Morrison, are given in the *American Federationist*, XVI (1909), no. 2.

[2] These men were J. J. Darlington, Daniel Davenport and James M. Beck.

[3] Gompers tells the story in *Seventy Years of Life and Labor*, II, chap. xxxiii. See also Laidler, *Boycotts and the Labor Struggle*, chap. viii, and 450-454 as far as 1913; *American Federationist*, XV (1908), 1072-1076; XIX (1912), 601 ff.

free speech, free press and peaceable assemblage.[1] For a quarter of a century the indiscriminate and novel use of the injunction had been growing in the United States until it had become an instrument which greatly increased the power of the judiciary and one which was used to discriminate against the interests of labor. The danger of normal lawful activities being interfered with by biased and class-conscious judges was so real that the fight to curtail the use of "labor injunctions" became one of the chief interests of organized labor. Not only was the issue one of concern to the representatives of the organized worker, but it provoked protest from thoughtful jurists as well.

From 1894 to 1914 every session of Congress but one had the question before it in one form or another, and in 1903 considerable data were collected on the subject.[2] California in 1903, Arizona, Iowa, Kansas and Oregon in 1913, Massachusetts and the federal government in 1914, passed anti-injunction legislation, and other states did so in succeeding years. The Clayton act, which Gompers hailed as "Labor's Magna Charta," declared that strikes, peaceful picketing and refusal to patronize were not violations of any federal law. It prohibited injunctions in labor disputes growing out of the terms and conditions of work, unless necessary to prevent irreparable injury, and granted jury trial to persons accused of violations of injunctions through acts indictable as criminal offenses.[3] After a long and persistent struggle the efforts of labor appeared to be crowned with victory, but the courts, as in the case of the boycott provisions, speed-

[1] Gompers, *Seventy Years of Life and Labor*, II, 206.

[2] Felix Frankfurter and Nathan Greene, *The Labor Injunction* (N. Y., 1930), chap. iv. See also Committee on the Judiciary, *Anti-Injunction Bill* (Wash., 1904).

[3] *U. S. Statutes at Large*, XXVII, pt. i, 738 ff.; *American Federationist*, XXI (1914), 957-974.

ily nullified the intent of Congress, leaving only that part relating to jury trial as good law.[1]

Labor found an enemy not only in the courts but also in the state police. State constabularies were little known before the twentieth century though Massachusetts had supported a small force since 1865. The Arizona rangers were established in 1901, Connecticut began the same practice in 1903, the New Mexico mounted police were organized in 1905 and an emergency force in Nevada in 1908.[2] The most important development, however, was the establishment of the Pennsylvania state constabulary in 1905. Denounced by labor as the "American Cossacks," and as a tool of capital to break up strikes, the state police system was viewed by others as the most effective means of preserving law and order both against rural criminality and industrial outbreaks. Although the Pennsylvania state police gave less than one sixth of their time during the first sixteen years of their existence to strike duty,[3] their invariable presence at major industrial conflicts and the frequently alleged incidents of brutality in dealing with strikers[4] incurred the enmity of labor. Labor's opposition at least prevented for some years the extension of the system and kept its advocates on the defensive.[5]

While the labor movement had to be constantly on

[1] J. R. Commons and J. B. Andrews, *Principles of Labor Legislation* (N. Y., 1916), 103-106; Frankfurter and Greene, *Labor Injunction*, 192-198.

[2] Bruce Smith, *The State Police* (N. Y., 1925), 36-46, 54-65. The Arizona and New Mexico forces were later disbanded.

[3] Pennsylvania State Police, *Biennial Report for 1920-1921*, 65.

[4] Pa. State Federation of Labor, *The American Cossack* (Phila., 1915). The Nevada police were established as a direct result of the Goldfield strike. *Papers Related to Labor Troubles at Goldfield, Nevada* (60 Cong., 1 sess., *House Doc.*, no. 607).

[5] A state police was established in New York, Colorado (later disbanded) and Michigan in 1917, in West Virginia in 1919, in New Jersey in 1921.

guard against enemies outside its ranks, its development was also handicapped by internal dissensions. Though Gompers and his lieutenants were able to hold the Federation to a steady course, their policies upon even such fundamentals as political action and form of organization were under constant attack. The Federation persistently refused to countenance a distinct labor party, preferring to work for its demands within the channels of the old parties. Its policy, definitely laid down by the executive council in 1906, called for the defeat of political aspirants who were antilabor, the nomination of a straight labor candidate if neither party was favorable and the unqualified support of the men "who have shown themselves friendly to labor." [1] Since the Republican party was the party of big business, organized labor tended to throw in its lot with the Democrats. Thus, in 1908 when Gompers and other members of the executive committee appeared at the Republican convention to plead for an anti-injunction plank, "James Van Cleave and the Republican reactionaries told Labor to 'go to Denver,'" where the Democrats were to meet.[2] There they went, and the incorporation of the desired plank in the Democratic platform, along with the Republican nomination of Taft, long odious to labor as an "injunction judge," led Gompers and other leaders to espouse the cause of the Democracy. Four years later they openly indorsed Wilson, and the Democratic party, as we have seen, reciprocated two years after with the Clayton act.

A radical minority in the American Federation still cherished hopes of committing the body to socialism. But, as Daniel DeLeon's attempts in the 1890's had

[1] *American Federationist*, XIII (1906), 529-531.

[2] Gompers, *Seventy Years of Life and Labor*, II, 262; also résumé by Gompers in *American Federationist*, XX (1913), 585-616, and in American Federation of Labor, *Rep. of the Proceeds. of the Thirty-Second Ann. Conv.* (1912), 31-34.

shown, all such expectations were doomed to certain failure. Far from wishing to abolish the capitalistic system, the typical wage-earner desired merely to open the doors wider so that he might share more generously in its benefits. Socialism, however, as a political movement showed signs of steadily increasing strength during these years, partly as a result of a swelling tide of protest votes against the policies of the old parties,[1] and partly because of the ability of new leaders who entered the movement. Earlier socialist agitation had been largely in the hands of recent immigrants unacquainted with American conditions, but with the formation in 1897 of a new party, presently known as the Socialist party, men like Eugene V. Debs and Victor Berger undertook to broaden the appeal of the cause and to work in such a way as to conciliate organized labor.[2] Its popular vote increased from about ninety-five thousand in the presidential election of 1900 to more than nine hundred thousand in 1912, at which time Socialist officeholders were to be found in more than three hundred cities and towns.[3] Officially the American Federation of Labor continued to maintain its distance and the party made no progress in the rural South. Its support came mainly from among skilled manual workers, clerical workers, merchants and professional people in the urban districts of Ohio, Pennsylvania, New York, Illinois, California and Wisconsin. Though the Socialists failed to win a single electoral vote, a political party of some significance, based primarily upon the labor vote, now actually ex-

[1] In the election of 1912 the Socialist popular vote was about eight times the enrolled party membership.

[2] Morris Hillquit, *History of Socialism in the United States* (N. Y., 1903), pt. ii, chap. iv.

[3] R. F. Hoxie, "The Socialist Party in the November Elections," *Journ. of Polit. Economy*, XX, no. 3, 205-223; C. E. Merriam, *The American Party System* (N. Y., 1922), 93 ff.

isted, and the pressure to swing the American Federation of Labor officially into line was persistent. As late as 1914 the United Mine Workers insisted that the time had arrived "for the laboring people to come together in a political labor party." [1]

Another bone of contention within the Federation had to do with the old question of whether the wage-earners should not organize as "one big union" rather than be split off in separate crafts. Such bodies as the United Brewery Workers and the United Mine Workers of America, in which industrial unionism had persisted, formed a radical bloc in the Federation inclined to regard dubiously the traditional craft emphasis. One of them, the Western Federation of Miners, was so insubordinate that in 1902 it led in the formation of the American Labor Union. This proved to be the first step toward the founding of a more powerful labor body on the same principle, the Industrial Workers of the World, which sprang full blown from a meeting of radical socialists and industrial unionists in Chicago in June, 1905. Among those in attendance were Debs, the popular standard bearer of the Socialist party, William D. ("Big Bill") Haywood, soon to emerge as the real leader of the new organization, and others of the ablest and most respected labor leaders, many of them American-born and with a long experience in the labor movement.

The delegates, who represented perhaps fifty thousand workmen in forty distinct occupations, committed themselves unreservedly to industrial unionism and revolutionary socialism. "The working class and the employing class have nothing in common . . . ," asserted the preamble to their constitution. "Between these two classes a struggle must go on until all the toilers come together . . . and take hold of that which they produce by their

[1] Groat, *Organized Labor in America*, 372.

labor through an economic organization of the working class, without affiliation with any political party." [1] In a later revision they went even farther, proclaiming that, "Instead of the conservative motto, 'a fair day's wage for a fair day's work,' we must inscribe on our banner the revolutionary watchword, 'Abolition of the wage system.' It is the historic mission of the working class to do away with capitalism." [2] Moreover, unlike the American Federation of Labor, they set about to organize skilled and unskilled alike. "We don't propose," said Delegate Charles O. Sherman, "to organize only the common man with the callous hands but we want the clerical force," while Haywood declared: "We are going down in the gutter to get at the mass of workers and bring them up to a decent plane of living." [3]

Overloaded with strong leaders, the I. W. W. was handicapped from the start by factional quarrels, which eventually left the radical direct-actionist group in control. Its paid-up membership was never large, amounting to but four or five thousand at the commencement of its great activity in 1912 and probably never exceeding sixty thousand; [4] but the activities of its leaders and the revolutionary ardor of its members gave it an influence far beyond its numerical strength until it threatened to become a serious rival of the American Federation of Labor. Its radical appeal won a following among the unskilled factory hands of the East and, in particular, among the migratory "wobblies" who cut the timber and followed the harvests—the wandering casual laborers, exploited, persecuted, homeless, but with grit enough

[1] Vincent St. John, *The I. W. W., Its History, Structure and Methods* (3d edn., Cleveland, 1913), 5; P. F. Brissenden, *The I. W. W.; a Study of American Syndicalism* (Columbia Univ., *Studies*, LXXXIII), app. ii.

[2] St. John, *The I. W. W.*, 9.

[3] Brissenden, *The I. W. W.*, 87.

[4] Brissenden, *The I. W. W.*, app. iv, table D.

to fight back at a system which they had learned to hate.[1] Because of its bitter antagonism to the existing economic order, its willingness to employ sabotage, and its success in handling the unskilled and unorganized toilers, the I. W. W. was vigorously denounced and relentlessly opposed by capital and conservative labor alike. Nevertheless it brought improved conditions in certain industries, and it eventually forced the American Federation of Labor to give greater recognition to the unskilled worker.

The I. W. W. first attracted attention in the Goldfield, Nevada, strikes of 1906-1907, and the strike of the Pressed Steel Car Company at McKees Rocks, Pennsylvania, in 1909; [2] but its real fame came late in the latter year when at Spokane, Fresno and other places on the Pacific Coast it made a fight for free speech. The tactics of the I. W. W., when a member was arrested for speaking, was to descend upon the town in large numbers and force the authorities to arrest them until the expense to the town became so great that the battle was won. Over five hundred went to jail and four lost their lives in the Spokane fight. The crest of their power came, however, in 1912 when they took the aggressive lead in the strikes at Lawrence, Passaic and elsewhere.

The Lawrence outbreak involved an uprising of over twenty thousand employees, who demanded a considerable increase in wages and radical changes in working conditions.[3] Receiving no coöperation from the craft unions, the unskilled workers, mostly recent immigrants, invited the I. W. W. to help them and, under the leadership of Joseph J. Ettor and "Big Bill" Haywood, the men were heartened for a bitter and protracted struggle.

[1] Carleton Parker, *The Casual Laborer* (N. Y., 1920), 108.

[2] St. John, *The I. W. W.*, 20 ff.; André Tridon, *The New Unionism* (N. Y., 1913), 105 ff.

[3] C. P. Neill, *Report on the Strike of Textile Workers in Lawrence, Mass., in 1912* (62 Cong., 2 sess., *Sen. Doc.*, no. 870), app. A.

In clashes with the authorities an Italian woman was shot and a young Armenian bayoneted to death. Hoping to discredit the strikers a Lawrence business man "planted" dynamite in several places, and, as a last resort, two leaders, Ettor and Arturo Giovanitti, were thrown into prison. Despite such provocations Ettor and Haywood did what they could to keep their followers in order and at the same time they skillfully combated the employers' propaganda against them. Public sympathy and publicity were cleverly secured by sending companies of strikers' children out of the city to spend "vacations" at the homes of strike sympathizers.[1] In the end victory lay with the strikers.

If Lawrence marked the crest of I. W. W. power, Paterson marked the beginning of the decline. A strike there in the broad-silk mills on February 25, 1913, quickly spread to the ribbon factories and dye shops until almost three hundred establishments and over twenty-five thousand workers were affected. The workers' demands included an eight-hour day, higher wages, better sanitary conditions and opposition to the three and four-loom system. Two factors explain the long and relentless battle. The introduction of the three and four-loom system, which involved the question as to whether Paterson should invade the cheap-silk field in opposition to the Pennsylvania mills, caused fear among the workers that, in such an event, greater strain, lower wages or loss of work would result. In the second place, there was the embittered opposition of the employers to the tactics of the I. W. W., who, on their part, believed that their

[1] Neill, *Report*, 44, 51, 58; Samuel Gompers, "The Lawrence Dynamite Conspiracy," *Am. Federationist*, XIX (1912), 815 ff.; E. D. Fosdick, "After the Strike—in Lawrence," *Outlook*, CI, 340-346 (June 15, 1912). Margaret Sanger describes the children in Committee on Rules, *Hearings on the Strike at Lawrence, Mass.* (62 Cong., 2 sess., *House Doc.*, no. 671), 226-232.

future progress depended on winning the strike. Their best leaders, Haywood, Ettor, Patrick Quinlan, Carlo Tresca and Elizabeth Gurley Flynn, hastened to Paterson and what funds they could raise were thrown into the campaign. In spite of police brutality, infringement of constitutional rights by the judiciary and the imprisonment of their leaders on the most flimsy excuses, the I. W. W. held their ranks intact for five months. In the end, lack of funds and loss of morale caused the strikers to surrender.

Nothing harmed the cause of labor more than the lessening of public confidence which resulted from the persistent antilabor propaganda and in part from the extralegal, if not criminal, activities of the more radical labor leaders. Two incidents in particular, the Steunenberg case and the dynamiting of the *Los Angeles Times*, were significant in this respect. On December 30, 1905, Frank Steunenberg, who by his course as governor of Idaho during the Coeur d'Alene strike of 1899 had incurred the hatred of labor, was murdered in front of his home at Caldwell. A certain Albert E. Horsely confessed to the murder, but alleged he had been hired to do it by Haywood, George H. Moyer and George W. Pettibone, officers of the Western Federation of Miners. Extradited to Idaho upon the false assertions of a county attorney, and failing to win their freedom under habeas-corpus proceedings, Haywood and Pettibone were tried for murder. In the public prints the accused were widely denounced as criminals and anarchists, and even President Roosevelt found time to condemn them as "undesirable citizens." Gompers and other friends of labor, on the other hand, bestirred themselves to see that the men had the benefit

[1] *American Year Book for 1913*, 411-413; Gregory Mason, "Industrial War in Paterson," *Outlook*, CIV, 283-287 (June 7, 1913); J. A. Fitch, "The I. W. W., an Outlaw Organization," *Survey*, XXX, 355-362 (June 7, 1913).

of a proper legal defense. In the end both men were acquitted, and the charge against Moyer dropped.[1]

More damaging to labor was the case of the McNamara brothers, an incident in the warfare between capital and labor on the Pacific Coast. On October 1, 1910, the building of the *Los Angeles Times,* whose proprietor was one of the bitterest foes of organized labor, was destroyed by a dynamite charge causing the death of twenty-one people. Through the efforts of the detective William J. Burns, three members of the International Association of Bridge and Iron Workers, John I. and James B. McNamara and Ortie McManigal, were arrested for the crime. McManigal made a confession involving the others, but the McNamaras so vehemently protested their innocence that the American Federation of Labor took vigorous steps for their defense. All over the country liberal opinion was aroused, but in the end the brothers pleaded guilty. Though the Federation promptly repudiated them, Burns talked much about the men "higher up" who were implicated and asserted that Gompers had known for some time of the guilt of the McNamaras.[2] No evidence, however, was ever produced to prove it. The incident did much to discredit the labcr cause and the ordeal was one of the most trying that American labor had ever had to face.[3]

The prestige of the labor movement was further affected by humiliating and costly defeats, such as that sus-

[1] U. S. Bureau of Labor, *Report on Labor Disturbances in the State of Colorado* (58 Cong., 3 sess., *Sen. Doc.*, no. 122); Gompers, *Seventy Years of Life and Labor,* II, 182; Theodore Roosevelt, *Autobiography* (N. Y., 1919), 487-491.

[2] "Gompers and Burns on Unionism and Dynamite," *McClure's,* XXXVIII (1912), 363 ff.

[3] Gompers, *Seventy Years of Life and Labor,* II, 183 ff.; *American Year Book for 1911,* 352-354; *American Federationist,* XVIII (1911), 433-450, 606, 611; XIX (1912), 17-23, 44-48, 132-135, 201-206; American Federation of Labor, *Rep. of the Proceeds. of the Thirty-First Ann. Conv.* (1911), 41-45.

tained in the Colorado coal strike which lasted from September, 1913, to December, 1914. In the southern counties of Colorado industrial conditions were found at their worst. Here were mining towns, isolated from civilization, owned or controlled politically, socially and economically by mine officials representing absentee stockholders—towns devoid of decent living accommodations, elementary sanitation, chances for recreation or medical attention, where drinking water unfit for use was pumped out of the mines and peddled by the companies at twenty-five cents a barrel and the saloon was the one place of public resort.[1] So absolute was the domination of the companies that even a United States congressman asserted, "I myself had to get a pass to enter one of the incorporated towns of the State of Colorado, situated upon the property of the Colorado Fuel and Iron Co., and I had to get a pass to get out." [2] Eighty per cent of the thirty thousand inhabitants of these mining settlements were unable to speak English. They were described by one of the militia as "essentially as good as the average man," but "being rapidly debauched and degraded by conditions over which they have no control," and "living under a despotism so absolute that the radical labor press is not far wrong in calling them slaves." [3]

These workers were partially organized in 1913 by the United Mine Workers of America and went on strike for recognition of the union, higher wages and the enforcement of the state labor laws regarding mining. Moving out of the company houses, the miners and their families established themselves in tent colonies. Some

[1] W. T. Davis, "The Strike War in Colorado," *Outlook*, CVII, 70 (May 9, 1914).

[2] Subcommittee of the Committee on Mines and Mining, *Conditions in the Coal Mines of Colorado* (Wash., 1914), II, pt. x, 2880.

[3] Davis, "Strike War in Colorado," 73.

armed clashes occurred between the workers and the imported detectives and deputy sheriffs, and the state militia was called out. The friction reached a climax on April 20 when a pitched battle at Ludlow caused the burning of the tent colony there and the death of six men, two women and eleven children.[1] Without avail President Wilson urged John D. Rockefeller, jr., who controlled one of the largest of the companies involved, to submit the dispute to arbitration, and when the situation got beyond the control of Colorado, he sent two thousand federal troops to restore order. Again in September the president proposed a plan for a "three-year truce," but, while acceptable to the miners, it was refused by the operators. Undiscouraged, he appointed a commission to settle future labor disputes in Colorado. With the mines thoroughly protected and operated by strike breakers the strike collapsed, though not before it had given the nation a picture of almost unbelievable industrial feudalism—of an employing and exploiting class whose social and economic ideas had hardly advanced beyond the ethics of a private warfare carried on with machine guns and dynamite.[2]

In spite of growing opposition without and within, the Federation and its allies, the great Railway Brotherhoods, hung on doggedly to their well-established policies. Profiting by the rising tide of prosperity and the growing humanitarianism of the bourgeoisie, labor could contemplate at the opening of the World War a decided advance in status. The percentage of labor organized had doubled in the decade 1900-1910 and the membership of the American Federation of Labor had grown to over

[1] *American Year Book for 1914*, 416-417.

[2] Subcommittee of the Committee on Mines, *Coal Mines of Colorado*, II, pt. x, 2841 ff.; testimony of J. D. Rockefeller, jr., in American Federation of Labor, *Rep. of Proceeds. of the Thirty-Fifth Ann. Conv.* (1915), 70-73.

two million by 1914.[1] Economists differed over the question as to whether labor was gaining its fair share of the enormous wealth produced, but there was general agreement that the standard of living had risen since 1898. This rising standard in no small measure was due to the immense amount of labor legislation which had been placed upon the statute books. As far as the federal government was concerned, such legislation had been slow in coming; for it was 1912 before Congress passed an effective and far-reaching eight-hour law for government contract work,[2] 1913 before a separate cabinet department was created for labor, 1914 before an effort was made to exempt labor from prosecution under the Sherman act, and 1915 before the La Follette law for insuring decent conditions for American sailors was passed.

Of greater concern to the toiling masses, however, was the legislation passed by the states. In this respect the period stands apart from all others in its accomplishments. Additional legislation for the protection of children was passed in all the states,[3] and a distinct impetus was given to laws protecting women after the United States Supreme Court held the Oregon ten-hour law constitutional.[4] Many states prohibited or limited night work, and sought to safeguard women from "sweating" and from labor which would endanger health. Massa-

[1] G. E. Barnett, "Growth of Labor Organizations in the United States, 1897-1914," *Quar. Journ. of Econ.*, XXX, 780 ff., puts the wage-earners as 3.5 per cent organized in 1900 and 7 per cent in 1910. Leo Wolman's estimate of 7.7 is in approximate agreement. See his "The Extent of Trade Unionism," Am. Acad. of Polit. and Social Sci., *Annals*, LXIX, 118 ff.

[2] Earlier laws of 1868 and 1892 had been so restricted as to be of little value. Commons and Andrews, *Labor Legislation*, 226 ff.

[3] See later, chap. vi.

[4] Muller *v.* Oregon, 208 U. S., 412 (1908); G. G. Groat, *Attitude of American Courts in Labor Cases* (Columbia Univ., *Studies*, XLII, no. 108), 297 ff.

chusetts passed the first minimum-wage law in 1912, to be followed in 1913 by eight other states.[1] Even men, particularly in hazardous trades, were benefited by special legislation, while a large number of laws were passed to regulate and improve physical conditions of employment.[2]

Even more significant was the widespread adoption of laws for workmen's compensation. Notwithstanding the high rate of industrial accidents the United States was the last great industrial nation to recognize the principle that responsibility for occupational accidents should rest upon the industry rather than the individual. Maryland (1902) and Montana (1909) enacted insurance laws with compensation features, but they were limited in their application and were soon declared, in part or in whole, unconstitutional.[3] Massachusetts passed an optional law in 1909, which was a dead letter, and when New York enacted a compulsory one in 1910, it was speedily declared unconstitutional as the taking of property without due process of law.[4] By means of constitutional amendments and carefully framed laws judicial opposition was finally obviated. Eleven states passed employers' liability acts in 1911, three in 1912, eight in 1913, two in 1914 and eleven in 1915, until by 1921 all but six and the District of Columbia had fallen in

[1] In 1912 Ohio adopted a constitutional amendment allowing minimum-wage laws for all classes of workers, and California in 1914 adopted one applicable to women and minors.

[2] Commons and Andrews, *Labor Legislation*, chap. vii; G. S. Watkins, *An Introduction to the Study of Labor Problems* (N. Y., 1922), chap. xxv.

[3] Employers' Liability and Workmen's Compensation Commission, *Report* (62 Cong., 2 sess., *Sen. Doc.*, no. 338); U. S. Bureau of Labor Statistics, *Bulls.*, nos. 45, 57, 203. The U. S. Philippine Commission had granted compensation to insular employees (1905) and the Federal Congress (1908) to certain employees.

[4] Ives *v.* the South Buffalo Railroad Company, 201 N. Y., 271; 94 N. E., 431 (1911).

line.[1] While compensation scales were grossly inadequate and the administration of the laws left much to be desired, they marked an important advance in according justice to the workers.[2]

The agitation for workmen's compensation aroused also much interest in other types of social insurance, such as old-age pensions, mothers' pensions and sickness and unemployment insurance, which had been experimented with in Europe and for which there appeared to be a decided need in America. Insurance and benefit funds had long existed in trade unions and fraternal organizations, and in some cases pension funds had been provided for city and state employees; but the state had not hitherto taken measures to safeguard its citizens as a whole against sickness, unemployment or old age, unless the wide distribution of Civil War pensions in the North might be so considered.[3] In spite of the staggering economic loss each year from sickness, it was estimated in 1907 that but 1,300,000 wage-earners out of 20,000,000 were covered in any way by sickness insurance through trade-union or other funds.[4] State insurance existed nowhere in America, and during this period remained in the preliminary stage of agitation except in the case of Wisconsin which in 1911 provided such a system.[5] The same was true of unemployment

[1] Missouri, Arkansas, North Carolina, South Carolina, Mississippi and Florida. Missouri, which was the only one of these states of industrial importance, submitted a compensation act to popular referendum twice (1920 and 1922), but it was defeated both times.

[2] U. S. Bur. of Labor Statistics, *Bulls.*, nos. 45, 57, 203, 240; E. H. Downey, *Workmen's Compensation* (N. Y., 1924), chap. vii; I. M. Rubinow, *Social Insurance* (N. Y., 1913), chap. xi; D. H. Van Doren, *Workmen's Compensation and Insurance* (N. Y., 1918).

[3] C. R. Henderson, *Industrial Insurance in the United States* (Chicago, 1907); *Workmen's Insurance and Benefit Funds in the United States* (U. S. Commissioner of Labor, *Twenty-Third Ann. Rep.*, 1908).

[4] Rubinow, *Social Insurance*, 292.

[5] Massachusetts instituted in 1907 a plan proposed by Louis D. Brandeis of voluntary insurance through savings banks under public administration.

insurance, although some advance was made in the handling of this problem by the establishment of free city and state employment agencies. Interest in unemployment reached its height in the industrial depression early in 1914 when the first National Conference on Unemployment was held and the New York legislature established a state-wide system of labor exchanges.[1]

The chief obstacle in the way of social legislation was the opposition of the courts rather than the indifference of the public. Grounded in eighteenth-century legal philosophy, unacquainted with modern industrial conditions and conservative by nature, the judiciary at some time or other has held practically every type of labor legislation unconstitutional on the ground that it was "class legislation" or that it took away property without due process of law.[2] Thus, in the first Ritchie case in 1895 the Illinois supreme court held invalid an eight-hour day for women; [3] the Colorado supreme court in 1899 threw out an eight-hour law in the smelting industry as "an unwarrantable interference with the right of both the employer and employee in making contracts"; [4] the United States Supreme Court in 1905 declared that the Lochner ten-hour law for bakers in New York state had "reached and passed the limit of the police power"; [5] and as late as 1907 the New York court nullified a law prohibiting night work for women.[6]

But these decisions were overruled or reversed as time went on. Some years before the Lochner decision, the

[1] *American Year Book for 1913*, 435; *for 1914*, 409; Watkins, *Labor Problems*, 242-247.

[2] Commission on Industrial Relations, *Final Report* (Wash., 1916), I, 48.

[3] Ritchie *v.* People, 155 Ill., 98 (1895).

[4] *In re* Morgan, 26 Colo., 415; 58 Pacific, 1071 (1899).

[5] Lochner *v.* New York, 198 U. S., 45 (1905).

[6] People *v.* Williams, 189 N. Y., 131; 80 N. E., 778 (1907).

federal judiciary sustained the right of Utah to limit the hours of work in mines and smelters, and subsequently upheld the Oregon ten-hour law in 1908 and a California eight-hour law in 1915.[1] The state courts likewise showed a change of heart, for the Illinois tribunal in part reversed itself in the second Ritchie case, and the New York state supreme court totally did so in 1915 on the question of night work for women.[2] While the activities of labor continued to be limited by legal interpretations and the wholesale use of injunctions, in other respects the judiciary gave clear evidence of yielding to the humanitarian emphasis of the times as the minds of the judges were touched by the new spirit of the age.

[1] Holden *v.* Hardy, 169 U. S., 366; Muller *v.* Oregon, 208 U. S., 412; Miller *v.* Wilson, 236 U. S., 373.

[2] Ritchie *v.* Wayman, 244 Ill., 509; People *v.* Charles Schweinler Press, 214 N. Y., 395.

CHAPTER IV

The New Democracy

To many thoughtful men in the opening years of the twentieth century it seemed that America in making her fortune was in peril of losing her soul. What had become of that precious concern of the Fathers, the "general welfare," when affairs of far-reaching social significance were settled outside legislative halls by contests between big business and little business, between capital and labor, between urban business interests and the embattled farmer? The infection indeed had spread to the legislatures themselves where the enactment of important laws was too often dictated by powerful lobbies which did not hesitate to employ outright corruption and bribery to accomplish their purposes. Despite the occasional victories of labor big business was in the saddle, and it was the unorganized and inarticulate public that was being whipped and spurred. The tocsin of revolt sounded in 1896 against "Wall Street" had been hushed by the bewildering new interests and the outburst of prosperity which came with the Spanish-American War. The death of Henry George in the midst of the New York mayoralty campaign of 1897 stilled the voice of the most acute critic of American economic life. Yet the fires of revolt, though burning low, were not quenched. Soon they were to blaze forth into hot and consuming flame.

Nowhere were conditions so bad as in state and municipal politics. Here the party machinery was at the beck and call of railroad and corporation interests which understood all too well the means whereby legislators were made their pliant tools. Indeed, bribery was so common in political life that Judge H. S. Priest of Missouri affirmed extenuatingly that it was, "at the most, a conventional crime," [1] and the grand jury for one of Folk's trials declared,

> We have listened to the confessions of State senators, and were we at liberty to make known all they have told us, the recital would appall and astound the citizens of this State. . . . Our investigations have gone back for twelve years, and during that time the evidence before us shows that corruption has been the usual and accepted thing in State legislation, and that, too, without interference or hindrance.[2]

"That bribery exists to a great extent in the elections of this state," said Governor L. F. C. Garvin of Rhode Island in a special message to the legislature in 1903, "is a matter of common knowledge." [3] Indeed, General Charles R. Brayton, boss of the Rhode Island "system," freely admitted that he was "an attorney for certain clients and looked out for their interests in the legislature," adding that he was retained annually by the New York, New Haven and Hartford Railroad Company and by other prominent corporations doing business in the state.[4] Such corporations as the railroad just

[1] Quoted by Lincoln Steffens, *The Struggle for Self-Government* (N. Y., 1906), 16.

[2] Quoted by F. C. Howe, "Joseph W. Folk," *Cosmopolitan*, XXXV (1903), 555. On Folk, who was circuit attorney of Missouri from 1900 until 1904, when he was elected governor, see also W. A. White, "Folk: the Story of a Little Leaven in a Great Commonwealth," *Cosmopolitan*, XXXV (1903), 545-560.

[3] Quoted by Lincoln Steffens, "Rhode Island: a State for Sale," *McClure's*, XXIV (1905), 340; "A Short View of Bribery," *Nation*, LXXVII, 45 (July 16, 1903).

[4] Steffens, *Struggle for Self-Government*, 133-134.

mentioned held the legislature of not one but a half-dozen states in the hollow of their hands.

Although the people exercised the forms of democracy, wherever they possessed anything worth stealing "interests" were at work in the state legislatures to take it away. A reform wave in Ohio in 1905 helped purify the legislature of that commonwealth, but how far even this body fell short of perfection is clear from one member's description of the last day of the session.

> Enmities were forgotten and by a tacit agreement each member was permitted to call up some bill that bore his name and if it was not too controversial it was permitted to pass. Thus members had something to show their constituents. These last hours were pandemonium. Many of the law-makers were drunk. . . . Scores of bills went through by gentlemen's agreement. Nobody knew what they contained and nobody cared. . . . I came away from the legislature with scant respect for the laws of the land. I had seen how they were made. Some were frankly bought and paid for. . . . Only occasionally were bills in the public interest forced through by the pressure of public opinion, and they were so crippled with amendments that they were of little value.[1]

How recreant to its trust a state legislature could be was dramatically illustrated in 1907 by the amazing exposure of the graft involving millions of dollars connected with the building of the new Pennsylvania state house.[2]

With the multiplying evidences of public betrayal before their eyes the voters, jarred out of their apathy or

[1] F. C. Howe, *Confessions of a Reformer* (N. Y., 1925), 165-166.

[2] Louis Seaber, "Pennsylvania Palace of Graft," *Independent*, LXII, 1235-1241 (May 30, 1907); Owen Wister, "The Keystone Crime," *Everybody's*, XVII (1906), 435-443.

complacency, resolved upon drastic measures to reform the law-making departments of their governments. The years from 1898 to 1914 were years of almost ceaseless constitutional tinkering, and the one constant thought in the minds of the members of the conventions was to curb the powers of the legislatures. Five states framed new organic laws,[1] in addition to those of the new states of Oklahoma (1907), New Mexico (1912) and Arizona (1912), and the comprehensive revisions made in Ohio (1912), Vermont (1913) and other states. More than fifteen hundred amendments to state constitutions were, in fact, proposed between 1900 and 1920, of which three out of five were adopted.[2] New York, which had accepted a new constitution in 1894, wrote a modern and scientific revision in 1915 which was voted down. Of the other states where the movement failed, an interesting example is Connecticut. Its legislature, under the control of rural delegates chosen through a "rotten-borough" system, acceded to the popular clamor for a constitutional convention, but made certain that the rural delegations would control it. The resulting constitution consequently offered little relief from existing abuses and was voted down in 1902.[3]

In general, these constitutional changes reveal an effort to strengthen the power of the executives, centralize administration and increase popular control over the government. So far did the tendency go that one expert queried whether it would "ultimately prove worth while to retain an expensive legislature to exercise its small residue of petty powers"; and when the movement had about run its course, another was led to assert that the

[1] Alabama (1901), Virginia (1902), Michigan (1908), New Hampshire (1912), Louisiana (1913).

[2] W. F. Dodd, *State Government* (2d edn., N. Y., 1928), 107.

[3] J. B. Phillips, *Recent State Constitution-Making* (Univ. of Colo., *Studies*, II, no. 2), 79-80.

"most serious impediment to a right kind of legislature and a proper kind of legislators seems to me to lie in the fact that they are individually and collectively powerless." [1] But if the new constitutions erred in reducing too radically the function of the legislative branch, they made long strides in the direction of greater executive efficiency and in the perfection of democratic machinery.

Of the democratic innovations the initiative, the referendum, the recall, the primary system, woman suffrage and the popular election of United States senators stand out. By means of the initiative a small percentage of the voters acquired the power of forcing upon the legislature the consideration of a measure, and by the referendum they could take it out of the hands of the legislature and compel its submission to the people. As early as 1898 South Dakota under Democratic-Populist leadership adopted an amendment providing for the initiative and referendum, and its example was followed two years later by Utah. But the widespread interest resulted when Oregon committed herself to the experiment in 1902.[2] In the next ten years fifteen other commonwealths followed her lead with some form of state-wide initiative and referendum.[3] Though the movement slowed up after 1912, Mississippi, North Dakota, Maryland and Massachusetts joined the procession between 1914 and 1918.

An even more radical innovation was the recall, a device for enabling dissatisfied voters to force a public official to submit himself and his policies to the test of a

[1] J. Q. Dealey, "General Tendencies in State Constitutions," *Am. Polit. Sci. Rev.*, I, 211; H. G. James, "Reorganization of State Government," *Am. Polit. Sci. Rev.*, IX, 297-298.

[2] J. D. Barnett, *The Operation of the Initiative, Referendum and Recall in Oregon* (N. Y., 1915).

[3] Nevada (referendum 1904, initiative and recall 1912), Montana (1906), Oklahoma (1907), Maine (1908), Missouri (1908), Michigan (1908), Arkansas (1910), Colorado (1910), California (1911), New Mexico (1911), Arizona (1911), Idaho (1912), Nebraska (1912), Ohio (1912), Washington (1912).

new election. First appearing in the Los Angeles city charter of 1903 and embodied in the Seattle charter of 1906, the recall spread most rapidly in the field of municipal government. Oregon gave it state-wide application in 1908, and ten other states followed before the close of 1914, of which all but one were west of the Mississippi.[1] The whole question was given wide publicity in 1911 when President Taft vetoed the resolution authorizing the admission of Arizona to the Union because of a clause in the constitution permitting the recall of judges. Though Arizona was forced to withdraw the clause, she reinserted an even more drastic provision after she had been safely admitted. Roosevelt in 1912 went so far as to approve the Colorado plan for the recall of judicial decisions, a stand which did more than anything else to alienate the conservatives in the campaign of that year.[2] The recall, as a matter of fact, has not been used with the same frequency as the initiative and referendum, the average through the country being not more than six recall elections annually in the past twenty years.

This generation was not content, however, to lock the barn door after the horse was stolen: it was determined that there should be a proper keeper of the stable. To this end it took steps to remove the choice of candidates from the machine-ridden party conventions and place it in the hands of the people. Wisconsin in 1903, under the influence of La Follette, was the first state to adopt the direct primary for all nominations and Oregon followed two years later. By 1915 the system, in some

[1] California, 1911; Arizona, Idaho, Washington, Colorado and Nevada, 1912; Michigan, 1913; Louisiana, North Dakota and Kansas, 1914. The laws regarding the recall, like those governing the initiative and referendum, vary considerably, being usually limited to administrative and elective officials. Dodd, *State Government*, 554, gives tables.

[2] The Colorado plan provided for a referendum to make valid a statute which, after passage by the legislature and approval by the governor, had been set aside by the supreme court.

form or other, was recognized in all of the states and adopted in its state-wide form in at least two thirds. Before interest in this innovation subsided, at least twenty of the states extended their laws to include preferential presidential primaries.[1]

Another important political change, facilitated by the primary system and further strengthening popular control of the government, was the direct choice by the people of United States senators. The Populist party had demanded it in the nineties, the Democratic party was on record for it from 1900 on, and the legislatures of more than two thirds of the states favored it before the Senate itself showed any interest. The demand was in part the result of the democratic tide sweeping the country and in part due to very definite abuses. Corruption was rife in the choice of senators by the legislatures and the feeling was strong that the Senate represented the special interests rather than the electorate. Bryce asserted in 1888 that "some, an increasing number, are senators because they are rich; a few are rich because they are senators," [2] and there was little a decade later to revive the faith of the people in the upper house. Tired of waiting, and quite contrary to the letter and spirit of the federal Constitution, twenty-nine states by 1912 had framed a method whereby electorates might indirectly work their will. In Oregon and Nebraska, for instance, the members of each party chose senatorial nominees in the primaries and these names were then submitted to all of the voters in the general election.[3] The candidates for the state legislature were required to indicate on the ballot whether or not they would support the popular choice. Invariably

[1] In spite of the widespread interest in the presidential preferential primary, at no time has it been a deciding factor, and with the exception of the 1912 campaign it has been of little significance.

[2] James Bryce, *American Commonwealth* (London, 1888), I, 158.

[3] A. H. Eaton, *The Oregon System* (Chicago, 1912), chap. viii.

they said they would do this, with the curious result that in 1908 a Republican legislature in Oregon was committed to the election of a Democrat, George E. Chamberlain. As members selected by popular choice began to take their seats in the Senate, that august body could hold out no longer. The Seventeenth Amendment passed both houses in 1912 and on May 31, 1913, became part of the Constitution.

The political reformation we have traced and the social legislation which followed in its wake were not obtained without strenuous effort and valiant leadership. In Oregon, where so many democratic innovations were tried out that the whole movement came to be called the "Oregon system," the battle was led by William S. U'Ren, a gentle but persistent crusader. Born in Wisconsin of parents who had emigrated from Cornwall, U'Ren had spent his boyhood in his father's blacksmith shop and upon various frontier farms. After studying law in Denver he had wandered about the West in search of health and opportunity until a reading of George's *Progress and Poverty* led him to a life of political reform. U'Ren held public office only once, but as secretary of various voters' organizations he was a leading influence behind the adoption of the Australian ballot (1891), the registration law (1899), the initiative and referendum (1902), the direct-primary law (1904), the corrupt-practices act (1908) and the recall (1910).[1] "In Oregon," asserted a contemporary observer, "the state government is divided into four departments—the executive, judicial, legislative and Mr. U'Ren—and it is still an open question who exerts the most power." [2]

[1] Lincoln Steffens, *Upbuilders* (N. Y., 1909), 285-320; Eaton, *Oregon System*; Barnett, *Initiative, Referendum and Recall*. On the laws, see also G. L. Hedges, *Where the People Rule* (San Francisco, 1914).

[2] *Oregonian*, July 17, 1906, 8; quoted by Barnett, *Initiative, Referendum and Recall*, 17.

Quite opposite in type from the self-effacing U'Ren was the battling politician, Robert M. La Follette, who, as part of a lifelong struggle against special privilege, won the governorship of Wisconsin in 1902, 1904 and 1906, forced a direct-primary law through the legislature, and rescued his state from railroad domination by championing a tax-equalization law and the establishment of a railroad commission.[1]

If Oregon was the outstanding example of progressive politics on the Pacific Coast and Wisconsin in the Middle West, the boss-ridden state of New Jersey toward the end of the reform period rather unexpectedly assumed that rôle in the East. A reform agitation had already been started in the state Republican party by Everett Colby and George L. Record when the Democratic machine nominated Woodrow Wilson, then president of Princeton, for governor in 1910. "I earnestly commend to your careful consideration," said the newly elected governor in his inaugural address, "the laws in recent years as adopted in the State of Oregon, whose effect has been to bring government back to the people and to protect it from the control of the representatives of selfish and special interests." [2] To the dismay of the politicians he proceeded straightway to demolish the reactionary Democratic machine in the state and took the lead in a thoroughgoing campaign for reform. His achievements embraced a strong public-utilities law, a workingmen's compensation act, a sweeping primary law including presidential preferential primaries, a corrupt-practices act governing campaign expenditures and methods and effective legislation for restraining corporate abuses. Long the refuge of trusts, New Jersey was at last brought

[1] R. M. La Follette, *Autobiography* (Madison, 1913); A. O. Barton, *La Follette's Winning of Wisconsin* (Madison, 1922).

[2] Hester E. Hosford, *Woodrow Wilson and New Jersey Made Over* (N. Y., 1912), 78.

by Wilson's efforts into line with the antitrust legislation of other progressive states.[1]

La Follette and Wilson were but outstanding examples of the new type of political leaders who were springing up in many parts of the country. Roosevelt, elected governor of New York state upon his return from the Spanish-American War, injected a cleaner atmosphere into New York politics and secured a reënactment of the civil-service law, much labor legislation, improvement in the conservation laws and the appointment of better state officials.[2] Charles Evans Hughes, who served two terms after defeating William Randolph Hearst for governor in 1906, gave New York state an efficient and distinctly reform administration, achieving among other things a commission to control public utilities, a law prohibiting race-track gambling and the enactment of a primary law. Even the Tammany governor, William Sulzer, made a stand for a far-reaching primary system, an action which so enraged the party bosses that they secured his impeachment and removal in 1913 on the charge of making a false statement in reference to his campaign fund.[3] In Missouri Folk carried his fight for clean government, begun in St. Louis, to the entire state and was elected governor in 1904. Albert B. Cummins, governor of Iowa from 1902 to 1908, secured the better regulation of railroads and the direct primary, while Hiram W. Johnson, who had come to the fore as the result of his activities in prosecuting

[1] Chaps. xiii-xix of the *Laws of New Jersey for 1913*; summarized in *American Year Book for 1913*, 344-345, and Mark Sullivan, *Our Times* (N. Y., 1926-), II, chap. xvii. These laws were soon withdrawn and New Jersey again became the "mother of trusts."

[2] Theodore Roosevelt, *Autobiography* (N. Y., 1913), chap. viii.

[3] S. B. Thomas, *The Boss, or the Governor* (N. Y., 1914); J. W. Forrest and James Malcolm, *Tammany's Treason* (N. Y., 1913); Gregory Mason, "William Sulzer and the Invisible Government," *Outlook*, CV, 356-360 (Oct. 18, 1913).

San Francisco grafters, won the Republican gubernatorial nomination in 1910 on the slogan, "The Southern Pacific Railroad must be kicked out of state politics." [1]

It is true many of these men found their quickest road to political preferment through the adoption of new rules of the game favorable to themselves, but with political conditions as bad as they were there was little reason in most cases to doubt their sincerity. With the exception of John P. Altgeld, governor of Illinois (1893-1897), there was hardly a state executive who stood out during the nineties as the representative of a better political day; yet within a decade of Altgeld's retirement to private life amidst a storm of abuse, the people of the various states were placing in the gubernatorial chairs men whose schemes of reform were more radical than Altgeld's.

If conditions in the states cried for reform, those in the great cities were, if possible, even worse.[2] Such centers were likely to be ruled by political machines of the lowest order, which found no type of graft too petty to exploit. In New York the widespread toils of Tammany Hall reached out in an alliance with the underworld. In Philadelphia the Republican machine, controlled by the state bosses, Matthew S. Quay and Boies Penrose, maintained power by the most scandalous election frauds and grew fat by "selling out" the people to the public-utility companies. In Pittsburgh Christopher L. Magee and William Flinn attained a finesse in robbing the city which enabled them to control it for years with an appearance of keeping within the law. In St. Louis Edward R. But-

[1] See later, 98.

[2] On this subject, see the annual review of graft prosecutions appearing in the *National Municipal Review* after 1912, and on earlier phases the books by Lincoln Steffens, *The Shame of the Cities* (N. Y., 1904), *Struggle for Self-Government* and *Upbuilders*. On San Francisco, see also Fremont Older, *My Story* (San Francisco, 1919).

ler ("Colonel Ed") acted as go-between for the franchise grabbers and the city council, supervising the distribution of graft while the councilmen turned over municipal property to private interests. Farther to the north Mayor Albert Alonzo ("Doc") Ames of Minneapolis boldly allied himself with commercialized vice, even allowing his police force to coöperate with thugs in perpetrating robbery upon the citizenry. On the Pacific Coast the labor government of Ruef and Schmitz turned the city of San Francisco over to the grafters after the fire of 1906.

It made little difference where one went, whether the older, thickly populated immigrant cities on the Eastern seaboard or the newer frontier cities of the West, the story was the same—inefficiency and corruption extending from the city through the state governments even into the national legislature, and behind the politicians to the business men and great corporations. It was customary—and convenient—to blame the evil conditions on the newly arrived immigrants, but Mrs. Older has pointed out that the San Francisco reformers received their best aid from Irish and German Americans and their greatest opposition from the descendants of New England and Southern aristocrats,[1] while Lincoln Steffens, who studied the conditions from coast to coast, found little to choose between the hill-town Yankee of Rhode Island who regularly sold his ballot and the newly arrived immigrant who, hurried through the formalities of naturalization, was lined up at the polls to vote as ordered. One of the most corrupt and at the same time contented cities was Philadelphia, which boasted of a higher percentage of native-born Americans than any other large city, yet the graft ran all the way from the

[1] Mrs. Fremont Older, "The Story of a Reformer's Wife," *McClure's*, XXXIII (1909), 292-293.

city councilor, who took fifty thousand for a vote, to the police captain who pocketed the miserable earnings of a prostitute. An idea of the extent to which graft was carried may be seen in Pittsburgh, where disorderly houses were safe from interference only when rented from a ward syndicate, furniture for them bought from the "official furniture man," beer purchased from the "official bottler," liquor from the "official liquor commissioner" and clothes from the "official wrapper maker." [1]

The traditional leadership for broader popular rights, so long borne by the rural frontier, had begun to pass with the failure of Populism. Though it was the newer states that led in democratic legislation in the new century, Western radicalism reached out to Eastern radicalism—a radicalism emanating from the population centers. Long regarded by political philosophers as sores on the body politic, the great city now began to stand forth as "the hope of democracy." [2] Thus at a time when municipal corruption was at its height reformers began to spring up here and there—in Toledo, Cleveland, Detroit and elsewhere—to battle for the restoration of government to the people. As in the case of state misrule, the disease bred its own antidote.

Of the new municipal leaders, one of the most picturesque and forceful was Samuel M. Jones, who in 1897 became mayor of Toledo, Ohio. Brought to America at the age of three, he had won a fortune as an oil pioneer

[1] Steffens, *Shame of the Cities*, 166. How it was done in the Harlem district of New York is illustrated by Captain Walsh's testimony before the Curran committee in 1913: "I collected from saloons, gambling places and disorderly hotels. Fifteen to twenty per cent went to Eugene Fox, a patrolman who collected for me. The rest I divided with Inspectors Thompson, Hussey, Murtha and Sweeney as they took charge of the district in turn," a method which was believed to have netted $500,000 annually. C. R. Atkinson, "Review of Graft Prosecutions and Exposures," *Natl. Municipal Rev.*, II, 440.

[2] F. C. Howe, *The City the Hope of Democracy* (N. Y., 1905).

and as manufacturer of improved apparatus for oil wells. A big sandy-complexioned Welshman with a ready smile and a rich gift of humor, Jones's one ambition in his later years was to improve the lot of mankind. His factory he conducted on the principles of the Golden Rule and as mayor he sought to carry the same ideal into municipal affairs. His philosophy was that of the Tolstoyan anarchists; his quarrel was with society which produced the evildoer, not with those who had fallen foul of the law. "I don't want to rule anybody," said Jones; "nobody has a right to rule anybody else. Each individual must rule himself." [1] In his administration he showed his zeal for social justice by advocating the public ownership of public utilities and the abolition of the private-contract system of doing city work. He took the clubs away from the policemen, telling them that theirs was to help, not to hurt; he introduced free kindergartens into the public schools, established public playgrounds for the children, instituted free concerts in the parks and secured an eight-hour day for city employees.[2]

His attempt to apply Christian principles to municipal politics brought about his speedy repudiation, not only by the Republican machine but also by the churches. "Every one was against him," says Howe, "except the workers and the underworld." [3] Nevertheless "Golden-Rule" Jones was reëlected three times on an independent ticket, and the impetus which he gave to nonpartisanship in politics was salutary and lasting. When he died in office in 1904, he was succeeded the following year by his disciple and former secretary, Brand Whitlock, whose

[1] Howe, *Confessions of a Reformer*, 187; Brand Whitlock, *Forty Years of It* (N. Y., 1914), 113; N. O. Winter, *A History of Northwest Ohio* (Chicago, 1917), II, 1166-1173.

[2] Whitlock, *Forty Years of It*, 112 ff., and his "Golden Rule Jones," *World's Work*, VIII (1904), 5308-5311.

[3] Howe, *Confessions of a Reformer*, 186.

philosophy was very close to that of Jones and who carried on the administration of the city in much the same spirit.[1] Among the many things which Whitlock accomplished during his four successive terms was the securing of a new city charter providing for the initiative, referendum, recall and direct nominations.[2]

When in 1901 Cleveland elected Thomas Lofton Johnson for its mayor, the new democratic movement was strengthened by the accession of one of the ablest men which the period produced. In the savage economic competition of the eighties and nineties Tom Johnson, the son of an impoverished Confederate colonel, had risen to fortune as a steel manufacturer, a manipulator of street railways and the inventor of street-railway apparatus. At the height of his business career, however, he was completely captured by the economic philosophy of Henry George, and relinquished his business activities to work for the single tax and other reforms. As congressman (1891-1895) he could do little, but as mayor of Cleveland for eight years a field was provided for his remarkable talents. Johnson's energies were chiefly expended in bringing the street railways under municipal control and in reducing the fare to three cents, but his program included city planning, a reassessment of city real estate and many other reforms. He was, as Steffens expressed it, the "best mayor of the best governed city in the United States." [3] Endowed with keen intellect and a

[1] See Brand Whitlock, *On the Enforcement of Law in Cities* (Indianapolis, 1913).

[2] Whitlock, in *Forty Years of It*, 176, tells how, on the morning after Jones's death, the stock of the Toledo street railway company went up twenty-four points and some brokers issued a letter saying that now that Jones had died "the securities of that enterprise offered a golden investment—about the most authentic extant illustration, I suppose," says Whitlock, "of the utter contemptibility of privilege in these states."

[3] Lincoln Steffens, "Ohio: a Tale of Two Cities," *McClure's*, XXV (1905), 302.

magnetic personality, he was never more at home than in handling a hostile audience; his charm and utter sincerity won him the support of young and able lieutenants—such men as Newton D. Baker, Frederic C. Howe, Peter Witt, Fred Kohler and Harris R. Cooley. Like Jones, his opposition came from the "interests" and others in high places. Cleveland gained enormously from Johnson's administration, though his defeat in 1909 by a few hundred votes prevented a full fruition of his program.[1] Much was saved two years later, however, when the voters returned to the Johnson ideals by electing Newton D. Baker as mayor.[2]

Jones and Johnson were only the most famous of the prophets who were endeavoring to lead the citizens of the great American municipalities out of the wilderness of political inefficiency and corruption. Joseph W. Folk between 1900 and 1904, as district attorney and later governor, attacked municipal corruption in St. Louis. Ben Lindsey fought to shake the rule of the bosses in Denver. In Minneapolis Hovey C. Clarke, foreman of the grand jury for the summer term of 1902, almost single-handed uncovered the graft of the Ames ring, forced the district attorney to prosecute the leaders, and freed the city from their toils. In Jersey City Mark Fagan fought valiantly to free the city from railroad and public-service domination. The election of the Socialist, Emil Seidel, as mayor of Milwaukee in 1910 opened a new era for that city. Even New York in one of its periodic uprisings against Tammany elected Seth Low mayor in 1901.

Of the efforts to reform municipal conditions perhaps the story of San Francisco is the most astonishing, al-

[1] T. L. Johnson, *My Story* (N. Y., 1911); Howe, *Confessions of a Reformer*, 85 ff.; Whitlock, *Forty Years of It*, 164 ff.

[2] E. C. Hopwood, "Newton D. Baker's Administration as Mayor of Cleveland and Its Accomplishments," *Natl. Municipal Rev.*, II, 461 ff.

though there was little that was unusual in the graft disclosed there. In 1901 Eugene E. Schmitz, a member of the Musicians' Union and candidate of the Union-Labor party, was elected mayor. The real head of the city government, however, was an unprincipled lawyer, Abram Ruef, who dominated the mayor and dictated policies to the board of supervisors, the legislative branch of the government. Unfortunately for the Ruef-Schmitz machine, an honest man, William H. Langdon, had been elected district attorney; and Langdon with the backing of Fremont Older, editor of the *Bulletin,* Rudolph Spreckels, who guaranteed the expenses, James D. Phelan, later United States senator, and other public-spirited citizens began investigations. For this purpose Francis J. Heney, prosecutor in the Oregon land-fraud cases, was made assistant district attorney and William J. Burns was hired to do the detective work. Thrown into a panic, the machine hastily secured the suspension of the district attorney, but Langdon ignored the action and continued his work. Indictments were eventually obtained against Ruef and Schmitz for taking money from "French restaurants," or assignation houses, since the more serious charge, that of distributing the slush funds of the great public-utility concerns, though generally known, could not be proved.[1] In spite of powerful backing and an array of high-paid legal talent Schmitz and Ruef were convicted of extortion and sentenced to jail.

The real fight, however, had just begun, for as soon as the prosecutors began to attack the bribe-givers as well as the bribe-takers the massed influence of California wealth and power was thrown against them. The higher courts freed Ruef and Schmitz, and only after a long

[1] With the aid of Golden M. Roy, proprietor of a well-known café, Burns trapped three of the supervisors, and finally, upon promise of immunity, the entire board of supervisors pleaded guilty of taking bribes.

legal battle was Ruef sent back to jail; at least one jury was tampered with. Fremont Older was kidnaped and barely escaped with his life, while an attempt was made on Heney's life during a recess in one of the trials. Newspapers were subsidized to fight the prosecution; even Hearst's *Examiner*, which posed as the enemy of corruption, threw its powerful influence against the prosecution and allowed the cartoonist, "Bud" Fisher, to poke daily fun at it in his series of "Mutt and Jeff" comic strips. The prosecution, forced to enter politics in self-defense, carried the 1907 election, but was unable to do much against the corporation bribe-givers. Though Louis Glass, manager of the Pacific States Telephone and Telegraph Company, was found guilty of bribery, efforts to convict General Tirey L. Ford and Patrick Calhoun of the United Railroads failed, and when the reformers lost the campaign of 1909 the graft cases were speedily dismissed. Even Ruef would probably have escaped further confinement if the election of Heney's assistant, Hiram W. Johnson, as governor in 1910 had not precluded the possibility of a pardon. The old régime returned in San Francisco, as it usually did elsewhere, but the three-year battle against intrenched corruption had stirred the people sufficiently to bring a state-wide victory for the progressive forces in 1910.[1]

The leaders for municipal improvement in most cases were partial to some particular reform. Thus, Jones and Johnson were firm believers in the municipal ownership of public utilities. All the reformers, however, were one in their belief that what was needed first of all was the elimination of corruption, a return of power to the people and the development of efficiency in municipal

[1] A full account is in Franklin Hichborn, *"The System" as Uncovered by the San Francisco Graft Prosecution* (San Francisco, 1915). See Mrs. Older, "Story of a Reformer's Wife," 292-293.

administration. In this they were assisted by various nonpartisan organizations composed of men interested in better government. The National Municipal League, formed in 1894, offered in 1900 a general program which included city home rule, government by experts, the establishment of official responsibility through the simplification of governmental machinery and full publicity of accounts, and the protection of the city's property from the raids of franchise grabbers.[1] It also proposed specific constitutional amendments and drew up a model municipal-corporations act.[2] In carrying out this program the League's exertions were soon augmented by nonpartisan associations of voters and "city clubs," which sprang up in many large centers to study municipal problems and assist the cause.

To put these efforts on a more scientific basis, bureaus of municipal research were established in many of the leading cities, including New York, Philadelphia, Chicago, Rochester, Detroit, Cincinnati, Minneapolis, and temporarily in other places. The prototype of these organizations was the New York Bureau of Municipal Research established in 1906 through the enthusiasm of R. Fulton Cutting and maintained during the first six years by private contributions aggregating upwards of five hundred thousand dollars.[3] Under the direction of Henry Bruère, Charles A. Beard and Frederick A. Cleveland the New York bureau not only maintained a staff of experts to advance efficient government and promote

[1] National Municipal League, *Proceedings of the Chicago Conference for Good City Government and the Tenth Annual Meeting* (Phila., 1904), 182.

[2] *A Municipal Program* (N. Y., 1900) is a report of a committee of the National Municipal League. The amendments and model charter were revised in 1915. See C. R. Woodruff, ed., *A New Municipal Program* (N. Y., 1919), 297 ff.

[3] The Bureau of City Betterment (1906), incorporated as the Bureau of Municipal Research (1907), and now the National Institute for Public Administration.

scientific methods of administration, but established in 1911 a school, likewise supported in its early years by private subscription, for the training of experts in municipal government.[1] Soon the College of the City of New York and the University of Cincinnati began to offer practical courses in municipal administration, research agencies were established in various universities, and the whole subject of municipal government was taken up with greater seriousness in the colleges and graduate schools. For the first time in American history trained intelligence was being brought to bear upon the complex problems of the city. It was high time, for under the new conditions of American life successful government of the cities was essential to national welfare.

The demand for more efficient municipal government received unexpected impetus from a catastrophe in the South. More than once in history has an event tragic and disastrous at the time worked in the end to further social progress. Confronted with the necessity for instant and efficient action, the community sloughs off its outworn precedents and customs and rises to new heights of coöperative activity. In 1900 Galveston was visited by a great tidal wave and storm which in a single night drowned one sixth of the population and destroyed one third of the property. In desperation the citizens threw aside their unwieldy government and put the task of rehabilitation in the hands of a commission of five. The commission form of government thus improvised was made permanent in the new charter of 1901. As amended in 1903, it placed the government in the hands of five elected commissioners who, at open meetings and by a majority vote, should enact municipal ordinances,

[1] E. M. Sait, "Research and Reference Bureaus," *Natl. Municipal Rev.*, II, 48-56.

make appropriations, determine all appointments and award contracts. The four main city departments were to be each under the direction of one of the commissioners, while the fifth, who was to be the mayor-president, was to exert a coördinating influence on all of them. The new plan was so successful that the near-by city of Houston adopted one somewhat similar in 1905.[1]

Soon these experiments began to attract attention in other parts of the country. James G. Berryhill told his fellow citizens in Des Moines of the improved conditions in Galveston; a committee of Kansas citizens visited Texas to study the results; and in October, 1906, George Kibbe Turner published a magazine article on the subject which provoked widespread discussion.[2] In 1907 the growing interest began to produce results. Iowa passed a general act authorizing the adoption of the commission form by cities of over twenty-five thousand, and Des Moines immediately inaugurated the system, adding new features in the form of popular checks on the activities of the commission. The commission form had been attacked as autocratic, but the Des Moines plan proved that efficiency and democracy might be skillfully blended.[3]

Hoping to approximate even more closely the efficiency of big business, certain variations of the commission form, known as the city-manager or commission-manager, were evolved, the essential feature being the employment of a manager to run the government, while

[1] The Houston plan varied from that of Galveston in that it accorded greater power to the mayor, required the commissioners to give full time to the city business and contained stricter regulations respecting the award of franchises.

[2] G. K. Turner, "Galveston: a Business Corporation," *McClure's*, XXVII (1906), 610-620.

[3] E. C. Lytton, comp., *The Des Moines Plan of Commission Government* (Des Moines, 1912). The charter is reprinted in J. J. Hamilton, *The Dethronement of the City Boss* (N. Y., 1910), 185 ff.

the people's representatives or commissioners merely supervised in much the same manner that a board of directors supervises the president of a corporation. Although this method was authorized by the New Mexico legislature in 1909 and inaugurated in Staunton, Virginia (1908), Sumter, South Carolina (1912), and other places, its most notable experiment was at Dayton, Ohio. Under the privilege granted by the home-rule amendment made to the Ohio constitution in 1912, Dayton was already evolving such a scheme when the severe flood of March, 1913, inundated the city. As at Galveston some years earlier, the exigencies of the situation speeded the adoption of the new plan, which demonstrated an efficiency in the work of rehabilitation that continued in the normal years to follow.[1] By 1912 commission government in some form had been adopted by two hundred and ten communities, and it was still growing in favor. It was especially popular in Texas and in sections of the Middle and Far West, but examples were also to be found in New England.[2]

One excellent result of the movement was the impulse given to the demand for municipal home rule—the right of cities to frame their own charters. The power which the state legislature had assumed over cities in days when American civilization was primarily agricultural and rural had outlasted its usefulness. On the one hand, the

[1] C. E. Rightor, *City Manager in Dayton* (N. Y., 1919); Tso-Shuen Chang, *History and Analysis of the Commission and City-Manager Plans of Municipal Government in the United States* (Iowa City, 1918), 158-220.

[2] Although most of the adoptions took place in small cities, a number of large centers including Oakland (1909), Kansas City and Memphis (1910), Trenton and Birmingham (1911), New Orleans and St. Paul (1912), Jersey City and Portland, Oregon (1913), Omaha (1914) and Buffalo (1916) experimented with the scheme. E. S. Bradford, *Commission Government in American Cities* (N. Y., 1911), 5, gives the list of adoptions up to 1909, and C. R. Woodruff, ed., *City Government by Commission* (N. Y., 1911), up to 1911. The *American Year Book for 1914*, 214, lists 45 city-manager cities.

state legislatures needed to be freed from handling the details of many purely local problems and, on the other, the cities needed greater autonomy for looking after their own special concerns. "Whenever we try to do anything," complained George R. Lunn, the Socialist mayor of Schenectady in 1913, "we run up against the charter. It is an oak charter, fixed and immovable." [1] Furthermore, reformers often found themselves powerless as long as the system they fought extended into the state legislatures and grafting politicians sought aid and protection there. Tom Johnson, for example, finding his efforts to remake Cleveland continually balked by the invisible government in the state legislature, made a state-wide campaign for the principle of home rule; the defeat of his candidacy for governor in 1903 delayed, but did not permanently prevent, its achievement. Only four states had home-rule provisions in their constitutions before 1898,[2] but by 1915 they were joined by Colorado, Oregon, Oklahoma, Michigan, Arizona, Ohio, Nebraska, Texas and Maryland.[3] As this enumeration shows, the movement was limited almost entirely to the Middle and Far West. As a step in the same direction, however, other states passed general acts giving cities the option of forming commission governments according to a standard pattern.

While the improvement in municipal government was notable, it was not universal nor was it continuous. Reform efforts were likely to be spasmodic; even in a reform age it was not easy to keep the electorate ceaselessly vigilant. Thus New York, after electing Seth Low

[1] L. H. Pink, "Socialism on Trial," *Outlook*, CV, 492 (Nov. 1, 1913).

[2] Missouri (1875), California (1879), Washington (1889) and Minnesota (1896).

[3] A. R. Hatton, "Constitutional Municipal Home Rule," Woodruff, *A New Municipal Program*, 73-94.

mayor in 1901 and enjoying a brief respite of honest government, turned back to Tammany in 1903 with the election of George B. McClellan, and in the following years was in frequent turmoil over police-graft scandals and the attempts of Tammany to rewrite the city charter.[1] In some cities, as Philadelphia and Pittsburgh, little effort was made to oust the corrupt rings. Even in the "reform cities" the old interests, hungry for power and ever watchful for opportunities, managed to creep back. Nevertheless some of the gains were too great to be lost, a new sense of civic responsibility was awakened in the urban populations, and an impetus to good government was given from which the next generation was richly to benefit.[2]

Though the movement for political reform was in general from the bottom up, the national parties also made their contributions. Indeed, it might be said that in the nineties the discredited Populists had anticipated most of the demands which were carried to victory and popular acclaim by the anointed leaders of the early years of the new century. Roosevelt, to mention no lesser person, was the direct heir and beneficiary of the Populism he had once so bitterly assailed. Suddenly finding himself the leader of a party which had completely succumbed to special privilege during the leadership of Hanna and McKinley, he strove mightily to give it a distinct progressive tone. In this his personal inclinations fitted nicely with political expediency. The nation was ready for a swing to the left, and Roosevelt gave voice to the unspoken aspirations of the common man with an accuracy achieved by few politicians. Instinctively he re-

[1] L. A. Tanzer, "The Defeat of the Tammany-Gaynor Charter," *Natl. Municipal Rev.*, I, 61-68.

[2] See P. W. Slosson, *The Great Crusade and After* (*A History of American Life*, XII), 407-408.

sponded to the widespread desire for a better civilization and, rushing to the head of the movement, he rose to unprecedented heights of popularity as the reform wave surged onward. Assemblyman, police commissioner, civil-service reformer, historian, assistant secretary of the navy, roughrider, governor, vice-president—the exemplar of the strenuous life with a long career of public service behind him—Roosevelt typified as have few others the ideal of his generation. What the many would like to be, he was, and his unerring journalistic sense enabled him to dramatize his actions and discomfit his enemies. Children in the nursery played with Teddy Bears,[1] and leading intellectuals considered him one of the greatest men of his day. The very initials T. R. came to have an almost magic symbolism.

From the point of view of uncompromising progressives, like La Follette, his devotion to the progressive cause had in it an element of charlatanry,[2] while many of his political associates accused him of ingratitude, insincerity and personal ambition. To his friends, however, his railroad legislation, his prosecutions of the trusts, his efforts in behalf of pure-food laws and conservation, placed him in the forefront of the newer statesmen.[3] Whatever may be the final opinion as to Roosevelt's contribution to the newer America, his domestic policies while president were aggressive and forward looking. Not only was he personally influential in the enactment of progressive legislation, but he helped give momentum to forces in our national political life which his more conservative successor in the White House could not stop.

[1] Sullivan, *Our Times*, II, 445-446, explains the origin of this term.

[2] La Follette, *Autobiography*, chap. xiii.

[3] Eugene Thwing, *Life and Meaning of Theodore Roosevelt* (N. Y., 1919), 154 ff.

With the great mass of voters the Rooseveltian policies were undeniably popular, representing as they did the hopes of a new political and social era, and the voters had no hesitancy in supporting William Howard Taft, whom Roosevelt had handpicked as his successor in 1908. Although the Taft administration saw the fruition of much advanced legislation [1] and the president himself was far from the whole-souled reactionary which his political enemies pictured him, it was not long before Taft found himself out of touch with the more progressive of the Roosevelt followers. The tariff issue, which his predecessor had so skillfully and persistently avoided, proved, in particular, to be his undoing, and the Democratic success in the 1910 elections was a strong indication of the growing unpopularity of his régime.

As the Taft administration drew stormily to a close, the progressive movement, which had been steadily growing in strength, reached its climax. Roosevelt, returning from a hunting trip in Africa, threw in his lot with the insurgent Republicans and, in a famous speech on "The New Nationalism" delivered at Osawatomie, Kansas, assumed an advanced progressive position.[2] The insurgents, planning to contest the renomination of President Taft, first rallied around La Follette, and then, scenting victory in the air, they stampeded to their old idol, Roosevelt. Though Roosevelt had asserted he would not run again, he yielded to the importunities of his friends and the promptings of his own ardent nature,

[1] This included the Mann-Elkins act, a bill establishing a commerce court, one authorizing the interstate commerce commission to undertake a valuation of the railroads, acts establishing postal-savings banks and a parcels-post system, an expense-publicity act, an employers' liability law and an act making an appropriation for a scientific study of the tariff.

[2] Theodore Roosevelt, "The Progressives, Past and Present," and E. H. Abbott, "Mr. Roosevelt in the West," *Outlook*, XCVI, 19-30, 64-67 (Sept. 3, 1910).

and on February 26, 1912, announced that he would accept the nomination if it were offered to him by the Republican national convention.[1] To many the future of political and social reform seemed to rest on the outcome of the ensuing campaign. Charging from state to state in his whirlwind campaign, Roosevelt undoubtedly won the indorsement of the rank and file of the Republican voters,[2] but in the nominating convention he was flattened by the same "steam-roller" which but four years before had so efficiently cleared the way for Taft. Hot with wrath and loud in their cries of fraud, the Roosevelt delegates launched the Progressive party, nominated their chief for president and wrote a platform which epitomized the hopes of reformers.[3] "We stand at Armageddon, and we battle for the Lord," shouted Roosevelt in concluding his keynote speech to a convention which in its fervor resembled an old-time religious revival.

Flushed with the hope that the Republican schism might open the way for victory the Democratic party met to choose their candidate. The political bosses in the convention labored under no illusion that they were battling for the Lord, but the more liberal element under the leadership of Bryan succeeded in mastering the situation and in nominating Woodrow Wilson on a liberal

[1] On the Roosevelt-La Follette controversy, see La Follette, *Autobiography*, chaps. xii-xiii; and B. P. DeWitt, *The Progressive Movement* (N. Y., 1915), 76 ff.

[2] With the exception of North Dakota and Wisconsin which went for La Follette and Massachusetts which Taft won by a small majority, Roosevelt carried all of the presidential-primary states.

[3] It called for direct primaries including presidential primaries, the initiative, referendum, recall, short ballot, direct election of United States senators, woman suffrage, recall of judicial decisions, an easier method of amending the federal Constitution, an inclusive program of social legislation, downward revision of the tariff, income and inheritance taxes and better control over corporations by means of a federal commission.

platform.[1] The Socialist party which had grown steadily in power during the previous decade again nominated its hero, Eugene V. Debs, on a platform more radical than that of the Progressives. Even the Republicans were forced to promise reforms which in an ordinary campaign might have given their platform a complexion of liberalism.

For the progressive voter the millennium in national politics seemed to have been reached. Each of the platforms was progressive and three out of the four candidates were reformers—even crusaders. However the election turned out, it appeared, for once, that the cause of reform would win. Reckoned by the popular vote Wilson was elected as a minority president, but gauged by public sentiment as well as by the decision of the electoral college he represented a majority. For the only time perhaps in its history the nation contained a progressive majority and the new chief executive stood for that group.

The Underwood tariff with its income tax, the Clayton antitrust act, the federal-reserve act and other important legislation which marked the early years of Wilson's presidency may have stopped short of the full progressive program, but they represented an extraordinary advance. The nation had made vast strides since the complacent plutocracy of the McKinley era and since the days when the Populists had been repudiated as dangerous radicals. A "social consciousness" had developed which demanded not only clean politics but a better world in which to live.[2] If the battle waged across

[1] W. F. McCombs, *Making Woodrow Wilson President* (N. Y., 1921), tells the story of the convention and nomination of Wilson, but his account in certain details must be accepted with caution.

[2] Roosevelt's introduction to S. J. Duncan-Clark, *The Progressive Movement* (Boston, 1913), chap. xvi.

a long front can be epitomized in the lives of a few men such as Tom Johnson, Robert La Follette or Theodore Roosevelt, the fact remains that their efforts would have been largely futile had they not represented the aspirations of the common man.

CHAPTER V

THE DECLINE OF LAISSEZ FAIRE

THE extraordinary success attained in democratizing the mechanics of government paved the way for employing the energies of government to new purposes. The political instrumentalities devised by this generation furnished the means by which the new leaders succeeded in regaining for the people a measurable control over their economic destinies. "The United States," wrote a British journalist in the early years of the century, "is like an enormously rich country overrun by a horde of robber barons, and very inadequately policed by the central government and by certain local vigilant societies." [1]

Those who had not, envied those who had; and materialism seemed to rule the thoughts of all sections of society. "Success" in life ordinarily meant business success, and "businesslike" was the most complimentary term that could be applied to any undertaking. Notwithstanding the fact that some five hundred thousand workers were either killed or maimed in the United States each year, an inventor is reported to have remarked that he could sell a time-saving invention in twenty places, but he could not sell a life-saving invention at all.[2] Those corporations which were beginning to dabble in welfare work felt obliged to excuse themselves on the ground that it was "simply to augment output." The widespread commercial philosophy bade fair even to degrade

[1] William Archer, "The American Cheap Magazine," *Fortnightly Rev.*, LXXXVII (1910), 930.

[2] E. A. Ross, *Sin and Sanity* (N. Y., 1907), 95.

religion and education. Indeed, not only churches and colleges but also charity must be institutionalized, made "businesslike" and directed by trustees in the same manner as a packing house. Efficiency and financial success, the twin gods of big business, held more firmly than ever the popular imagination.

This glorification of individualism and *laissez faire* and the money madness which accompanied it were not new; they had been evident at least since the "moral collapse" following the Civil War.[1] Nor had they gone unrebuked. Economic discontent had long been rife, but the discontent of the eighties and nineties was chiefly a restlessness of the city proletariat over low wages and of the farmers over declining prices. The discontent of the first decade of the twentieth century, on the other hand, was a general protest against economic, social and political injustices which gained its great strength from the middle class and attracted to itself also many of the wealthy.

Why great numbers of the people should suddenly awake to a realization of the failure of *laissez faire* and engage in a crusade for constructive social control requires explanation. The rapid consolidation of business which went on in the years from 1899 to 1903 furnished a striking example both of the danger to a people from lack of social control and, at the same time, of the benefits which would accrue to business from the abandonment of unbridled individualism. With the closing of the open frontier, moreover, the nation had reached the stage where it well might pause to examine the errors of the past. Possibly, too, the economic strain of the eighties and nineties had shaken the naïve faith of the masses that all existing institutions were perfect. To fan

[1] Allan Nevins, *The Emergence of Modern America* (*A History of American Life*, VIII), chap. vii.

the flames of discontent came the new generation of political leaders and social workers.

In encouraging the movement for reform no influence was greater than that of the popular magazines. At the opening of the century the only high-class magazine that consistently agitated for social change was the *Arena.*[1] But between the years 1902 and 1905 at least half a dozen widely read magazines were devoting much space to a militant and sensational exposé of existing abuses.[2] Roosevelt likened the more rabid writers to the character in *Pilgrim's Progress* "who could look no way but downward with the muckrake in his hands." The apt phrase, applied to the few, was caught up and used to designate all writers who made it a practice to reveal corruption in business or politics.

The "era of the muckrake" was really inaugurated by *McClure's.* According to the owner, S. S. McClure, the new policy was not deliberately planned. "It came," he says, "from no formulated plan to attack existing institutions, but was the result of merely taking up in the magazine some of the problems that were beginning to interest the people a little before the newspapers and the other magazines took them up."[3] Believing that the public was interested in the trusts and that the Standard Oil was the "mother of trusts," McClure assigned to a staff writer, Ida M. Tarbell, the task of studying this organization and writing a series of articles concerning it.[4] Shortly before the appearance of the first installment of

[1] Edited at different times by B. O. Flower, J. C. Ridpath and Frank Parsons. See B. O. Flower, *Progressive Men, Women and Movements of the Past Twenty-Five Years* (Boston, 1914).

[2] C. C. Regier, The Era of Muckrakers (Ph.D. thesis, State Univ. of Iowa), is an excellent study.

[3] S. S. McClure, *My Autobiography* (N. Y., 1914), 246.

[4] Ida M. Tarbell, "The History of the Standard Oil Company," *McClure's*, XX (1902-1903), 3-16, 115-128, 248-260, 390-403, 491-508, 606-621; XXI (1903), 73-87, 202-215, 312-327.

Miss Tarbell's history in November, 1902, Lincoln Steffens, on the staff of the same magazine, happened on the story of municipal corruption in St. Louis and published it under the title "Tweed Days in St. Louis," the first of a long series on political corruption.[1] It was simply a coincidence that these two series appeared almost simultaneously and also that Ray Stannard Baker and others later prominent in the movement happened to be affiliated with *McClure's* at the time.

The public response to the articles of Miss Tarbell and Steffens was immediate and McClure discovered his circulation mounting rapidly. Although more interested in this than in reform, he became so impressed with the exposures of Steffens and the connection between municipal corruption and crime that he pursued this topic in a true crusading spirit. Other editors, influenced in varying degrees by motives pecuniary and altruistic, followed the lead; and by 1904 *Everybody's, Munsey's,* the *Cosmopolitan, Hampton's, Pearson's* and many others were in the thick of the fray. In that year Steffens, Baker and Miss Tarbell took over the *American* and quickly infused it with the McClure spirit.

Of the hundreds of articles and books comprising the literature of the muckrake, some were ephemeral and unnecessarily sensational, but a large part furnish an invaluable commentary on the merits and defects of contemporary American civilization. A high standard was set by McClure himself who believed in paying his writers "for their study rather than for the amount of copy they turned out,"[2] and the painstakingly accurate work produced by Miss Tarbell, Steffens and Baker gave their articles great weight. Miss Tarbell spent five years in the

[1] C. H. Wetmore and Lincoln Steffens, "Tweed Days in St. Louis," *McClure's*, XIX (1902), 577-586.

[2] McClure, *Autobiography*, 246.

investigation and preparation of fifteen articles, and Lincoln Steffens averaged but four a year.[1] Though many of the muckraking articles were packed with apparently libelous matter, the court records reveal no important suits sustained against the magazines or the authors. Among the most notable achievements were the artistic and thoroughgoing articles of Steffens on municipal and state corruption,[2] the scholarly work of Miss Tarbell on the Standard Oil Company and the protective tariff system, the careful studies by Ray Stannard Baker on the railroads and the Negro problem,[3] the contributions of Burton J. Hendrick on life insurance,[4] the lurid picture of "Frenzied Finance" by Thomas W. Lawson [5] and the equally sensational series by David Graham Phillips on the "Treason of the Senate." [6] Charles Edward Russell wrote on the "beef trust" and many other subjects; George Kibbe Turner on vice in Chicago and New York; Samuel Hopkins Adams on patent medicines and fraudulent advertising; and Upton Sinclair on conditions in the meat-packing industry. A roster of the Muckrakers includes a majority of the leading novelists and journalists of the day.[7]

Muckraking, declining in 1908, was given a new lease

[1] McClure, *Autobiography*, 244.

[2] *McClure's*, XX (1902-1903), 227-239, 545-560; XXIV (1904-1905), 337-353, 649-664; XXV (1905), 41-55, 84-92; *American*, LXV (1907), 26-40, 140-151, 390-400, 527-540, 614-625; LXVI (1908), 120-130, 339-356.

[3] "Railroads on Trial," *McClure's*, XXVI (1905-1906), 47-59, 179-194, 318-331, 398-411, 535-549; "Following the Color Line," *American*, LXIII (1907), 562-579; LXIV (1907), 3-18, 135-148, 297-311.

[4] "The Story of Life Insurance," *McClure's*, XXVII (1906), 36-49, and following numbers.

[5] *Everybody's*, XI (1904), 1-10, 154-164, 289-301, 435-468, 601-613, 747-760; XII (1905), 40-53, and following numbers.

[6] *Cosmopolitan*, XL (1905-1906), 487-502, 628-638; XLI (1906), 3-12, and following numbers.

[7] See later, chap. xi.

of life in 1909 by the failure of the Republicans to reform the tariff, and it gradually merged into the progressive movement culminating in 1912. Thus for approximately ten years there had been an incessant hammering at abuses in the most widely read magazines and at a time when many people were looking to the magazines rather than to the newspapers for their editorial guidance. The combined circulation of the leading muckraking magazines totaled several million; the circulation of *Everybody's* alone, during the publication of the Lawson articles (1903-1905), jumped from 197,000 to 735,-000. The literature of the muckrake was both a symptom of the social unrest which was sweeping the country and an influence which deepened and widened that discontent. Although the Muckraker was in most cases destructive rather than constructive in his criticisms, he did stimulate the general progressive movement and was primarily responsible for several specific reforms. The decline of the movement by 1912 is attributed not alone to the natural reaction, but to the widespread belief that general conditions were rapidly improving. To a lesser degree this decline was due to a persistent attack upon the magazines by the business interests which forced them to soften their attacks or drove them into bankruptcy.[1]

The breakdown of *laissez faire* effected changes in many phases of political, social and economic life, but its most spectacular victories are to be found in federal and state legislation. Although the Muckrakers did not particularly emphasize the shortcomings of the railroads, it was upon the interstate carriers that the wrath of the reformers first fell. Controlling as they did one tenth of the nation's wealth, holding in their hands the

[1] Upton Sinclair, *The Brass Check* (Pasadena, 1920), 230; George French, "Masters of Magazines," *Twentieth Century*, V (1912), 501 ff.; C. E. Russell, "The Magazines Soft Pedal," *Pearson's*, XXXI (1911), 179 ff.

economic fate of vast areas and multitudes of people, the roads had long alienated the masses by their indifference to the public welfare and to the laws of the land. While their lawyers whittled away the power of the interstate commerce commission and their lobbies dictated the policies of state legislatures, their executives flouted with impunity the federal legislation of 1887.

Fortunately for the advocates of railroad legislation a strong ally was found in Roosevelt who in his first message to Congress advocated a firmer regulation of large corporations.[1] Under his leadership the law against rebating was strengthened in 1903, and an effort made to speed railroad cases in the federal courts.[2] These measures, however, were but preliminary skirmishes in the battle for effective public control of rates which finally came in the Hepburn act of 1906. This statute not only empowered the commission to determine just and reasonable rates, but enlarged its power of regulation to include express and sleeping-car companies, pipe lines, switches, spurs, tracks and terminal facilities.[3] It offered a reasonably successful compromise between the theories of unrestricted private operation and government ownership, and marked a milestone in the development of the regulatory power of the federal government. But to the more radical advocates of government control it was merely an opening wedge. Stimulated by the insurgency during the Taft régime, Congress further increased the powers of the commission and extended its regulatory interest to matters of labor.[4] At the same time several of

[1] J. D. Richardson, comp., *Messages and Papers of the Presidents* (Wash., 1910), IX, 6641 ff.

[2] *U. S. Statutes at Large*, XXXII, 823, 847.

[3] *U. S. Statutes at Large*, XXXIV, 838.

[4] The Mann-Elkins act gave the commission power to suspend rates for six months. *U. S. Statutes at Large*, XXXVI, 539. A law was also passed authorizing the commission to report on the value of railroad property. For labor legislation, see the hours-of-service law, *U. S. Statutes at Large*,

the states, including Iowa, Wisconsin and later California, moved aggressively to break the political power of the railroads.

Although Roosevelt repeatedly emphasized his friendliness toward honest business and his opposition to government ownership, he early made it clear that his administration would not tolerate illegal monopolies. The Sherman antitrust act, which had almost died from inanition, was suddenly revived in 1901 when suit was instituted against the Northern Securities Company on the ground that it effected a monopoly of transportation in the Northwest.[1] The complete victory for the government in 1904 Roosevelt regarded as one of the "great achievements" of his administration, emphasizing "in signal fashion, as in no other way could be emphasized, the fact that the most powerful men in the country were held to accountability before the law." [2] Struck with the inadequacy of state regulation because of the "utter lack of conformity in the state laws," the president held further that the nation itself should, without interference with the rights of the states, assume power of supervision and regulation over all corporations doing an interstate business.[3] In line with this policy the Union Pacific was forced to separate its Southern Pacific property,[4] the New Haven to disgorge some of its holdings,[5] and suits were instituted against monopolies which were

XXXIV, 1415; the employers' liability act, XXXV, 65; XXXVI, 291; the Newlands act, XXXVIII, 1, 103 ff.; also R. M. La Follette, *Autobiography* (Madison, 1913), 425.

[1] U. S. *v.* Northern Securities Company, 120 Fed. Rep., 721; 193 U. S., 197; W. Z. Ripley, *Railroads; Finance and Organization* (N. Y., 1915), 555 ff. See earlier, chap. ii.

[2] Theodore Roosevelt, *Autobiography* (N. Y., 1919), 428-430; J. B. Bishop, *Theodore Roosevelt and His Time* (N. Y., 1920), I, 325.

[3] Richardson, *Messages and Papers*, IX, 6646.

[4] 226 U. S., 61 (Dec. 2, 1912).

[5] U. S. *v.* N. Y., N. H. & H. R. R., District Court Southern District of N. Y. See earlier, chap. ii.

believed to exist in anthracite coal, in oil, tobacco, powder, meat packing, salt, paper and other commodities. Taft not only aggressively carried on his predecessor's policy of prosecuting monopolies, but proposed a plan for the federal licensing and supervision of all corporations doing an interstate business and the setting up of a federal corporation commission equal in dignity to the interstate commerce commission.[1]

Although the efforts to enforce the Sherman act were widely acclaimed by the masses, the trusts, which had enjoyed practical immunity for so long, were dumfounded. After the Northern Securities prosecution was launched Morgan hastened to Washington to "fix it up" and seemed surprised that terms could not be made.[2] Hill was aggrieved at the necessity of fighting "for our lives against the political adventurers," [3] but the cynical Harriman, less perturbed, is reported to have said that if he wanted state legislation he could buy it and, if necessary, he could buy Congress and the judiciary as well.[4] The comment of one paper that "Wall Street is paralyzed at the thought that a President of the United States should sink so low as to enforce the law" contained not a little truth.[5]

Wall Street, however, was unduly disturbed. These actions under the Sherman act demonstrated beyond doubt the power of the federal government over corporations doing an interstate business, but, as we have seen,

[1] During the Taft administration there were 46 bills in equity, 43 indictments and one contempt proceeding, more than twice the number under Roosevelt. They included actions against the International Harvester Company, the American Sugar Refining Company, the United Shoe Machinery Company and the "beef trust." See J. W. Jenks and W. E. Clark, *The Trust Problem* (rev. edn., Garden City, 1917), 280-281.

[2] J. F. Rhodes, *The McKinley and Roosevelt Administrations* (N. Y., 1922), 223; Bishop, *Theodore Roosevelt*, I, 185.

[3] Quoted by Mark Sullivan, *Our Times* (N. Y., 1926-), II, 415.

[4] Rhodes, *McKinley and Roosevelt*, 332.

[5] Quoted by Sullivan, *Our Times*, II, 415.

they had little effect in permanently delaying the trend toward business consolidation. Certain large units, as the Standard Oil Company and the American Tobacco Company, were indeed broken up, but ways were found to continue monopoly practices without falling afoul the law. There might be informal understandings or gentlemen's agreements, such as those reached at the famous Gary dinners where the policies of the steel business for the coming year were discussed,[1] or those achieved by a trade association maintaining a secretary and a publicity bureau, as in the case of the "cement trust." Interlocking directorates, interlocking stock ownerships, community of interest produced by concentration of the ownership of capital, all tended to undo the results of judicial decrees. The stock of the Standard Oil companies was actually more valuable after the dissolution of the holding company in 1911 than before.

Few could doubt the futility of the antitrust drive of Roosevelt and Taft after the revelations of the Pujo committee,[2] and few likewise doubted that the Democrats, coming into power in 1913, would seek to strengthen the hands of the government. Fortified by brave words against trust domination when out of power, they were led to victory by a man fresh from his successful efforts to stiffen the corporation laws in New Jersey. Wilson had emphasized in his campaign speeches what he called the "New Freedom" and pledged himself to the restoration of the earlier conditions of competition and opportunity. "American industry is not free, as it was once free," he said, ". . . the man with only a little capital is finding it harder to get into the field, more and more impossible to compete with the big fellow. Why? Because the laws of the country do not prevent the strong

[1] Ida M. Tarbell, *Life of Elbert H. Gary* (N. Y., 1925), chap. ix.
[2] See earlier, chap. ii.

from crushing the weak." [1] The remedy of the Democrats took the form of two important statutes.[2] In the Clayton antitrust act of 1914 they sought to obviate monopoly by attacking price discrimination, tying contracts and interlocking directorates, at the same time exempting labor unions and farmers' organizations from prosecution as conspiracies in restraint of trade. Simultaneously they created a federal trade commission endowed with power to investigate corporations engaged in interstate commerce (with the exception of banks and common carriers) and take action in the courts against unfair practices.

From legislation designed to restrain harmful practices in big business, it was but a step for the government to embark in business on its own accord. Postal-savings banks had operated successfully for almost half a century in Europe, the Populists had advocated them in their platform of 1892, and both Roosevelt and Taft strongly urged their establishment in messages to Congress.[3] Hailed as socialistic and opposed "almost without exception" by private bankers, they were finally authorized by an act of June 25, 1910.[4] Although the primary object was to encourage thrift, the leading financial paper of the country was of the opinion that the two-per-cent rate of interest was not large enough "to attract a very large volume of deposits," [5] and in this it was correct. After four years the number of depositors amounted to 388,000, but the total deposits aggregated but

[1] Woodrow Wilson, *The New Freedom* (N. Y., 1913), 15.
[2] *U. S. Statutes at Large*, XXXVIII, 717, 730.
[3] Richardson, *Messages and Papers*, X, 7482, 7667, 7802.
[4] *U. S. Statutes at Large*, XXXVI, 814. See *Financial and Commercial Chronicle*, LXXXI, 9 (July 2, 1910), for the bankers' point of view.
[5] *Financial and Commercial Chronicle*, LXXXI, 12. The law looked forward to the possibility that the deposits might provide a new market for government bonds.

$43,000,000, an amount so small as not to involve appreciable competition with private banking. Furthermore, as this represented money hitherto largely hoarded, and as the government distributed some of the deposits among state and national banks, it was not long before the bankers hailed the act as an "enlightened reform."

Two years later the government extended its program of public ownership by the creation of a system of parcels post.[1] Like the postal-savings bank, the parcels post had long been a great boon to Europeans and, like the former system, it had been long agitated here. It was opposed by the express companies, by the country merchants who feared competition from the great mail-order houses and city stores, and by the conservatives in general. That the mail-order houses were especially benefited is undoubtedly true, but the general effect was also advantageous. Unlike the postal-savings system, it quickly passed into general use.

Great as had been the advance in American banking inaugurated by the national banking act of 1863, many defects remained. The inelasticity of credit, the expensive and cumbersome transfer system, the decentralized gold supply and other shortcomings obvious to the banker were brought into bold relief by the Panic of 1907.[2] As an emergency measure the Aldrich-Vreeland act was passed the following year, which, while making temporary provision to improve conditions, authorized the appointment of a national monetary commission to make a thorough study of the situation. Banking legislation would have come if there had been no spirit of change in the air, but it would have been of a different sort. The "Aldrich plan" offered by the commission, which

[1] *U. S. Statutes at Large*, XXXVII, 557. See Roosevelt's messages to Congress on the subject, Dec. 3, 1907, and Dec. 8, 1909. Richardson, *Messages and Papers*, X, 7482, 7607.

[2] National Monetary Commission, *Report* (Wash., 1912), 6-9.

provided for a central bank dominated by private bankers, was impossible in the highly charged atmosphere at Washington, and it was left for the Wilson administration to draw the final plan.

The federal reserve act of 1913 called for public control and supervision through a commission appointed by the president, and provided for a paper currency which might expand or contract with the needs of business.[1] Through greater integration and elasticity, it was hoped to minimize the danger of panics and provide a system which would more equitably serve the whole nation. The ingenious method by which efficiency and public control were welded into a national institution was, in its way, as striking an example of the new America as any piece of legislation of the period. Interesting also was the readiness with which the experts in laying out the reserve districts recognized the nation as a group of economic sections rather than an agglomeration of states.

While the nation's banking system was being revamped, a fundamental change was taking place in the method of financing the federal government. Indirect taxation through tariffs and excises was no longer adequate to the rising costs of government, and to meet the need for revenue Taft in a special message to Congress on June 16, 1909, advocated an income-tax amendment. For a number of years it had been a pet scheme of the Democratic party, and its eventual advocacy by a Republican president led more than one Democratic organ to point out sorrowfully the thievish propensities of their opponents. If European experience is taken as a criterion, direct taxation was, in any case, inevitable, but the

[1] J. L. Laughlin, *Banking Progress* (N. Y., 1920); E. W. Kemmerer, *The A. B. C. of the Federal Reserve System* (Princeton, 1918); H. P. Willis, *The Federal Reserve System* (N. Y., 1923).

readiness with which the American public accepted the innovation can be explained only in relation to the rising demand for social justice and the successful use of such taxes in Europe and Australia. A federal income tax had been tried in America during the Civil War and again in 1894, but in the latter instance had been declared unconstitutional in a legal battle surcharged with class feeling.[1] So rapidly had the nation swung to the left, however, that in 1909 a constitutional amendment passed the Senate unanimously and the House by an overwhelming majority, and by 1913 had received the consent of the requisite number of states. An income tax was immediately added by the Democrats to the Underwood-Simmons tariff of that year, which within five years yielded the major portion of the federal revenue.[2]

The acceptance of direct federal taxation was no indication that the nation had lost its faith in the protective-tariff system. The growth of "trusts" and the rising cost of living, however, developed a rather critical attitude toward exorbitant duties, which inspired the Republican party in 1908 to promise "unequivocally for the revision of the tariff." [3] The failure of the Payne-Aldrich act of 1909 to meet the wishes of the reformers gave a great impetus to the progressive movement and helped pave the way for the Democratic victory of 1912. The Underwood-Simmons bill, passed by the Democrats in 1913, was undoubtedly the most thoroughgoing effort to reduce the tariff for over half a century, but the average rates were still high. Protection had not been deserted, and there was little likelihood that any business which both parties so glibly described as "legitimate"

[1] Pollock *v.* Farmers' Loan & Trust Company, 158 U. S., 42.

[2] Alzada Comstock, *Taxation in the Modern State* (N. Y., 1929), 71.

[3] Fourteenth Republican National Convention, *Official Report of Proceedings* (Columbus, 1908), 117.

would suffer. Whether the lower tariff would check monopolies or the rising cost of living remained to be seen.[1]

An added significance attaches to the federal legislation during these years in that it marks not only a distinct drifting away from the philosophy of *laissez faire* but an exaltation of the central government. State prestige, which had received a severe blow by the outcome of the Civil War, was now further shaken by the extension of national authority in many directions. Though the trend toward centralization of power was a part of the nationalistic movement widespread throughout the world, its great impetus came from indigenous causes. With the Economic Revolution rapidly standardizing people and communities, uniformity of government control in economic life followed as a matter of course. Moreover, the many abuses resulting from a checkerboard division of political functions made it evident that local authority was inadequate to deal with many of the problems of an industrialized state.[2]

The decline of *laissez faire,* so strikingly illustrated in federal legislation, in a large measure mirrored a similar tendency in states and municipalities. There was scarcely a state in the Union whose laws did not reflect the popular discontent and which did not make progress in establishing greater control over public utilities and promoting the general public welfare through social legislation. The most conspicuous example was Wisconsin, a state largely inhabited by people of Scandinavian and German stock, who from their antecedents had no antipathy to the extension of state authority. This sturdy and cautious element formed the backbone of the progressive movement, and their children, trained at the

[1] *American Year Book for 1913,* 28-38; F. W. Taussig, *The Tariff History of the United States* (6th rev. edn., N. Y., 1914), chap. ix.

[2] Walter Thompson, *Federal Centralization* (N. Y., 1929), pt. iv.

state university, furnished the bulk of the leadership. From this "German university of the German state of Wisconsin" [1] emanated Robert M. La Follette, whose election to the governorship in 1900 opened the way for a remarkable program of social legislation. A strong railway commission (1905) and a public-utility commission (1907), with power to regulate rates and determine valuation, brought the most powerful corporations under effective state control; an industrial commission was created to enforce labor legislation and promote the interests of labor, and a tax commission was appointed to evolve a more equitable and scientific system of taxation. A workmen's compensation act, a state insurance system and a state income tax were among the many innovations. At the same time, through a board of public affairs, a policy was promoted which combined conservation of natural resources with a wise development of economic wealth.[2] In all this work the state government had so depended on the experts of the state university that the latter virtually became a fourth department of the state.[3] Not merely did the professors sit upon the state commissions but, through lectures and extension courses, explained and popularized the new laws.

This remarkable "lesson of scientific popular self-help, and of patient care in radical legislation," [4] as Roosevelt described it, made a deep impression during these restless years, and other states were aroused to adapt the "Wisconsin Idea" to their own needs. When it further appeared that under these laws Wisconsin was enjoying unprecedented economic prosperity, conservative critics were dumfounded, and much encouragement was given

[1] Charles McCarthy, *The Wisconsin Idea* (N. Y., 1912), 28.

[2] F. C. Howe, *Wisconsin; an Experiment in Democracy* (N. Y., 1912), chap. ix.

[3] Howe, *Wisconsin*, 39.

[4] Roosevelt's introduction to McCarthy, *Wisconsin Idea*, x.

to the belief that legislation for the benefit of the masses might be as beneficial to sound business as that for the classes. At all events, the electorate in many states turned their attention to the consideration of laws which would afford protection from exploitation and give a fairer chance to the common man.

In the large cities the need for protection against the special interests was, if possible, even more acute. Students of municipal problems were obliged to agree with Howe that "in most of our cities the public service corporation is the 'invisible government' behind the boss and the political parties," [1] and with Heney when he said that "in the Pacific coast city all corruption flowed from two sources," the public-service corporations "that wanted something from the public for nothing," and the "disorderly houses and dives." [2] Again and again this fact was hammered home to the average citizen as he read the exposures of Steffens and other Muckrakers in the popular magazines. How to control these vultures with their ill-gotten franchises, their watered stock and their bribing of officials was difficult, for the influence of the public-service corporations extended to the courts and the state legislatures. Tom Johnson's efforts to establish municipal control over the street railways resulted in more than fifty court injunctions against him, a decision by the Ohio supreme court that the Cleveland charter was unconstitutional, and the passing of a special legislative act for creating a state municipal code which, it was believed, would tie the hands of the reformers.[3] One obvious check was the establishment of public-utility

[1] F. C. Howe, *The Modern City and Its Problems* (N. Y., 1915), 154.

[2] Howe, *Modern City*, 157. See also National Civic Federation, *Municipal and Private Operation of Public Utilities* (N. Y., 1907), I, pt. i, 38.

[3] T. L. Johnson, *My Story* (Elizabeth J. Hauser, ed., N. Y., 1911), 163-166.

commissions equipped with adequate power. At the behest of citizens of Kansas City, Governor Folk in 1907 called a special session of the legislature to pass a bill authorizing cities to establish public-utilities commissions,[1] but the system ordinarily followed was to put local utilities under a state commission. The latter method, begun by Wisconsin and New York in 1907, speedily spread to the other states.[2]

The difficulty of safeguarding the interests of the public even where a commission existed converted many to the belief that municipal ownership was the only solution. Public ownership of municipal waterworks increased from about one half of the total in 1896 to over two thirds in 1915; at the latter date every one of the thirty-six largest cities, with the exception of Indianapolis, either owned or operated its waterworks.[3] In other utilities, however, the trend toward public ownership was not so rapid. Less than one per cent of the gas sales and but four per cent of the electric-power output came from publicly owned stations in 1917, but there had been a significant increase in the number of municipal plants.[4] Several cities built municipal docks and embarked in business in various ways; others, as Boston and New York, built their subways, but allowed them to be operated by private companies. Restrictions in their charters and limitations on their borrowing power alone prevented Cleveland, Toledo, Detroit and Chicago from

[1] C. L. King, *The Regulation of Municipal Utilities* (N. Y., 1912), chaps. xii-xiii.

[2] King, *Municipal Utilities*, chap. xiv; Leo Sharfman, "Commission Regulation of Public Utilities," Am. Acad. of Polit. and Social Sci., *Annals*, LIII, no. 142, 1-18.

[3] C. D. Thompson, *Public Ownership* (N. Y., 1925), chap. viii; Bureau of the Census, *General Statistics of Cities for 1915*, pt. iv.

[4] Municipal electric plants increased from 386 in 1895 to 2318 in 1917, a growth in per cent of total plants from 18.5 to 35.43. Municipal gas plants increased from 14, or 1.5 per cent of the total in 1899, to 126 or 5.3 per cent in 1916. Thompson, *Public Ownership*, 260, 269, 273.

ownership and operation of their street railways, and only one of the larger cities, San Francisco, took over its electric trolleys before the World War. That the popular support for municipal ownership was strong in certain cities, however, is seen in the backing given to Jones and Whitlock in Toledo, to Johnson in Cleveland, to Dunne in the Chicago election of 1905 [1] and to the mayoralty candidates in Des Moines in 1910 and Los Angeles in 1911. Professor Beard, after careful study, concluded in 1912 that "the principle of public ownership seems to be slowly gaining in favor." [2]

Regardless of the Muckrakers, the increasing complexity of urban life and the need for many things which could be best supplied through governmental agencies would inevitably have enlarged the scope of municipal activities. The interest of the municipality in social welfare, which hitherto had been confined chiefly to public day schools, was rapidly extended in the larger cities in many directions. Municipal hospitals, medical and dental clinics, free meals for impoverished school children, playgrounds, evening schools, public baths, free libraries, lectures and music were but a few of the fields into which the cities were extending to supplement private enterprise. Furthermore, there was a tendency for the city governments to be more exacting in their laws regarding tenement-house architecture, sanitation and fire control, and a willingness to attempt a stricter regulation of the social evil. This extension of municipal functions, begun in the larger centers where the need was greatest, extended slowly but surely into the smaller cities.

The willingness of the people to increase the power of the government came, curiously enough, at a time when

[1] E. F. Dunne, "Our Fight for Municipal Ownership," *Independent*, LXI, 927-930 (Oct. 18, 1906).

[2] C. A. Beard, *American City Government* (N. Y., 1912), 229.

the masses were becoming cognizant of the corruption and inefficiency which permeated almost every branch. But it came also at a time when the initiative, referendum, recall, direct primary, short ballot, commission government and other methods of insuring democratic control were being adopted.[1] In a great measure, however, the tendency was inevitable. The nation had reached a stage of economic development in which *laissez faire* had outlived its usefulness. The Economic Revolution had created problems of transportation, banking, industrial consolidation, health, sanitation and general social welfare which could only be solved through effective community action. The way was undoubtedly made easier by the experiments of the more economically advanced nations of western Europe and by the coming to America of millions of immigrants, but the movement was due primarily to conditions here. Unlimited opportunity had begun to depart with the frontier and economic liberty unscrupulously used was bringing its own retribution.

[1] See earlier, chap. iv.

CHAPTER VI

THE REVOLUTION IN TRANSPORTATION

WHILE the political attention of the nation was fixed on problems arising from the growth of giant industry, active-minded inventors, going about their proper business, were quietly effecting changes in the essentials of American living, which had far-reaching social consequences. In the field of transportation the new inventions, in their immediate and remoter effects, amounted to nothing less than a revolution. Just as in the first half of the nineteenth century the speed and ease of travel had been transformed by the application of steam power to locomotion on land and water,[1] so distances were once more dramatically shortened by new applications of electrical energy and the introduction of gasoline as a source of motive power. The new conquests were not limited to the earth's surface: even the atmosphere above the land was successfully invaded.

To people living at the time, the most significant of the discoveries was the self-propelled motor vehicle. The automobile had no single inventor; its lineage goes back to the first man who conceived the idea of putting an engine on wheels—perhaps Nicholas Cugnot, a French artillery captain, who in 1769 constructed a three-wheeled wagon equipped with a boiler and engine.[2] It came down through such men as the American, George

[1] C. R. Fish, *The Rise of the Common Man* (*A History of American Life*, VI), 78-87.

[2] J. E. Homans, *Self-Propelled Vehicles* (6th edn., N. Y., 1907), 1.

B. Selden, who in 1879 applied for a patent on a vehicle driven by an internal-combustion engine; the German, Gottlieb Daimler, who in 1883 perfected the "hot-tube" system of ignition; the German, Carl Benz, who built the first successful gasoline-driven motor car; and such Frenchmen as Panhard, Levassor, Serpollet and the Renault brothers, who added many refinements. Undoubtedly the automobile was the result of many minds, chiefly European, and had a substantial historical background before any real development occurred in America.[1]

Although other lands contributed the underlying inventions, it was America which succeeded in standardizing the processes and reducing the costs of manufacture so as to bring the motor car within the reach of the average pocketbook. As news of the "horseless carriages" came to our shores—how, for instance, Levassor had achieved an average of fifteen miles an hour in 1895 on a race from Paris to Bordeaux, and how this had been bettered to twenty-five miles in 1897 in a Paris-Dieppe race [2]—innumerable mechanics all over the country began to dream of the fortunes to be made out of the new idea.[3] At least six different motive powers were tried by

[1] The greatest early development was in France, and it is probable that as late as 1905 there were more motor vehicles in Great Britain than in the United States.

[2] Beckles Willson, *The Story of Rapid Transit* (N. Y., 1903), 177.

[3] When in 1925 the National Automobile Chamber of Commerce determined to honor the American pioneers of the industry, it conferred medals upon John D. Maxwell, Edgar L. Apperson, A. L. Riker, John S. Clarke, Rollin H. White, H. H. Franklin, Charles E. Duryea, Charles B. King, Elwood Haynes, Alexander Winton and R. E. Olds, but these men were only the outstanding living representatives of the early mechanics who in their little shops laid the practical foundation of the industry between 1886 and 1899. R. C. Epstein, *The Automobile Industry* (Chicago, 1928), 26. Other pioneers were S. H. Roper of Roxbury, Massachusetts, who experimented for thirty years with steam-driven cars; George E. Whitney of Providence, Rhode Island, who built in America the first practical steam car; the Stanley brothers who developed the leading concern

these experimenters—electricity, gasoline, steam, compressed air, carbonic-acid gas and alcohol—though only the first two, electricity and gasoline, were ever extensively used.

Typical of these pioneers were Duryea, Haynes, Ford and Olds. Charles E. Duryea of Chicopee, Massachusetts, a bicycle designer for the Ames Manufacturing Company, constructed with the help of his brother a gasoline motor, mounted it on wheels, and in the summer of 1893 made a successful road demonstration. Continuing to build cars, he won most of the American races during the years 1894-1896 and for a time was easily the outstanding figure in the automobile field.[1] Meanwhile Henry Ford, eldest son of a Michigan farmer, whose mechanical interests had driven him to desert the farm for a machine shop in Detroit, was constructing a car in the little barn behind his Bagley Street house, which, when placed on the road in 1893, accomplished twenty-five miles an hour.[2] Still a fourth, Ransom Eli Olds, "that pioneer exponent of quantity production" in motor cars,[3] brought out the first three-wheeled horseless carriage in 1887, a practicable four-wheeled automobile in 1893 and a gasoline-driven car in 1896. Elwood Haynes, field superintendent of a natural-gas company in Kokomo, Indiana, desiring to cut down the time he was forced to spend on the road, purchased a gasoline engine and, with the help of Elmer and Edgar Apperson, local mechanics, constructed a car which was successfully tried out on July 4, 1894. Haynes has been called the "father

in the manufacture of steam cars; and William Morris of Des Moines, credited with the first successful electric vehicle.

[1] Mark Sullivan, *Our Times* (N. Y., 1926-), I, 486.

[2] H. L. Arnold and F. L. Faurote, *Ford Methods and the Ford Shops* (N. Y., 1915), 8 ff.

[3] Epstein, *Automobile Industry*, 209.

of the automobile in America," but, as we have seen, his was not the first car built here.[1]

Years before any of these men had constructed a practicable car George B. Selden, a graduate of the Sheffield Scientific School of Yale and a patent lawyer at Rochester, New York, had built in 1877 a gasoline engine and designed a vehicle which it could propel. Though a patent was soon applied for, it was not granted until 1895.[2] Selden spent the intervening years in a fruitless search for capital to develop his project, but his patent when issued included so many ideas fundamental to automobile construction that manufacturers consented to pay him a small royalty and themselves organized an Association of Licensed Automobile Manufacturers to protect the basic patent agreement. This association in 1902 and 1903 brought suits against Alexander Winton, Henry Ford and others for infringement, and were upheld by the lower court. Led by Ford, the defendants fought the case until 1911 when the United States circuit court of appeals held that, while the patent was valid, it was not infringed by the defendants in the test cases, as they were using an engine of a different type from the Selden.[3] This decision prevented an automobile monopoly protected by patents and opened the way for a period of free competitive development.

The sixteen years after 1898 mark the advance of the automobile from an obsession of tinkering mechanics or a "plaything of the rich" to a widely used pleasure and business vehicle. The mechanical improvement from the "one-lung" motors of Ford, Olds and Winton to the smooth-running "sixes" and "eights" of a few years

[1] Sullivan, *Our Times*, II, 456; R. C. Epstein, "Industrial Invention: Heroic or Systematic?," *Quar. Journ. of Econ.*, XL, 246 *n.*

[2] U. S. Patent No. 549,160.

[3] Waldemar Kaempffert, ed., *A Popular History of American Invention* (N. Y., 1924), chap. iv.

later was nothing short of marvelous. Regarded dubiously by the more conservative in its earlier years, the automobile appealed to too many human traits, both good and bad, to languish. The convenience, the feeling of power, the chance for show, made some willing to mortgage even their homes to obtain the coveted car. The four automobiles registered in 1895 and the eight thousand in 1900 grew to two and a half million in 1915, the capital invested in manufacturing from $5,-760,000 in 1899 to $407,730,000 in 1914.[1]

Two main problems confronted manufacturers: the production of a practicable car simple enough for the layman to operate, and the reduction of the cost as the market among the wealthier classes was exhausted. Even the shortest spin in the early years was accompanied by every kind of uncertainty and almost sure mechanical difficulty. Furthermore, manufacturers were far from agreed on many essential features of construction. The power, for example, used at the opening of the century was about evenly divided between electricity and steam; at the first real automobile show, held in 1900, one third of the space was taken up with electric vehicles, including models from the Pope, Riker, Waverley and Barrows factories. It was some years before engineers and the general public swung to the gasoline-driven engine.

From the start the public benefited from the keen competition of rival makers.[2] This not only led to the solution of many mechanical difficulties, but also brought the price within the range of the average man. Henry

[1] Epstein, *Automobile Industry*, 316-317.

[2] Epstein, *Automobile Industry*, 163 ff. Sullivan gives the following fifteen companies, which started in the early days of the industry, as still in operation in 1925: Haynes, 1896; Olds, 1897; Studebaker, 1898; Locomobile, 1899; Franklin, 1900; Peerless, 1900; Stearns, 1900; Apperson, 1901; Pierce-Arrow, 1901; Cadillac, 1902; Overland, 1902; Packard, 1902; Buick, 1903; Ford, 1903; Maxwell, 1904.

Ford, in the first year of factory production, sold "Model A" runabouts for as little as $850 and, although in subsequent years some of his models went above $2000, he attempted a progressive reduction of prices after 1908.[1] In 1903 two thirds of American cars sold at $1375 or under, but in the years following the proportion of low-priced automobiles fell off until 1908 when there was a swing back and an increasing percentage of cheap cars sold.[2]

At all events, the number of automobiles grew by leaps and bounds, the advance being vastly more rapid than the increase in either manufactures in general or national income in the aggregate, making it evident that automobile expenditure was in part diverted from the purchase and production of other commodities.[3] Already in 1907 a New Yorker could speak of "the throngs of cars of every description upon Fifth avenue, the theater 'buses at night, the endless procession of automobiles faring out in the country of a week-end, the industrious little electrics."[4] But the most successful of the early manufacturers—the Olds Motor Works at Detroit, when the famous "curved-dash" Oldsmobile was at the height of its popularity in 1903—turned out only 4000 machines for the year; while the Ford Motor Company alone manufactured 258,356 in 1914, by methods which represented the acme of efficiency in a mechanical and industrial age.[5] The popularity of the automobile was undoubtedly increased by the improvement in design which

[1] Henry Ford and Samuel Crowther, *My Life and Work* (Garden City, 1926), 54 ff. A Ford touring car in 1904 without equipment sold for $1200; in 1924, without self-starter, for $290.

[2] Epstein, *Automobile Industry*, 75 ff.

[3] Epstein, *Automobile Industry*, 81 ff.

[4] W. F. Dix, "Conquerors of the Road," *Independent*, LXIII, 1092 (Nov. 7, 1907).

[5] P. W. Slosson, *The Great Crusade and After* (*A History of American Life*, XII), 223-227.

took the engine from underneath and placed it in front, making the car look less like a horseless carriage, and by the widespread introduction in 1913 and 1914 of the self-starter.

It is doubtful if any mechanical invention in the history of the world has influenced in the same length of time the lives of so many people in an important way as the motor car. As it passed into general use, it took the city to the country and country to the city, mitigating rural isolation and provincialism and widening the business as well as the intellectual life of the farmer. Hardly a phase of American rural life remained untouched, its influence upon education in promoting the consolidation of schools into larger and more effective units being particularly notable. It helped promote the suburban developments which the railroad and "trolley" had already started, while in the nation as a whole it provided work for hundreds of thousands. By 1914 it was obvious that the motor car had not only contributed a new form of recreation, but by means of more rapid facilities for social and economic intercourse had accelerated the whole tempo of our civilization.[1]

The extent to which this revolution in transportation would go was not fully apparent even in 1914, for the rapid economic development of the preceding years had called for draft animals as well as automobiles. The number actually increased by two million between 1900 and 1914, and the number of farm horses continued to grow until 1918. But the noble animal who for two hundred years had provided the primary means of internal transit and had been an essential factor in agriculture and business, had met an invincible rival. His part in the building of America had been an important

[1] T. W. Allen and others, *Highways and Highway Transportation* (U. S. Dept. of Agr., *Bull.*, no. 914), 178-181.

one, but the complexities of our mechanized civilization had become too much for him.

More spectacular, though less significant in the life of these times, was the progress made in flying. The century opened with much interest in aeronautics, particularly in France, but the experiments were largely limited to various types of balloons. The Aero Club of America, founded in 1905, had as its chief objective "the popularization of ballooning as a sport, especially among the more wealthy class," [1] and few people, even in aeronautical circles, believed that a practicable heavier-than-air machine could ever be built. Though Sir Hiram Maxim in England and C. E. Ader in France had constructed airplanes in the nineties, the outcome of their efforts was not encouraging. In America Samuel P. Langley, secretary of the Smithsonian Institution, devoted study to the building of airplanes and devised large steam-driven models which made successful flights of from one-half to one mile in 1896. After a favorable report from a board of army and navy officers, the war department in 1898 granted fifty thousand dollars for further experiments. With his assistant, Charles M. Manly, Langley built a man-size airplane which in October and December, 1903, made two unsuccessful attempts to fly over the Potomac.[2]

The sight of Langley's machine nose-diving into the Potomac aroused more merriment among the public than serious interest. It was now quite evident, said the *Chicago Tribune*, that there was "little possibility" that man would fly "until we become angels," while the *Boston Herald* urged Langley "to drop work on his flying machine and turn his attention to the construction of a

[1] Aero Club of America, *Navigating the Air* (N. Y., 1907), xiii.

[2] S. P. Langley, "Experiments with the Langley Aerodrome," Smithsonian Institution, *Ann. Rep. for 1904*, 113-125; Sullivan, *Our Times*, II. 557-568; newspaper reports for October 8 and December 9, 1903.

diving or submarine craft, his efforts seeming to result in success in this direction rather than upward." [1] Langley always maintained that the trouble was not with the airplane, but with the failure to launch it properly,[2] and his belief was in part vindicated in 1914 when Glenn Curtiss, after installing a more powerful motor, drove the Langley plane successfully.

Just nine days after the Langley fiasco, and while the press was still jeering at the Smithsonian scientists for attempting the impossible, Orville Wright at Kitty Hawk on the North Carolina coast made a flight which "lasted only 12 seconds, but it was nevertheless the first in the history of the world in which a machine carrying a man had raised itself by its own power into the air in full flight, had sailed forward without reduction of speed, and had finally landed at a point as high as that from which it started." [3] The next day Wilbur Wright stayed in the air fifty-nine seconds.

The Kitty Hawk flights of December, 1903, were but one step in the experiments of the Wright brothers, whose interest in aviation had begun when Wilbur read a newspaper account of the death in 1896 of Otto Lilienthal, the great German experimenter with gliding machines.[4] Neither Orville nor Wilbur Wright, who were bicycle mechanics in Dayton, Ohio, had had a theoretical engineering education, but, like the automobile experimenters, both were expert practical mechanics and both were endowed to a superabundant degree with persever-

[1] *Chicago Tribune,* Dec. 10, 1903, 6; *Boston Herald,* Dec. 10, 1903, 6.

[2] Langley, "Experiments with the Langley Aerodrome," 124-125.

[3] Orville Wright, "How We Made the First Flight," *Flying,* II (1913), 36. See also Aero Club of America, *Navigating the Air,* 6-12, and Henry Wodehouse, "History of the Conquest of the Air," *Flying,* V (1916), 229-242.

[4] Wilbur Wright, "Some Aeronautical Experiments," Smithsonian Institution, *Ann. Rep. for 1902,* 133-148.

ance and "Yankee ingenuity." Profiting by the work of Lilienthal, Chanute and others,[1] but departing in some respects radically from their predecessors, the Wrights up to 1902 devoted their attention almost exclusively to experimentation with gliders. They next attached a motor to the wings, and with the Kitty Hawk flights the Wrights realized that success was in their grasp. Their further experiments were made near Dayton where in 1904 they succeeded in turning a complete circle in the air and in 1905 in making several flights lasting over half an hour.

Their work had been carried on very quietly, but when the inventors in the spring of 1908 returned to Kitty Hawk, the daily press awoke to the fact that something of vast importance was happening on the lonely Carolina coast. Reporters verified the rumor that flights were actually made by a heavier-than-air machine, and the news was broadcast to the world. Abandoning secrecy, the Wrights now demonstrated their machine in Europe and America, where they were joined in their labors by scores of enthusiastic engineers. The greatest interest was evinced in Europe and there the chief advances of the next ten years were made. America, however, had one further contribution to make before the close of the period in the hydroplane, designed by Glenn E. Curtiss, which was first successfully flown above the Hudson in 1911. Slow as was the relative progress in America between the years 1906 and 1914, the fundamental inventions were developed, new records were constantly made, and preparations were even under way for a transatlantic flight when the World War unexpectedly intervened.

[1] In particular, Professor J. J. Montgomery, whose work was of the highest importance. See Victor Lougheed, *Vehicles of the Air* (Chicago, 1919), 138-146.

These revolutionary applications of gasoline power to locomotion were attended by a tremendous development of the sources of electrical energy. Though most of the basic uses of electricity had been discovered by the preceding generation, it was for this one to realize more fully its possibilities. The few tiny power stations of the early 1880's had grown to over two thousand in 1898 and more than five thousand in 1914, delivering their current not only to homes but also to factories, and with each new demand for electricity the primary problem of distributing the power took on new significance.[1] The fundamental researches of the brilliant Austrian immigrant, Nicola Tesla,[2] in the rotating magnetic field and the work of his successors lengthened the delivery point by 1914 to over one hundred and fifty miles, a factor which gave power producers a wide radius within which to find the cheapest place for manufacture.

The great project to "harness Niagara" had already been accomplished by the opening of the century, and producers turned with increasing interest to water as the cheapest form of power. The decade from 1904 to 1914 was characterized by a widespread development of hydroelectric projects, culminating in 1913 in the successful inauguration of service on the finished half of the great Keokuk Dam on the Mississippi, destined at its completion to be the largest power plant in the world.[3] As in other industries, the dictates of efficiency and the hope of greater profits soon led the power producers to

[1] Bureau of the Census, *Central Electric Light and Power Stations, 1902*, 106; C. D. Thompson, *Public Ownership* (N. Y., 1925), 269. Condensed statistics on the increased use of electric power in manufacturing are given in Bureau of the Census, *Abstract of the Fourteenth Census, 1920*, 1034-1050. See also C. O. Ruggles, "Problems in the Development of a Super-Power System," *Harvard Business Rev.*, II (1924), 161.

[2] Born in Austria, he was a Serb by race. T. C. Martin and S. L. Coles, *The Story of Electricity* (N. Y., 1919), I, 420.

[3] *New International Year Book for 1913*, 230.

consolidation and to the extension of a network of giant power cables over large areas.[1]

Electricity played its part in solving the transportation problems of this generation, especially in the case of short distances. In the earlier years at least, it seemed little affected by the growing competition of the automobile. As once the nation had turned enthusiastically to the construction of canals and railroads, so now with equal ardor it embarked upon the building of street railways. The annual increase of track averaged well over two thousand miles in the years from 1902 to 1907, though falling to about half that amount in the next five-year period.[2] Such engineers as Charles J. Van Depoele, Stephen D. Field, Frank J. Sprague and Elihu Thompson turned their inventive genius to the field, and many *entrepreneurs* of the type of Mark Hanna, Tom Johnson and August Belmont provided executive ability and financial leadership for the new roads.

To meet the intolerable conditions of congestion New York and Chicago had earlier built elevated systems,[3] and Boston followed in 1901; but the overhead railroad left much to be desired until electric power replaced steam. The first trains operated by electricity ran on the New York elevated system in 1901 and this power was soon afterward installed in Chicago and Boston. The needs of traffic, however, in the larger cities seemed always in advance of facilities. At the close of the nineties two of them, following the example of London, attempted to solve the problem by building subways. Bos-

[1] Federal Trade Commission, *Supply of Electrical Equipment and Competitive Conditions* (70 Cong., 1 sess., *Sen. Doc.*, no. 46), 4-13, 159 ff.

[2] Bureau of the Census, *Electric Railways, 1922* (*Census of Electrical Industries*, Wash., 1925), 5-6. See also E. P. Burch, *Electric Traction* (N. Y., 1911), and F. J. Sprague, "The Electric Railway," *Century*, LXX (1905), 434-451, 512-527.

[3] See A. M. Schlesinger, *The Rise of the City* (*A History of American Life*, X), chap. iv.

ton, the pioneer in this respect, completed the first unit of her system in 1898. New York began hers in 1900 and the portion to be put into operation first, that part from City Hall on the south to 145th Street and Broadway on the north, was opened by Mayor McClellan in October, 1904.[1] A year later trains were running under the East River to Brooklyn and by 1908 connection had been achieved with New Jersey by the tube under the North River.[2]

At first chiefly useful as a substitute for the old-fashioned city horse car, the electric trolley after 1898 spread increasingly into the suburbs and soon came to link one community with another. So far had this development proceeded by 1910 that, in the more thickly settled regions, most towns were connected by electric railways. By the close of the period it was possible to travel from New York City to Portland, Maine, and from New York to Sheboygan, Wisconsin, entirely by electric road.[3] The extension of interurban service reacted upon the steam railways, forcing fare reductions in some instances, the purchase of the lines by the steam roads in others, and eventually in certain cases the actual electrification of the railways.[4] The New York Central began operation by electricity from the Grand Central Station in New York City in 1906 and two years later the New York, New Haven and Hartford inaugurated complete electric

[1] Herbert Croly, "The New York Rapid Transit System," *Am. Rev. of Revs.*, XXX (1904), 306-311.

[2] J. B. Walker, *Fifty Years of Rapid Transit* (N. Y., 1918), 289. Even more remarkable from an engineering point of view was the tunnel under the Detroit River at Detroit, built by the Michigan Central and opened for regular service October 16, 1910, after four years of construction.

[3] Burch, *Electric Traction*, 13 ff.

[4] The New York, New Haven and Hartford had acquired by 1909 about 1500 miles of trolley line in New England, and the New York Central about half as much in the Mohawk Valley. Burch, *Electric Traction*, 21.

passenger service between the same terminal and Stamford, Connecticut. Competition from interurban trolleys was, however, but one of the causes of electrification. The electric engine was cheaper, faster, cleaner and much better adapted to the crowded conditions of the inclosed city terminals than the puffing, smoky steam locomotive, besides being more dependable on mountain grades and in zero weather. Notwithstanding the heavy initial cost, railroads in many sections of the country were laying plans for electrification as the period closed.[1]

In spite of the competition of other modes of travel and transport, railroads expanded their mileage at more than the normal rate during the early years.[2] The marked decline after 1907 was attributed by some to the Hepburn act and other federal legislation, but the chief causes seemed rather to be declining profits, competition from interurban electrics and the approach to a saturation point. Something of the romance which surrounded the early railroad building continued into these years. Plans to connect Los Angeles and its harbor, San Pedro, with Salt Lake City by a line running over the old Mormon trail had for years fired the imagination of farseeing Westerners. The project, however, had been blocked by Collis P. Huntington who, in the interests of the Southern Pacific, wished to develop the rival port of Santa Monica. Although the Union Pacific had built southward as far as Milford, Utah, Harriman lost interest in the project after his acquisition, upon the death of Huntington, of the Southern Pacific. His hand was forced, however, in 1902 by Senator W. A. Clark, the copper magnate, who obtained control of franchises and

[1] Most of these plans were, however, delayed for years because of the precarious financial condition which confronted many of the companies. Burch, *Electric Traction*, chap. xv.

[2] The annual average for the half-century ending in 1900 had been approximately 3800. The average for the next fourteen years was 4000.

trackage around Los Angeles and began to build the line himself. Harriman now made terms and the new San Pedro, Los Angeles and Salt Lake Railroad—a line 778 miles long—was thrown across the Sierras, and opened for business on May 1, 1905. The road not only made accessible large mineral regions to the outside world, but reduced by twenty-four hours the running time of fruit express trains between California and the Eastern market.[1]

This important railroad project was the exception. For most American railroads the era of mileage expansion had long since passed, and the restless railroad executives turned aggressively to the problems of integration and the improvement of existing facilities. With the completion of the South Station in Boston in 1898 an era of huge station construction commenced. The truly beautiful Washington depot, an important feature in the plans for a more attractive capital city, was completed in 1907. Important stations in the West included the Chicago station of the Chicago and Northwestern, completed in 1911, and the Kansas City Union Station, opened in 1914, where twelve great railway systems united to build a terminal.[2] Other railroads, such as the Delaware, Lackawanna and Western, found the means to build strings of new and architecturally pleasing stations along the whole line.

In the combination of magnitude, æsthetic qualities and utilitarian purpose American architecture reached perhaps its highest achievement in the Pennsylvania and Grand Central stations in New York, completed respec-

[1] Montgomery Schuyler, *Westward the Course of Empire* (N. Y., 1906); French Strother, "Swinging the March of Empire Southward," *World's Work*, XI (1906), 7073-7081.

[2] Slason Thompson, *A Short History of American Railways* (N. Y., 1925), 276-283, 331-352; Edward Hungerford, *The Modern Railroad* (Chicago, 1911), chap. vi.

tively in 1910 and 1913. The former, which Arnold Bennett described as "full of the noble qualities that fine and heroic imagination alone can give," stirred him as did few sights in America. "That there existed," he exclaimed, "a railroad man poetic and audacious enough to want it, architects with genius powerful enough to create it, and a public with heart enough to love it—these things are for me a surer proof that the American is a great race than the existence of any quantity of wealthy universities, museums of classic art, associations for prison reform, or deep-delved safe-deposit vaults crammed with bonds." [1]

Despite the apparent absorption of this generation in rail and highway traffic there occurred a surprising revival of interest in canal transportation. Since the advent of railroads inland water transportation in the United States had been on the wane, with almost half of the original canal mileage abandoned by 1908.[2] In the face of this decline the insufficiency of rail facilities in periods of prosperity directed attention to the need of utilizing waterways. Other influences worked to the same purpose: the dramatization of canal possibilities in the building of the Panama Canal, the opposition to railroads and railroad monopolies, the desire to reduce freight rates, the example of successful operation of waterways in Europe and the agitation of interested speculators. Convention after convention assembled to advocate the building of canals, the deepening of rivers and the improvement of harbors, until finally in 1907 President Roosevelt appointed an inland waterways commis-

[1] Arnold Bennett, *Your United States* (N. Y., 1912), 100.

[2] The decline of river transportation can be gauged by the fact that the river shipments from St. Louis fell away almost ninety per cent between 1880 and 1910. Only traffic on the Great Lakes seemed to keep pace with the nation's growth. Inland Waterways Commission, *Preliminary Report* (Wash., 1908), 204; *Final Report* (Wash., 1912), 485, 511.

sion to survey the whole subject.[1] With this commission he floated down the Mississippi from Keokuk to Memphis amid the acclaim of the populace and the incessant shrieking of whistles and rattle of fireworks. State governments also became interested in the possibilities.

The first important project to be undertaken was the improvement and enlargement of the existing New York canals, an enterprise involving 440 miles of improvement or new construction and the canalization of 350 miles of lakes and rivers. Though agitation for a "barge canal" had been continuous since the early nineties and a preliminary appropriation had been made in 1895, it was not until 1903 that the people of New York state voted over one hundred millions for it. By means of the enlarged canal a cheaper freight route was provided from the Lakes to the sea and, since over two thirds of the state's area is within fifty miles of the canal, many other benefits came to the people of New York.[2] Interest was also revived in the century-old plan of Gallatin for an intercoastal waterway along the Atlantic, and in 1909 Congress authorized the war department to make surveys.[3] While the government was still engaged in the preliminary work, a private corporation headed by the capitalist, August Belmont, jr., and the engineer, William Barclay Parsons, undertook to build the first unit of the system. After a labor of five years and a cost of twelve millions the Cape Cod Canal was opened in July, 1914, marking the consummation of a project which had had warm advocates ever since the Puritan worthy,

[1] H. G. Moulton, *Waterways versus Railways* (rev. edn., N. Y., 1926), 1 ff.

[2] N. E. Whitford, *History of the Barge Canal of New York State* (Albany, 1922), and his *History of the Canal System of the State of New York* (Albany, 1906); A. B. Hepburn, *Artificial Waterways of the World* (N. Y., 1914), 34-108.

[3] *Intercoastal Waterways* (62 Cong., 2 sess., *House Doc.*, no. 391).

Judge Samuel Sewall, had noted in his diary the possibility of such a cut.[1] West of the Alleghanies the federal government authorized approximately sixty million dollars in 1911 for the improvement of the Ohio, and the state of Illinois was building the first link in the projected "Lakes-to-Gulf Deep Waterway."

Wide as was the interest in these projects all of them were overshadowed by the construction of the Panama Canal. Even the least imaginative caught something of the significance of the tremendous conception, and thrilled to see this greatest engineering feat brought to a successful conclusion. Before the canal was started there were unsuccessful negotiations with Colombia, a revolution in Panama, and the purchase of rights from the defunct French company.[2] It was necessary, further, to decide between a sea-level and a high-level canal, organize an executive staff, import tens of thousands of laborers, and perfect a government for the zone. Above all, it was necessary to improve the conditions of health in the isthmus, for upon this depended the success or failure of the whole enterprise. The sanitary program carried out under the direction of Colonel William C. Gorgas included the building of hospitals and of sewerage systems, the paving of streets in Panama and other towns and a relentless war upon the yellow-fever and malaria-carrying mosquito. So successful were the efforts that Gorgas turned a pestilential tropical wilderness into an inviting, livable region with a death rate lower than the average American city.[3] The task of cutting the

[1] Oct. 26, 1676: "Mr. Smith, of Sandwich, rode with me and showed me the place which some had thought to cut, for to make a passage from the south sea to the north." See W. B. Parsons, "Cape Cod Canal," Am. Acad. of Polit. and Social Sci. *Annals,* XXXI, 81-91.

[2] See later, 313-314.

[3] W. A. Gorgas, *Sanitation in Panama* (N. Y., 1915); Isthmus Canal Commission, *Annual Reports* (1904-1914).

isthmus was undertaken by three commissions, the last one headed by Colonel George W. Goethals. Literally the engineers removed one mountain to let through the waters at the Culebra Cut and built another to form the Gatun Lake. Opened in 1914, the Panama Canal cost approximately $375,000,000 and the labor of thirty-five thousand men for ten years, but the expense was trivial in comparison with the gains. Thousands of miles were slashed from the all-sea routes of ships bound for the west coast of the Americas to Europe and from the east coast of the Americas to the Orient.[1]

Beside this remarkable achievement—"the greatest liberty man has ever taken with nature," James Bryce called it—the story of highway development seems a prosaic one. Yet in this mode of transportation as in others this generation set a pace of its own. Begun by the bicycle craze of the 1880's and 1890's, the good-roads movement reached its full momentum as a result of the introduction of the automobile. Organizations were formed, the most important of which was the American Association for Highway Improvement, founded in 1910, and the first International Good Roads Congress convened in Paris in 1908. As late as 1909 there were nearly two million miles of dirt roads in the country out of a total of 2,210,000.[2] Improvement, however, was rapid. Engineers offered new types of road construction, for the old dirt, gravel and even "water-bound macadam" were found unequal to the strain of motor traffic. In the course of time some form of bituminous macadam or bitulithic pavement became the standard for the more permanent road construction, although

[1] J. B. Bishop, *The Panama Gateway* (N. Y., 1913); G. S. Mills, *The Panama Canal* (London, 1913); W. J. Abbott, *Panama and the Canal* (N. Y., 1914); John Barrett, *Panama Canal* (Wash., 1913).

[2] L. W. Page, *Roads, Paths and Bridges* (N. Y., 1912), 79.

these types were already being challenged by concrete roads.[1]

The movement for better roads in Connecticut may be taken as typical of the more progressive states. Realizing in 1895 that the maintenance of good roads was of more than local interest, the legislature established a highway commission to administer a scheme of state aid, the state contributing seventy-five thousand dollars annually for that purpose provided the town and county each pay one third of the local improvement. By subsequent legislation the amount offered by the state was gradually increased, as were the powers exercised by the central authority in determining which roads should receive state aid. In 1906 the commission was authorized to lay out trunk lines through the state, in 1907 it was given full power to make final selection of the highways to be improved, and in 1911 the state undertook to pay the entire cost of repairs on the main arteries.[2]

The reconstruction of the highways involved the rebuilding of thousands of bridges and, for these, concrete or reënforced concrete became increasingly popular. While steel had many advantages, the greater permanency of concrete, its ease in shaping and the declining prices of Portland cement brought it into wide use from the smallest culverts to such great structures as the three concrete bridges built over the Great Miami River at Dayton, Ohio, 1902-1906, and the famous Tunkhannock Viaduct constructed by the Delaware, Lackawanna

[1] *Good Roads Year Book for 1912*, 187 ff.; J. P. Beck, "Concrete Pavements for Small Cities," *Am. City*, VII (1912), 352-353. A. H. Blanchard and H. B. Drowne, *Text Book on Highway Engineering* (N. Y., 1913), 583, says: "The first concrete pavement in the United States was laid in Bellefontaine, Ohio, in 1893. It was not until 1900, however, that this material was used to any extent."

[2] U. S. Bureau of Public Roads, *Report of a Survey of Transportation of the State Highway System of Connecticut* (Wash., 1926), 19 ff.

and Western Railroad (completed in 1915).[1] Such uses of concrete were but one phase of the increasing employment of that material. Scientists began to talk of the "cement-stone" or "concrete age" just as glibly as of a stone age or an iron age. Cities used it in sidewalks, waterworks and sewage disposal; railroads and corporations for posts, fences, telegraph poles, wharves and reservoirs. Perhaps the most important use, however, was in the construction of buildings.[2] Numerous experiments in concrete structure were made, notably the use of building blocks which enjoyed some popularity; but the chief application came to be in reënforced concrete buildings of various types, particularly apartment houses, factories and other industrial buildings, sometimes, as in the case of apartment houses, with an outside brick facing. In particular, the modern factory was influenced by steel and concrete, materials which made it possible to erect at moderate cost fireproof buildings with immense windows.

Compared with the achievements in the field of transportation, the advances made in the facilities for communication seem less impressive. Yet here, too, this generation improved greatly upon the work of its predecessors. For the first time, for example, the telephone entered significantly into the life of the common man. The 677,000 telephones belonging to the Bell system in 1900 grew to 3,500,000 in 1910 and to nearly six million in 1915.[3] From being an exception, a telephone installation by the last date had become the

[1] H. C. Tyrrell, *History of Bridge Engineering* (Chicago, 1911), 425-426.

[2] L. C. Sabin, *Cement and Concrete* (N. Y., 1905), 410; R. W. Lesley, *History of the Portland Cement Industry in the United States* (Chicago, 1924).

[3] The independent companies operated 1,053,866 telephones in 1902 and 3,644,565 in 1912. "Telephone Systems," *Encyclopedia Americana*, XXVI, 384.

rule in the middle-class home, making life easier for the city dweller and helping further to break down the isolation of rural life. This growth was in part the cause, and in part the result, of the important discoveries of the large research staff maintained by the Bell holding corporation, the American Telephone and Telegraph Company, which was especially active in solving the problems of underground and long-distance communication.

The range of overhead conversation was gradually lengthened until by January, 1915, Alexander Graham Bell, inventor of the telephone, speaking in New York into an exact reproduction of his original instrument, was clearly heard in San Francisco by Thomas A. Watson, who thirty-nine years before, as Bell's assistant, had caught the first telephone message ever spoken.[1] Long-distance conversation by underground cable began in 1902 over a ten-mile stretch from Newark to New York. Owing to a disastrous sleet storm Washington was without wire communication on the day of President Taft's inauguration, but the year that his successor took office saw underground installations from Boston to Washington. Nor were these advances all. Wireless telegraphy, still in its infancy in 1898, was so rapidly developed that on December 12 and 13, 1901, its inventor, the Italian Guglielmo Marconi, caught with the aid of a kite at St. John's, Newfoundland, the signal sent from Poldhu Station, Cornwall. This dramatic demonstration seized the imagination of the public; and a Marconi Wireless Telegraph Company of America was established the next year. Wireless installations within a half-dozen years became standard equipment on all large ships; and many scientists, of whom the American, Lee

[1] See Allan Nevins, *The Emergence of Modern America* (*A History of American Life*, VIII), 88-89.

De Forest, was perhaps the best known, contributed numerous improvements.[1] Americans living in 1914 might well have marveled at the changes in transportation and communication that had occurred within their short span of years. How little they dreamed of the miracles that still lay ahead!

[1] *Yearbook of Wireless Telegraphy and Telephony for 1914*, 17-34; O. E. Dunlap, jr., *The Story of the Radio* (N. Y., 1927), chaps. i-iii; Kaempffert, *History of American Invention*, 351-378.

CHAPTER VII

WOMEN IN THE NEW CENTURY

THE new conditions of American life affected the position of women in many vital respects. In the first decade of the century the number of female wage-earners increased both numerically and relatively though, in contrast with earlier times, the greatest relative advance took place in office and store employments.[1] While fewer women lawyers and ministers were listed in 1910 than in 1900 and but few more physicians and surgeons, women continued to invade the educational field in ever greater proportions. The enlarging rôle of the sex in economic life was, however, purchased at a cost. Of the women sixteen years of age and over at work outside the homes and professions, almost half earned less than six dollars a week in 1914 and approximately three fourths less than eight dollars.[2] Probably the most comprehensive wage statistics on women's labor ever published were those gathered in the years 1907-1909 by the United States bureau of labor for the cotton, men's clothing, glass and silk-manufacturing industries. "One of the most significant facts brought out by the investigation," asserted the bureau, "was the large proportion of women

[1] Of the female population ten years of age and over, which numbered 28,246,000 in 1900, 5,317,000 are given as breadwinners, and of the 34,553,000 in 1910, 8,076,000 are so listed, a relative increase of 3.8 per cent. See *U. S. Thirteenth Census* (1910), IV, 30, 41.

[2] Economists generally agreed in 1914 that for women under American conditions $7.00 a week provided a bare subsistence and that more than $8.00 was necessary for a "living wage." C. E. Persons, "Women's Work and Wages in the United States," *Quar. Journ. of Econ.*, XXIX, 207, 209.

wage earners who were paid very low wages—wages in many cases inadequate to supply a reasonable standard of living for women dependent upon their own earnings for support." [1]

Various explanations were advanced for the low wages: the immobility of the female labor force; the youth and inexperience of the individual laborer; the large number of immigrant women among the mill workers; and the fact that seven out of ten lived in families where there were other breadwinners. Women's position in industry was still somewhat subordinated to the home.[2] The real labor unit was the family rather than the woman worker; and as a member of the family group she suffered either because it might not be necessary for her to earn her full way or because she was forced to find work where her family was located. Moreover, many women considered work as a temporary expedient until an eventual escape was found in matrimony; at least one half the women in manufacture and trade, it was discovered, were under twenty-five years of age. Such conditions retarded the progress of trade unionism among women. To improve the situation, the National Women's Trade Union League was formed in 1903. Composed chiefly of women labor leaders and social workers, the league strove with increasing success to affiliate women wage-earners with the labor movement.[3]

As in the 1880's and 1890's, the movement of women was not only from the home to the factory and office, but also from the country to the city. Just as the first women operatives moved from rural New England to the mill villages of Waltham and Lowell, so now their

[1] U. S. Department of Labor, *Summary of the Report on Condition of Women and Child Wage Earners in the United States* (U. S. Bur. of Labor Statistics, *Bull.*, no. 5), 21.

[2] Persons, "Women's Work and Wages," 212 ff.

[3] Alice Henry, *The Trade Union Woman* (N. Y., 1915), 62 ff.

granddaughters, aspiring to be stenographers, saleswomen or librarians, sought the towns and cities, while the newly arrived immigrant girl found her best opportunity in domestic service in city homes. The factory system had already modified the economic importance of the home and it was now changing its physical aspect. The pressure of population on land had so raised its value that the single-family house was rapidly being supplanted in the great cities by apartment houses and even by apartment hotels. The number of private houses annually built in Manhattan dropped from over thirteen hundred in 1886 to about forty in 1904 while apartment houses were springing up everywhere, a tendency greatly hastened after 1897 when the cost of elevator service was reduced by the opportunity to buy electric power from the street conduits.[1] The alteration, commented Charlotte Perkins Gilman in 1904, "is so great and so swift as to force itself upon us with something of a shock," and with many others she protested against seeing the American home "lifted clean off the ground—yardless, cellarless, stairless, even kitchenless." [2] Such conditions, however, were little known in the smaller towns.

Whatever the objections to the new type of home, it was of great service in reducing household drudgery. The difficulty of obtaining domestic servants, the rising cost of building materials and the decline in the size of the American family, all contributed to a distinct reaction from the large houses of the last half of the nineteenth century to the small compact homes of the new era. At the same time mechanical inventions continued to lighten the labors of the housewife. The telephone in 1898 was

[1] Herbert Croly, "The New York Rapid Transit Subway," *Am. Rev. of Revs.*, XXX (1904), 310.

[2] Charlotte P. Gilman, "The Passing of the Home in Great American Cities," *Cosmopolitan*, XXXVIII (1904), 139.

more commonly found in offices than in homes, but in the succeeding years it became a household necessity.[1] The incandescent light, widely used in the cities by 1898, now spread rapidly into the suburban districts. Installation of wiring for lighting purposes opened the way for such devices as electric irons, washers, toasters, stoves and vacuum cleaners which ingenious inventors speedily placed on the market. Better plumbing and improved bathroom and kitchen fixtures further simplified housework as did changing styles in house furnishings. Hardwood floors were banishing carpets for the more sanitary rugs, and the smaller rooms of the new type of dwelling had no space for the wondrous arrays of bric-a-brac which so often cluttered up the living rooms of the previous generation.[2]

Of great benefit to women also was the simpler diet which was being widely adopted. The heavy food and groaning boards which had been characteristic of a rural population were less needed as American life became increasingly urbanized. The discussion which accompanied the pure-food laws made the American pay more attention to food values, while the mania for efficiency led him to lend ready ear to the propaganda for the new "health foods" which flooded the market. The change began with the introduction of new and in some cases "predigested" breakfast foods, which were so widely and persistently advertised in the opening years of the century as to be a chief financial support for many periodicals.[3] The legends which accompanied the smiling features of the ubiquitous Negro chef[4] or the chubby

[1] In 1900 there were 1.33 telephones per hundred population in the United States; in 1905, 4.02, and by 1915, 10.09.

[2] See A. M. Schlesinger, *The Rise of the City* (*A History of American Life*, X), chap. v.

[3] "Breakfast Foods," *Independent*, LX, 1577-1578 (Dec. 26, 1906).

[4] For many years the Negro chef accompanied advertisements for Cream of Wheat.

"Sunny Jim" [1] may have exaggerated the merits of their respective wares, but they helped revolutionize the national breakfast table. Not only was the American eating different food but he was eating less. Lunch in the urban business districts declined in importance until a sandwich and a drink at a saloon or soda fountain served to satisfy the noonday hunger. The only meal of importance to many was now the evening dinner and even here there was less consumption of meat.

The smaller and simpler dwelling of the new century amply served its purpose. The father spent his working day elsewhere, the children spent most of theirs in school, and the mother, relieved of much household drudgery, devoted more time to outside interests. Recreation, intellectual stimulation and the means of subsistence were now so largely obtained away from home that in many instances the city dwelling had become primarily a place to sleep. But important as were the effects of household improvements on the women of the middle class, large numbers of the sex were entirely unaffected. The rapid growth of cities, the flood of immigrants, the unequal distribution of wealth and inadequate housing laws, all contributed to the development of congested areas where thousands of human beings were huddled into unbelievably close quarters and where, deprived of proper light, air, sanitary appliances and privacy, it was but a question of time before many fell victims to vice and disease.

Although the problem of the slums was an old one and existed in some degree in every large American city, it was most acute in New York. Of the three and a half million inhabitants of Greater New York in 1900, more than two thirds lived in about ninety thousand tenement

[1] "Vigor, Vim, Perfect Trim,
"Force Made Him Sunny Jim."

houses, the majority of them of the so-called "dumb-bell type" in which but four rooms out of fourteen on each floor had direct air and light.[1] The New York Commission of 1900, in fact, found that New York presented "the most serious tenement house problem in the world," with conditions that could hardly be duplicated in western Europe and that harked back to Manchester and Liverpool of a century before. New York had not been oblivious of the growing evil; official commissions had reported at various times and legislation had been enacted, but it had proved quite inadequate to cope with the situation.[2] In 1898, partly through the influence of Lawrence Veiller, the Charity Organization Society took up the problem, drafted a model law and in 1900 conducted a model-tenement competition. So much interest was aroused that the legislature appointed a tenement-house commission and in 1901 passed a special tenement-house law for the greater cities (250,000 or over). The new code required that all rooms and hallways be lighted and ventilated, and imposed strict regulations regarding size of rooms, running water, fire escapes and sanitation.[3] The recommendations of the commission also included a separate tenement-house department for New York City, which was created under the new charter of that metropolis when it went into operation under Mayor Seth Low in 1902.

Although the law was bitterly attacked by the speculators and small owners, its constitutionality was upheld[4] and it inaugurated a new era in tenement legislation. New Jersey in 1905 passed a law modeled on that

[1] R. W. De Forest and Lawrence Veiller, *The Tenement House Problem* (N. Y., 1903), I, 3-4. Of course a tenement house is not necessarily a slum.

[2] See Schlesinger, *Rise of the City*, chap. iv.

[3] De Forest and Veiller, *Tenement House Problem*, II, app. v.

[4] Tenement House Department *v.* Katie Moeschen, 179 N. Y., 325.

of New York, but applying to cities of all classes in the state; Pennsylvania legislated in 1903 for cities of the second class and in 1907 amended her legislation for first-class cities by requiring licensing of tenement houses and quarterly inspection; Connecticut in 1905 enacted a general law for cities of over twenty thousand. While these few commonwealths set up state-wide standards, many cities—Chicago in 1905, Boston, Cleveland and San Francisco in 1907 and Baltimore in 1908—enacted new regulations or revised the existing building codes. By the end of the period the problem of slum housing had been squarely met and notable progress had been made.

From the slum districts came many of the victims of commercialized vice. Though the new building laws constituted an oblique attack on that ancient uncleanness, the leaders of this generation were not content with indirect or halfway measures. Prior to 1898 little of a systematic character had been done in American cities to regulate the "social evil" or to lessen it, and practically nothing in the way of scientific study. New York was so startled by the spread of prostitution that in 1900 a meeting of citizens appointed a committee of fifteen to investigate the situation.[1] This committee not only presented an excellent report based upon a study of conditions here and abroad, but prosecuted some offenders of the law, presented a series of recommendations for better control and, in fact, inaugurated in America the first serious attack upon the evil. The report had noted especially the connection between the so-called "Raines-law hotels" and prostitution,[2] and in 1905 a new and

[1] Committee of Fifteen, *The Social Evil* (N. Y., 1902).

[2] Committee of Fifteen, *Social Evil*, app., 159. Under the Raines law only hotels having at least ten rooms to rent above the basement could sell liquor on Sunday, with the result that thousands of saloons were turned into assignation houses and loitering places for prostitutes.

permanent organization, known as the Committee of Fourteen, was formed to fight the Raines law, though its work soon widened to include an attack upon all forms of prostitution.[1] A ten years' crusade distinctly improved conditions in New York City. The Raines-law hotels, numbered literally by the thousands in 1905, had practically disappeared; all of the famous resorts had been closed; and disorderly houses which had operated openly by the hundreds were greatly reduced in number and forced to conduct their business with secrecy. A direct result of the work of this committee was an investigation of the courts of minor criminal jurisdiction in New York and the passage of the Page law which revolutionized the procedure in the city magistrates' courts.[2]

Though the experience of New York was watched in other cities, it was not until George Kibbe Turner in a sensational article in *McClure's* laid bare the connection between liquor, gambling, crime, political corruption and prostitution that other centers were stirred to action. Turner asserted that there were ten thousand prostitutes in Chicago who were exploited by criminal hotels, houses of ill-fame, cheap dance halls and saloons, and that the whole business was organized from the snaring of young girls to the drugging of older and less salable women out of existence.[3] At the urgence of the Federation of Churches of Chicago the Mayor appointed a vice commission in 1910, and similar studies were made by

[1] Committee of Fifteen, *The Social Evil* (2d edn., N. Y., 1912), chap. iii.

[2] Committee of Fifteen, *Social Evil* (2d edn.), 216, 231 ff.; see also Committee of Fourteen, *Annual Report for 1914*.

[3] G. K. Turner, "The City of Chicago," *McClure's*, XXXVIII (1907), 575-592; also "Tammany's Control of New York by Professional Politicians," *McClure's*, XXXIII (1909), 117-134.

official bodies appointed in Minneapolis, Portland, Oregon, Hartford, Connecticut, and other cities in the next few years.[1]

The wide extent and highly organized character of the traffic in women came as a shock to the public. The Chicago commission believed that there were at least five thousand in that city who devoted their entire time to prostitution; [2] a Pittsburgh survey found two hundred disorderly houses in one section alone in the summer of 1907; [3] and the Portland vice commission in their comparatively small city reported one hundred and thirteen places wholly given up to prostitution or assignation. There was scarcely a city of any size which did not have its "red-light district." These reports, however, by pointing to poverty, liquor, defective mentality and lack of wholesome places of amusement as contributing causes suggested thereby means of remedy. At the same time they endeavored to break down the complacent attitude of many that organized prostitution and segregated districts were necessary, if not desirable.

The conditions described by the investigations were greatly modified by 1914, and improved even more during the war years as the federal government coöperated with the local police in eliminating open prostitution. More careful efforts were made to regulate places of amusement and to separate the saloon from the prostitute. The new juvenile courts played their part in rescue work and in many cities the red-light districts were eliminated. In the meantime the medical aspect was be-

[1] Vice Commission of Chicago, *The Social Evil in Chicago* (Chicago, 1911); Minneapolis Vice Commission, *Report* (Minneapolis, 1911); Portland Vice Commission, *Report* (Portland, 1913); and Hartford Vice Commission, *Report* (Hartford, 1913).

[2] Vice Commission of Chicago, *Social Evil*, 70.

[3] P. U. Kellogg, ed., *Wage-Earning Pittsburgh* (same ed., *The Pittsburgh Survey*, Russell Sage Found., N. Y., 1909-1914, VI), 350.

ginning to receive the attention it deserved through the organization of the American Society of Sanitary and Moral Prophylaxis in 1905.[1] Efforts were also made to check one source of prostitution by laws against the white-slave traffic. After a period of investigation and agitation in America, Roosevelt issued a proclamation declaring the adhesion of the United States to the international white-slave treaty; the immigration law of 1908 was strengthened to provide adequate punishment for those engaged in this traffic, and in 1910 the Mann act sought to deal with it through the federal power over interstate commerce.[2] Beginning with Illinois in 1908 most of the states also enacted stringent legislation against it.[3]

Less successful were the efforts directed from high quarters against family limitation. Not a new phenomenon, the tendency was greatly intensified by the new conditions of life. The woman who had tasted economic independence was slower to marry and insisted on a higher level of comfort when she did so. Nor was she willing to submerge all her interests in motherhood, however precious that estate, when once she took the fateful step. The cramped living quarters of the modern city and the stern "No children or dogs" of the apartment-house owner, as we have seen, provided further deterrents to maternity. These and numerous other social and economic causes were producing the inevitable. The rate of population increase had fallen in each decade but one since 1880 and had done so in spite of tremendous

[1] American Society of Sanitary and Moral Prophylaxis, *Transactions*, I (1906); II (1908); III (1910).

[2] *U. S. Statutes at Large*, XXXVI, pt. i, 825; C. G. Roe, *Panders and Their White Slaves* (N. Y., 1910).

[3] Committee of Fifteen, *Social Evil* (2d edn.), 207 ff.; Commission for the Investigation of the White Slave Traffic, So Called, *Report* (*Mass. House Doc.*, no. 2281).

immigration.[1] Although the census of 1910 failed adequately to cover the subject of birth rate, it showed a slight loss in each decade since 1890 of the number of "persons to a family." [2]

The decline in birth rate was greatest among the more educated and prosperous classes and among the native stock, although a similar tendency was at work among the second generation of immigrants. In New England the birth rate of the native stock appeared to be less than the death rate,[3] while a study made of Americans of native parentage in the central United States showed a shrinkage of the family between the present generation and their parents of 38.5 per cent. Over a tenth of the unions recorded in this study were found to be infertile and about one fifth produced but one child.[4] College women, recruited from the most intellectual group of each generation, married two years later than other girls of the same social class and averaged less than two children; only one out of two married, whereas in the whole population the ratio was nine out of ten.[5]

Generally speaking, the higher the social, intellectual and economic status, the smaller the family; but the declining birth rate was also evident among the "white-collar proletariat" of the cities. One student of the subject in New York City visited twenty-two apartment houses containing four hundred and eighty-five families

[1] Bureau of the Census, *Abstract of the Thirteenth Census, 1910*, 22. The rate of population increase was 26 per cent from 1870 to 1880; 24.9 from 1880 to 1890; 20.7 from 1890 to 1900; 21 from 1900 to 1910; and 15 from 1910 to 1920.

[2] Bureau of the Census, *Abstract of Thirteenth Census*, 260. In this census the term "family" means a household or group of persons, whether related by blood or not, who share a common abode and usually the same table.

[3] E. A. Ross, *Principles of Sociology* (N. Y., 1923), 35.

[4] R. E. Baber and E. A. Ross, *Changes in the Size of American Families in One Generation* (Univ. of Wis., *Studies*, no. 10), 3.

[5] Ross, *Principles of Sociology*, 392.

which possessed but fifty-four children, or about one child to every nine families. Twelve New York physicians practising among people in comfortable circumstances agreed, in substance, "that the large family does not exist and is not desired," while a woman physician with long practice on the West Side in the upper Sixties went so far as to say that "having a family is not an American ideal. Among my patients I find that the majority do not want any children; certainly not more than one. I should say that as a rule the second is an accident, the third is a misfortune, and the fourth a tragedy." [1]

To many this situation appeared deplorable. Ignoring the influences which made the tendency almost universal and inevitable, they attributed it merely to the selfishness of the "new woman." The leadership in this cause was taken by President Roosevelt when he scathingly denounced "race suicide" and used his great powers to popularize the idea of larger families. Roosevelt's propaganda called attention to the situation, but it obviously did not change it.[2] The primary motive in the restriction of birth appeared to be economic and social, and the views of a wealthy statesman might have little bearing on the problems of a twenty-dollar-a-week clerk or a twelve-dollar-a-week laborer. Roosevelt's blast helped, however, to stir up interest in the question of both eugenics and birth control. Already the Carnegie Institution (1904) had established a eugenics laboratory at Cold Spring Harbor, New York, and enough popular interest in eugenics was aroused by 1907 to induce Indiana to pass a law providing for the sterilization of cer-

[1] Lydia K. Commander, "Has the Small Family Become an American Ideal?," *Independent*, LVI, 836-840 (April 14, 1904).

[2] Theodore Roosevelt, *Autobiography* (N. Y., 1913), 176-184; Lydia K. Commander, "Why Do Americans Prefer Small Families?," *Independent*, LVII, 847-850 (Oct. 13, 1904).

tain types of defectives and criminals, an example followed by eleven other states by 1914.[1]

Meanwhile an earnest movement for scientific regulation of the size of families took form under a small group of reformers, who coined the term "birth control" as best expressing their aims. The idea was not new in America. An important early agitation had occurred in the 1830's, but the modern movement developed during the first two decades of the twentieth century. American and European advocates of family limitation joined in the First International Neo-Malthusian Conference in Paris in 1900; Moses Harmon, editor of *Lucifer,* was sentenced to Leavenworth in 1906 for publishing a serious discussion of matrimonial relations. A forward step was taken in 1912 when Dr. Abraham Jacobi, in his presidential address to the American Medical Association, indorsed the hygienic prevention of pregnancy. But the obstacles confronting the spread of such ideas were formidable. Not only was the circulation of contraceptive information or devices prohibited by a federal statute of 1873 and by laws in many of the states,[2] but contraception was opposed by numerous groups, especially the Roman Catholic Church, on theological, moral or social grounds.[3] The movement awaited vigorous and devoted leadership.

Such championship appeared when Mrs. Margaret Sanger, a visiting nurse in the East Side of New York, became convinced through her social work of the importance of family limitation, and began in 1912 to study practical methods. In 1914 she published the first

[1] H. H. Laughlin, *Eugenical Sterilization: 1926. Historical, Legal, and Statistical Review of Eugenical Sterilization in the United States* (New Haven, 1926), *passim.*

[2] Mary W. Dennett, *Birth Control Laws* (N. Y., 1926), 7 ff., app. i.

[3] For a statement of the position of the Catholic Church, see P. J. Ward, "The Catholics and Birth Control," *New Republic,* LIX, 35-38 (May 29, 1929).

issue of the *Woman Rebel,* immediately barred from the mails, and began the formation of the American Birth Control League. Her arrest and indictment under the federal statutes for mailing her pamphlet *Family Limitation,* and her consequent enforced absence from the country for over a year, delayed progress in the movement, but allowed her valuable time for further study. The movement was reorganized as the National Birth Control League in 1915, and other groups under the leadership of Mrs. Mary Ware Dennett formed the Voluntary Parenthood League in 1918. The two groups coalesced in 1921 to form the American Birth Control League, and worked to legalize the dissemination of contraceptive methods by properly qualified physicians, at the same time preaching the doctrine of better rather than more children, of the child's right to be wanted, of the proper spacing of children and of the right of the poor to scientific knowledge of contraception, a knowledge obviously possessed by the wealthy. Efforts to change existing laws failed, but in the postwar years the movement was to take on increasing strength and a number of birth-control clinics were established, though always in the face of continued vocal opposition.[1]

The chief advantages of the new age fell to women of the comfortable classes in the cities. Relieved of much of their former work, they found themselves with more leisure on their hands than they had ever before enjoyed and more, indeed, than some of them knew wisely how to use. The new woman, said Mrs. Gilman, "too ignorant, too timid, too self-indulgent to do other work, simply plays most of the time, or labors at amusement,

[1] Dennett, *Birth Control Laws,* chaps. ii-iii; Theodore Shroeder, *List of References on Birth Control* (N. Y., 1918); Julia E. Johnson, *Selected Articles on Birth Control* (N. Y., 1915); F. H. Hankins, "Birth Control," *Encyclopaedia of the Social Sciences,* II, 561-564.

salving her conscience with charity." [1] "My mountain of mail," wrote a woman journalist, "is often a volcano of seething unrest," an unrest resulting from the questioning of older values as well as from a failure to meet new opportunities.[2] At such a time the age-old complaint that the younger generation were faster and less bound by convention was frequently heard, and it seems probable that in this case the complaints had some foundation in fact. In 1898, if etiquette books are to be believed, no self-respecting girl would be seen at a public restaurant or tea room with a gentleman, unless a chaperon was present, and in the "same category of offenses" was ranked that of maidens visiting places of public amusement under the escort of young men alone.[3] This sort of convention was pretty largely an importation from Europe, and the earnest efforts of dictators of manners to impose them upon America were doomed to failure except in select circles in the large Eastern cities. "In many parts of the West and South," mourned an etiquette counselor in 1906, "society may grant a girl the privilege of visiting places of public refreshment or amusement alone with a young man, or of accepting his escort to or from an evening party. . . ." [4] Indeed, the standard of conduct in rural and urban parts varied throughout the nation.

More significant of the new position of women was the alarming increase of divorce. Much interest in this question was excited by Roosevelt's special message to Congress in 1905 and by the publication three years later

[1] Charlotte P. Gilman, "The Passing of the Home in Great American Cities," *Cosmopolitan,* XXXVIII (1904), 139.

[2] Ella W. Wilcox, "The Restlessness of the Modern Woman," *Cosmopolitan,* XXXI (1901), 314-317.

[3] Mrs. Burton Harrison, *The Well-Bred Girl in Society* (Phila., 1898), 86; One of the Four Hundred (*pseud.*), *Bad Breaks* (N. Y., 1897), 41.

[4] Mrs. Frank Learned, *The Etiquette of New York Today* (N. Y., 1906), 286.

of the results of a federal investigation.[1] This report demonstrated conclusively that the tendencies toward a high divorce rate, already apparent in the 1870's and 1880's, had continued.[2] Thus the rate, which had been 53 per 100,000 population in 1890, was 73 in 1900, 84 in 1906, and 112 in 1916. Although seven of the states and the District of Columbia showed a lower rate in 1916 than in 1906,[3] in others the increase was astounding. Divorces in Oregon had grown over 100 per cent, in New Jersey 120 per cent, in Idaho 150, in Arizona nearly 190 and in California over 200. With the exception of Japan the United States had a higher divorce rate than any other civilized country and granted a greater number of divorces than all the rest of the world, Japan again excepted.

Such classifications as adultery, cruelty, desertion, drunkenness and neglect to provide used by the statutes in describing the grounds for divorce conceal much of the truth. The underlying causes were as complex as civilization itself; and as the speed and intensity of life became greater, the marriage tie became increasingly regarded as a convenience rather than a sacred obligation.[4] By some the rising divorce rate was hailed as a favorable sign, but the great majority deplored it as a dangerous tendency. Remedial suggestions, however, were largely futile; neither the fulminations of the clergy nor the warning cry of statesmen appeared to have any effect.

[1] J. D. Richardson, comp., *Messages and Papers of the Presidents* (Wash., 1910), X, 7072; Bureau of the Census, *Marriage and Divorce, 1887-1906*. See also Bureau of the Census, *Marriage and Divorce, 1916*.

[2] See Allan Nevins, *The Emergence of Modern America* (*A History of American Life*, VIII), 215-216; Schlesinger, *Rise of the City*, chap. v.

[3] Colorado, South Dakota, West Virginia, Maine, Mississippi, Alabama and North Dakota.

[4] Julia E. Johnson, ed., *Selected Articles on Marriage and Divorce* (N. Y., 1925); R. L. Hartt, "The Habit of Getting Divorces," *World's Work*, XLVIII (1924), 402-409, 519-524; W. E. Carson, *The Marriage Revolt* (N. Y., 1915), 157 ff.

The discussion did, nevertheless, help call attention again to the curious legal situation which existed with reference to divorce. The grounds for divorce varied from none at all in South Carolina to fourteen in New Hampshire, and while a majority of the states recognized the divorce laws of the other states, at least eight did not recognize them unconditionally. The period of residence required for bringing suit ranged from six months to three years, thus encouraging an exodus to Nevada, where the city of Reno became famous for its six-month settlers. At the same time the laws on marriage also differed widely.[1] The chaotic legal aspect of the divorce problem led to an increasing demand that something be done through state agreement or federal amendment to standardize the laws. Leadership in the movement was assumed by Pennsylvania where Governor Samuel W. Pennypacker in 1906 called a National Congress of Uniform Divorce Laws which drafted a model act.[2] Discussed again by the conference of governors in 1913, the problem was presented to Congress in 1915 and again in 1923. Although supported by the American Bar Association, prominent churches and leading women's clubs, federal action was not achieved.

Probably never before did so large a proportion of American women strive to keep abreast the latest fashions in dress. As of yore, the styles were set by Paris, but the models once imported were quickly copied by the wholesale garment makers who brought neat imitations of the new modes within reach of the slenderest pocketbook. Even before the period opened, strong influences

[1] F. S. Hall and E. W. Brooke, *American Marriage Laws in Their Social Aspect* (N. Y., 1919).

[2] *Proceedings* of the National Congress on Uniform Divorce Laws held at Washington on Feb. 19, 1906, and *Proceedings* of the Adjourned National Congress on Uniform Divorce Laws held at Philadelphia on Nov. 13, 1906; E. W. Huffcut, "The National Congress on Uniform Divorce Laws," *Independent*, LXI, 1265 (Nov. 9, 1906).

were at work to modify the cumbersome costumes of earlier years. The coming of the bicycle and the participation of women in sports put an end to the bustle, and the growing activity of women in business and the professions tended to make the skirt discreetly shorter. In the early years of the century well-dressed women still wore large picture hats set on pompadours artificially enlarged, with tight-sleeved, high-necked blouses and bell-shaped ruffled skirts trailing in the dust. With modifications this style prevailed until 1904 when the waist and skirt were separated and the shirt waist appeared. This innovation was joyfully received, especially by the outdoor girl, and America's only contribution to fashion, the Gibson girl, with her stiffly starched shirt waist and dark skirt, flourished for a brief span. By 1908 the unsanitary trains had been eliminated and it was now proper to wear dresses at least an inch from the ground, though the vogue a few years later of the "hobble skirt" seemed to be a backward step. At the same time the massive corsets which had been in vogue in the early years of the century grew simpler and the half-dozen starched petticoats which had hung on them in 1900 decreased to one or two. After many decades women again appeared in a costume which revealed their forms, and with the further shortening of the skirt, about 1915, a serviceable costume for a practical age was at last on its way.[1]

While increased leisure merely gave some women additional time to fritter away, for other women it opened new vistas for self-improvement and community service. Many of them made excellent use of their new leisure in athletic sports, in study, in club activities, and in the

[1] Frances A. Allen, "Fig Leaves," *Am. Mercury*, XIII (1928), 59-66; Mary Blossom, "The Well Gowned Woman," *Cosmopolitan*, XXXI (1901), 135-144.

social-welfare, prohibition, suffrage and peace movements. The rosy-cheeked "athletic girl" with golf club or tennis racquet, whose picture adorned the magazine covers, had an existence in reality, while women's clubs in the churches and elsewhere throve as never before.

As good a barometer as any of the new women is the growth of the General Federation of Women's Clubs, which through its affiliated clubs embraced a membership of fifty thousand in 1898 and had increased to considerably over a million by 1914. Working through its standing committees on art, civics, civil-service reform, conservation, education, home economics, industrial and social conditions, legislation, literature, music, public health and library extension, the organization did much to assist many excellent movements in an era of rapid change. The more advanced leaders tried to laugh out of existence the old literary study clubs, the president-elect in 1904 urging her followers to drop the study of Dante's *Inferno* "and proceed in earnest to contemplate our own social order." [1] "We have no platform," said the president at the tenth biennial convention in 1910, "unless it is the care of women and children, and the home, the latter meaning the four walls of the city as well as the four walls of brick and mortar," and continued in her address to point out the kind of work which women's clubs had undertaken in behalf of child life and health conservation.[2] In some communities the woman's club was the only organization devoted to civic improvement.[3]

As the participation of women in affairs outside of the home broadened, their political enfranchisement could

[1] Rheta C. Dorr, *What Eight Million Women Want* (Boston, 1910), 42.

[2] Mary I. Wood, *The History of the General Federation of Women's Clubs* (N. Y., 1912), 249-250.

[3] Mary R. Beard, *Women's Work in Municipalities* (N. Y., 1915).

not be long delayed. Already by the close of the nineteenth century the chief inequalities in civil status had been removed in most of the states. Differences still remained. In general, the status of women was higher in those states where they took an active part in public affairs. Thus Colorado, the second state to obtain equal suffrage, more clearly recognized sex equality whereas the Southern states were by far the most backward in this respect, with Louisiana, still dominated by the old French civil code, bringing up the rear. In that commonwealth the husband received the dowry, controlled his wife's earnings and was legal guardian of the children, his wife being unable to appear in court, to be an executor, or to execute business pertaining to her own estate without his authorization.[1] The age of consent was still as low as ten years in Georgia and Mississippi although in most of the states it had been raised to sixteen or eighteen.[2] In certain states women were not admitted to the bar or to the practice of medicine, and in some, even at the close of the period, married women had little or no control over property or earnings, and their legal position as respects control of children was inferior to that of the father.[3] Yet, even in the backward states, steady improvement was registered during these years, and the feminist leaders were able to center their efforts on securing equality at the polls.

Although this question had been discussed for almost three quarters of a century, the fruits of the agitation by 1898 seemed very small. Partial suffrage existed, to be sure, for specific purposes in many states, but only four, Wyoming, Colorado, Utah and Idaho, had granted full

[1] E. A. Hecker, *A Short History of Woman's Rights* (2d edn., N. Y., 1914), 196-197; G. J. Bayles, *Women and the Law* (N. Y., 1901), 172-173.

[2] Summarized by Hecker, *History of Woman's Rights*, 174-225.

[3] Dorr, *What Eight Million Women Want*, chap. iv.

political power to women.[1] The leaders of the suffrage movement attributed the slowness of the advance to many causes, such as the opposition of the liquor interests and the low standard of political morality in the eighties and nineties; [2] but more potent than any of these influences was the active hostility of a minority of women and the passive indifference of the great majority of both men and women.

A Frenchman's observation that woman's status had "reached its maximum of progress in the Far West of America, on the shore of the Pacific," was tenable as far as it applied to the suffrage movement in this country.[3] It was in the state of Washington in 1910 that the cause was given a new impetus by the adoption of a suffrage amendment to the constitution, a precedent followed the next year by a hard-won victory in California.[4] In the fall elections of 1912 similar amendments were submitted to the voters of six states. Oregon, with suffrage states on three sides of her, carried the amendment by a small majority; in Kansas, where women had been voting in municipal elections since the Populist uprising of the eighties, victory was easy, while in the new state of Arizona the amendment was carried in every county by a vote of almost two to one.[5]

This success in the Far West was not duplicated in the Middle West. Suffrage advocates twice let victory slip through their fingers in Michigan, the proposal was

[1] See Schlesinger, *Rise of the City*, chap. v.

[2] Carrie C. Catt and Nettie R. Shuler, *Woman Suffrage and Politics* (N. Y., 1923), chaps. ix-xi.

[3] P. H. B. d'Estournelles de Constant, *America and Her Problems* (N. Y., 1915), 61.

[4] Catt and Shuler, *Woman Suffrage*, 174, 176; Abigail S. Duniway, *Path Breaking* (Portland, Ore., 1914); Ida H. Harper and others, eds., *The History of Woman Suffrage* (N. Y., 1881-1922), IV, 27-58.

[5] Harper and others, *Woman Suffrage*, VI, 14.

badly beaten in Wisconsin, while in Ohio other problems of more pressing interest prevented a clear decision on this issue and the amendment was defeated.[1] A bill granting presidential suffrage passed the Illinois legislature in 1913 and was upheld by the state supreme court in 1914. In the latter year suffrage referenda took place in seven states, but in only two, Montana and Nevada, were they successful.[2] Notwithstanding these defeats the number of equal-suffrage states had reached eleven by 1914.

But this progress was too slow for the ardent feminists. Their failure in many of the states the leaders ascribed to "the mobilization of the foreign vote . . . under the direction and probable pay of the liquor interests, and with the collusion of local bipartisan election officials, if not that of state central committees,"[3] and they decided to concentrate on the federal government. A federal amendment had, indeed, been pending since 1878, but Congress had shown little interest in it. As late as 1908 Roosevelt had refused to recommend woman suffrage to Congress and advised a deputation of workers to "go, get another state."[4] During the next administration, however, a petition of 404,000 signatures was presented to Congress (1910), and headquarters for the Congressional Committee of the National Woman Suffrage Association opened in Washington. In the presidential election of 1912 Taft and Wilson sidestepped the issue, but the Progressive party came out unequivocally for it. Roosevelt who had admitted in

[1] Catt and Shuler, *Woman Suffrage,* chap. xiv.

[2] Montana, Nevada, North Dakota, South Dakota, Nebraska, Missouri and Ohio.

[3] Catt and Shuler, *Woman Suffrage,* 195.

[4] Catt and Shuler, *Woman Suffrage,* 235.

1911 that he was only "tepidly in favor" now supported it enthusiastically.[1]

During the following months the American suffrage movement began to feel the influence of the more militant English tactics. Alice Paul was given the chairmanship of the Congressional Committee and the full backing of the Association in the organization of a suffrage parade to be held in Washington the day before the inauguration of Wilson.[2] Although the parade was broken up and the participants disgracefully abused by the Washington populace, it was successful in advertising the cause.[3] The hostility of the Washington mob was not a true indication of the status of the movement. The pioneer work had been done and success was in sight. Mrs. Elizabeth Cady Stanton, who for decades had encountered abuse and ridicule, died full of honor in 1902, and her coworker, Susan B. Anthony, when she laid down the reins of office in 1900, had won world-wide esteem.[4] It was left to their coworkers and successors, Mrs. Carrie Chapman Catt and Dr. Anna Howard Shaw, to complete the task.

On the very brink of success the suffrage movement had to meet squarely in 1912 the question of tactics. Certain of the leaders, notably Alice Paul, advocated the more militant tactics adopted by their English sisters and the English theory that the party in power should be held accountable, but the majority leaders of the National Woman Suffrage Association under the presidency of Dr. Shaw held that these theories were not applicable

[1] Harper and others, *Woman Suffrage*, VI, 44; Catt and Shuler, *Woman Suffrage*, 237 ff.

[2] Doris Stevens, *Jailed for Freedom* (N. Y., 1920), chap. ii. "Where are the people?" Wilson is reported to have asked on his arrival in Washington. "On the Avenue watching the suffragists parade," was the answer. Stevens, *Jailed for Freedom*, 21.

[3] *N. Y. Times*, March 4, 5, 1913.

[4] Ida H. Harper, *Life of Susan B. Anthony* (Indianapolis, 1908), III.

to American conditions and ousted Miss Paul from the chairmanship of the Congressional Committee. Miss Paul, however, had already organized a Congressional Union, which carried on during the next five years an aggressive campaign by means of picketing and other methods of publicity, and in the end helped force the Wilson administration to take a definite stand for woman suffrage.[1]

Suffrage agitation occupied so much of the attention of the women leaders chiefly because in most other ways the equality of the sexes was established in law and custom. Colleges of the type of Wellesley, Mt. Holyoke and Bryn Mawr, brilliantly administered by women executives, were giving collegiate training on a par with the leading colleges for men.[2] The best of the state universities had long since opened their professional schools to women and the great Eastern universities, somewhat grudgingly to be sure, were following their example. Columbia admitted them to the Graduate School of Political Science in 1900, though it was not until 1914 that Pennsylvania allowed women in its medical school, followed in 1916 by Columbia and in 1918 by Harvard. As writers they were turning out their share of the "best sellers" of the period. In some spheres of activity, indeed, women had a clear advantage over men. As school teachers and as social workers they were definitely in possession of the field. If in sculpture, painting and music their participation was less, their influence as arbiters of culture and patrons of the arts seemed often predominant.

[1] See P. W. Slosson, *The Great Crusade and After* (*A History of American Life*, XII), 160.

[2] Lavinia Hart, "Women as College Presidents," *Cosmopolitan*, XXXIII (1902), 72-79.

CHAPTER VIII

CHILDREN'S RIGHTS

IT was characteristic of the age that the quest for social justice should embrace children's rights as well as women's rights. Perhaps the shrinking size of the family caused parents to value more highly the individual child, and certainly the teaching of the new psychology tended to place increasing importance upon the years of infancy. Most significant of all, however, was the fact that, while the nation had reached a stage where sufficient wealth was available to give greater opportunities to youth, it was still young enough for the industrious and talented child to achieve a brilliant career. The immigrant himself might not go far, but in a land of hope and opportunity there was nothing to which his children, if properly trained, might not aspire, and this same attitude was prevalent in groups higher up the social and economic scale. A society with its eyes on the future very naturally glorified the child.

A community placing new values on child life could not long overlook the appalling rate of infant mortality with its attendant human suffering. In certain states of civilized America, in 1900, it was found that one hundred and sixty infants died out of every thousand, and that the death rate for children under five years was one in every twenty.[1] Experts affirmed that probably half of this mortality was preventable, and that the causes, which sprang from unsanitary surroundings, improper

[1] Bureau of the Census, *Mortality Statistics for 1911*, 23-25; G. B. Mangold, *Problems of Child Welfare* (N. Y., 1914), chaps. i-iii.

food, parental ignorance and other factors, in part or entirely attributable to poverty, might be greatly lessened. The problem had many ramifications; it extended into the field of labor legislation in laws governing the work of prospective mothers; into the whole question of tenements, tenement-house legislation and city sanitation; into the problem of the milk supply, the proper feeding of infants and the instruction of the mother in the care of the child; and into the medical care of mother and child. Indeed, it encompassed the whole range of preventive medicine.

The cities, which surpassed the rural districts in the rate of infant mortality, took the lead in the warfare on death.[1] The pioneer was Rochester, New York, where in 1897, under the direction of Dr. George W. Goler, two milk stations were established in which experiments were carried on, pasteurized milk distributed at cost and mothers instructed in diet and the proper care of infants. The next step was to obtain a milk supply produced under clean and sanitary conditions. Through a wise intermingling of education and compulsion this was eventually secured in spite of political interference and the opposition of private interests.[2] Following the footsteps of Rochester, most of the large cities worked out milk codes covering various aspects of sanitation, pasteurization and the number of bacteria per cubic centimeter and made investigations into the source of disease bacteria. Most of them also eventually had milk depots where clean milk, upon a physician's certificate, was sold at or below cost or given away to needy mothers. New York City, especially, after the division of child hygiene was established in 1908, did excellent work. Certain of the states, notably Massachusetts, came to the aid

[1] Bureau of the Census, *Mortality Statistics for 1911*, 74.
[2] Mangold, *Child Welfare*, 84 ff.

of the cities in requiring commercial milk to have a certain amount of butter fats, in requiring cows to be tuberculin-tested and in providing for dairy inspection.

As an adjunct of the milk depots many cities established baby clinics where the growth and condition of infants could be regularly checked. Supplementing the clinics was the work of the visiting nurse, by whose means state and private philanthropy was carried into the home and the progress of the baby supervised in its normal environment. The extraordinary success attending the work of the visiting nurses in New York City is indicated by the fact that during four and a half months in 1911 only 1.4 per cent of the 16,987 babies under their care died, which was less than half the prevailing rate for the entire city. Other efforts were directed along the lines of prenatal care, first attempted by New York City and by the Woman's Municipal League of Boston in 1908; toward more effective control of midwifery; and toward legislation covering the working conditions of the wage-earning mother. That real progress had been made was shown in Rochester, New York, where the death of children under five years was one third less for the decade following 1897 than for the ten preceding years.[1] The census for the registration area of 1911 showed a decline of twenty-two per cent in the death rate of children under one year for the decade, and a decline of twenty-seven per cent for those under five years. Whereas approximately one sixth of the children in the registration area under one year died in 1900, but one eighth died in 1911.

Day nurseries where working mothers might leave their infants had been introduced into the United States as early as 1854, but their rapid extension came after 1897. In that year the Association of Day Nurseries of

[1] Mangold, *Child Welfare*, 87.

New York City was founded and in the following year the National Federation of Day Nurseries held its first meeting. Following quite naturally after the day nursery came greater attention to community playgrounds, especially where children's play was responsibly supervised. In 1898 Mayor Quincy of Boston opened twenty school-yard playgrounds and in the following year New York City through its Board of Education opened thirty-one. By 1910 more than 150 cities reported playgrounds and five years later 432 cities were maintaining a total of 3294 managed by 2883 men and 4624 women.[1] The Playground and Recreation Association of America, organized in 1906, did much to integrate the work of local societies and to extend the movement.

Massachusetts set an example to other states in 1908 by making it compulsory for all cities of over ten thousand to hold a referendum on the question as to whether the municipality should provide at least one public playground for the physical education of the minors of such city, and at least one playground for every additional twenty thousand of population.[2] Within a year forty-one out of forty-two cities had voted affirmatively.[3] The impetus for such a law came not alone from the desire to promote amusement and health, but also from the hope that juvenile crime might be lessened. But whatever the motives the supervised city playground was a great success. It might lack the spontaneity and charm of "the old swimmin' hole," but it marked a new era in the recreational life of the city youngster.

[1] C. E. Rainwater, *The Play Movement in the United States* (Chicago, 1922), 19, 31; E. B. Mero, *American Playgrounds* (Boston, 1918), 20; E. A. Rice, *A Brief History of Physical Education* (N. Y., 1926), 259-261; L. F. Hammer and C. A. Perry, *Recreation in Springfield, Illinois* (Russell Sage Found., N. Y., 1914).

[2] *Acts and Resolves of Massachusetts for 1908*, chap. dxiii, 464.

[3] Third Annual Playground Congress, *Proceedings* (N. Y., 1910), 56.

Important as were the city playgrounds, they fell far short of solving the entire recreational problem of childhood. The instinct of youth to play together in some sort of club and the necessity of turning the gang energy into useful and constructive activities had not been met. The expanding recreational activities of the Y. M. C. A. were of great value, but it was left to the Scout movement to make the chief contribution in this respect. The Boy Scouts originated in England in 1908 through the work of General Sir Robert S. S. Baden-Powell for the purpose of training boys between twelve and eighteen years in self-reliance, manliness and good citizenship. Immediately successful in England, the organization was quickly introduced into America where two similar clubs—the Woodcraft Indians, founded by Ernest Thompson-Seton, and the Sons of Daniel Boone, founded by Dan C. Beard—coalesced in 1910 to form the Boy Scouts of America and received in that year a charter under the laws of the District of Columbia. These American forerunners and the phenomenal growth which the organization quickly experienced indicate that one underlying explanation for its success was the desire to restore to American youth the normal experiences of earlier generations of boys.

With almost unanimous backing, including interdenominational church support, and with an undeniable appeal to youth, the Boy Scouts speedily became the preëminent boys' organization of the country, numbering at the end of 1913 about eight thousand Scout Masters, representing as many organizations, and approximately three hundred thousand members. The oath of the organization was a promise made by each Scout "to do my duty to God and my country" and "to help other people at all times," and the three classes of the order were based upon accomplishments in woodcraft and in various useful activities pertaining to outdoor life.[1] Although the Scout movement was quite democratic, its greatest work was done among the children of the middle and upper classes rather than among the poor and potentially delinquent children of the cities. It, however, brought into its membership the children of many immigrants whose instruction in Indian lore and woodcraft science constitutes perhaps the most curious episode in the current Americanization movement.

The undoubted success of the Boy Scouts resulted in an organization designed to do much the same thing for girls. The Campfire Girls, founded in 1912 by Dr. and Mrs. Luther Gulick, not only served to promote the health of girls by outdoor life but to instill thrift and other excellent qualities among them as well as to develop an interest in the technique of the homely tasks of everyday life. Quite similar were the Girl Scouts founded in the same year by Mrs. Juliette Low. Their growth was slower than the boys' organization, but they steadily gained in favor.

Much as organized and supervised play might contribute to minimize juvenile crime, it could not wholly obviate the handicap of bad heredity or environment. It is significant of this period that probably the greatest change made in criminology was in the handling of the delinquent and defective child. Though Massachusetts as early as 1869 had provided for separate trials for children, children's courts in the modern sense did not originate in the United States until the Illinois law of 1899. Juvenile courts were established in Milwaukee and Buffalo in 1901, in New York, Baltimore and Cleveland in 1902, and within a decade in every large city in the country; between 1903 and 1907 no fewer than

[1] L. W. Barclay, *Education Work of the Boy Scouts* (U. S. Bur. of Educ., *Bull. for 1919*, no. 24).

eighteen states had adopted legislation to make possible their establishment. Juvenile delinquency was no longer to be handled like that of adults—the problem of the judge was not to mete out punishment, but to save and redeem the child. The plan included not only separate courts with private hearings before especially qualified judges but also a probationary system. By reducing the number of juveniles committed to institutions of various kinds it was a source of large saving to the taxpayer, but what it accomplished in the saving of children is beyond calculation.

Fortunately for the juvenile-court movement many of the early judges were in sympathy with the idea and labored with marked success.[1] The best known of this group was Judge Ben B. Lindsey, who was chiefly responsible for the Colorado law of 1901 and was judge of the Denver juvenile court from its foundation until 1927. Through lectures and articles Lindsey contributed greatly to the movement not alone for juvenile courts but for every type of child conservation. When his enthusiasm for social justice widened to include reforms in election procedure, the elimination of child labor and prevention of franchise exploitation in the city of Denver, both political parties in 1908 refused to indorse him, and his dramatic fight with the corrupt interests of the city served the good purpose of giving wider publicity to the work of his children's court.

While juvenile courts were doing much to redeem the moral delinquent, many children with physical defects were being aided as a result of the medical inspection of

[1] Such men as Judges Richard S. Tuthill and Julian W. Mack of Chicago, N. B. Neelen of Milwaukee, G. W. Murphy of Springfield, Ill., George W. Stubbs of Indianapolis, Robert M. Foster of St. Louis, Curtis D. Wilbur of Los Angeles, Robert Wilkin of Brooklyn and Willard H. Olmstead, William E. Wyatt and Julius Mayer of New York. For a picture of a typical juvenile court, see H. K. Webster, "The Square Deal with Children," *American*, LI (1906), 394 ff.

school children. Boston in 1894, the first to establish a regular system of medical inspection of school children, was followed during the next three years by Chicago, New York and Philadelphia. In 1899 Connecticut passed a law providing for the testing of vision in all public schools; in 1903 New Jersey authorized boards of education to employ medical inspectors; and in 1904 Vermont required annual examination of eyes, ears and throats. Massachusetts, however, was the first state (1906) to introduce medical inspection in all its schools; but so rapidly did the movement spread that by 1912 seven commonwealths had passed mandatory laws,[1] ten had passed permissive laws, and two states and the District of Columbia carried on medical inspection under regulations promulgated by the boards of health.[2] Dental inspection, starting in Rochester in 1906 through the public spirit of Henry Lomb, rapidly progressed until at the close of 1911 such work was carried on in eighty-nine American cities, most of them in the North Atlantic and North Central divisions.[3] What medical and dental inspection meant, not alone in alleviating immediate misery and detecting contagious diseases but in the way of preventive medicine, can never be gauged, but it remains one of the movements of this period most productive of absolute benefit.

In its various phases child labor had existed in America from the earliest times, but it did not become a serious menace until the later decades of the nineteenth century when increasing numbers of children were caught in the toils of the spreading factory system. By 1900 the num-

[1] Massachusetts, New Jersey, Pennsylvania, Minnesota, Louisiana, Utah and Colorado. L. H. Gulick and L. P. Ayres, *Medical Inspection of Schools* (N. Y., 1913), 13, 164.

[2] Of the 1038 cities reporting in an investigation conducted by the Russell Sage Foundation, 443 (43 per cent) had medical inspection in 1911. Gulick and Ayres, *Medical Inspection of Schools*, 15-20.

[3] Gulick and Ayres, *Medical Inspection of Schools*, 122.

ber under sixteen engaged in gainful occupations was at least 1,700,000, and some students of the child-labor problem placed the figure even higher.[1] The majority (60 per cent) were agricultural workers who labored under conditions which might not be deleterious, but the reports which came in of the twelve-hour day in the berry fields of New Jersey, of the congestion, overwork and immorality among the young workers in the vegetable gardens of Delaware and Maryland, the beet-sugar fields of Michigan, Nebraska and Colorado, and the tobacco fields and stripping farms of Connecticut, Kentucky, Virginia and Pennsylvania were anything but encouraging.[2]

The worst conditions, however, prevailed in manufacturing in which about sixteen per cent of the child workers were engaged. The picture of children kept awake during the long night in a Southern mill by having cold water dashed on their faces, of little girls in canning facttories "snipping" sixteen or more hours a day or capping forty cans a minute in an effort to keep pace with a never exhausted machine, of little ten-year-old breaker boys crouched for ten hours a day over a dusty coal chute to pick sharp slate out of the fast-moving coal, of boys imported from orphan asylums and reformatories to wreck their bodies in the slavery of a glass factory, or of a four-year-old baby toiling until midnight over artificial flowers in a New York tenement—these were conditions which might well shame a civilized people into action.[3] "Capital has neither morals nor ideals," cried a Socialist critic in 1906; in the United States of the

[1] John Spargo, *The Bitter Cry of the Children* (N. Y., 1906), 145.

[2] O. R. Lovejoy, "Some Unsettled Questions about Child Labor," Fifth Ann. Conf. on Child Labor, *Proceeds.* (N. Y., 1909), 59.

[3] Spargo, *Bitter Cry*, 146, 150, 154, ff., 163 ff.; "Child Labor in Canneries," *Child Labor Bull.*, I, no. 4, 28, 40. See also Mrs. John Van Vorst, *The Cry of the Children* (N. Y., 1908), *passim*.

twentieth century it "calls for children as loudly as it called in England a century ago." [1]

In certain of the older industrial states such as Massachusetts, child-labor legislation, chiefly in the interest of education, existed on the statute books prior to 1898, but the laws were not far-reaching or adequately enforced. Some improvement, however, was in sight. The spectacle of thousands of children caught in a ruthless economic system and crushed in soul and body before they had barely escaped from infancy stirred certain socially minded reformers. Working through labor unions, women's clubs, the National Consumers' League and other organizations, the movement for child-labor legislation rapidly gathered momentum, the most important step perhaps being the organization in 1904 of the National Child Labor Committee in order to encourage and coördinate the work of various state committees and other interested groups.

The climax of the early movement came in the years 1905-1907 when two thirds of the states either initiated protective legislation or greatly improved and strengthened the existing laws. In the latter year Congress appropriated one hundred and fifty thousand dollars for an investigation of conditions, which resulted in an exhaustive nineteen-volume report,[2] and in the creation in 1912 of a children's bureau in the department of commerce and labor to study the problems of child labor and systematize inquiries into conditions of child life.[3] In the hope of crystallizing public opinion the Child Labor Committee drew up in 1912 a model law,

[1] Spargo, *Bitter Cry*, 141.

[2] Summarized in U. S. Bureau of Labor Statistics, *Bull.*, no. 175.

[3] Sentiment in favor of the latter act had, in part, been stimulated by a national conference on the care of dependent children held in Washington in 1909 at the call of President Roosevelt, which was followed by a special message urging legislation. "Child Labor Laws in All States,"

the adoption of which was urged upon the states. To bring the more backward sections in line pressure for federal legislation began with the introduction into Congress in 1907 of a bill to exclude from interstate transportation goods offered for shipment from mines and factories employing children under fourteen years of age. In spite of wide backing this bill was not passed until 1916 when it was speedily declared unconstitutional, and an attempt in 1919 to accomplish the same object by the imposition of a ten-per-cent tax on the net profits of factories employing children under fourteen met the same fate.[1]

The state laws relating to child labor adopted during these years generally fixed a minimum age limit, prohibited certain employments as dangerous to health and morals, limited the hours a child under a certain age might work and, in many cases, fixed an educational requirement which must be met before children could be released for labor. By 1914 every state but one had some minimum age limit, varying from twelve years in several Southern states to fifteen years in South Dakota and sixteen in Montana. At least twenty-one states had restricted the working day for children in factories to eight hours, and some had extended the limit to other occupations, though ten hours was the usual maximum. A majority of the states prohibited children and young persons from certain occupations and over half of the states forbade night work under a specified age. A majority also made some effort to insure literacy before the child could be put to work. Certainly the decade which closed with the year 1914 marked a tremendous progress in child-

Child Labor Bull., I, no. 2, 80-107; summary in Mangold, *Child Welfare*, 324-325; Conference on the Care of Dependent Children, *Proceedings* (Wash., 1909).

[1] Hammer *v.* Dagenhart, 247 U. S., 251; Bailey and Bailey *v.* Drexel Furniture Company, 259 U. S., 20 (1922).

labor legislation. Unfortunately, however, many states still lacked adequate regulations, and even such advanced states as Massachusetts, Illinois and New York failed effectively to enforce the excellent laws which had been passed. Child labor in 1914 was still a problem and plenty of opportunity remained for the efforts of the Child Labor Committee.[1]

Dilatory as had been the nation in attacking the curse of child labor, it had not failed to appreciate the importance of education. Like other phases of American civilization, education, as it developed during the lifetime of this generation, was the result of numerous and intricate forces long in the making. The industrialization and urbanization of the nation, accompanied as it was by the inundation of millions of immigrants, opened new opportunities to the city schools, but at the same time staggered them by the complexity of the task. The declining influence of the church upon the home and the relaxation of parental discipline raised the question of the rôle of the school as a moral mentor, while the living conditions of the crowded slums obliged the school to contribute to the solution of such problems as recreation, hygiene and health. While the needs of a changing civilization forced educational leaders to wrestle with the question of methods and curricula, a rapidly expanding school system confronted civic authorities with problems of architecture and finance. At the opening of our period the American people were more than ever convinced that the hope of democracy rested largely upon a free, tax-supported public-school system, but as to the lines along which it should develop there was wide divergence of opinion.

Educational philosophy in 1898 was decidedly in

[1] Helen L. Sumner and Ella A. Merritt, *Child Labor Legislation in the United States* (Children's Bur., *Industrial Ser.*, no. 1, 1915).

flux. The principles of Froebel had long been revising kindergarten procedure and the new Herbartian theories introduced into America about 1890 by Charles De Garmo and others were winning many adherents among students of elementary education.[1] Hardly, however, had the National Herbart Society for the Scientific Study of Education been organized in 1895 before American students and philosophers began to undermine the major tenets of Herbart. Most influential in pointing out the direction which the new education would take was John Dewey, for some years head of the School of Education at the University of Chicago and after 1904 professor of philosophy at Columbia University. Following the new psychology in stressing the importance of early environment and training, and holding to the belief that the public school was the chief remedy for the ills of society, Dewey argued that social efficiency and not mere knowledge was the aim of education. To obtain this social efficiency the activities of the school must be closely connected with real life, and the education of the child must go beyond book learning and include play, the use of tools, contact with nature and the development of personal expression. The school was a place where the child should learn life by living life.[2]

That one of America's leading philosophers devoted his chief efforts and interest to the field of education was of incalculable benefit during this important period of development, but his influence would have been limited without the aid which came from the psychological and other scientific research which played continuously upon the problem of education. Fortunate likewise was

[1] See A. M. Schlesinger, *The Rise of the City* (*A History of American Life*, X), chap. vi.

[2] John Dewey, *The School and Society* (Chicago, 1899), and *Democracy and Education* (N. Y., 1916); John and Evelyn Dewey, *Schools of Tomorrow* (N. Y., 1915).

the fact that America's foremost psychologists were primarily interested in education. The books of William James in the early nineties embodied "an earnest and direct and scientific attack on the scholastic psychology" then existing; [1] G. Stanley Hall's monumental studies of adolescence marked a milestone in educational psychological research; while Edward L. Thorndike in his *Educational Psychology* (1903) went far to subject old conceptions of education to the acid test of scientific psychology and to open new fields for research. At all events Dewey's philosophy of modern education together with the work of the new psychology was warmly accepted by trained educators, and deeply influenced the trend of twentieth-century educational reform. Henry Adams's cynical observation that "the chief wonder of education is that it does not ruin everybody concerned in it, teachers and taught," was certainly less applicable in the year 1914 than it had been at the beginning of the period.[2]

While philosophers and pedagogues struggled to evolve a more intelligent system of instruction, the nation carried on with unprecedented enthusiasm a program of educational expansion. The children in elementary schools increased between 1898 and 1914 from less than sixteen million to more than twenty while the registration in high schools and colleges more than doubled.[3] For every day of the calendar years between 1890 and 1918 one public high school was established, and the total high-school pupils per thousand of the population rose from less than five to more than seventeen, and the

[1] D. B. Leary, "Development of Educational Psychology," I. L. Kandel, ed., *Twenty-Five Years of American Education* (N. Y., 1924), 104.

[2] Henry Adams, *Education of Henry Adams* (Boston, 1918), 55.

[3] U. S. Commissioner of Education, *Report for 1898-1899*, I, xi; *Rep. for 1916*, II, 1.

increase was to gather momentum in the years which followed.[1]

Especially striking was the advance in the South where the states, says Cubberley, "experienced the greatest educational awakening in their history—an awakening to be compared with that of Mann in Massachusetts and Barnard in Connecticut and Rhode Island."[2] Active campaigns for better schools were generally promoted, beginning in North Carolina in 1902, in Virginia in 1903, in Tennessee and Georgia in 1904 and soon spreading to the states of the Lower South. Improvement appeared in many ways: the educational provisions of the constitutions and laws were revised and strengthened; school revenues doubled or trebled in a single decade; the enrollment of white children increased almost a third between 1898 and 1914. Impetus was also given to the development of high schools—hitherto neglected by the South—which now, for the first time, came to be accepted by the rural communities as an integral part of the state school system. Though most of the Southern commonwealths continued to lag behind their sister states, the remarkable educational progress after 1898 both in quality and quantity may be regarded as nation-wide. In spite of this advance it was disturbing to note that in 1914 the average number of years (of 200 days) of schooling received by the American youth was but 6.16.[3]

[1] These estimates are for both private and public schools. U. S. Comr. of Educ., *Rep. for 1917*, II, 511; U. S. Bur. of Educ., *Bull. for 1919*, no. 91, 127-128, 310. Discussed by A. J. Inglis in Kandel, *Twenty-Five Years of American Education*, 251 ff. See also P. W. Slosson, *The Great Crusade and After* (*A History of American Life*, XII), chap. xii.

[2] E. P. Cubberley, *Public Education in the United States* (Boston, 1919), 361. See also E. W. Knight, *Public Education in the South* (Boston, 1922), chaps. xii-xiii; and U. S. Comr. of Educ., *Rep. for 1916*, II, 586.

[3] The average for 1900 was 5.23. U. S. Comr. of Educ., *Rep. for 1916*, II, 6.

The most important feature of the educational system, if judged by the number of pupils directly touched, remained the elementary school. Twenty times as many students attended the early grades as found their way into the high school and the instruction at these lower levels continued to be the only formal education received by well over ninety per cent of American youth. Though buttressed by compulsory-attendance laws in two thirds of the states and hailed as the bulwark of democracy, the elementary school at the opening of the century still had wide room for improvement.[1] The average child attended for perhaps sixty-eight days out of a one-hundred-and-forty-three-day year a one-room school where he was taught formal subjects in a mechanical manner by a young woman who had had little if any training beyond the elementary grades and whose services were valued at the munificent sum of around $38 a month.[2] The situation by 1914 was far better: the school year had been lengthened to 158.7 days, the average attendance to 86.7 days, and the salaries of women teachers to approximately $66.

More encouraging than the lengthening of the school term was the general improvement apparent. As never before, elementary education was being subjected to scientific study by the teachers and students of the great graduate schools of education which became veritable laboratories of educational research and experiment. At the same time large amounts of concrete data were accumulated by surveys of educational systems. Chicago led the way in 1897, Cleveland followed in 1906, and their example was soon emulated by several states and numerous cities.[3]

[1] C. L. Robbins, "Elementary Education," Kandel, *Twenty-Five Years of American Education*, 228.

[2] U. S. Comr. of Educ., *Rep. for 1898-1899*, I, lxxv, lxxix.

[3] U. S. Comr. of Educ., *Rep. for 1914*, I, chap. xxiv.

An effort was made to raise the educational qualifications of elementary teachers, which were surprisingly low.[1] That real progress was made was indicated by the slightly higher standards set by some states, the establishment of teachers' training classes in high schools, and by the growth and improvement of normal schools.[2] The cities, as usual, showed the chief gains; but the rural districts too shared in the advance, particularly in the tendency to combine scattered district schools into one union school with a better equipped building, more highly trained teachers and division into grades. Great impetus was given this movement by the rapid improvement of roads and the increasing use of motor busses.

Even more important in the field of elementary education was the modification of the curriculum. Music, drawing, domestic science, manual and physical training, which since the 1880's had been gradually pushing their way into the schools, were now adopted with real enthusiasm. These practical subjects fitted in with the pragmatic philosophy of the time and it was Dewey's great contribution to rationalize and popularize these changes. Perhaps the most interesting experiment along the line of the newer education was that made at Gary, Indiana, by William A. Wirt. Forced in a rapidly growing industrial center to economize in space and money, Wirt worked out a scheme for a school plant which contained not only classrooms, but playgrounds, gardens, workshops, a library and a social center. Specialization of instruction and departmental instruction running through the grades; outdoor activities and shop work

[1] "An Educational Study of Alabama," U. S. Bur. of Educ., *Bull. for 1919*, no. 41, 349; "The Rural Teacher of Nebraska," *Bull. for 1919*, no. 20, 31; "Status of the Rural Teacher in Pennsylvania," *Bull. for 1921*, no. 34, 31.

[2] *Biennial Survey of Education for 1916-1918* (U. S. Bur. of Educ., *Bull. for 1919*, nos. 88-91), IV, 9-121.

carried on at the same time as the indoor classes, thus doubling the capacity; the holding of school in all seasons of the year; the use of the plant in the evening for continuation schools and as a social and recreational center—these were some of the features which attracted the attention of administrators seeking to curtail expenses and students of education looking for improved methods.[1]

The doubling between 1898 and 1914 of the number of high schools and of the enrollment of students shows clearly that the American taxpayer accepted the high school as an essential community obligation and as necessary to the success of the democracy. The private secondary schools might continue to attract the children of the wealthy, but they were declining in relative importance,[2] and there were now few cities or towns which did not support a high school. The high school of the nineteenth century had been largely dominated by the idea of training for college; but this old conception, already yielding in the 1890's, declined rapidly with the new century as it came more directly under popular influence and as the followers of Wirt and Dewey gained greater recognition. Old courses were made more flexible and new ones added. Before 1898 commercial and home-economics courses were almost the only nonacademic training provided in high schools, but after that date vocational training of many kinds was introduced, including instruction in agriculture, industry, trade and commerce. In the larger cities high schools devoted to commerce and mechanics were established. At the same time some of the older courses, such as those in Greek, geology and astronomy, began to be dropped. While the

[1] Deweys, *Schools of Tomorrow*, 175-204, 251 ff.

[2] A. J. Inglis, "Secondary Education," Kandel, *Twenty-Five Years of American Education*, 252; U. S. Comr. of Educ., *Rep. for 1898-1899*, 1843 ff.; *Rep. for 1916*, chap. viii.

extraordinary growth of high schools showed an insistence upon an opportunity for all to get a higher education, the simultaneous development of vocational training indicated a conviction that not all were capable of achieving it.

Nothing illustrates the growing popularity of the high school more than its extension downward into the junior high school and upward into the junior college. The impetus to add the seventh and eighth grades to the old high-school system came less from a desire to train better for the colleges and more from the need to afford a broader education in the lower grades and to provide earlier for individual differences among children. In its first stages the junior high school was merely an expansion of the upper grades with administration providing for departmental instruction, some opportunity for elective courses and segregation from the six elementary grades. Beginning spontaneously about 1910 in many parts of the country, this movement became one of the outstanding developments of the subsequent years.

More slowly proceeded the movement for the junior college, advocated during the 1890's by Dean A. F. Lange of the University of California and by President William R. Harper of the University of Chicago which in 1898-1899 inaugurated the degree of Associate for those students who finished the work of the freshman and sophomore years.[1] The establishment of junior colleges was urged to alleviate the overcrowding of the older colleges, to provide facilities for two years' work nearer home and to supply a shorter academic training for those who could not go farther. Some struggling small colleges gave up their last two years to become accredited junior colleges; universities and normal schools also developed the junior college, while in Joliet, Illinois, there

[1] U. S. Comr. of Educ., *Rep. for 1898-1899*, II, 1561-1562.

was introduced in 1902 the first junior college in connection with a city high school. By 1914 over fifty public and private institutions of this type were in operation, all in the South and Middle or Far West.[1] Six of these were in California where legislation had been passed in 1907 enabling high schools to add the first two years of standard college work to the traditional four-year course, thus approximating the scope of European secondary schools.

Many of the same tendencies were also characteristic of the higher education. Though the number of colleges and universities, exclusive of junior colleges, slightly declined between 1893 and 1916, the students in attendance increased threefold, and the financial support fivefold. This remarkable showing was due in part to the normal growth in population and wealth, and in part to the exuberant belief, stimulated by the marvelous development of the high school, that "not only should college education be open to everybody, but that nearly everybody should have it."[2] In 1914 one in every twenty-five of the population between nineteen and twenty-three years was attending college, a considerable increase over the figures of 1898.[3] Although the inundation of students was not nearly so rapid in the years previous to the World War as in the years following,[4] it was sufficient not only to influence the curricula, but also to convince even enthusiastic devotees of democracy that many who entered college were debarred by lack of interest or innate mental limitations from achieving much of value.

[1] F. M. McDowell, "The Junior College," U. S. Bur. of Educ., *Bull. for 1919*, no. 35.

[2] *Biennial Survey of Education for 1916-1918*, I, 7, 56.

[3] H. R. Bonner, comp., "Statistics of Universities, Colleges and Professional Schools, 1917-1918," U. S. Bur. of Educ., *Bull. for 1920*, no. 34, 19.

[4] See Slosson, *Great Crusade and After*, 333-334.

To meet the demand of the throngs pressing at their gates, colleges and universities widened and subdivided their graduate and professional courses. Although every aspiring university at the opening of the century already embraced a wide variety of specialized colleges and "schools," their number tended to grow rather than lessen during these years. Especially notable was the multiplication of colleges of education, organized under the stimulus of state laws requiring additional professional training of prospective teachers. Equally noteworthy was the establishment of schools of journalism for which the proprietor of the *New York World,* Joseph Pulitzer, set the pattern when he announced in 1903 that he would bequeath to Columbia University one million dollars to build and endow such a college. The Pulitzer school at Columbia was opened in 1912 and was quickly followed elsewhere by similar experiments.

Even more significant perhaps was the rapid rise of the business college connected with the college or university. For years instruction in typewriting, stenography and rudimentary business knowledge had been given by private agencies and to some extent by the public high schools; but with the exception of the Wharton School of the University of Pennsylvania scarcely any university had entered the field. Now, responding to the commercial trend of the times, colleges generally began what they called the process of "professionalizing business." This was done by combining some of the more "practical" studies of the old liberal-arts curriculum with courses on economics and business and calling the result a professional school. When the oldest of American colleges gave birth in 1908 to the Harvard Graduate School of Business Administration the odor of exalted respectability invested the new movement. It had yet to receive the stamp of approval of big business, but this came fifteen years later in a gift to Harvard of $5,000,000 from the aged George F. Baker. The business college by 1914 had not yet subordinated the higher learning to a secondary position, but its growing importance was causing alarm among upholders of the older academic traditions.

More than ever before, the keynote of the history of higher education during the early years of the century was popularization. In the tax-supported state universities the tendency was perhaps carried farthest. By study centers, lecture courses, traveling libraries and exhibits and by correspondence study, thousands who had never trod a university campus were brought into touch with the newest scholarship.[1] At the forefront was the University of Wisconsin which at the end of 1914 had an extension enrollment of 7113 students, and recorded that during the previous two years 1251 lectures had been given in 525 communities to estimated audiences totaling 370,750 people.[2] But here again it must be remarked that the tendency had not yet attained its full strength, and the subsequent years were to witness a further advance.

For the great universities the period was one of change and expansion. Woodrow Wilson (1902-1910) strongly but unsuccessfully opposed the establishment of a graduate school at Princeton isolated from the undergraduate institution, and at the same time sought to improve the grade of the undergraduate work by the introduction of the preceptorial system.[3] Ira Remsen, Gilman's successor to the presidency of Johns Hopkins

[1] L. E. Reber, "University Extension in the United States," U. S. Bur. of Educ., *Bull for 1914*, no. 19, 6-7.

[2] A. J. Klein, "Correspondence Study in Universities and Colleges," U. S. Bur. of Educ., *Bull. for 1920*, no. 10, 6 ff.

[3] E. E. Slosson, *Great American Universities* (N. Y., 1910), 75 ff.; R. S. Baker, *Woodrow Wilson* (Garden City, 1927), II, chaps. xv, xvii.

(1901-1912), by limiting graduate work to courses for the Ph.D. and the medical degree and maintaining them at the highest possible standard, carried on unswervingly the purposes of the founder. Nicholas Murray Butler of Columbia (1902-), who ran "the University with the nonchalance and efficiency of the head of a railroad system or a department store, combined with the ideals of a philosopher," saw grow up around him some of the strongest graduate schools in the country, including perhaps the foremost social-science faculty of the period and the greatest college of education.[1] Charles R. Van Hise of Wisconsin, although president (1903-1918) of the university which above all others had allied itself with the life of its state, at the same time upheld the highest ideals of scholarship and defended his liberal professors from the onslaughts of reactionary politicians. At Michigan James Burrill Angell (1871-1907) developed a great institution which set a standard for the state university, while at Chicago Harry Pratt Judson (1907-1923), building on the money of Rockefeller and the genius of Harper, was carrying on educational experiments which rivaled Columbia and was expanding the facilities with a like rapidity. For decades the intellectual freshness of Eliot had prevented stagnation at Harvard, and his successor, A. Lawrence Lowell (1909-), signalized his administration by the introduction of the tutorial system and the general-examination plan. Ably led, generously supported by gifts and state appropriations, with the democracy pressing at their gates, the universities found the years following 1898 a period of rapid growth and educational achievement.

That there were unfortunate and even dangerous tendencies at work, however, few leading educators would

[1] Slosson, *Great American Universities,* 452.

deny. One resulted from the fact that the ultimate control of American colleges had come to rest in a board of trustees, regents or fellows, composed usually of clergymen, lawyers and business men who conducted the institution through their agent or employee, the college president. In the last analysis this meant that the policies were often determined by outsiders, noneducators and representatives of the capitalistic interests, a situation which sometimes existed even in the state universities where the legislatures were likely to be dominated by big business or bad politics. In too many instances the result was interference with the academic freedom of those teachers whose economic or social philosophy was liberal. According to one trenchant critic, there was substituted for the old rule of the clergy that "of business men and politicians; which amounts to saying that it is a substitution of business men." [1] It seemed as if almost any economic heterodoxy might result in dismissal though it is only fair to record that the dismissed professor was usually able to secure appointment elsewhere.

The most famous breach of academic freedom occurred at the University of Pennsylvania where the appointment of Professor Scott Nearing, a brilliant and extraordinarily successful teacher, was terminated because, according to the trustees, "his efforts . . . although doubtless perfectly sincere . . . were so consistently misunderstood by the public and by many parents," the "misunderstood" efforts being his advanced social and economic ideas.[2] Even more astonishing was the demand for the resignation of Willard Clark Fisher, for

[1] Thorstein Veblen, *The Higher Learning in America* (N. Y., 1918), 64. See also Upton Sinclair, *The Goose Step* (Pasadena, 1923), a book crammed with facts generally accurate but giving an exaggerated picture of the situation. For a contemporary view of the situation, see H. C. Warren, "Academic Freedom," *Atlantic Mo.*, CXIV (1914), 689-699.

[2] American Association of University Professors, *Bull.*, II, no. 3, 27.

twenty years professor of economics at Wesleyan University, Connecticut, because of an incidental utterance on churchgoing and Sunday observance made in an address, not intended for publication, before a literary club at Hartford. The official reason for his resignation was so absurdly flimsy that those acquainted with the situation were quick to ascribe the real cause to the professor's advocacy of social legislation and his strong position in state progressive politics.[1] The desire to counteract such invasions of academic freedom was one of the causes which led in November, 1914, to a call for the organization of the American Association of University Professors to represent the "common interests of the teaching staffs" and consider "the general problems of University policy."[2]

Why was it that the conspicuous cases of dismissal were of professors who were critics of the economic order? Some explanation for the horror with which college trustees looked upon unconventional economic views may perhaps be found in the vast sums which millionaires were contributing to higher education. The enlargement of endowments and college plants was well-nigh universal during the early years of the century, but the philanthropy which had perhaps the most important nation-wide influence resulted from the foundation in 1902 of the General Education Board by John D. Rockefeller. Incorporated by Congress in 1903, its object was set forth as "the promotion of education within the United States of America, without distinction of race, sex, or creed."[3] To this foundation Rockefeller

[1] Professor Fisher was twice mayor of Middletown, Connecticut, and in 1914 candidate on the Progressive ticket for governor of the state. Am. Assoc. of Univ. Profs., *Bull.*, II, no. 2, pt. ii, 75-76. See also case of Joseph H. Brewster at the University of Colorado in the same *Bull.*, 3-71.

[2] Am. Assoc. of Univ. Profs., *Bull.*, II, no. 1, 11.

[3] 61 Cong., 2 sess., *Sen. Rep.*, no. 405.

gave before 1909 approximately $53,000,000, of which $13,500,000 went to the University of Chicago, over $10,000,000 to the Rockefeller Institute for Medical Research and approximately $16,000,000 to various other activities initiated by the board. These last included endowments to colleges usually on condition that a similar amount be raised, contributions to medical schools, gifts to Negro education, and coöperation with federal and state agencies in the betterment of secondary education and the carrying out of farm demonstrations. The board was particularly interested in improving the backward educational conditions in the South, and its policy of "coöperation, not interference," had a helpful and stimulating effect wherever it was tried.[1] Gifts of this type not only encouraged other millionaires to contribute in a similar way, but induced state and municipal authorities to be more liberal in their educational appropriations.

While the emphasis in education was, of course, in providing facilities for youth, some progress was made in adult education. The rapid development of women's clubs provided opportunity for group study which the simultaneous growth of public libraries stimulated. Correspondence schools sought to enroll the adult as well as the youth, and especial efforts were made by various organizations to reach the adult immigrant. A few far-seeing individuals realized the educational possibilities in the open forum and a valuable movement was launched with the establishment in 1908 of the Ford Hall Forum in Boston under the leadership of George W. Coleman.[2] Another agency of similar kind was the Chautauqua which had steadily increased its influence

[1] *The General Education Board, an Account of Its Activities, 1902-1914* (N. Y., 1915), *passim.*

[2] R. L. Lurie, *The Challenge of the Forum* (Boston, 1930), chaps. ii-iv.

since the founding of the parent body in 1874.[1] In order to improve the standard of the programs and bring some system out of the existing chaos, the International Chautauqua Alliance was launched in 1899. Though it went out of existence in 1915, the regional circuits proved widely successful, especially in the rural regions. It was a far cry from the great gatherings at Lake Chautauqua to the prairie tent where the farmer listened under flickering gas lights to a peripatetic spellbinder, but these gatherings marked a high point in the community life and provided intellectual stimulation where it was most needed.[2] The Chautauqua was likewise not without its political influence, for it was upon its circuits that the progressive politicians of the new political day expounded their reform programs.

When the balance sheet is drawn, however, it is clear that the chief educational gains of the period fell to the younger generation. To them also, as we have seen, came other substantial benefits, cultural and physical. Never before had collective childhood been so much the center of the American scene, never before so important a concern of public policy. To a bewildered European visitor it seemed that "children reign supreme in the United States."[3] Yet the record shows that this generation did not succeed in doing all it set out to accomplish, and its unfinished task it had to pass on to its successors.

[1] See Allan Nevins, *The Emergence of Modern America* (*A History of American Life*, VIII), 239-240; and Schlesinger, *Rise of the City*, chap. vi.

[2] U. S. Comr. of Educ., *Rep. for 1899-1900*, I, 318; J. L. Hurlbut, *The Story of Chautauqua* (N. Y., 1921), chaps. xviii-xxi, xxv; H. A. Orchard, *Fifty Years of Chautauqua* (Cedar Rapids, Iowa, 1923), chaps. vi-xi.

[3] P. H. B. d'Estournelles de Constant, *America and Her Problems* (N. Y., 1915), 267. See also Sir Philip Burne-Jones, *Dollars and Democracy* (N. Y., 1903), 33 ff.

CHAPTER IX

RELIGION AND REFORM

FOR American Christianity the years following 1898 fairly bristled with problems. The immense tide of foreign immigration flooding the cities, the extraordinary mobility of population, the draining of rural districts and the abandonment of country churches, and the difficulties of financing new churches, hospitals, schools and other similar projects in a period of rapid growth created situations which taxed the enthusiasm and skill of religious leadership to the utmost.[1] The Sunday newspaper, Sunday excursions, Sunday ball games and Sunday moving pictures crowded in to break the erstwhile Sabbath monopoly of the church. Pastors who a few years earlier denounced Sabbath breaking in sermons on such themes as "You cannot serve God and skylark on a bicycle" now had greater competition in the automobile and the golf course.[2]

In meeting these new problems American Christianity displayed striking resourcefulness and virility. Though science continued to give opportunity for theological exegesis and doctrinal controversy, religious leaders wisely turned their attention from these interesting topics to the rôle which the church must play in the new society. Religious activities were directed in many new channels, both social and political. While still maintaining and enlarging the schools, colleges, hospitals,

[1] H. K. Carroll, *The Religious Forces of the United States* (rev. edn., N. Y., 1912), lxix.

[2] *N. Y. Times Book Rev.*, Nov. 28, 1920, 3.

orphanages and relief organizations typical of the nineteenth century, the church entered actively into the campaign for reform measures, carrying out its own projects for social redemption and participating frequently in politics. The hand of the church seemed everywhere. Its membership increased by approximately sixteen million between 1900 and 1914, an advance which can be explained in a large measure by its willingness to face squarely the problems of the new day.[1]

Of the growth in membership the Roman Catholic Church was the chief beneficiary. One half of its five million new adherents were immigrants from Italy, Austria-Hungary and other Catholic countries, who tended to concentrate in the great industrial centers of New England, the Middle Atlantic states, Illinois, Wisconsin and Michigan.[2] As earlier in the case of the Irish and French Canadians, this new inundation, in spite of official repudiation of Cahenslyism, was cared for in many instances by priests of the same racial stocks.[3] Usually successful in holding the allegiance of the immigrant, the Catholic Church made especial efforts during these years to prevent defection. A Church Extension Society was founded in 1905, which proved an important aid in bringing religious ministration to scattered communities,[4] and six years later a Catholic Colonization Society was

[1] Membership as given by the *World Almanac for 1900*, 334, estimates the Protestants at 27,710,004 and the Catholics at 8,447,801, while the estimates of H. K. Carroll as given in the *Bulletins of Church Statistics*, published by the Federal Council (1914), give the Protestants at 38,059,428 and the Catholics at 13,673,787. The Bureau of the Census, *Religious Bodies, 1916*, pt. i, 526-527, gives total church membership as 21,699,000 in 1890, 35,068,000 in 1906 and 41,927,000 in 1916.

[2] Gerald Shaughnessy, *Has the Immigrant Kept the Faith?* (N. Y., 1925), chap. x.

[3] The Cahensly movement which aimed to foster national groups within the Catholic Church in America was opposed by Cardinal Gibbons. A. S. Will, *Life of Cardinal Gibbons* (N. Y., 1922), I, chaps. xxix-xxx.

[4] Shaughnessy, *Has the Immigrant Kept the Faith?*, 261.

organized to promote colonization projects under proper church auspices. With Catholics of longer American residence the prestige of the American church was undoubtedly strengthened in 1908 when the pope removed it from the supervision of the missionary department (Congregation of Propaganda), thereby giving it complete ecclesiastical status, and by the creation of three new American cardinals in 1911.[1] The church was particularly fortunate in its leader, the scholarly Cardinal Gibbons, whose enthusiasm for the American Constitution and indorsement of the separation of church and state gave a distinctly national trend to the American branch of his church.[2]

Among the Protestant churches the Methodist group with its seventeen bodies or offshoots continued to rank as the most powerful denomination, but neither its growth of nearly two million communicants nor the increase of the Baptists or Lutherans was as rapid as that of the Catholics.[3] The most notable Protestant gains were made in the South where every state but four showed a greater increase in communicants than in population. The Southern Protestant advance was to no small extent due to Negro accessions, for their number of communicants grew forty per cent in the two decades 1890-

[1] John Farley, an Irish immigrant; William O'Connell, a son of Irish immigrants; and Monsignor Diomede Falconio, a naturalized American citizen then serving as apostolic delegate at Washington.

[2] James Cardinal Gibbons, *A Retrospect of Fifty Years* (Balt., 1916), 210-234; Will, *Cardinal Gibbons*, I, 508.

[3] Carroll, *Religious Forces*, lxxi, puts the denominations showing the largest absolute increase during the period 1890-1910 as follows: Roman Catholic 6,183,680 or 99 per cent; Southern Baptist 1,003,000 or 78 per cent; Methodist Episcopal, 946,508 or 42 per cent; Disciples of Christ (older branch) 667,065 or 104 per cent; Methodist Episcopal Church, South, 641,173 or 53 per cent; Presbyterian (Northern) 540,490 or 69 per cent; Colored Baptist 441,176 or 33 per cent; Northern Baptist 410,263 or 51 per cent; Lutheran Synodical Conference 409,128 or 115 per cent; Protestant Episcopal 396,726 or 75 per cent; and Congregational 222,629 or 43 per cent.

1910, while the race as a whole increased but thirty-one per cent. As a social and intellectual factor the church was undoubtedly declining in certain Protestant communities in the Northeast, but in the rural districts of the South and West it was still playing in 1914 a rôle hardly less important than in seventeenth-century colonial New England.

Three tendencies in American Christianity during the early years of the period are clearly discernible: a trend toward church unity, a further liberalizing of theology and an increasing emphasis upon socialized religion. Interrelated as these influences were, each strengthened the other, with the result that Protestant Christianity was distinctly modified. Practical considerations as well as a softening of theological differences aided the movement toward unity, particularly in the rural districts where denominational splits and the keen religious rivalry of earlier decades had left an oversupply of churches. Many communities which a half-century earlier could support several churches were now barely able to keep one alive. Decline in economic prosperity, the drain of population to the cities or to the West, immigration which replaced Protestants by Catholics, the decline of sectarianism and the development of the community spirit—these and many other influences led to the pooling of the remaining resources in fewer units. Though some steps in this direction had been taken in New England before the period opened, everywhere long-established prejudices had to be overcome and the movement gained momentum slowly. A careful survey during the years 1922-1925 disclosed nine hundred and seventy-seven united churches in town and country in the Northern and Western states, the majority organized after 1900. These churches included a number of types: federated churches, interdenominational churches and denominational united churches; but whatever the name, they represented an impressive decline in sectarian spirit.[1]

While churches in the depleted country districts were combining for efficiency, various groups of the same denomination found it possible to draw closer together, an analogous development to that in industry where, as we have seen, bitter competition had given way to consolidation.[2] Northern Presbyterians in 1906 formulated a basis for union with the Cumberland Presbyterian Church which was carried through in spite of strong minority opposition and much litigation. Three groups of the Northern Baptists effected a loose union in 1907, and in 1910 the Northern and Free Will Baptists took the first step toward confederation when they merged their missionary and denominational work. The various Methodist branches, after effecting minor reunions, made unsuccessful efforts to heal the breach which slavery had made in 1845,[3] while Lutherans, Disciples of Christ and other denominations, large and small, were taking steps toward unification.

Simultaneously with the movement for denominational integration, there developed a demand for interdenominational coördination of activities, the greatest triumph of which was the organization of the Federal Council of the Churches of Christ in America, the consummation of years of slow development. For many years Protestants of various sects had coöperated in such organizations as the Young Men's and Young Women's Christian associations, the International Sunday School Association, the American Bible Society and the American Tract Society. Especially was the need of coöpera-

[1] Elizabeth R. Hooker, *United Churches* (N. Y., 1926), 23-25.

[2] H. K. Rowe, *The History of Religion in the United States* (N. Y. 1924), chap. xii.

[3] See C. R. Fish, *The Rise of the Common Man* (*A History of American Life,* VI), 289-290.

tion strong in the home and foreign mission fields, and the various coördinating mission boards which had appeared in America were "in the nature of a reflex action" from efforts of foreign missionaries to the same end.[1] An impetus also came from local organizations such as the New York City Federation of Churches, established in 1895, and the Massachusetts Federation of Churches (1902). The success of these local federations, particularly that in New York, led to the founding in 1901 of the National Federation of Churches and Christian Workers, a federation of local federations which served as a stepping-stone to a greater union. At its annual meeting in 1902 plans were laid for a nation-wide conference to be held in 1905 at Carnegie Hall, New York, to which all the evangelical denominations were invited to send delegates. It was this conference that adopted the constitution of the Federal Council of the Churches of Christ in America, which, after ratification by the constituent churches, brought about the establishment of that body three years later.[2]

The Federal Council as organized in 1908 was the work of delegates from thirty-three evangelical bodies representing seventeen millions of communicants and in numbers and adherents more than half the population of the United States. Powerful as was this backing, the actual functions of the Council were limited. Controlled by quadrennial conferences and a large executive committee, its chief business was the study of problems vital to American Protestantism and the recommendation of policies to be followed. It was to act as a clearing house for interdenominational activities, as a spokesman for the evangelical churches of America and as a constant en-

[1] C. S. Macfarland, *The Churches of the Federal Council* (N. Y., 1916), 246.

[2] E. B. Sanford, *Origin and History of the Federal Council of the Churches of Christ in America* (Hartford, 1916), gives a detailed history.

couragement to further unity. Dominated by progressive and socially minded leaders, the Federal Council kept one step ahead of the great body of church thought and did much to direct the energies of Protestantism into constructive channels.

This tendency toward coöperation would have been impossible without some softening of the harsh lines which had separated the Protestant denominations. The old-fashioned theology had never recovered from the staggering blow dealt to it by the evolutionary hypothesis and the higher criticism,[1] and each new discovery in the realm of science served to put it increasingly on the defensive in spite of the continued efforts of learned men to reconcile science and the old religion.[2] In America the higher criticism was centered primarily in the theological seminaries. Union Theological Seminary, associated with Columbia, and the Chicago University Divinity School went over wholeheartedly to the new theology; Andover, which had been founded in 1808 to counteract the Unitarianism of Harvard, gave up the struggle to be orthodox and returned to Cambridge just one hundred years later, where it was soon absorbed by the Harvard Divinity School.[3] Conservatism at the seminaries of the Episcopalians at Cambridge, of the Congregationalists at Hartford and of the Presbyterians at Princeton was pretty well forced to the wall, while even those time-honored bulwarks of the old theology, the Methodist seminaries, Drew and Garrett, were rapidly crumbling before the onslaught of the new views. From the centers of advanced theological thinking a constant stream of

[1] A. M. Schlesinger, *The Rise of the City* (*A History of American Life*, X), chap. ix.

[2] *E.g.*, W. N. Rice, *Christian Faith in an Age of Science* (N. Y., 1903).

[3] J. A. Faulkner, "The Tragic Fate of a Famous Seminary," *Bibliotheca Sacra*, LXXX, 449-464.

students went forth to man the pulpits of the nation, young men sympathetic with a more liberal theology and willing to lead in the transition. They found in their pews some communicants who through college courses had come to eye critically certain of the old beliefs,[1] but the great majority continued to be more orthodox than their pastors, and, as a natural consequence, tended in most cases to exert a dampening influence on their liberal aspirations.

Modernism by 1898 was already in the ascendency in Congregationalism,[2] while the hidebound conservatism of the Northern Presbyterians broke down in 1902 when the general assembly adopted a brief statement of the reformed faith, not as an official standard but as an interpretation of the confession, in which they repudiated the doctrine of infant damnation while insisting upon the consistency of predestination and of God's universal love.[3] The Southern Presbyterian Church, however, refused in 1910 and again in 1911 to disavow infant damnation. Conservative as was this church in the South, Northern leaders of the type of Henry Sloane Coffin were at the forefront of the modernist movement. Meantime Baptist theology was being strongly influenced by the Divinity School of Chicago, while liberalism in the Episcopal Church found powerful champions in Bishop

[1] One of the most interesting and most widely discussed series of muckraking articles was that by Harold Bolce, starting with one entitled "Blasting at the Rock of Ages," *Cosmopolitan*, XLVI (1909), 665-676, which purported to tell how ruthlessly college professors in the leading institutions of learning dealt with age-old religious and moral beliefs. Although these articles confirmed the opinion of many that the colleges were hotbeds of infidelity and radicalism, they helped to awaken the church to a realization that a new day had come.

[2] G. A. Gordon, *My Education and Religion* (Boston, 1925), chap. xvii.

[3] General Assembly of the Presbyterian Church, *Minutes*, n. s., II, no. 2, 93-97.

William Lawrence and the Episcopal Theological School at Cambridge.[1]

The Methodist Church, while not seriously rocked by doctrinal controversies, was confronted by at least one notable heresy trial in the case of Borden P. Bowne, professor of philosophy in Boston University; but the powerful support elicited by Professor Bowne within the church and his acquittal formed a striking demonstration of the leftward tendency of that denomination.[2] On the part of its younger constituency there was also a continual pressure for a liberalization of its attitude toward dancing, theatergoing and card playing which could not indefinitely be ignored.[3] Of the great churches only the Catholic maintained a steadfast front against the new theology, and the papal decree *Pascendi* (1907) against modernism was more readily accepted in America than by many priests of Germany and France.[4]

This modernist trend, although strong in certain circles, was not universally approved. The great mass of churchgoers, whether in city or country, knew little and cared less about it. The average pew holder, living in a hurried and nervous age, wanted a shorter sermon and one unencumbered with theology. Conservative by nature, he was willing to accept the old dogma if it was presented in an attractive form and, as a consequence, services tended to become shorter and more ornate. Furthermore, the new theology, strong as it might be in the scholastic corridors of a metropolitan seminary, hardly penetrated the great hinterland. Here the old doctrine was

[1] William Lawrence, *Fifty Years* (London, 1924), and *Memories of a Happy Life* (Boston, 1926).

[2] *Outlook*, LXXV, 927-928 (Dec. 19, 1903); *Independent*, LVI, 869 (April 14, 1904). Some flurry was caused in the Episcopal Church by the ousting of Dr. Algernon S. Crapsey of St. Andrew's Church, Rochester, for beliefs pronounced heretical.

[3] *American Year Book for 1912*, 731.

[4] *American Year Book for 1911*, 735.

fervently preached and here evangelism was revamped to suit a rapidly moving age. There had been just enough of sensationalism in the meetings of Moody and Sankey to give them spice,[1] but the methods of those evangelists were mild in comparison with the "high-pressure" tactics used by their successors. The best known of them was William A. ("Billy") Sunday, an ex-baseball player and ordained Presbyterian clergyman, whose circus antics, free use of slang and general disregard of dignified pulpit procedure attracted large numbers of curious people to his exciting services. Sunday was only one of scores of traveling evangelists who succeeded in maintaining a "spiritual ferment" in the small towns and rural regions of America and who aimed to confound the cunning emissaries of Satan turned out by the theological schools.[2]

Whatever the fate of the older churches, America has never been too preoccupied to give a hearing to new religions, and of these none has enjoyed a more astonishing development than Christian Science in the years following 1898. Conservative estimates placed the membership in 1913 at eighty-six thousand members with many more adherents, while branch churches were being established at the rate of a hundred a year.[3] The famous Christian Science Temple in Boston adjoining the "Mother Church" was dedicated in 1906 and two years later the sect established the *Christian Science Monitor*, a daily newspaper which quickly assumed a leading position especially in news of national and international interest.

[1] Allan Nevins, *The Emergence of Modern America* (*A History of American Life*, VIII), 260, 345; W. R. Moody, *The Life of Dwight L. Moody* (N. Y., 1900), chap. xxiv.

[2] Lindsay Denison, "The Rev. Billy Sunday and His War on the Devil," *American*, LXIV (1907), 451-468.

[3] *World Almanac for 1914*, 538; *American Year Book for 1911*, 748-750.

The growth of Christian Science occurred in spite of an almost unceasing barrage of ridicule and criticism [1] and of adverse judicial decisions directed against the practice of Christian Science "healers." Some concession to public opposition was made in 1902 when Mrs. Mary Baker Eddy advised that, "until public thought becomes better acquainted with Christian Science, the Christian Scientists shall decline to doctor infectious or contagious diseases," an order which followed close after the indictment of three Christian Scientists for manslaughter at White Plains, New York, in connection with the death of a child.[2] At the opening of the century almost any news regarding Christian Science was considered by newspapers as sensational copy, but by 1910, the year in which the venerable Mrs. Eddy passed away at her Chestnut Hill mansion near Boston, the sect she had founded was looked upon as an established religion and excited no unusual attention.[3]

To adherents of the faith its success in winning converts was, of course, ascribed to the messiahship of Mrs. Eddy. Others, however, attributed it to the "receptivity of the American mind to religious novelties—the ripeness of America for a reaction from mere materialism, the native talent of the founder for meeting emergencies, the preparation for a health-cult by a number of moderately successful experimenters" and the undoubted value of mental therapy as an aid in combating disease.[4] But

[1] The inimitable Mr. Dooley, giving both sides of the controversy as usual, concluded, "I think that if th' Christyan Scientists had some science an' th' doctors more Christyanity, it wudden't make anny diff'rence which ye called in—if ye had a good nurse." F. P. Dunne, *Mr. Dooley's Opinions* (N. Y., 1901), 9.

[2] *New International Year Book for 1902*, 167; *Literary Digest*, XXV, 586, 663 (Nov. 8, 22, 1902). See also Sibyl Wilbur, *The Life of Mary Baker Eddy* (rev. edn., Boston, 1913).

[3] *American Year Book for 1911*, 749.

[4] *Outlook*, XCVI, 843-844 (Dec. 17, 1910).

Christian Science was not the only religious proponent of mental therapy. This was also recognized as a part of the religious function within certain orthodox churches, the most conspicuous early example of which was the Emanuel movement in the Episcopal church.[1]

A somewhat different movement, generally known as New Thought and showing a distinct heritage from the Transcendentalism of an earlier day, with an added mysticism derived from Eastern philosophies, also made some headway.[2] Like Christian Science, its activities were chiefly confined to problems of mental healing; and its teachings appeared in magazines, often short-lived, radiating optimism and success.[3] Some of its leaders eventually went over to the Bahaist and other Oriental cults which had gained adherents, particularly on the Western coast, and others devoted themselves increasingly to magazine advertisements of short cuts to business success, health and culture, or to pseudoscientific, pseudoreligious lectures with one eye on the door receipts. The most famous of such prophets was Elbert Hubbard, "the sage of East Aurora," New York, who after a successful business career established the Roycrofters, an arts and crafts group engaged mostly in wrought-iron work and artistic printing and binding. He edited the *Philistine* and the *Fra,* "arty" magazines arousing in dilettantes a sense of intellectual superiority. Elbert Hubbard's sayings were regarded by many as those of a great iconoclast; others saw in him only shrewd Yankee wit and good showmanship.

The receptivity of Americans to religious novelties

[1] Elwood Worcester, Samuel McComb and I. H. Coriat, *Religion and Medicine* (N. Y., 1908); Elwood Worcester and Samuel McComb, *The Christian Religion as a Healing Power* (N. Y., 1909).

[2] Its first national conference was held in Boston in 1899.

[3] Typical of these were the *Nautilus* (1898-) and *Success* (1897-1911, resumed in 1918 as the *New Success*), edited by O. S. Marden.

was never better illustrated than in the case of the Christian Catholic Church of Zion, founded in 1896 in Chicago by John Alexander Dowie.[1] A Scotchman educated at the University of Edinburgh and ordained a Congregational minister in Australia, Dowie landed in America at the age of forty-one and speedily gained a reputation as a preacher and faith healer. His new church had prospered sufficiently by 1899 for him to organize the Zion Land and Investment Association, which purchased six thousand five hundred acres of land in Lake County, Illinois, about forty miles from Chicago, and established there a city for the faithful. The first houses were ready for occupancy in the late summer of 1901 and it was not long before the community embraced a population of over five thousand. This religious settlement Dowie proceeded to fashion after his heart's desire.

At Zion City were allowed no saloons, no drug or tobacco stores, no physicians, no theaters, dance halls, secret-lodge rooms, or the selling or eating of swine's flesh. Factories, stores, the bank and all other industries were under the absolute ownership and control of Dowie; and the city government was conducted by the "Theocratic Party" whose sole wish seemed to be to carry out the wishes of the leader. Most of the spare time was given to religious exercises which centered in the great Shiloh Tabernacle where Dowie, looking like the pictures of Moses in the old family Bibles, held healing séances and laid down the law to his people.[2] Originally content with the title of general overseer, Dowie became increasingly autocratic. "You have to do what I tell you," he thundered, "because what I tell you is in accordance with the word, and because I am the Messenger of the Coven-

[1] The name was altered in 1904 to the Christian Catholic Apostolic Church of Zion.

[2] W. S. Sadler, *The Truth about Mind Cure* (Chicago, 1928), 49.

ant, Elijah the Restorer." [1] The literalness with which he interpreted his own words was evidenced in 1904 when he commanded all members of his church throughout the world to sell all they had, come to Zion City and place their money in his hands.

All went well with the prophet until personal extravagance, financial mismanagement, unwise projects and charges of personal immorality brought about his undoing; but before he was ousted from power he treated the nation to one of the most interesting religious spectacles of the period. This was no less than an invasion, with his flock, of the sin-stricken city of New York to save it, if possible, for God. The press of the nation was almost unanimous in conceding that there was room for improvement in the great metropolis, and when Dowie descended upon the city with some three thousand followers in mid-October of 1903, he found himself well press-agented. Madison Square Garden was packed nightly, but New York refused to take the bearded patriarch with his huge retinue, blooded horses and liveried coachman as anything but a big show.[2]

Roaring evangelists, soft-voiced teachers of peace, prosperity and plenty, and Oriental swamis sitting in silent mystery attracted the attention of the casual observer of religious institutions; but the rank and file of the people were little affected, and invoked still the faith of their fathers. Even here, however, new forces were at work. Nineteenth-century theology had been essentially orthodox and religion essentially personal, but a rapidly changing economic and social order called both

[1] Rolvix Harlan, *John Alexander Dowie and the Christian Catholic Apostolic Church in Zion* (Evansville, Wis., 1906), 38; Gilbert Seldes, *The Stammering Century* (N. Y., 1928), 394.

[2] Harlan, *John Alexander Dowie*, 1-27; Seldes, *Stammering Century*, 389-401; *Literary Digest*, XXVII, 532, 572, 820 (Oct. 24, 31, Dec. 12, 1903).

for a theology less unbending and for a church with a more versatile technique. That organized religion was able to maintain itself during this period of readjustment was due in part to a willingness to desert the older methods and face squarely the new social problems, and in part to a willingness to place the emphasis upon the social teachings of Christ. First in the cities, and later in all types of communities, the churches interested themselves in social work, educational activities and benefit societies. They extended their activities to include the physical and intellectual as well as the purely spiritual welfare of mankind.

This change was not a sudden one, for it had been foreshadowed by the teachings of men like Josiah Strong and Washington Gladden in the preceding period, and in the 1890's had led to the development of the so-called "institutionalized" church of the city with numerous philanthropic enterprises radiating from it, carefully organized charities, paid welfare workers, athletic clubs and social halls.[1] Much inertia and opposition remained, however, to be overcome; and the record of the church, even after 1898, contained puzzling inconsistencies. In spite of the fact that the quest for social justice was so distinctively Christian in character that it might conceivably have enlisted the leadership of the church, it did not always do so. Generally speaking, the church floated on the current of a great popular tide, participating prominently at times, but neither initiating nor directing the movement. The religious world was far too large and too many forces were playing upon it to enable it to present a united front one way or the other. While certain metropolitan churches were engaging in the most advanced

[1] Schlesinger, *Rise of the City*, chap. ix. W. M. Tippy, *The Church a Community Force* (N. Y., 1914), describes the work of Epworth Memorial Church, Cleveland, Ohio, a typical "institutionalized" church.

social experiments, reformers like "Golden-Rule" Jones and Brand Whitlock encountered the bitterest opposition from organized Christianity.[1] As soon, however, as the mantle of respectability was thrown around a humanitarian crusade, the coöperation of the church became more enthusiastic.

The first decided change in the official attitude of the church toward social reform is apparent in its attitude toward the labor movement. The struggle of organized labor for more humane conditions had met with little sympathy from the church and many labor leaders had come to denounce the church as "organized hypocrisy" and an "ally of capital," and considered it hostile to their aspirations.[2] In an effort to break down this antipathy the Protestant Episcopal Church as early as 1887 had established a Church Association for the Advancement of the Interests of Labor,[3] but its example was not followed until 1901 when the National Council of the Congregational Churches appointed a labor committee, known after 1904 as the Industrial Committee, to study such questions as organized labor, child labor, immigration and socialism, and at its national meeting in 1904 urged its churches "to take a deeper interest in the labor question, and to get a more intelligent understanding of the aims of organized labor." [4] To the same end the Presbyterian Church established in 1903 a department of church and labor under the board of home missions, placing at its head Charles Stelzle, a clergyman who had

[1] Brand Whitlock, *Forty Years of It* (N. Y., 1914), 112 ff.

[2] Charles Stelzle, *The Workingman and Social Problems* (N. Y., 1903); C. B. Thompson, *The Churches and the Wage Earners* (N. Y., 1909), 108; H. F. Perry, "The Workingmen's Alienation from the Church," *Am. Journ. of Sociology*, IV, 622 ff.

[3] *Encyclopedia of Social Reform*, 211-212.

[4] National Council of the Congregational Churches, *Minutes of 1901*, 37; *Minutes of 1904*, 414-429.

served an apprenticeship at the machinist's trade.[1] At its general conference in 1908 the Methodist Episcopal Church likewise took an affirmative stand, recognizing

> that the organization of labor is not only the right of laborers and conducive to their welfare, but is incidentally of great benefit to society at large in the securing of better conditions of work and life, in its educational influence upon the great multitude concerned and particularly in the Americanization of our immigrant population,

and in the episcopal address definitely advocated child-labor legislation, workingmen's compensation and other reforms.[2]

Taking its cue from this Methodist conference of 1908, the Federal Council from the outset advocated such far-reaching measures as the protection of the worker from dangerous machinery and occupational diseases, the abolition of child labor, the suppression of the sweating system, the reduction of the work day, the six-day week, a living wage, workers' compensation, old-age insurance and "the most equitable division of the products of industry that can ultimately be devised." [3] If these declarations meant anything, it appeared that the strength of organized Protestantism had definitely allied itself with the labor movement.[4]

[1] Charles Stelzle, *A Son of the Bowery* (N. Y., 1926), chap. vii.

[2] "Report on the Church and Social Problems," Methodist Episcopal Church, *Journal of the Twenty-Fifth Delegated General Conference* (1908), 121-150, 545-549.

[3] Federal Council of the Churches of Christ in America, *Report of the First Meeting* (Phila., 1908), 239.

[4] Though certain English Catholics, basing their policy on the great Encyclical of Leo XIII, and believing that the time was ripe to take an active part in the great social movements of the day, organized in England in 1909 the Catholic Social Guild, it was not until the World War that American Catholics, through the National Catholic War Council (1917) and its successor, the National Catholic Welfare Council (1919), formu-

Other evidences also appeared. In many cities the ministerial associations appointed "fraternal delegates" to the city central labor union, and in 1905 the American Federation of Labor at its Pittsburgh meeting reciprocated by recommending that its state and city bodies follow this example wherever practical.[1] In the theological seminaries "practical theology" and home missions were stressed as never before; courses in "Christian Sociology" were widely introduced and some effort was made to prepare prospective ministers to become "social engineers."[2] What organized religion could do for the laboring classes in a definite way and in a restricted area was demonstrated by Stelzle in 1910 when he took over an old church about to close at the corner of Fourteenth Street and Second Avenue in New York and speedily made it a humming center of community interest and social service.[3]

The increasing interest of the church in social problems was not accomplished without a certain amount of the same type of muckraking which had brought improved conditions elsewhere. Ray Stannard Baker in a series of articles on "The Spiritual Unrest" pointed out the estrangement between the church and large classes of the population and accused it of failure to grasp its great opportunities.[4] Charles Edward Russell scathingly attacked Trinity Church of New York for the miserable tenements which it owned. "I have tramped the Eighth

lated a definite social program. Henry Parkinson, "Catholic Social Guild," *Cath. Encyc.*, XVII (sup. 1), 168; National Catholic War Council, *Social Reconstruction* (Wash., 1919).

[1] American Federation of Labor, *Report of the Proceedings of the Twenty-Fifth Annual Convention* (1905), 155; Stelzle, *Son of the Bowery*, 88.

[2] Shailer Mathews, "The Development of Social Christianity in America," G. B. Smith, ed., *Religious Thought in the Last Quarter Century* (Chicago, 1927), 228-239.

[3] Stelzle, *Son of the Bowery*, chap. xi.

[4] *American*, LXVIII (1909), *passim*.

Ward day after day with a list of Trinity properties in my hand," he declared, "and of all the tenement houses that stand there on Trinity land, I have not found one that is not a disgrace to civilization and to the city of New York." [1] A widely read series in *McClure's* on Christian Science marked the climax of popular attack upon that religion,[2] and a new outburst of denunciation against Mormonism and its economic and political power occurred in 1910.[3] A powerful plea for a new evaluation of Christ's teachings was made in fiction by Winston Churchill in *The Inside of the Cup* (1913), and on the stage by such plays as Charles Rann Kennedy's "The Servant in the House" (1908) and the English drama, Jerome K. Jerome's "The Passing of the Third Floor Back" (1909).

The new attitude of the church represented but a small part of the contribution of Christianity to the movement for social welfare. From the churches, as earlier, came the chief support for temperance and prohibition, for the movement for social purity, for the Salvation Army, the Young Men's and Young Women's Christian associations and numerous other social and philanthropic organizations; and it was from the churches that the social workers themselves emanated. No public question so greatly affected the problem of moral standards and con-

[1] C. E. Russell, "The Tenements of Trinity Church," *Everybody's*, XIX (1908), 54.

[2] Georgine Milmine, "Mary Baker G. Eddy: the Story of Her Life and the History of Christian Science," *McClure's*, XXVIII-XXXI (1907-1908), later published in book form.

[3] J. C. Welliver, "The Mormon Church and the Sugar Trust," *Hampton's*, XXIV (1910), 82-93; A. H. Lewis, "The Viper on the Hearth," *Cosmopolitan*, LX (1910), 439-450, "The Trail of the Viper," 683-703, "The Viper's Trail of Gold," 823-833; Richard Barry, "The Political Menace of the Mormon Church," *Pearson's*, XXIV (1910), 312-330, "The Mormon Evasion of Anti-Polygamy Laws," 443-451, "The Mormon Method in Business," 571-578; B. J. Hendrick, "The Mormon Revival of Polygamy," *McClure's*, XXXVI (1911), 245-261, 449-484.

duct with which the religious minded were concerned as that involving the liquor traffic. After more than a half-century of agitation but five states were legally dry in 1898—Kansas, Maine, North Dakota, New Hampshire and Vermont—and of these the last two were to revert to local option in 1903. This situation, however, by no means reflected the true strength of the movement. Quite apart from the effects of drinking on the drinker, the liquor business was in bad repute as a prolific source of political corruption. Roosevelt, for example, asserted that "more than half of the political leaders in Tammany Hall have at one time or another been in the liquor business." [1] Although the saloon was called the "poor man's club" and admittedly supplied "a legitimate want in the life of the workingman," [2] it was so widely denounced as the ally of every evil interest that even the liquor manufacturers agreed it needed reformation.[3] Temperance agitation had advanced beyond the stage of freak reform and now received support from the most conservative sources. An increasing number of thoughtful people were convinced that the consumption of alcoholic beverages was physically and economically wasteful and that therefore the best interests of the nation would be served by its elimination.

Although the prohibition movement commanded a growing support from employers demanding sober workmen and the backing of social reformers who believed it essential in their warfare on prostitution, disease, poverty and other ills, its chief impetus came from organized religion. Each of the leading denominations, including the Catholic Church, had its temperance com-

[1] J. M. Barker, *The Saloon Problem and Social Reform* (Everett, Mass., 1905), 32.
[2] Raymond Calkins, *Substitutes for the Saloon* (Boston, 1901), 25.
[3] *Literary Digest*, XXV, 338 (Sept. 20, 1902).

mittee or abstinence society,[1] but the brunt of the battle was borne by three organizations: the Temperance Society of the Methodist Episcopal Church, the Women's Christian Temperance Union and the Anti-Saloon League. Though the Methodist Church had been somewhat late in its hearty espousal of prohibition,[2] by 1912 its official representatives were asserting that "all the woes of perdition lurk in the bar-room" and that "the liquor traffic cannot be legalized without sin." [3] Eventually the Temperance Society of that church moved its headquarters to Washington where its lobby became almost as powerful as that of the Anti-Saloon League. "We must realize," said a leading liquor organ in 1914, "that the entire Methodist Church is a solidified, active, aggressive and obedient unit in this war on our trade." [4] The same year the secretary of the Liqaor Dealers' Association asserted, "It is only necessary to read the list of those preachers who are active in the present propaganda for legislative prohibition to realize that it is the Methodist Church which is obsessed with the ambition to gain control of the government." [5] Such statements, however, did less than justice to the other two groups.

Quite as ardent in the cause was the Woman's Christian Temperance Union which, after a quarter-century of activity, claimed in 1898 ten thousand local branches

[1] Many of these are listed in the *Anti-Saloon League Yearbook for 1913*, 280-281. In 1908 a National Interchurch Temperance Federation was organized to secure the coöperation of the various temperance boards of the church.

[2] Its Committee on Temperance was first appointed in 1892.

[3] M. E. Church, *Journ. of the Twenty-Sixth Del. Gen. Conf.* (1912), 654-663.

[4] *Bonfort's Wine and Spirit Circular*, Oct. 25, 1914. According to the president of the Brewers' Association, E. A. Schmidt, the strongest forces arrayed on the side of the bills for a constitutional amendment were the members of the Methodist and Baptist churches, the W. C. T. U., the Epworth League and the Anti-Saloon League. U. S. Brewers' Association, *Yearbook for 1914*, 9.

[5] *The Pocket Cyclopedia of Temperance*, 241-242.

and a membership, including affiliated societies of children, of well-nigh half a million. One of its unique achievements had been the introduction into the nation's schools of antialcoholic propaganda, in the form of "scientific temperance" instruction, at public expense.[1] Even more effective in its practical measures was the American Anti-Saloon League, a union of several state leagues and local organizations formed in 1893. Essentially a religious organization, it insisted that it was not a rival of any sectarian league, but was simply engaged in coördinating the work of militant Christianity and directing the legislative battle. Eyed coldly by the Catholic Church, whose leaders eventually repudiated it, and but tepidly supported by the Episcopalians[2] and Lutherans, its chief backing came from the remaining Protestant denominations whose churches were opened to League exhorters and whose membership was urged to contribute to the movement. The Anti-Saloon League became "the Church in Action." It was the spearhead of the militant movement.

Ably led by men of the type of Wayne B. Wheeler and William H. Anderson, who had mastered every detail of political action, its methods were quite as sophisticated

[1] "All of the states in the Republic except two have laws requiring the study of scientific temperance in the schools, and all these laws were secured by the W. C. T. U.," exulted Frances E. Willard in 1898. These two were soon to be added. *World Almanac for 1898*, 302; F. C. Inglehart, *King Alcohol Dethroned* (N. Y., 1917), 339; Mark Sullivan, *Our Times* (N. Y., 1926-), II, 192.

[2] In the summer of 1904 a number of New York reformers opened a saloon at the junction of Bleeker and Mulberry streets, known as the "subway tavern," which hoped to promote temperance by providing a clean and wholesome place where men would "feel impelled to drink little rather than much, where the beverages will be the best of their kind at moderate price, and where every influence will discourage rather than induce drunkenness." This saloon was formally dedicated by Bishop Henry C. Potter of the Episcopal Church, but his action was denounced with equal virulence by the Anti-Saloon League and the liquor dealers. *Literary Digest*, XXIX, 185-186, 233-234 (Aug. 13, 20, 1904); *Independent*, LVII, 339, 465 (Aug. 11, 25, 1904).

and much more successful than those of its opponents.[1] It set out to do two things and in the end accomplished both: first, like the W. C. T. U., to convince a majority of the American people that the drinking of alcoholic liquors was morally wrong; and, secondly, to organize the sentiment of rural Protestantism to ban the liquor trade by political means, a method made possible by the "rotten-borough" system existing in the state and federal governments.[2] Within a decade after its organization the League had a budget of four hundred thousand dollars a year with a hundred well-equipped business offices, a staff of five hundred employees and a reputation so deadly that politicians feared it as the plague.[3]

To this union of moral crusade and political action many influential public men lent their aid. Representative Richmond P. Hobson, the hero of Santiago, stumped the country for prohibition, and Bryan for some years devoted his oratorical talents primarily to its advancement.[4] Except in certain districts it became unsafe politically for a man to be known as a "wet." Roosevelt, charged by a Michigan editor with inebriety on one occasion, was so concerned for his reputation as a temperate drinker that he brought suit for libel and won the verdict.[5] On their part the liquor interests were by no means inactive, but their propaganda was ineffectual against the moral crusade and their old-time political power was shaken. Public support came to them from the foreign population, especially the Germans, Irish and

[1] P. H. Odegard, *Pressure Politics* (N. Y., 1928), chap. i, 107-113, 228-240. See also Justin Steuart, *Wayne Wheeler, Dry Boss* (N. Y., 1928).

[2] Odegard, *Pressure Politics*, 29-34, 36 ff.

[3] *Anti-Saloon League Yearbook for 1908*, 15; Odegard, *Pressure Politics*, chaps. iv-v.

[4] Inglehart, *King Alcohol Dethroned*, chap. xiv.

[5] *Literary Digest*, XLVI, 1262, 1321 (June 7, 1913).

Italians, but this influence was relatively small and concentrated in the larger centers.

The fruits of a century of prohibition agitation were at last to be garnered, and the first harvest was to be in the South where the desire to remove strong drink from the Negroes, the willingness to curtail the political power of the liquor trade and the belief that economic efficiency would be promoted may have played as prominent a part as moral motives in bringing success. Georgia took state-wide action in 1907, Alabama in 1907 (wet again 1911-1915), Mississippi and North Carolina in 1908, West Virginia in 1912, Virginia two years later and Arkansas and South Carolina in 1915. The movement now swung to the Middle and Far West. State-wide prohibition was voted in 1914 in Arizona, Colorado, Oregon and Washington, to go into effect during 1915 or 1916, and the legislatures of Idaho and Utah by statute sought to make their respective states dry by January 1, 1916. It was certain that by that day at least nineteen states would be officially dry, with an excellent prospect that others would fall into line in the succeeding years.[1]

The extension of state-wide prohibition, however, did not measure the full success of the movement. Local option, when state prohibition was impossible, had by 1914 largely dried up rural America.[2] The last stronghold of the liquor interests was in the cities. There they were so heavily intrenched that the League, convinced that nation-wide prohibition could be obtained only through federal action, exerted increasing pressure upon Washington. The government's liquor policy in Alaska

[1] In spite of these legislative victories for prohibition, the total consumption of wines and liquors was greater in 1913 than in any previous year and the per-capita consumption greater than in all years but two. *Anti-Saloon League Yearbook for 1915*, 47.

[2] See maps in Odegard, *Pressure Politics*, 164-165, showing progress, 1904-1917, and in the *Anti-Saloon League Yearbook for 1915*, 105 ff.

and in the Indian reservations was carefully watched, bills to control liquor more effectively in the District of Columbia were introduced, and on March 1, 1913, the Webb-Kenyon bill was passed over the veto of President Taft.[1] Its purpose was to prohibit the shipment of intoxicating liquors into any state, territory or district where they were intended to be used in violation of the local law. It marked the first important federal victory of the League. In spite of the delicate constitutional questions involved in the bill itself and in the supporting state legislation, the rapidity with which it was passed over President Taft's veto and the numerous judicial decisions supporting both it and the state legislation demonstrate with great certainty the growth of the movement. The prohibition forces through Senator Morris Sheppard and Representative Hobson presented their first resolution in December, 1913, to provide for national prohibition by constitutional amendment, only to have it die in committee. The following year it actually reached the floor but failed of the two-thirds vote. The prohibitionists were forced to wait until America's entrance into the war offered a new opportunity.[2]

[1] *U. S. Statutes at Large,* XXXVII, pt. i, 699; *Anti-Saloon League Yearbook for 1913,* 20-21; Odegard, *Pressure Politics,* 144-147.

[2] See P. W. Slosson, *The Great Crusade and After* (*A History of American Life,* XII), 105-112.

CHAPTER X

SCIENCE AND HEALTH

SCIENCE, no less than religion, made its contribution to human welfare and happiness. The research spirit of the 1880's and 1890's was now attaining its full growth and the new century proved a veritable harvest time. Although some of the new scientific information, particularly that originating in commercial laboratories and designed for private gain, remained secret or was protected by patents, most of it speedily became a part of the world's knowledge and equipment. To attempt to trace the history of science on a nationalistic basis would be misleading, for the contributions of many laboratories in widely scattered countries may all play their part in establishing some fact or principle. The discoveries of a scientist in Europe may be as great a boon to America as to his native land. Thus the work, culminating in 1898 and 1899, of the Englishman, Donald Ross, and the Italian, Giovanni Battesta Grassi, in demonstrating that malaria is transmitted by the *Anopheles* mosquito proved basic to sanitary hygienists everywhere in combating that disease.[1] Likewise the discovery of the X-ray in 1895 by the German professor, Conrad Roentgen, and the isolation of radium by M. and Mme. Curie in their Paris laboratory in 1898 had far-reaching effects on the labors of American scientists in many fields.[2]

Into this world stream of scientific advance America merged with ever increasing effectiveness. On every hand

[1] Paul De Kruif, *Microbe Hunters* (N. Y., 1926), chap. x.

[2] Ray Wilbur, "The Harvest Time of Medicine and Surgery," F. H. Hooper, ed., *These Eventful Years* (London, 1924), II, 508.

were indications that, scientifically, America had come of age. Endowed institutions and privately maintained laboratories, especially those connected with the great electrical industry, were doing notable work, while in scores of college laboratories important contributions were being made. Particularly was this true of medicine, where epochal progress was accomplished in conquering tropical disease—one beneficent result of the new imperialism.

England had made a beginning under the influence of Sir Patrick Monson in the establishment at London and Liverpool of the first schools of tropical medicine, and now the United States, impelled by her new possessions in hot climes, turned aggressively to the same field. Upon its entrance into Cuba the American army found itself confronted with that terrible scourge of the tropics, yellow fever. Working on the prevalent theory that the disease was spread through contamination, Major William Crawford Gorgas of the army medical corps used heroic measures to clean up the city of Havana. His work was to little purpose, and in 1900 a yellow-fever commission, composed of Doctors Walter Reed, Jesse W. Lazear, Aristides Agramonte and James Carroll, was appointed to study the problem. When after exhaustive experiments he failed to discover the bacillus, Reed decided to test a theory long held by a Cuban doctor, Carlos J. Finlay, that the disease was transmitted not by contact, but by a female mosquito of the variety *Stegomyia*. Lazear and Carroll both submitted to being bitten by mosquitoes which had fed on yellow-fever patients, and many others heroically offered themselves for experimentation.[1] At Camp Lazear, near Quemedos, Reed and his

[1] The first of these were Private John R. Kissenger and Civilian Clerk John J. Moran, both of Ohio, who, refusing the proffered reward, volunteered solely for the cause of humanity and in the interest of science.

associates during the final weeks of 1900 proved by every test that human ingenuity could devise that Dr. Finlay's theory was valid.[1] A few minutes before the old century closed Reed wrote to his wife:

> Here have I been sitting reading that most wonderful book, 'La Roche on Yellow Fever,' written in 1853. Forty-seven years later it has been permitted to me and my assistants to lift the impenetrable veil that has surrounded the causation of this most wonderful, dreadful pest of humanity and to put it on a rational and scientific basis. I thank God that this has been accomplished during the latter days of the old century. May its cure be wrought in the early days of the new! [2]

During the experiments of the commission Lazear died of yellow fever and Carroll's health was broken, but their martyrdom was fruitful to mankind. When four years later the problem of building the Panama Canal confronted the nation, the knowledge thus gained made it possible to complete that epoch-making project without the frightful loss of life which had attended the French efforts. Because of his experience at Havana Gorgas was appointed head of the sanitary department, and made his chief task the elimination of yellow fever. So thorough was his work that from May, 1906, to the completion of the canal in 1914 not a single case of this disease originated in the Canal Zone, while remarkable success was also achieved in eradicating malaria. A second demonstration of the practical application of Reed's dis-

[1] Finlay was Cuban-born of English parents. Popular accounts are in De Kruif, *Microbe Hunters*, chap. xi; Mark Sullivan, *Our Times* (N. Y., 1926-), I, 432-474; H. A. Kelly, *Walter Reed and Yellow Fever* (N. Y., 1906). See also U. S. Commission of Medical Officers to Investigate the Cause of Yellow Fever, *Report* (Wash., 1899), and W. C. Gorgas, *Sanitation in Panama* (N. Y., 1915), chaps. i-ix.

[2] Kelly, *Walter Reed and Yellow Fever*, 152. Reed's hope was not fulfilled, and the next great step in combating the disease was not made until the brilliant Japanese scientist, Hideyo Noguchi, a member of the Rockefeller Institute, described the *spirochete* in 1919.

coveries was simultaneously given in New Orleans where an epidemic of yellow fever in 1905 was speedily crushed by a thorough antimosquito campaign.

The great work of Ross and Reed demonstrated beyond doubt the importance of insects as carriers of disease, and this clue was pursued with enthusiasm in the following years. The Canadian, Dr. Harris Graham, working at Beirut, Syria, in 1902 found a connection between mosquitoes and *dengue* or breakbone fever, a disease common in tropical countries,[1] and his conclusions were later verified in the Philippines by Percy M. Ashburn and Charles F. Craig of the American army. The discovery by Colonel David Bruce of the British army that an African cattle disease was caused by a protozoan of the genus *Trypanosoma,* transmitted by a tsetse fly, created international interest among medical entomologists, resulting in the demonstration that the tsetse fly was also the transmitter of the dreaded sleeping sickness.

A somewhat similar development occurred in America. The belief held by certain entomologists that the Rocky Mountain spotted fever which affected mankind in that region was a tick disease was fully established by Dr. Howard T. Ricketts of the University of Chicago in 1906. Turning his attention to typhus, Ricketts and his colleague R. M. Wilder proved by experiments in Mexico the communicability of that disease by body lice, a conclusion already reached independently by French scientists in Tunis the previous year. Like Lazear, Ricketts sacrificed his life for mankind, but the facts disclosed by his Mexican investigations were soon to prove invaluable in fighting typhus in the war-stricken nations of Europe.

[1] Dr. Graham's medical degree was taken at the University of Michigan, 1885, after which he was commissioned by the American Board as a missionary to Turkey. *Medical Record,* CI (1922), 426.

When the United States army entered Porto Rico, medical officers found a surprisingly large number of the natives suffering from anæmia. An intensive study convinced Major Bailey K. Ashford that the cause was the hookworm, and his persistent efforts finally brought the establishment in 1904 of the first Porto Rican anæmia commission.[1] Since it was already known that the hookworm larva could penetrate the skin, thus reaching the intestines by a devious route, this knowledge made it easier to devise effective means of prophylaxis. When the Porto Rican commission found ninety per cent of the natives affected with the disease, there could be no doubt of its devastating effect in the island. Specimens of the Porto Rican worms had been submitted by Ashford to the zoologist, Dr. Charles W. Stiles, who identified them in 1902 as a new species peculiar to America. Stiles was firmly convinced that much of the backwardness of the Southern poor-white class could be traced to the hookworm parasite, and such strength was given to his theories by the remarkable results accomplished in Porto Rico that the Rockefeller Sanitary Commission was established, through a million-dollar gift in 1909, for the specific purpose of eradicating the hookworm in the Southern states.[2] Of 415,000 children examined between 1910 and 1913 nearly one half were found infected, but, through their own clinics and through the wide coöperation of medical organizations, boards of health and public educators, a great improvement was effected in a comparatively few years. If, as many contended, the slow development of the South was due primarily to the

[1] B. K. Ashford and P. G. Igaravidez, *Uncinariasis in Porto Rico* (61 Cong., 3 sess., *Sen. Doc.*, no. 808).

[2] See the *Publications* and *Annual Reports* of the Rockefeller Sanitary Commission (1910-); B. K. Ashford, "The War on the Hookworm," Julius Stieglitz, ed., *Chemistry in Medicine* (N. Y., 1928), 639-664.

hookworm, its eradication would be comparable to the Industrial Revolution in hastening the regeneration of that section.

The important discoveries relative to insects and other parasites as carriers of disease were significant primarily in preventive medicine. In the field of curative medicine chemistry lent to bacteriology a valiant hand. Of specific remedies which it contributed during the early years of the century, that offered to combat syphilis was perhaps the most important. This great work was performed almost entirely in Germany where Fritz Schaudinn discovered the parasite (1905), August von Wassermann introduced a reliable hemolytic diagnosis (1907),[1] and finally the indefatigable Paul Ehrlich, the greatest contributor since Pasteur and Koch to the science of infectious diseases, introduced in 1909 his salvarsan, one of the miracles of modern medicine.[2] Though this pioneer work was done by Germans, through the transit of civilization its benefits were shared in America where, according to war estimates, from ten to twelve million people were afflicted with the disease in some form.[3] But Ehrlich's salvarsan meant more to mankind than the cure of syphilis; it stirred scientists to attack with renewed courage the problem of the chemical destruction, without injury to the patient, of the deadly cocci and bacilli which infect the human body, and this attack was to yield important results in the war and postwar years.

In line with the efforts to destroy invading bacteria by means of chemicals was the research in vaccines and serum therapy. Immunization to a greater or less degree against typhoid was achieved through vaccine inocula-

[1] Improved in 1909 by Hideyo Noguchi.

[2] F. H. Garrison, *An Introduction to the History of Medicine* (3d edn., Phila., 1924), 744-748; De Kruif, *Microbe Hunters*, chap. xii.

[3] Julius Stieglitz, *Chemistry and Recent Progress in Medicine* (Balt., 1926), 6.

tion and a very definite aid to the cure of diphtheria was afforded by antitoxin injections; but greatly to the disappointment of the medical profession, with the exception of diphtheria the usefulness of antitoxin serums seemed limited. Chemotherapists in coöperation with famous surgeons opened an almost unexplored field in the study of gland functions and gland secretions, one of the early triumphs occurring in 1905 when Edward C. Kendall of the Mayo Foundation isolated a pure crystalline compound from the thyroid gland which proved useful in preventing diseases resulting from thyroid inactivity.[1] In the field of surgery chemistry made a new contribution in 1905 in the local anesthetic, novocaine, which quickly proved itself invaluable to dental surgery.[2]

Perhaps at no point was the life of the people touched so constantly by chemistry as in the matter of food. Diet was more carefully watched and there was much anxious talk of calories and food constituents. Commercially this interest was exploited by manufacturers of health breakfast foods and coffee substitutes, but it contributed also to an interest in food chemistry and to important discoveries. The pioneer in this field in America was W. O. Atwater who in his laboratories at Wesleyan University, Connecticut, and Washington, D. C., devised ingenious respiration calorimeters, and won the wholesale denunciation of prohibitionists by his thesis that alcohol was a food.[3] When Atwater tabulated in 1906 the exist-

[1] Garrison, *History of Medicine*, 732-734; Stieglitz, *Chemistry and Recent Progress*, 18 ff.; E. C. Kendall, "The Story of Thyroxine," Stieglitz, *Chemistry in Medicine*, 232-238.

[2] E. H. Volwiler, "Local Anesthesia," Stieglitz, *Chemistry in Medicine*, 465.

[3] "If we define food," said Professor Atwater, "as that which, taken into the body, either builds tissue or yields energy, alcohol is a food, but it is a very one-sided food." W. O. Atwater, "The Nutritive Value of Alcohol," J. S. Billings, ed., *Physiological Aspects of the Liquor Problem* (Boston, 1903), II, 314.

ing data regarding American foodstuffs, he expressed no doubt of the physiological adequacy of a diet composed of proteins, carbohydrates, fats and mineral salts,[1] but already scientists were suggesting that something more was necessary to maintain life. The climax of interest in food chemistry came with the experiments after 1909 of three Americans, Thomas B. Osborne of the Connecticut agricultural experiment station, Lafayette B. Mendel of Yale and Elmer V. McCollum of Johns Hopkins, who proved beyond doubt the existence and necessity of certain food substances, presently to be widely known as vitamins. McCollum soon carried the work a step further by proving that more than one vitamin existed. These pioneers and other ingenious scientists immediately set to work on scurvy, rickets, beriberi, pellagra and other diseases believed to be caused by deficient diet and it was not long before the new knowledge of vitamins was being advertised to the public and having valuable application.[2]

In the hands of the unscrupulous the discoveries of the chemists held certain dangers for the public. By the manufacturers of foodstuffs the new knowledge was welcomed with open arms. Improving on past practices, they found new and ingenious ways by which stale meat and rancid butter could be freshened and food artificially preserved for an indefinite time. They found it possible to produce artificial coloring matter and flavors so convincing that it was no longer possible to tell whether the

[1] W. O. Atwater, *Principles of Nutrition and Nutritive Value of Food* (U. S. Dept. of Agr., *Farmers' Bull.*, 2d. edn., 1906), 14 ff.

[2] Benjamin Harrow, *Vitamines* (N. Y., 1921); E. V. McCollum and Nina Simmonds, "The Story of the Discovery of the Vitamines," Stieglitz, *Chemistry in Medicine*, chap. iv; H. C. Sherman, "Chemistry and Economy of Food," O. W. Caldwell and E. E. Slosson, eds., *Science Remaking the World* (Garden City, N. Y., 1924), 247 ff. See also P. W. Slosson, *The Great Crusade and After* (*A History of American Life*, XII), 380-381.

food was the genuine article. Not only were substitutes and adulterants freely used, but the chemicals employed were often harmful. Even more objectionable were the tragic results attendant upon the patent-medicine fraud. Grossly exaggerated and utterly untruthful claims were advanced for these so-called remedies, concoctions which soothed babies by means of morphine and opium, and "cured" consumption by alcohol. Many of the most famous and most widely advertised, when subjected to chemical analysis, were found to be either useless or harmful—rarely curative.

It was apparent that these abuses could be greatly curtailed by some sort of a bill which required all compounds, combinations, imitations or blends to be so labeled, and for some years a campaign for federal legislation was carried on, led by such persons as Edwin F. Ladd, state chemist of North Dakota, Robert M. Allen, secretary of the National Association of State Dairy and Food Departments, and, above all, by Dr. Harvey W. Wiley, for twenty-nine years chief chemist of the department of agriculture.[1] Legislation to stamp out this evil was introduced in 1902, but it was effectively shelved by the Senate.

Sentiment, however, was rapidly aroused. In 1904-1905 the *Ladies' Home Journal* exposed the patent-medicine fraud in a series of articles, and in 1905 *Collier's Weekly* published a similar series by Samuel Hopkins Adams and others. Unexpectedly reënforcement came in the same year when the Muckrakers trained their guns upon the packing industry. Charles Edward Russell published eight articles entitled "The Greatest Trust in the World," showing that the packers were raising prices notwithstanding the declining value of beef cattle, and

[1] P. N. Leech, "The Safeguarding of Drugs," Stieglitz, *Chemistry in Medicine*, 395-416; Sullivan, *Our Times*, II, 471-552.

were illegally accumulating millions through rebates disguised as "private-car charges."[1] While these articles were being published, Upton Sinclair, a young Socialist writer, was living in the Chicago stockyards to obtain material for a novel which appeared in 1906. *The Jungle,* which pictured the story of a Lithuanian immigrant peasant caught and destroyed in the toils of an economic system essentially vicious, was intended as a piece of Socialist propaganda and the shocking revelations of conditions in "Packingtown" were incidental. To the surprise of the author it was his picture of the unbelievable filth connected with the packing industry which caught the attention of the public and stirred the nation from end to end. Investigations by Doubleday, Page and Company,[2] and by a Roosevelt commission composed of James B. Reynolds and Charles P. Neill, confirmed the charges of Sinclair, and the publication of the first part of the Neill-Reynolds report made inevitable the passing of the food and drugs act of June 30, 1906.[3] Although investigators for the *New York Herald* a year later found conditions in the packing industry as bad as ever,[4] in its final effect few federal acts have been more salutary.

The passage of this law represented but one aspect of the growing concern of the government in matters touching the physical well-being of the people. State and municipal boards of health had, of course, been in existence for many years, but with the new knowledge came the establishment in the larger centers of well-equipped lab-

[1] C. E. Russell, "The Greatest Trust in the World," *Everybody's,* XII (1906), 147-156, and following numbers.

[2] Several articles in *World's Work,* XII (1906), 7490-7514, 7700, 7813, 8152 ff.

[3] *U. S. Statutes at Large,* XXXIV, 768; G. A. Weber, *The Food, Drug and Insecticide Administration* (Balt., 1928).

[4] Upton Sinclair, *The Brass Check* (Chicago, 1920), chap. v, 50-52.

oratories and a wider diversification of activities.[1] War was declared in many communities upon the mosquito, and as it was proved that the common house fly might be the carrier of typhoid, infantile diarrhea and many other diseases, there started about 1908 a crusade against this pest in which civic associations of many types coöperated with the official health bodies.[2] As we have seen, medical inspection of school children brought better control of disease, while the new laboratory science made it possible to inspect milk, to diagnose diseases and to manufacture, distribute and administer antitoxins. To solve the problems of pure water and sewage disposal, which were always acute in the overgrown cities, bacteriology and chemistry continued to lend aid. An important advance was achieved with the chlorination of water, first introduced in America in 1908 and rapidly adopted after 1913.[3] This method proved superior to water filtration as a protection against water-borne diseases.

With equal vigor governmental agencies joined in the fight against tuberculosis. Abundant wealth and the optimism characteristic of America made the United States the natural leader in this rising combat with the great white plague. It was Theobald Smith of Harvard who made the first clear differentiation between the bovine and human tubercle bacilli in 1898, and Edward L. Trudeau who demonstrated at Saranac Lake the curative value of outdoor living and the proper diet

[1] C. V. Chapin, "History of State and Municipal Control of Disease," M. P. Ravenel, ed., *A Half Century of Public Health* (N. Y., 1921), 133-160.

[2] L. O. Howard, "A Fifty Year Sketch History of Medical Entomology," Ravenel, *Half Century of Public Health*, 433.

[3] G. C. Whipple, "Fifty Years of Water Purification," Ravenel, *Half Century of Public Health*, 161-180; J. F. Norton, "Safeguarding the Water We Drink," Stieglitz, *Chemistry in Medicine*, 323-339. For the related subject, see Rudolph Hering, "Sewage and Solid Refuse Removal," Ravenel, *A Half Century of Public Health*, 181-196.

for turbercular patients.[1] Trudeau's work, begun in the late eighties, bore fruit in the early years of the century in the foundation throughout the country of private, municipal and state sanitariums where tuberculosis might be treated, in the forming of the National Tuberculosis Association in 1904, and the nation-wide establishment of state commissions and local societies. The sinews of war were secured in part from the sale of Christmas seals, a method emanating from Norway and first made known to America by an *Outlook* article of Jacob A. Riis in 1907.[2]

As America became more of a neighborhood, concerted nation-wide efforts were necessitated as the capstone of the great edifice of preventive medicine. The functions of the old marine hospital service, which already included supervision of quarantine, medical inspection of immigrants and the prevention of the interstate spread of disease, were enlarged in 1902 and again in 1912.[3] Known after the later date as the public-health service, it became the chief federal tool in the investigation and prevention of disease.[4] But while the leadership was taken by the public-health service, scarcely any of the major federal departments were without agencies carrying on important health work.[5] Coöperating with the federal and

[1] E. L. Trudeau, *An Autobiography* (N. Y., 1916), *passim*.

[2] S. A. Knopf, *A History of the National Tuberculosis Association* (N. Y., 1922), chap. vi; J. A. Riis, "The Christmas Stamp," *Outlook*, LXXXVI, 511-514 (July 6, 1907).

[3] *U. S. Statutes at Large*, XXXII, 712, 728; XXXVII, 309.

[4] L. F. Schmekebier, *The Public Health Service* (Balt., 1923); J. A. Tobey, *The National Government and Public Health* (Balt., 1926); R. D. Leigh, *Federal Health Administration in the United States* (N. Y., 1927).

[5] Notable examples are the work of the children's bureau of the department of labor, which did much in the conservation of child life, that of the division of school hygiene of the bureau of education, the bureau of chemistry of the department of agriculture and the medical corps of the army and navy. J. A. Tobey, *The Children's Bureau* (Balt., 1925); G. A. Weber, *The Bureau of Chemistry and Soils* (Balt., 1928).

local governments in this beneficent service were the private foundations, the most important of which were the Rockefeller Institute for Medical Research, founded in 1901, and the Rockefeller Foundation, chartered by New York state in 1913. The American Public Health Association, founded in 1872 and composed of persons interested in public health, continued to do valuable work as a clearing house of information, in raising standards and in publishing after 1912 the *American Journal of Public Health.*[1]

Meantime medical education and practice continued to improve. Many of the old-time proprietary schools with their part-time instructors and inadequate facilities disappeared, and in their places emerged the great medical centers attached to universities, with well-equipped laboratories and research professors, institutions which were comparable to the marvelous medical schools of Germany.[2] Even more striking was the improved educational standard for nurses. The lead was taken in New York state in 1901 when a state association of trained nurses was formed and a bill secured from the legislature establishing a board of examiners and registration of nurses, a policy soon followed by other states.[3]

In spite of the growing complexity and speed of American civilization with its increased hazards of life and limb, the advance in medical knowledge and the widespread activity in preventive and curative medicine had its effect. The adjusted death rate for the registration area of the United States was 17 per thousand in 1900, 15.4 in 1910 and 13.2 in 1920, while the average length of life increased from 49 years in 1901 to 51 in 1910

[1] H. H. Moore, *Public Health in the United States* (N. Y., 1923), chap. xi.

[2] Abraham Flexner, *Medical Education* (N. Y., 1925), chap. i.

[3] Lavinia L. Dock, *A History of Nursing* (N. Y., 1912), III, 116-236.

and 56 in 1920.[1] Truly remarkable declines in the death rate were registered in typhoid, which dropped from 30.8 per 100,000 in 1900 to 5 in 1920, in diphtheria and croup which fell from 44 to 19.6, in tuberculosis which fell from 166.7 to 92.2 and in scarlet fever.[2] On the other hand, the death rates from influenza, from cancer, from diabetes, from cerebral hemorrhage and softening of the brain and from heart disease were greater.[3]

Especially was the increase in cancer—from 63 per 100,000 in 1900 to 83.4 in 1920—a cause for alarm.[4] Scientific research in this disease had begun in 1898 with a small grant from the New York legislature and constantly widened through the endowments of Caroline B. Croft, Collis P. Huntington, George Crocker and John D. Rockefeller; but the disease continued among the unconquered problems of medicine. Furthermore, tuberculosis, in spite of its decline, remained an important cause of death and continued to baffle the profession. Though interest in both these diseases was widespread after 1898 and ample funds for their study were available, the gains up to 1914 from investigation were slight.

Not alone in the realm of medicine and health but in almost every aspect of life science entered in a practical way to modify habits and environment. For chemistry in particular the early years of the twentieth century were a harvest time. Besides its contributions to public health, its wizardry in creating new products and remaking old ones inaugurated a new age of artificial commodities upon which no limit could be placed. Coal tar was turned into commodities ranging from high explosives to coloring matter for cake frosting, and cellulose

[1] Bureau of the Census, *Mortality Rates, 1910-1920*, 22; Moore, *Public Health*, 10.

[2] Bureau of the Census, *Mortality Rates*, 33, 45, 57, 69.

[3] Bureau of the Census, *Mortality Rates*, 63, 81, 87, 93, 99.

[4] Bureau of the Census, *Mortality Statistics for 1921*, 55 ff.

from wood pulp into sausage casings and rayon bloomers.[1] Owing to the scarcity of raw materials in Europe, the leadership in the discovery of synthetic products naturally fell to the chemists abroad, particularly those of Germany, but American workers enthusiastically followed. As in Europe, much of this research was financed by industrial corporations in search of profits, whose laboratories contributed not alone to creative chemistry but to practical physics and inventions of many types.[2]

The progress in physics, while less spectacular, was equally notable. In 1898 it seemed that all the fundamental principles had been discovered and that physicists might confidently rely upon the familiar concepts of the existence of the ether, the second law of thermodynamics and the electromagnetic theory of light. But with the discovery of the X-ray and of radium a revolution began, which was further to be extended by the quantum hypothesis of Planck and the intrusion of Albert Einstein's theory of relativity. The older idea of a mechanistic universe weakened: mechanics no longer served to unlock all the secrets of the physical world. In America, as elsewhere in the world, physicists set eagerly to work to test and extend the new insights. Of particular importance were the American contributions in the field of astrophysics, made by A. A. Michelson and others. Geology, on the other hand, revealed no startling new developments. The work of the state and federal geological surveys, the latter under Charles D. Walcott, was steadily pushed forward, while private research and the expeditions of the larger universities added constantly to man's knowledge of earth structure and resources.

In no field of science was research pursued with greater

[1] E. E. Slosson, *Creative Chemistry* (N. Y., 1919), chaps. iv-v; Caldwell and Slosson, *Science Remaking the World*, 48-77.

[2] E. F. Armstrong, ed., *Chemistry in the Twentieth Century* (London, 1925); Hugh Farrell, *What Price Progress* (N. Y., 1926), chap. xiii.

intensity than in biology. The work of the German monk, Gregor Mendel, which became known after 1900, and the theory of mutation propounded in 1903 by the Dutchman, Hugo de Vries, opened new vistas to the biologist, while in the years from 1909 to 1912 the successful transplantation of organs and tissues, the growth of living tissues of warm-blooded animals in vitro, and the artificial parthenogenesis in the eggs of a sea urchin induced by chemical means in the laboratory of the German American, Jacques Loeb, were all discoveries of far-reaching implications. In following these leads American biologists did significant work, particularly in furnishing conclusive evidence that the sex of an organism is determined by, or associated with, the nuclear constitution of the fertilized egg,[1] and in associating sex determinants with special chromosomes.

Important as the patient researches of myriad scientists might be for the future of the human race, their labors, for the most part, attracted little popular attention. One scientific enterprise, however, engaged the continuous interest of the public throughout the period, though, it must be confessed, more because of its sporting hazards than its scientific import. This was polar exploration. Although it was the Norwegian, Roald Amundsen, who in 1906 first passed by boat from the Atlantic to the Pacific, thus accomplishing the northwest passage which had been the goal of explorers for three centuries,[2] it was left to the American, Robert E. Peary, finally to achieve the North Pole. Peary had engaged in arctic exploration almost continuously since 1886 and his discovery of the North Pole on April 6, 1909, was a logical culmination

[1] E. S. Dana and others, *A Century of Science in America* (New Haven, 1913), 429.

[2] Roald Amundsen, *The Northwest Passage* (London, 1908); Roald Amundsen and Lincoln Ellsworth, *First Crossing of the Polar Sea* (N. Y., 1927).

of a lifetime devoted to solving the mysteries of the North.[1] The glory attending Peary's well-earned success was for the moment somewhat dimmed by the counter-claim of Dr. Frederick A. Cook who asserted that a year earlier, April 21, 1908, in the company of two Esquimaux, he had also reached the pole.[2] The nation was deeply stirred that two Americans had finally achieved the impossible, but its pride was soon marred by the unseemly controversy which ensued between the two explorers and which speedily divided the press and public into two camps. Peary denounced Cook's story as a fraud and this point of view was eventually widely accepted after the scientists of the University of Copenhagen found the proofs advanced by Cook to be insufficient. The actual discovery of the pole contributed little directly to the world's science, but it cleared the way for a more intensive study of arctic phenomena.

Just as the natural sciences stepped out of the laboratory to play their part in the everyday life of mankind, so the social sciences became distinctly more realistic. Thus William James, America's greatest philosopher since Emerson and a man who understood and shared if he "also transcended the American spirit,"[3] matured a philosophy of empiricism and pragmatism based on a wide knowledge of psychology. James's method, as we have seen, was elaborated and adapted concretely to education by his fellow pragmatist, John Dewey, and by other disciples to various branches of thought.[4] Psychology, which since the 1880's and 1890's had been outgrowing its tutelage to philosophy, turned increasingly, as its scientific technique developed, both to psychother-

[1] R. E. Peary, *The North Pole* (N. Y., 1910), chap. xxxiii.
[2] F. A. Cook, *My Attainment of the Pole* (N. Y., 1911), chap. xx.
[3] Josiah Royce, *William James and Other Essays* (N. Y., 1911), 36.
[4] See earlier, 189-190.

apy and to the investigation of social phenomena.[1] In the latter interest it worked hand in hand with sociology, a study which now assumed an important position in the graduate schools under the virile leadership of such men as William G. Sumner, Albion W. Small and Franklin H. Giddings.[2] In economics Thorstein Veblen, Wesley C. Mitchell, Allyn A. Young, John R. Commons and others, impatient with the dialectical quibbling over time-honored theories of classical political economy, sought, through the quantitative, inductive investigation of the evolution and operation of economic institutions, to lay the foundations for a new type of economic theory.[3] While the study of political science continued to be historical and analytic, it became more concerned with the functions than with the structure of government, more interested in practice than in theory.[4] In line with all this, progressive students of jurisprudence of the type of George W. Kirchwey, Roscoe Pound and Louis D. Brandeis called for an improvement in the form of the law and a restatement more in harmony with actual social conditions.[5]

With the popular attitude distinctly pragmatic, it was but a question of time before American history would be rewritten with a changed emphasis. A foundation was being laid in the monumental volumes of J. B. McMaster, James Ford Rhodes, H. L. Osgood and Edward Channing as they currently appeared, and in *The American Nation: a History*, edited by Albert Bushnell Hart; but even more important was the research of hundreds of

[1] Kimball Young, "Social Psychology," H. E. Barnes, ed., *The History and Prospects of the Social Sciences* (N. Y., 1925), 156-209; E. C. Givler, "Ethics," Barnes, *Social Sciences*, 480-521.

[2] A. W. Small, "Fifty Years of Sociology in the United States," *Am. Journ. of Sociology*, XXI, 721-864.

[3] K. W. Bigelow, "Economics," Barnes, *Social Sciences*, 392.

[4] W. J. Shepard, "Political Science," Barnes, *Social Sciences*, 396-443.

[5] Roscoe Pound, "Jurisprudence," Barnes, *Social Sciences*, 444-479.

students trained in the graduate schools where the German seminar method was in its full flower. As the time-worn myths were chipped away in the most unexpected places, leaders of historical thought found themselves more in sympathy with the economic emphasis and more convinced that history was not past politics but included every phase of human life and interest. Of the men whose influence was strongest in reformulating American history perhaps Frederick J. Turner and Charles A. Beard stand preëminent.[1] The former in the 1890's had urged that American history should be rewritten from the point of view of three centuries of moving frontier. The latter, convinced of the illuminating significance of the economic interpretation, ruthlessly thrust his keen rapier into many a vulnerable spot in our body of political knowledge. The work of these men, their followers and students built a foundation of realistic history which would make possible ere long a new synthesis of American development. In the field of European history a similar service was performed by Professor James Harvey Robinson, whose collection of essays, *The New History*, published in 1911, supplied a rallying point for protagonists of the new conception.[2] However the future student may appraise the contributions of this period of American thought, it will remain true that in all fields of science and scholarship the human mind was restless, inquiry was ceaseless, and learning was placed, more than ever before, at the service of society.

[1] See bibliographical notes in A. M. Schlesinger, *New Viewpoints in American History* (N. Y., 1922); also same author, "History," Wilson Gee, ed., *Research in the Social Sciences* (N. Y., 1929), 209-240.

[2] See H. E. Barnes, *The New History and the Social Studies* (N. Y., 1925), 3-39, and *Social Sciences*, 1-54.

CHAPTER XI

SOURCES OF CULTURE

MORE important than the discoveries of scientists and scholars in shaping the cultural background of America, more important even than the public-school system, was the influence of the newspapers and low-priced magazines. The "little red schoolhouse" might teach the youngster how to read and write, but it was the periodical press that provided reading matter for the great majority. "Yes, sir," commented Mr. Dooley, "th' hand that rocks th' fountain pen is th' hand that rules th' wurruld," [1] and this seemed increasingly evident as the newspapers enlarged their size, the magazines lowered their price, and the popular fiction came more and more to deal with the problems of everyday life. The basic mechanical inventions which went to make the modern newspaper—the high-speed power press, the linotype, the typewriter and the telephone—had all appeared before 1898, but their technique was improved and their scope widened to meet the needs of a more complex civilization. With the new century also came the wireless, the printing telegraph machine, the motor truck and other inventions which facilitated the collection of news and speeded its distribution.

While the mechanical processes for printing huge editions were being perfected, editors and publishers were ever on the alert to catch new readers. The great coöperative news-gathering agencies—the Associated Press

[1] F. P. Dunne, "Mr. Dooley on the Power of the Press," *American*, LXII (1906), 613.

Association and the Scripps-McRae Press Association, both dating from the 1890's—steadily increased the efficiency of their service, and were joined in 1906 by the International News Service, organized by the Hearst papers. Well-written news items, however, proved less effective in swelling subscription lists than attractive "feature" articles and special departments designed to cater to a wide variety of interests. Under the new impulse the Sunday edition became little less than a bulky, flapping magazine, divisible into many sections for the convenience of all members of the family. The special syndicated articles, the color and magazine supplements, the comic section and finally the rotogravure pages, introduced by the *New York Times* in 1914, all helped to promote its popularity. When Arthur Brisbane left the *World* in 1897 to join the staff of Hearst, he raised the circulation of the Sunday edition to the unheard-of figure of 600,000. In 1914 the Sunday edition of the *New York American* had 738,943 buyers and the *New York Times* 217,265.[1]

The daily paper was but the Sunday paper writ smaller. Every enterprising journal came to embrace a financial page, a sporting page, a theatrical page, a women's page, puzzles and bedtime stories for the children, and a series of "comic strips," theoretically for children but enjoyed by the simple-minded of all ages. Even the lovesick youth and maiden found guidance in such departments as "Marion Harland's Helping Hand," Beatrice Fairfax's "Advice to the Lovelorn," and Laura Jean Libbey's "First Aid to Wounded Hearts," columns which one sober authority believes "have played no

[1] W. G. Bleyer, *Main Currents in the History of American Journalism* (Boston, 1927), 339. The statistics for the *New York American* and the *New York Times* were obtained from the circulation departments of these papers.

mean part in the social service of the press." [1] Of the various newspaper features none attracted a wider following than the comic strips. Emulating Richard F. Outcault's success in the 1890's in originating the "Yellow-Kid" pictures,[2] popular comic artists in large numbers created characters which became household words.[3] To his original creation Outcault now added "Buster Brown" and other favorites; Frederick B. Opper originated "Alphonse and Gaston" and "Happy Hooligan"; Carl Shultz delighted the youngsters with "Foxy Grandpa," and Rudolph Dirks with the adventures of the Katzenjammers, while H. C. ("Bud") Fisher provided unfailing amusement with his "Mutt and Jeff." Though usually purveying humor of a slapstick variety, occasionally there were incorporated in these pictures sly digs at current conventions.

It was in the field of humor, if not in comic art, that the feature pages reached their highest development. Through this channel a new brand of American humor became popular. It was in the *Chicago Record* that George Ade's *Fables in Slang*—Aesop attuned to the times—first began to appear, and in the *Chicago Journal* that F. P. Dunne published his early comments on men and affairs through the medium of "Mr. Dooley," the Irish saloon keeper of Archey Road, Chicago, and his naïve but constant customer, Mr. Hennessy. Nor was it without significance that the Irish immigrant, Mr. Dooley, had taken the place of the early Yankee humorist. Even better adapted to the strap-hanging urban American of the twentieth century was the pungent and abbreviated humor produced by the group of "column-

[1] J. M. Lee, *History of American Journalism* (Boston, 1917), 392.

[2] See A. M. Schlesinger, *The Rise of the City* (*A History of American Life*, X), chap. vi.

[3] R. L. McCardell, "Opper, Outcault and Company," *Everybody's*, XII (1905), 763-772.

ists" rising to popularity about 1914, though the great development belonged to subsequent years.[1] "Don" Marquis in the *New York Evening Sun,* Franklin P. Adams in the *New York Evening Mail* and Bert Leston Taylor in the *Chicago Tribune* stood at the forefront of the humorists of their time. It was the free use of slang by comic artists and columnists that in many cases gave their work a humorous turn and it was here that many slang phrases were coined.

The influence of women upon the content of the daily paper, which had been evident since the eighties, reached full flower after 1898. The widening horizon of women as they moved from the home to the factory or office, the development of higher education for women and the suffrage movement which diverted their attention more definitely to current affairs, and the growth of the newspapers as an advertising medium were among the causes which contributed to the feminization of the press. From the time when McClure began in the eighties to syndicate cooking recipes to the day "when every page, possibly with the exception of that devoted to sports, had to be written so that the intelligent woman could understand it," [2] the tendency was evident, and as this policy developed it became possible for a growing number of women to find newspaper "careers" on the larger dailies.

Among the influences which contributed to expanding circulations was the increased emphasis on so-called yellow journalism. William Randolph Hearst had set a new pace when he acquired the *New York Journal* in 1895, one which even Joseph Pulitzer's *World* found it difficult to keep up with.[3] The *Journal's* exaggerated

[1] P. W. Slosson, *The Great Crusade and After* (*A History of American Life,* XII), 355-356.

[2] S. S. McClure, *My Autobiography* (N. Y., 1914), 179; Lee, *American Journalism,* 389.

[3] Schlesinger, *Rise of the City,* chap. vi.

handling of sensational news through headlines and feature stories, the special work of able writers and cartoonists, and the occasional fiery crusade against some existing abuse caught the attention of the masses and made the paper a sort of Bible to hosts of immigrants who found time to examine it on their long rides back and forth to work. In 1896 Hearst commenced the publication of the *Evening Journal,* and in the following year Arthur Brisbane, Sunday editor of the *World,* came to Hearst with the offer to edit the *Journal* at one hundred dollars a week, but with the stipulation that he receive a dollar a week raise for every thousand he added to the circulation.[1] With Brisbane's help the circulation increased by leaps and bounds until it surpassed all evening papers in numbers sold. Hearst's success with the *New York Morning* and *Evening Journals* led him to establish or acquire the *Chicago American* and the *Chicago Examiner* in 1900, the *Boston American* in 1904 and the *Atlanta Georgian* and the *Los Angeles Examiner* in 1912, and eventually to enter the magazine field;[2] and wherever he went the same general policies were followed. It also inspired dreams of a political career, but his efforts to win the Democratic presidential nomination in 1904, the New York governorship in 1906 and the mayoralty of New York in 1905 and 1909 all failed.[3]

The degradation of the public taste through yellow journalism was incalculable, but its influence was not entirely bad. If the more "respectable" papers felt it

[1] Will Irwin, "The Power of the Press," *Collier's,* XLVI, 17 (Feb. 18, 1911).

[2] In 1925 Hearst owned twenty-five papers in seventeen cities, and had acquired at least nine monthly magazines, published in America and Great Britain, the most important being the *Cosmopolitan* and *Good Housekeeping.* O. G. Villard, *Some Newspapers and Newspaper Men* (N. Y., 1923), 19.

[3] He was congressman from a Tammany district, 1903-1907.

necessary to become increasingly sensational, they also were forced to popularize their style and brighten their "make-up." Furthermore, the reforming efforts of these papers were often conducive to much benefit. The *New York World*, for instance, under the editorship of Joseph Pulitzer and Frank I. Cobb, struck repeatedly for social and political justice and remained the most independent and most ably edited paper in the East. It was the hammering of the *World* in editorials that was chiefly influential in forcing an investigation of the New York life-insurance companies in 1905, in exposing New York police corruption after the Rosenthal murder in 1912 and in forcing into the open the campaign contributions of large corporations.[1]

In spite of the sensationalism of many of the important dailies, no tendency was more obvious during these years than that toward standardization. The syndication of feature articles and pictures, the prevalence of great news-gathering associations and the decided sameness in the economic views held by the owners of the papers, all contributed strongly to this end. The use of the same cartoons, comic strips, photographs and news stories obviously broke down newspaper individuality and a paper came to be commonly known by the news service it purchased. It was either an Associated Press paper, a United Press paper,[2] an International News Service paper, or it belonged to one of the lesser associations. A system in which hundreds of newspapers received their news from a single source involved the danger, of course, that the source might become tainted or deliberately used for propagandist purposes. That this happened was a charge commonly made. The Associated Press was under

[1] J. L. Heaton, *The Story of a Page* (N. Y., 1913), chaps. xv-xvii, xx.

[2] The Scripps-McRae Press Association, after buying out the Publishers' Press in 1904, coalesced as the United Press in 1907.

almost continuous fire as a closed reactionary organization which deliberately withheld or colored its news and the United Press was accused of radicalism. When Upton Sinclair, the last of the great Muckrakers, published in 1920 his scathing attack upon the Associated Press, he gave unmistakable warning of the vast power of that organization in the formation of public opinion.[1]

As the new century progressed the American newspaper appeared increasingly impersonal, a business organization engaged in making money through selling news and entertainment and incidentally disseminating the economic and political doctrines of the dominant stockholders. This tendency toward standardization was also promoted by the consolidation movement which penetrated the newspaper business as it did so many others. Before 1898 the idea of the chain newspaper had been developed by Edward W. and George H. Scripps, who with Milton A. McRae owned by 1908 a score or more newspapers, chiefly on the Pacific Coast and in the Middle West. Their example was followed by Hearst, and then by Frank A. Munsey who by 1912 owned papers in five Eastern seaboard cities.[2]

Notwithstanding the trend toward standardization and consolidation certain papers continued to maintain a well-defined identity. As the Hearst papers were famous for their lurid sensationalism, so the *New York World* was noted for its progressivism, the *Kansas City Star* under William Rockhill Nelson for its independence and virility, the *Chicago Tribune* for its chauvinism, the *Christian Science Monitor* for the high level of its news policy, the *New York Herald* under the Bennetts for its appeal to the sporting element, and the *Boston Transcript* for the excellence of its musical and literary criti-

[1] Upton Sinclair, *The Brass Check* (Pasadena, 1920).
[2] Bleyer, *American Journalism*, 410, 414.

cism as well as for the staid conservatism of its editorial policy.[1] Although the editorial continued to decline in influence with the growth of the feature page, it was still possible for editors of the type of Cobb, Nelson, Henry Watterson or Fremont Older to exert a real power.

While the typical American continued to read the newspapers with avidity, his confidence in them was shaken. Repeatedly the venality of the press and its subservience to advertisers were described in the magazines. Samuel Hopkins Adams in a famous series in *Collier's* during 1905 and 1906 told how patent-medicine advertisers influenced the press by inserting clauses to the effect that the advertising contracts were void if any material appeared detrimental to the proprietary interests, and Will Irwin five years later showed again the willingness of all types of papers to prostitute their news columns and editorial policy to the wish of their advertisers.[2] How low the standard for advertising had fallen was revealed in 1907 when the *New York Herald* paid a fine of thirty thousand dollars for printing personal notices designed to call attention to houses of prostitution.[3]

The stronger newspapers, not so dependent for their prosperity upon fraudulent advertising, made some effort to protect their readers. As early as 1903 the Scripps-McRae league appointed a censor who in one year debarred five hundred thousand dollars' worth of advertising,[4] but it was not until 1913 that the Associated Advertising Clubs of America set up a "vigilance committee" to expose such humbuggery. The newspaper

[1] Villard, *Newspapers and Newspaper Men*, chaps. ii-iii, vi-vii, xi-xii.
[2] Will Irwin, "The American Newspaper," *Collier's*, XLVI, 15-18 (Jan. 21, 1911), and succeeding numbers.
[3] Lee, *American Journalism*, 390.
[4] M. A. McRae, *Forty Years in Newspaperdom* (N. Y., 1924), 123.

division of that organization indorsed some "Standards of Newspaper Practice" which marked out an excellent objective, and shortly after the *New York Tribune* took the bold stand of guaranteeing its readers "absolutely against loss or dissatisfaction through the purchase of any wares advertised in its columns." [1] Falling first upon habit-forming drugs and patent medicines, the crusade widened to include all fraudulent advertising. This heightened sense of social responsibility was not achieved without some prodding on the part of the state and federal legislators. Advertising was more carefully regulated and the libel laws made more drastic, while some of the courts tried to put a suppressing hand upon the sensational handling of divorce and criminal cases. In a similar spirit the postal department under the revised statutes attempted to prevent the delivery of mail and payment of money orders to fraudulent advertisers.[2]

That the sensational journalism of the period irritated the authorities is demonstrated by the libel suit which the federal government at the behest of President Roosevelt instituted against the *New York World* and the *Indianapolis News* for printing what Roosevelt claimed to be "deliberate misstatements of fact" in their exposure of the circumstances surrounding the acquisition of the Panama Canal strip. A federal judge speedily dismissed the suit against the *News*, and that against the *World* was thrown out of the federal courts because of lack of jurisdiction, thus preventing a probing of the murky depths of that adventure in imperialistic

[1] *Editor and Publisher*, XIV, 54-72 (June 8, 1914); *N. Y. Tribune*, Nov. 17, 1914.

[2] These laws, passed in 1912, required that all editorials or reading matter for which a consideration was received be plainly marked "advertisement" and provided that magazines and other publications file with the post-office department and publish semiannually a list of their officers and of the principal stock and bond holders. *U. S. Statutes at Large*, XXXVII, pt. i, 553-554.

diplomacy. It did, however, enable the *World* to fight an arbitrary procedure on the part of the government and, by winning a unanimous decision from the Supreme Court, strike an effective blow for the freedom of the press.[1]

The same influences which were changing the American newspaper were producing a somewhat similar effect upon the magazines. Large advertising sections and improvements in the process of half-tone engraving had made possible the ten-cent popular magazine of which *Munsey's* was the pioneer in 1893. With the lowering of the price, a sprightlier tone and engaging illustrations the purchasing public more than doubled in size when the "era of the muckrake" arrived to shoot circulations up again. The timely studies and attacks upon existing abuses which *McClure's* inaugurated provided a ready cue to others until the popular magazines were in keen competition for the most sensational exposés and a new crop of writers appeared to answer the demands.[2] The work of arousing public opinion, formerly performed by the newspapers, was now for a brief period taken over by the magazine press. The old-fashioned polite literary magazine seemed doomed. Conservative publications of the type of *Harper's, Scribner's,* the *Century* and the *Atlantic* sought to take on a more popular tone, while such magazines as the *Cosmopolitan, Munsey's, McClure's, Everybody's, Collier's,* the *American* and *Hampton's* flourished mightily.[3]

Muckraking, of course, was not the only influence which made the low-priced magazine popular. The

[1] Heaton, *Story of a Page,* chap. xix; Lee, *American Journalism,* 407-408; *Nation,* XC, 104-105 (Feb. 3, 1910). See later, 313-314.

[2] See earlier, chap. v.

[3] W. B. Cairns, "Later Magazines," W. P. Trent and others, eds., *The Cambridge History of American Literature* (N. Y., 1917-1921), III, chap. xix; Algernon Tassin, *The Magazine in America* (N. Y., 1910), chap. xiv.

Ladies' Home Journal, which under Edward W. Bok's editorship attained a circulation of two million a month, and the *Saturday Evening Post,* which under the editorship of George Horace Lorimer reached a million a week, managed to achieve this success with a minimum of sensationalism. The former engaged only mildly in moral crusades, but it indisputably unlocked the mystery of what women wanted in a magazine, and undoubtedly had an influence in raising standards of table decoration, gardening, home entertainments, dress fashions and domestic architecture. The *Saturday Evening Post,* which Cyrus H. K. Curtis bought in 1897 for a thousand dollars and nurtured for several years with the profits of the *Ladies' Home Journal,* soon became the great American weekly and a true mirror of the views of the multitude. Curtis and Lorimer divined intuitively the middle-class American—his ardent nationalism, his admiration of financial success, his belief in the economic *status quo,* his gospel of work and his mid-Victorian attitude toward sex. Although it generally ridiculed all deviations from accepted practices, the *Post* was primarily a business and not a propagandist enterprise and it published some of the best fiction of the period. It employed the ablest denizens of Grub Street and incidentally gave to the reader a big return for his nickel.[1]

The magazines of the period were legion, for besides those which tried to please everyone there were others which catered to the special interests of groups. A luxuriant growth occurred of periodicals devoted to sports and moving pictures. A more interesting phenomenon was the growth of the adventure magazine which supplied the demand for vicarious experience as the possibility of genuine adventure grew less. Thus the old Wild-West weeklies and "dime novels" written for the consump-

[1] Leon Whipple, "SatEvePost," *Survey Graphic,* XII (1928), 699 ff.

tion of youth now gave way to magazines which specialized in stories of adventure or the detection of crime—stories which were read by those who, at least in years, were adults. There was also a rapid growth of the "house organ," published sometimes to promote *esprit de corps* and sometimes for advertising purposes. For the few whose interest in public affairs went beyond the newspapers, the *Independent* maintained itself by becoming ever more popular in its make-up; the *Outlook* by calling to its editorial board Theodore Roosevelt; and the *Literary Digest* by condensing the news for the busy man. Nor was there any diminution in the patronage extended to the religious press. The large denominations possessed their weekly and monthly organs which reached into the humblest houses of their members, the Methodist Episcopal Church, for instance, maintaining a string of weeklies with an average circulation in 1915 of around 420,000 copies.[1] As earlier, magazines also abounded for children, farmers, professional men and other select groups in the population.

Many of the influences which affected the magazines also made themselves felt upon other types of literary production. Prior to 1898 few American novels had achieved a circulation of 100,000, while at the turn of the century such a record began to be common. In 1901 at least six novels ran to 150,000 copies and half as many more to 100,000. Indeed, at the end of that year *David Harum* had sold 520,000 copies, *Richard Carvel* 420,000, *The Crisis* 320,000 and *Janice Meredith* 275,000—sales which led the *Bookman* fourteen years later to refer to this period as the fat years of fiction.[2]

[1] This includes the circulation of about 20,000 distributed among four papers published in German, Swedish, Italian and Norwegian-Danish.

[2] Talcott Williams, "The Change in Current Fiction," *Am. Rev. of Revs.*, XXII (1900), 754 ff.; same author, "Fiction Read and Written in 1901," *Am. Rev. of Revs.*, XXIV (1901), 586 ff.

Undoubtedly one cause for this expansion of novel readers was the service of the low-priced magazine in familiarizing readers with better fiction or at least with the kind of fiction now published in book form. Other influences were also important. Improved processes of typesetting and binding helped make it possible to sell the average novel for a dollar or a dollar and a half. The lower-priced novel, it should be noted, was in part also made possible by a reduction in its size to 150,000 or 200,000 words, an indication that writers were adapting themselves to a more rapidly moving age. At the same time publishers discovered that display advertising would sell fiction as well as tooth paste and breakfast foods, and appropriated large sums for this purpose rather than for subsidizing the now disappearing book agent. Doubtless, too, a growing proportion of public-school graduates were turning to a better class of fiction to satisfy a taste hitherto appeased by dime novels and the effusions of E. P. Roe.

At least three tendencies are particularly noticeable in the fiction of this period, that toward historical fiction, that toward the rural novel and that toward the sociological novel. Although Henry James from the rarefied atmosphere of his London home continued to contemplate American civilization and William Dean Howells was still recognized as our chief novelist, their philosophizing and leisurely progress no longer satisfied. The public demand was for the quick action and romantic setting of the historical novel, or else for a courageous attack upon existing abuses. The romantic revival may have had its origin in the burst of patriotism and martial feeling which accompanied the Spanish-American War or from the pleasant feeling that the United States had had a long history. It may have come chiefly, as a novelist-historian himself explained it, from a revived interest in American history.[1] The origin of much of it, however, must have been the longing for a romantic escape from the grinding economic problems and conflicts which so completely filled the decade of the nineties, the same urge which made the war with Spain so popular. At any rate there was never a time in American history when the proportion of fiction to other books published was so large.[2]

Historical fiction, of course, was anything but new, and the revival was under way before the Spanish-American War. The most widely read book in 1898 was Henryk Sienkiewicz's *Quo Vadis,* a translation of which had appeared the previous year, but it had to share popularity with S. Weir Mitchell's *Hugh Wynne,* perhaps the greatest of the American historical novels of the period, and with other books of a different sort. With 1899, however, the historical novel was in full swing. Charles Major's *When Knighthood Was in Flower,* Winston Churchill's *Richard Carvel* and Paul Leicester Ford's *Janice Meredith* swept the country, their only rival in popularity being Edward Westcott's *David Harum.* Westcott's book was perhaps the most famous of a group of novels dealing with rural life whose *raison d'être,* like that of historical fiction, may well have been escape from urban reality. The trio of historical novels so popular in 1899 was soon augmented by Mary Johnston's *To Have and To Hold,* which easily led the sales for 1900. The most widely read novels in 1901—Maurice Thompson's *Alice of Old Vincennes,* Winston Churchill's *The Crisis* and Irving Bacheller's *Eben Holden*—were all historical,

[1] P. L. Ford, "The American Historical Novel," *Atlantic Mo.,* LXXX (1897), 721-728.

[2] The proportion of fiction to the whole reached 27.4 per cent in 1901, but was only 12.2 per cent in 1907 and 8.77 in 1914. F. E. Woodward, "A Graphic Survey of Book Publication, 1890-1916," U. S. Bur. of Educ., *Bull. for 1917,* no. 14.

although the last also cleverly combined the element of rural life with pictures of Greeley and Lincoln. But these books did not complete the list, for the year also marked the appearance of Bertha Runkle's *The Helmet of Navarre* and of George B. McCutcheon's *Graustark*. McCutcheon's book, a variation of the historical novel, dealt with an imaginary kingdom, a theme made popular by the Englishman, Anthony Hope, and one which attracted many readers.[1]

With the year 1902 the tide of historical fiction began to ebb. The most popular book was *Mrs. Wiggs of the Cabbage Patch* by Alice Hegan Rice although it was closely followed by the Englishman Gilbert Parker's *The Right of Way*. Major wrote another book, *Dorothy Vernon of Haddon Hall,* and Owen Wister's *The Virginian* and Emerson Hough's *The Mississippi Bubble* had their meed of popularity. The most widely read book in 1903 was Mrs. Ward's *Lady Rose's Daughter,* an English novel, and most of the popular fiction was not historical. Toward the end of the year, however, appeared John Fox's Civil War story, *The Little Shepherd of Kingdom Come,* which shared popularity with Churchill's *The Crossing.* Following 1904 the vogue of historical fiction passed. Fox, Churchill and others continued their efforts for a while, but the popular fancy was caught by many types of novels: the sentimentalism of Kate Douglas Wiggin or Alice Hegan Rice, the vivid north-woods stories of Rex Beach or Jack London, the legendary-kingdom stories of McCutcheon and Harold McGrath, the college tales of Owen Johnson and the studies of American character by Booth Tarkington. Mrs. Wharton, Mrs. Deland and Miss Wilkins, whose

[1] These estimates as to the popularity of books are based upon the *Bookman,* which in 1901 formulated a point system which probably comes as close to the truth as anything except the actual sales statistics of publishing houses.

work was well known before 1898, continued to be regarded as among the most highly esteemed of novelists. An examination of the best sellers during the next ten years reveals the fact that the great majority were written by Americans and deal with the American scene, and it is interesting to note the frequent appearance of women's names among the authors.[1]

Fortunately for American letters not all the literary talent was spent in providing amusement and romantic escape. Throughout there was a small group, influenced by the realism of Tolstoi and Zola, who believed it was the duty of the literary artist to paint his scene with a stark and utter truthfulness. Feeling that the realism of Howells and James was too attenuated, a group of younger writers—Hamlin Garland, Frank Norris, Henry Harland, Harold Frederic and others—attempted in the late nineties and at the turn of the century to give the American scene a more uncompromising treatment. Of this school no one made so deep an impression as Frank Norris who planned a trilogy of stories comprising the "Epic of Wheat." Only the *Octopus* (1901), which dealt with the struggle between the farmers and the railroads, and *The Pit* (1903), an epic of grain speculation in the Chicago market, were finished before his death at the age of thirty-two, but his contribution both to the literature of realism and to the social revolt was far-reaching. What Norris did for railroads and wheat, Upton Sinclair did for the packing industry in *The*

[1] *The Bookman* lists the best sellers as follows: 1905, Katherine Cecil Thurston's *The Masquerader;* 1906, Edith Wharton's *The House of Mirth;* 1907, Frances Little's *The Lady of the Decoration;* 1908, Frances Hodgson Burnett's *The Shuttle;* 1909, John Fox's *The Trail of the Lonesome Pine;* 1910, Florence Barclay's *The Rosary;* 1911, *The Rosary* sharing honors with Jeffrey Farnol's *The Broad Highway,* Mary Johnston's *The Long Roll* and others; 1912, Gene Stratton Porter's *The Harvester,* Harold Bell Wright's *The Winning of Barbara Worth* and Basil King's *The Street Called Straight;* 1913 and 1914, Winston Churchill's *The Inside of the Cup.*

Jungle (1906) and Jack London for capitalistic society in general in *The Iron Heel* (1907). Churchill turned aside from the romance of the past in *Mr. Crewe's Career* (1908) to attack the railroads, while the young novelist, David Graham Phillips, in a series of books published in rapid succession exposed the shortcomings of American society in many of its aspects, and a university instructor, Robert Herrick, opened to view some of the sorest spots of the capitalistic system. Some of this realistic fiction was strongly influenced by the "muck-rake" and was definitely propagandist in tone, but most of it simply painted the scene as it appeared and left the moral, if any, for the reader to draw.[1]

None of these novelists more clearly reflected the cross currents of American social life during these years than did Jack London. The son of a Western frontiersman and scout, Jack London had been successively a rancher, an oyster-pirate and a sealer. For a year he had followed the life of a tramp and had been one of the few who in the winter of 1897 had reached the Klondike over Chilcoot Pass. There were few of the cruder aspects of the modern capitalistic society which London did not know from personal experience, and socialism with him was a living gospel.[2] In his books are to be found the restless virility of the conquering pioneer and the frontier reaction against urbanization; in his fiery pen was fused the long agrarian unrest and the rising proletarian protest against American capitalism.

The American realists of the first decade of the century dealt primarily with political and social corruption rather than with problems of individual morality. Frank acceptance and discussion of sex met almost universal

[1] Rex Glendining, "Relation of the Novel to the Present Social Unrest," *Bookman*, XL (1914), 276-303.

[2] Charmian London, *Jack London* (London, 1921).

public disapproval. In 1900, the year that historical novels were selling literally by the hundred thousands, Dreiser's first novel *Sister Carrie* was peremptorily rejected by Harper & Brothers. When finally accepted by Doubleday, Page & Company, that concern attempted upon second thought to break its contract, but finding that impossible issued a small edition with unstamped covers. Condemned to a decade of hack work for Butterick and Street and Smith, Dreiser's next book *Jennie Gerhardt* did not appear until 1911, but the intervening years had seen such a change in the public attitude toward sex that Harper & Brothers gladly published it, as they did *The Financier* in 1912. When that house, however, published *The Titan* in 1914 it again became frightened and suppressed the book,[1] but Dreiser's vindication was not long in coming. Under the wet blanket of disillusionment following the World War a host of followers were to produce work which was to be predominant in the third decade.[2]

The ablest of the fiction writers did some of their best work in shorter sketches, but it was left to William Sidney Porter to occupy the most important position in that field. Just as Garland and others had drawn on rural scenes for their material, Porter typified the new urbanized America by his pictures of city life. Some of his earliest tales were written during a prison term which he served for the alleged embezzlement of funds from an Austin (Texas) bank, and were published under the pseudonym O. Henry. His later work, comprising some two hundred and fifty short stories written in the decade preceding his death in 1910, deal with his experiences in New Orleans, Texas and Central America, but above all with the types found in his later life in New York, the

[1] H. L. Mencken, *A Book of Prefaces* (N .Y., 1917), 67 ff.
[2] See Slosson, *Great Crusade and After*, 419-420.

city which he knew with an intimacy surpassed by no writer.

In American poetry the years from 1898 to 1914 marked a period of transition. The rural dialect poets, Will Carleton and James Whitcomb Riley, continued to write and were widely read, but their best work had already been done. Riley's last years were a series of triumphs; Yale and Pennsylvania awarded him honorary degrees, and his birthday in 1915 was set aside by the governor's proclamation as a time to do honor to "Indiana's most beloved citizen." [1] Of the poems written during these years the one which sank deepest into the American consciousness was Edwin Markham's "The Man with the Hoe." Composed in December, 1898, by a San Francisco schoolmaster, it sensed the questioning restlessness and rising social consciousness of the generation. The poem swept the country, many hailing it as "the battle cry of the next thousand years." [2] The new school of poetry, when it came, was to follow the influence of Whitman rather than the Victorians and it was destined to reflect the American scene with a realism more poignant than Riley or Carleton. The new note was tentatively sounded by William Vaughn Moody, who did not hesitate to question the existing order, and Edwin Arlington Robinson, who drew many of his characters from the frustrated and the unfit. About 1912 realism became dominant.[3] Vachel Lindsay began his ragtime boomings, Carl Sandburg his virile pictures of the West, and Robert Frost his sketches of New England. The movement was strongly under way when Amy Lowell's *Sword Blades and Poppy Seeds* appeared in 1914. Her

[1] Marcus Dickey, *The Maturity of James Whitcomb Riley* (Indianapolis, 1902), chap. xxii.

[2] Mark Sullivan, *Our Times* (N. Y., 1926-), II, 236 ff.

[3] Amy Lowell, "Two Generations in American Poetry," J. C. Bowman, ed., *Contemporary American Criticism* (N. Y., 1926), 277-285.

book not only proved a pioneer in freer forms of poetry, but it bestowed a touch of respectability upon *vers libre.* In 1898 American poetry was at a low ebb; in 1914 a significant group of younger writers had emerged who heralded a poetic revolution.

In music, too, new forces were astir. Realizing that the lack of originality in American composition was in part due to the paucity of historical background, certain enthusiasts sought a foundation for an autochthonous music among Indian and Negro melodies. Edward MacDowell led in the development of the Indian theme in his "Indian Suite" (1896); Charles Wakefield Cadman wrote Indian songs and later a one-act grand opera, "Shanewis"; Arthur Nevin, who had sojourned on an Indian reservation, used the theme operatically in "Poia" (1910), as did Victor Herbert in "Natoma" (1911).[1] The Negro influence, stimulated by the enthusiasm of the Bohemian composer, Antonin Dvořák, called forth Rubin Goldmark's "Negro Rhapsody" and several compositions by Henry F. B. Gilbert.[2] Though there were interesting possibilities in both Negro and Indian melodies and rhythms, neither by itself—nor both together—proved suitable as a musical embodiment of the American spirit.

The common man was content to take his Indian music in the bastard form of "Hiawatha," "Arawana" or "Tammany," and his Negro music in the form of "My Gal, She's a High Born Lady" or "Alexander's Ragtime Band." This type of song, along with the sentimental ballad and the more prominent "hits" of the cur-

[1] Arthur Farwell and W. D. Dailey, eds., *Music in America* (D. G. Mason, ed., *The Art of Music,* 1915-1917, IV), chap. ii. See also Natalie Curtis, *The Indian's Book* (N. Y., 1907), and Frances Densmore, *The American Indians and Their Music* (N. Y., 1926).

[2] H. E. Krehbiel, *Afro-American Folksongs* (N. Y., 1914); Dorothy Scarborough, *On the Trail of the Negro Folk Songs* (Cambridge, Mass., 1925).

rent musical comedies, provided the musical meat for the average American.[1] The musical comedy, "Floradora," unmercifully scored by the critics upon its New York opening, later became one of the most popular shows of the decade because, in the opinion of Harris, of one song, "Tell Me, Pretty Maiden." [2] The nearest to a "native music"—if that term may be used to describe a form popular with the masses—was a syncopated rhythm known as "ragtime," which flourished mightily in the decade before the war. To exploit this interest popular-song publishers sprang up like mushrooms. The centers of the industry were "tin-pan alley" (West Twenty Eighth Street, New York) where the leading publishers had their offices, and the vicinity of Tony Pastor's on Fourteenth Street where the "song pluggers" sought to inveigle variety stars into using their wares.

In spite of the failure to build a native music out of Indian or Negro themes and of the almost universal appeal of ragtime, the years from 1898 to 1914 marked a distinct broadening of musical appreciation. This came in part from the activities of the National Federation of Musical Clubs, formed in 1898; in part from an increased importation of great European artists such as Hofmann, Kreisler and Caruso; and in part from the perfection of the phonograph, which brought good as well as poor music into the home. The older musical-training centers—at Harvard under the direction of John Knowles Paine, at the New England Conservatory of Music under George Whitefield Chadwick, at Yale under Horatio W. Parker and at Columbia under Edward

[1] Typical of the ballad form were the exceedingly popular "In the Shade of the Old Apple Tree," by Harry Williams and Egbert Van Alstine, and "In the Good Old Summer Time," by George Evans and Ren Shields. For a list of popular songs, see C. K. Harris, *After the Ball* (N. Y., 1926), 215-219, and Isaac Goldberg, *Tin Pan Alley* (N. Y., 1930).

[2] Harris, *After the Ball*, 304-305.

Alexander MacDowell—continued to be influential. The influence of MacDowell in particular was perpetuated through the foundation (1909) of the MacDowell Colony at Peterborough, New Hampshire.[1] The Institute of Musical Art of the City of New York, founded in 1904 by Frank Damrosch through a half-million-dollar gift from the banker, James Loeb, started with an independence from tuition fees which put it at once in the forefront of musical institutions.

The symphony orchestra, which already existed in New York, Chicago and Boston, now made its appearance in smaller cities and in many sections of the country. Philadelphia established one in 1900, Minneapolis in 1902, St. Paul in 1905, New Orleans the next year and Seattle in 1908. The Symphony Society of New York was reorganized in 1905 and a Russian Symphony Society produced Russian music for several seasons. Henry Lee Higginson's Boston Symphony Orchestra moved into its new hall in 1900, and Theodore Thomas closed his notable career of forty years' leadership by seeing the Chicago Symphony Orchestra endowed and adequately housed in its own hall in 1904.[2] An important innovation in New York City's musical education was inaugurated by Walter Damrosch in his symphony concerts for children in the season 1897-1898.

In certain respects the early years of the century represent the golden age of opera in America. This was due primarily to the strenuous rivalry provided for the Metropolitan by Oscar Hammerstein in his newly built Manhattan Opera House. After four brilliant but finan-

[1] Carried on by the Edward MacDowell Association, Inc. See J. F. Porte, *Edward MacDowell* (N. Y., 1922), 27-37.

[2] G. P. Upton, ed., *Theodore Thomas, a Musical Autobiography* (Chicago, 1905), I, chap. xi; Rose F. Thomas, *Memoirs of Theodore Thomas* (N. Y., 1911), chap. xxi; C. E. Russell, *The American Orchestra and Theodore Thomas* (Garden City, 1927), 296.

cially unsuccessful years (1906-1910), Hammerstein sold out to the Metropolitan which under the successive direction of Maurice Grau (until 1903), Heinrich Conried (1903-1908) [1] and Giulio Gatti-Casazza (1908-), set the standard for American opera production and undertook a policy of encouragement to American artists.[2] Outside of New York City, however, the patronage was hardly great enough to maintain permanent companies. Hammerstein was unable to place his Philadelphia Opera on a permanent footing and sold out to the Metropolitan interests who organized a subsidized company which divided its time between Chicago and Philadelphia. The Boston Opera Company, organized in 1908, lasted but six seasons.[3] Unsuccessful as they were, these brave attempts were widely heralded as forerunners of an operatic revival which would place permanent companies in many cities.[4]

If this generation added little notable to the world's store of music, the same was not true of the art of dancing. While hardly more than a child Isadora Duncan reacted violently from the artificiality of the ballet and toe dance and sought by simple free draperies and flowing movements to bring back some of the naturalness of the classic dance. Unappreciated in America, she was enthusiastically received in Europe where her interpretations opened new possibilities for the art. Her influence in due course of time reached the land of her birth, though the interest in classic dancing in America was but

[1] Conried shared the direction for two years with Johann Andreas Dippel who then directed the Chicago-Philadelphia venture.

[2] A phase of this encouragement was the production in 1910 of "The Pipe of Desire" by Richard S. Converse, the first American opera to be produced at the Metropolitan.

[3] The building of both the Boston Opera House and the new structure for the New England Conservatory of Music were made possible by the munificence of Eben D. Jordan.

[4] Farwell and Dailey, *Music in America,* 174.

a pale reflection of the possibilities which the great Isadora perceived.[1]

Even less than in music was there a distinctive American school of painting. In general, American art tended to be highly imitative; its principal characteristic was an eclectic cosmopolitanism. The American exhibit at the Paris Exposition of 1900 was marked by a high general standard of craftsmanship, but it was criticised as lacking virility and individuality.[2] For the "irreproachable table manners" and "trite propriety" of much American work the responsibility rested largely upon the market which demanded it and upon an immaturity of taste which looked askance at the nude and saw only ugliness and distortion in the work of Cézanne, Matisse and other Continental modernists.

Yet not all American painting was of this sort.[3] Winslow Homer continued to produce marine paintings of great power and originality. Younger and of a more experimental turn were Robert Henri, George B. Leeks, William J. Glackens, George W. Bellows, John Sloan and Eugene Speicher, whose work, both in technique and subject matter, displayed a strongly realistic bent. The older impressionists, Theodore Robinson, Childe Hassam, J. H. Twachtman and J. Alden Weir, continued active; and John Singer Sargent reached the summit of his powers, limning with brilliant and audacious brush the figures of notables in both England and America. William M. Chase was perhaps the outstanding teacher of painting during the period. American art showed little trace of the formless expressionism which dominated the radical Continental school during these years. Bel-

[1] Isadora Duncan, *My Life* (N. Y., 1927).

[2] C. H. Caffin, *The Story of American Painting* (N. Y., 1907), 339-340.

[3] Walter Pach, "Art," H. E. Stearns, ed., *Civilization in the United States* (N. Y., 1922), 227-241.

lows, for example, insisted on natural appearances in his prize-fighting picture, "A Stag at Sharkey's," though he was a powerful rather than a fine draftsman and he splashed his canvas with bold, free strokes. At the New York Armory Show of 1913, however, Americans for the first time were privileged to see some of the best work produced by the new transatlantic school, and "postimpressionism," as it was called, soon began to win followers in the United States.

Late in its American development, mural painting made a rapid progress after 1898, stimulated as it was by the large number of newly erected public buildings. The first of these to be murally decorated with a consistent scheme were the Appellate Court in New York and the Library of Congress, buildings which offered opportunities for Henry Oliver Walker, Edward Simmons, Edwin H. Blashfield, John W. Alexander, Robert Reid and others. The new state capitol in Minnesota allowed Simmons to do some of his best work, and a similar chance was afforded Blashfield at Wisconsin and Edwin A. Abbey and Violet Oakley at Pennsylvania. In the Boston Public Library, constructed from 1896 to 1901, is to be found perhaps the best of the mural work of Sargent and the most striking of Abbey. American mural painting was, in general, of a high order, an exceedingly fortunate circumstance when its importance in democratizing the fine arts is considered.[1]

The illustrative arts fared less well. In reproductive engraving the old landscape line engraving was a thing of the past. Gustav Kruell, Henry Wolf and Timothy Cole were all doing excellent wood engraving with the new white line, but by 1910 that art was being pushed aside by the photomechanical relief-block process.

[1] F. J. Mather, jr., and others, *The American Spirit in Art* (R. H. Gabriel, ed., *The Pageant of America*, New Haven, 1926-1929, XII), 98 ff.

Under the spell of Whistler many of the leading painters turned aside momentarily to etch, particularly Joseph Pennell whose work more closely reflected the changing America than did that of his fellow artists. His early inspiration he found in lovely old houses and romantic European landscapes, but after 1898 he turned to the great locks of the Panama Canal, to skyscrapers and to other urban subjects. Excellent as was the work done on copper, the market was small and public appreciation meager. Work on stone attracted the best talent even less than did copper, and, with the exception of Pennell's contribution, was fragmentary.[1] Lithographic art came chiefly from abroad.

For this condition the changing tastes of the reading public were largely responsible. The hordes who read the new ten-cent magazine, the illustrated Sunday supplement and the historical best seller had little appreciation of technical skill in art; and publishers, impatient with the exacting work and high cost of reproducing woodcuts or copper prints, sought cheaper substitutes. Improvements in the processes of reproducing pictures enabled publishers to draw upon new kinds of talent, but they did not tend to improve illustration. Such men as Frederic Remington, A. B. Frost, Joseph Pennell, Edwin A. Abbey, E. W. Kemble, William T. Smedley and Arthur I. Keller were still illustrating after 1898, but their successors were of lesser stature. Even Howard Pyle (1853-1911), who bridged the period from the old to the new, and whose influence was for the best, failed to stay the retrogression. Typical of the new illustrations were Maxfield Parrish's fantasies, which had a wide appeal, and the drawing-room scenes with their "full-dress heroes" of Howard Chandler Christy, Charles Dana

[1] Frank Weitenkampf, *American Graphic Art* (2d edn., N. Y., 1924), chap. x.

Gibson and James Montgomery Flagg.[1] From this "long line of American girls and men of impeccable appearance" there emerged an idealized conception of the American girl, athletic, pretty, high-spirited and well groomed, which found countless imitators in real life. Gibson, Christy, A. B. Wenzell, Henry Hutt and Harrison Fisher had each a standardized type which pleased, if it did little to elevate, the public taste. Against the deluge of pulchritude the occasional sorties of greater artists like Glackens, Leeks and Sloan into illustration had little effect. By far the ablest illustrated magazine in America during the brief span of its life was the *Masses* (1911-1917), but its circulation was chiefly limited to the artistic and socially radical group.[2]

While the illustrative arts lost ground, sculpture flourished as never before.[3] The years following 1898, in fact, saw as much good work as in the whole previous century, work which retained a certain native individuality in spite of foreign influence. This was in part due to the residence of very able sculptors in America where their talents found ample employment and their genius appreciation. Some, moreover, received most of their schooling in America. John Quincy Adams Ward (1830-1910), whose life bridged the period between the classicism of Powers and the modern school, was trained entirely in America; Daniel Chester French spent but one year of study abroad and that under the

[1] Among the ablest of illustrators of the first decade of the century were Walter Appleton Clark, who illustrated for Mary Wilkins Freeman, James Lane Allen and Henry Van Dyke; F. Walter Taylor, who did the pictures for Margaret Deland's *Iron Woman;* F. C. Yohn, who followed Pyle in his historical scenes; Jules Guerin and Henry Patrick Raleigh.

[2] Mather and others, *American Spirit in Art,* 317. Among those illustrating for the *Masses* were "Art" Young, Maurice Sterne, Arthur B. Davies, Boardman Robinson, George Bellows, John Sloan and Mahonri Young.

[3] Lorado Taft, *The History of American Sculpture* (rev. edn., N. Y., 1924), 538-588.

American, Thomas Ball, at Florence. The greatest of the group, however, Augustus Saint-Gaudens (1848-1907), born in Ireland of a French father and an Irish mother but brought to America in infancy, received a thorough French training, as did George Grey Barnard, whom many place second only to him.

Historical themes provided the principal subject matter for this brilliant period of native sculpture. The aged J. Q. A. Ward, as productive as ever, chiseled the Soldiers' and Sailors' Monument in Syracuse (1907), the statue of General Sheridan in Washington and that of General Hancock in Philadelphia in 1908, while Saint-Gaudens produced his immortal statue of General Sherman in New York (1903). Notable work from the chisel of French appeared almost yearly, much of it commemorative of great Americans: his "Grant" at Philadelphia in 1899, his "Washington" in Paris the next year, his "Hooker" at Boston in 1903, his impression of Alice Freeman Palmer at Wellesley, Massachusetts, in 1907, his "Lincoln" at Lincoln, Nebraska, in 1912, and his "Emerson" at Concord, Massachusetts, in 1914. Barnard's "Hewer" came in 1902,[1] and in the following year he commenced his colossal commission for the two sculptured groups on the Pennsylvania state capitol, a work which he completed in spite of almost insuperable difficulties thrown in his way by grafting politicians.

These men were but the most famous of that notable group who almost overnight brought American sculpture on a par with the best in the world. Paul Wayland Bartlett designed his famous equestrian "Lafayette" which in 1900 was presented to the French nation by the school children of America. Frederick William MacMonnies, although for a decade (1903-1913) much interested in painting, found time to execute among other

[1] Owned by John D. Rockefeller.

works a statuette of Roosevelt (1905), one of McClellan at Washington (1906) and a monument at Denver commemorative of pioneer life. Charles Henry Niehaus produced perhaps his masterpiece in the colossal nude "The Driller" for the Drake monument at Titusville, Pennsylvania. Herbert Adams designed the Vanderbilt memorial doors in New York in 1902, and the monument to William Cullen Bryant (1911) in the same city. Lorado Taft, the historian-teacher-artist whose influence upon Western sculpture was notable, began in 1905 a grand scheme of sculptured decoration in Chicago, the first unit of which was "The Spirit of the Lakes" (1913). Herman Atkins MacNeil, Phimister Proctor, Cyrus Dallin and others with their stirring Indian conceptions were perpetuating the red man in art, while Solon Borglum roamed successfully over the whole range of frontier life—cowboys, animals, Indians, soldiers. His brother, Gutzon, did many things, but is best known in America for his colossal head of Lincoln in the capital and his Lincoln Memorial at Newark, New Jersey. These men and others, most of whom were born in the 1850's and 1860's, reached the full flower of their productive powers at the turn of the century, producing what may well prove to be a golden age in American sculpture.

American architecture by 1898 had raised itself from the almost unbelievable depths into which it had sunk in the Civil War and *post-bellum* periods and was on the threshold of a new and original era of activity. The rapid development of the nation and the immense wealth created necessitated an activity in building which provided ample opportunity for experimentation and at the same time stimulated architectural talent. Moreover the steel-framed skyscraper had brought into being new possibilities of loftiness and lightness of construction and "freed architecture from the limitations of massive walls which had for ages kept it from soaring otherwise than in the frail and beautiful but practically useless form of the spire." [1] In Chicago particularly, under the influence of Louis Sullivan, Daniel Burnham and John W. Root, much of the pioneering in steel structure was carried on, but it was the Flatiron Building of New York, one of Burnham's creations completed in 1902, that made the American public conscious that a revolution had arrived.[2] But the twenty stories of the Flatiron Building, which caused such a stir in 1902, pale into insignificance before the Woolworth and Singer buildings, the Metropolitan Tower, the Municipal Building and others which soon jagged the New York skyline.[3] The skyscraper was a product of the nineteenth century; it was the superskyscraper, designed to offset the fabulous land values of an island city, which came with the twentieth. The superskyscraper, however, was not the only architectural development of these years. Frank Lloyd Wright in his design of the Larkin Building in Buffalo struck a new note in industrial architecture, while Ernest Wilby of the firm of Albert Kahn of Detroit revolutionized the modern factory by virtually abandoning the solid wall and substituting glass.[4]

[1] T. F. Hamlin, "Twenty-Five Years of American Architecture," *Architectural Record*, XL (1916), 3. See also C. H. Edgell, *The American Architecture of Today* (N. Y., 1928); and T. E. Tallmadge, *The Story of Architecture in America* (N. Y., 1927), chap. x.

[2] There were at least six other New York buildings in 1903 with as many stories, and four that were higher. *World Almanac for 1903*, 533.

[3] The Woolworth Building, 785 feet above the sidewalk, completed in 1912, was designed by Cass Gilbert; the Singer (completed in 1908) by Ernest Flagg; the Metropolitan Tower (1908) by M. Le Brun and Sons; and the Municipal Building (1909) by McKim, Mead and White. *Scientific American*, XCVII, 168-169 (Sept. 7, 1907); CVIII, 224 (March 8, 1913).

[4] Fiske Kimball, *American Architecture* (Indianapolis, 1928), 196-198; F. L. Wright, "In the Cause of Architecture," *Architectural Record*, XXIII (1908), 166-173; Russell Sturgis, "The Larkin Building in Buffalo," *Architectural Record*, XXIII (1908), 311-321.

As in the case of office buildings, land values pushed the apartment house ever higher into the air. Humanitarianism, working through building laws,[1] put an end to the "dumb-bell" style of tenements, letting in air and light, while architects discarded the old-fashioned corridor apartment in designing the "cliff dwellings" for city tenants. Nor was the advance limited to the cities. In the suburbs and rural regions the mid-Victorian monstrosities were deserted for a colonial revival. Though the vogue of certain colonial types often tended to give suburban landscapes an atmosphere of sameness characteristic of the city, the revived colonial was a distinct improvement, and the skill of architects in developing the New England rambling farmhouse, the Dutch gambrel roof, the Pennsylvania stone house, the Southern Georgian style and the Spanish mission provided a pleasing variety and at the same time perpetuated provincial types in their respective regions.[2] The ubiquitous bungalow of mongrel origin was exceedingly popular and badly littered the suburban landscape, but with the passing years it assumed a more artistic form.

This architectural outburst brought with it better facilities for architectural education and an increasingly large number of excellent craftsmen. McKim had early become interested in the education of architects and had endowed traveling fellowships at Harvard and Columbia. After the Chicago Exposition he led a movement to establish an American Academy at Rome, a dream which was consummated in 1905 when a special act of Congress incorporated it. Universities established departments and new courses and some of the important professional journals were founded: *Architecture* (1899), the *Western Architect* (1901), the *Architect and Engi-*

[1] See earlier, 157-159.
[2] Edgell, *American Architecture*, 11.

neer (1905) and the *Journal of the American Institute of Architects* (1913). At the same time the popular illustrated magazines, particularly those which catered to women and which dealt with country life, carried news of the newer developments in suburban gardens and architecture, dwelt much on antiques and period furniture and played no small part in educating the public taste to better domestic styles. The colored photographs of Wallace Nutting contributed to the same end.

Like other cultural influences, that of the public library is difficult to estimate, but it is safe to say that it greatly increased in the new century. By 1898 the more advanced communities had reached the point where free, public and tax-supported libraries were held, like schools, to be an essential element in the equipment of a democracy.[1] It was for the new generation to improve library facilities and master the technique of service to the community. There were in the United States in 1900 over seventeen hundred libraries of more than five thousand volumes, a number which grew to nearly three thousand by the close of the period.[2] Undoubtedly the greatest single incentive to this growth came from the Carnegie fortune which had been pouring into the building of libraries since 1881. Carnegie alone was responsible during the decade 1906-1916 for the construction of over a thousand library buildings, most of them in the United States. The largest of his gifts was in 1901 when he wrote that he would "esteem it a rare privilege" to donate $5,200,000 to build sixty-five branches for the New York Public Library. To carry on the work of providing libraries and otherwise promote the advancement and diffusion of knowledge, he founded in 1911 the

[1] Schlesinger, *Rise of the City*, chap. vi.

[2] Public, society or school libraries. U. S. Commissioner of Education. *Report for 1899-1900*, I, 932; *Rep. for 1914*, I, 13.

Carnegie Corporation of New York and shortly endowed it with $125,000,000.[1] As the facilities increased, library administrators rose to meet the new opportunities. The libraries took up seriously the task of meeting the public needs and, where possible, of improving the public tastes. No longer was the public library a mere repository of culture; it had become by 1914 an aggressive and important factor in the shaping of American civilization.

[1] T. W. Koch, *A Book of Carnegie Libraries* (N. Y., 1917), vii-viii, 15.

CHAPTER XII

THE PEOPLE AT PLAY

THE tremendous interest in sports and outdoor life which characterized this generation can be explained in part by the growth of wealth and leisure and in part by the desire to recapture something of the benefits of rural life which were disappearing for large numbers of Americans. A nation scarcely two decades removed from a fighting frontier was hardly ready to forego the strenuous life, and Roosevelt's excoriation of the "over-civilized man" and the "life of slothful ease" fell on receptive ears.[1] Exponents of health fads and physical culture fostered the idea of individual exercise for personal efficiency, and the publicity given to amateur sports by the metropolitan press was both a stimulus to further endeavor and an indication of the public's spontaneous interest.[2] Unfortunately interest in athletics did not necessarily mean personal participation. College sports came to be less a matter of undergraduate exercise and more a means of visual recreation for alumni and others. The common man, especially the city dweller, who had neither opportunity nor energy to take part personally, looked to professional athletics for vicarious exertion.

In an age of rapidly growing cities it was but natural that the most significant recreational developments should concern the urban population. The first need was to provide the crowded tenement dweller with an oppor-

[1] Theodore Roosevelt, *The Strenuous Life* (N. Y., 1900), 1, 7.
[2] W. H. Nugent, "The Sports Section," *Am. Mercury*, XVI (1929), 328-338.

tunity to get into the open, but the problem was complicated by the fact that the typical American city had grown with but slight attention to recreational needs. Not until the 1890's had much interest been evinced in public parks, even in the large centers; [1] but the first decade of the new century witnessed the rapid extension of older systems and the creation of new parks and parkways.[2] Among the most notable examples were the Boston Metropolitan Park System extending from the Middlesex Fells on the north to the Blue Hills Reservation on the south, enlarged and improved during these years; the Essex County Park System along the Orange Mountains in New Jersey, including parks in Newark, Montclair, the Oranges and other towns; [3] and the Palisades Interstate Park, running from a point opposite 179th Street, New York City, nearly to Newburgh, and from the Hudson River to Tuxedo Park. Opened in 1909, it was enlarged the next year by a gift of ten thousand acres from Mrs. E. H. Harriman and further extended in subsequent years.

In 1903 Chicago entered upon a "second parkbuilding era" by an appropriation of $6,500,000 to be used not only for extending existing city parks and building new ones, but also for an outer belt of forests and meadows connected by parkways.[4] In 1908 New York began work on the Bronx River Parkway, the first link in the Westchester system, a parkway soon accorded nation-

[1] C. M. Robinson, *The Improvement of Towns and Cities* (N. Y., 1901), 154-155.

[2] *Public Recreation Facilities* (Am. Acad. of Polit. and Social Sci., *Annals*, XXXV, no. 2). See also A. W. Crawford, "The Development of Park Systems in American Cities," Am. Acad. of Polit. and Social Sci., *Annals*, XXV, 218 ff.

[3] F. W. Kelsey, *The First County Park System* (N. Y., 1905); Alonzo Church, *The Essex County Park Commission* (N. Y., 1913).

[4] H. G. Foreman, "Chicago's New Park Service," *Century*, LXIX (1905), 610-620.

wide recognition as a model of its kind. Cleveland under Tom Johnson made plans for an imposing civic center and an extensive park system; Washington under the supervision of George Burnap carried out after 1902 a program of intensive park development; [1] Seattle between 1907 and 1912 appropriated five million dollars for parks, playgrounds and boulevards; [2] St. Louis prepared plans for a group of outer parks, and Philadelphia organized for an even more comprehensive system.[3] These projects were but outstanding examples of what was going on in other cities. Frederick Law Olmsted, the pioneer of American landscape architecture and the genius behind many of the earlier parks, died in 1903 before this latest era of building was well under way, but his son, Frederick Law Olmsted, jr., and his pupil, John C. Olmsted, headed a firm which transmitted the ideas of the master to the new generation. Even the smaller towns began to take pride in their evidences of rusticity.

Such amusement resorts as Coney Island, New York, and Revere Beach near Boston, with their merry-go-rounds, shooting galleries, dancing floors, freak shows, restaurants and beer gardens, had long since become an important recreational outlet to the factory hand and the office-bound clerk, but they had been limited to the largest cities. The trolley-car companies, however, as they extended into the country, laid out amusement parks to which the public might go in the evenings or on Sunday when the business of the company was normally light. Shortly "trolley-parks" were to be found in

[1] R. R. Root, "Intensive Park Development," *Am. City*, VII (1912), 417-421.

[2] Roland Cotterill, "The Parks, Playgrounds and Boulevards of Seattle," *Am. City*, VII (1912), 204-207.

[3] A. W. Crawford and F. M. Day, *The Existing and Proposed Outer Park Systems of American Cities* (Phila. Allied Organizations, *Report*, Harrisburg, 1905), 36-42.

the outskirts of even the smaller cities, where throngs enjoyed dancing, band concerts, baseball games, bathing and boating and the usual shows of a typical trolley-park midway.[1] Some of these parks amounted to little more than a trolley station with a near-by pavilion, as at Neff Park near Xenia, Ohio; others boasted large auditoriums. That at Willow Grove, Philadelphia, seated ten thousand and supported the best musical talent of the nation.

An important impetus to this development had been the widespread popularity of the bicycle, but the zenith of the bicycle was rapidly passing. Pointing to a remarkable decline in general riding and club membership, the *International Year Book* in 1899 added that, "wheeling as a fad having now died out, a healthy growth is assured for the sport, while the bicycle itself is becoming more and more devoted to business uses, one example of which is the equipment of telegraph boys in New York with wheels." [2] But the vogue of the bicycle was threatened with something more serious than the changing winds of popular fancy; it was soon forced to meet the competition of a new means of locomotion, the automobile.[3] The recreational and amusement possibilities of the automobile were obvious, though with all its advantages it did not furnish the excellent exercise provided by the bicycle. It did, however, along with the bicycle and trolley car, contribute to keep alive among city dwellers an active interest in fishing, hunting and other outdoor recreations. In such contests as the annual Vanderbilt Cup race on Long Island and the hill-climbing events at Wilkes-Barre, Pennsylvania, the automobile in its earlier

[1] D. A. Willey, "The Trolley-Park," *Cosmopolitan*, XXXIII (1902), 265-272.

[2] *International Year Book for 1899*, 254.

[3] See earlier, chap. vi.

years also added interesting innovations to the world of competitive sport.

Unquestionably the premier position among American sports was held by baseball and it continued as popular on the village green as the city diamond. The expansion of the professional game, however, was distinctly urban.[1] Up to 1898 the parent professional organization, the National League of Professional Baseball Clubs, had succeeded in crushing any league which threatened to become national in scope, but shortly thereafter its hegemony was broken by the advent of the American League. Organized as the Western League in 1893, it became the American League in 1900 and began a bitter war with the older body. Securing a Chicago franchise in 1900, the new league, strongly financed, reorganized its circuit in the following year by abandoning Indianapolis, Kansas City, Minneapolis and Buffalo for Baltimore, Washington, Philadelphia and Boston. In 1902 it transferred its Milwaukee franchise to St. Louis and in 1903 the Baltimore franchise to New York.[2] This invasion of enemy territory, accompanied as it was by extensive raids upon the older organization for star players, considerably weakened the latter. The National League replied in kind, its chief coup being the purchase in mid-season of the Baltimore club and the transfer of John J. McGraw and most of his players to New York.[3] The election of Harry O. Pulliam as president of the National League in 1902 brought overtures of peace, and in the mid-season of 1903 a new agreement was adopted, which in-

[1] During the first part of the period many villages as well as cities had professional or semiprofessional teams and local leagues.

[2] A. G. Spalding, *America's National Game* (N. Y., 1911), chap. xxiii. See also G. W. Axelson, *"Commy," the Life Story of Charles A. Comiskey* (Chicago, 1919).

[3] McGraw has replied to those who criticized this deal in *My Thirty Years in Baseball* (N. Y., 1923), chap. xxiv.

cluded detailed rules for conducting professional baseball and a national commission to enforce them.[1]

Stabilized by this agreement, professional baseball entered upon a new era of popularity and of financial prosperity not to be interrupted again until the attempt in 1914 to organize a new Federal League. Whatever may have been the interest in local teams and minor leagues, the attention of the baseball world was chiefly drawn to the contests in the two major organizations and to the classic "world-championship" series held each year after 1903 between the victors of the two leagues. In the National League the two most important contenders between 1903 and 1914 were the Chicago team, led by Frank L. Chance, which won the pennant in 1906, 1907, 1908 and 1910, and the New York club, managed by John J. McGraw, which was victorious in five of the remaining years.[2] The noted Chicago infield trio, J. J. Evers, Joseph Tinker and F. L. Chance, has rarely been equaled, while the New York team included the famous pitchers "Christy" Mathewson and Joseph McGinnity and the catchers Roger Bresnahan and Frank Bowerman. These were also the years when John P. ("Honus") Wagner, believed by McGraw to be the "greatest of all players," played shortstop for Pittsburgh.[3] In the American League the chief honors were divided between Philadelphia, which won the pennant six times, and Detroit which enjoyed three years of victories after 1906.[4] The former club, under the crafty generalship of Cornelius McGillicuddy ("Connie Mack") and containing such players as Charles Bender,

[1] See F. C. Richter, *History and Records of Baseball* (Phila., 1914), 213 ff.; Spalding, *America's National Game*, chap. xxxiii.

[2] New York won in 1904, 1905, 1911, 1912, 1913, Pittsburgh in 1909 and Boston in 1914.

[3] McGraw, *Thirty Years in Baseball*, 205.

[4] Other victors were Boston, 1903, 1904, 1912 and Chicago, 1906.

Edward Plank, J. W. Coombs, E. T. Collins, Jack Barry, J. Frank Baker and John McInnis, also won the world championship in 1910, 1911 and 1913,[1] while the latter, under the leadership of Hugh Jennings and aided by the batting of Tyrus Cobb, was a constant contender for honors. Financial prosperity attended the increasing popularity of the sport with the result that greater stadiums were built and unheard-of prices paid for players. The world series of 1913 had an attendance at the five games of 151,000 and gate receipts approximating $326,000.

Viewed askance by the more respectable elements and circumscribed in many states by legal restrictions, boxing enjoyed immense popularity among the "sporting fraternity" and remained the sport *par excellence* of the underworld. Although amateur boxing made progress, pugilism was largely professionalized, and the chief interest centered in the championship contests of the different classes, especially the heavyweight championship. The Australian, Robert Fitzsimmons, who had captured the crown from James J. Corbett in 1897 in a fourteen-round battle at Carson City, Nevada, was forced to relinquish it two years later to James J. Jeffries at the old Coney Island Athletic Club. The mighty Jeffries defended his title in subsequent matches with both Fitzsimmons and Corbett until he voluntarily retired in 1905, handing on to lesser men the task of combating for the world's title. The best of these proved to be the colored boxer, Jack Johnson, who established his preeminence at Reno, Nevada, in 1910, when he worsted Jeffries who had been induced to emerge from a five-

[1] In the remaining years the world championship was won by Boston (A. L.) 1903, New York (N. L.) 1905, Chicago (A. L.) 1906, Chicago (N. L.) 1907 and 1908, Pittsburgh, (N. L.) 1909, Boston (A. L.) 1912 and Boston (N. L.) 1914. There was no series in 1904.

year retirement as the only remaining "white hope." [1] These matches helped to stimulate an interest in boxing which was quickly reflected in the press. The *New York Tribune,* which had given the Corbett-Fitzsimmons battle two columns on an inside page, gave the Johnson-Jeffries fight six columns and the place of honor on the front page.[2] In spite of the growing popularity of the sport, boxing was denounced as a brutal pastime and vigorous efforts were made either to abolish or carefully regulate it. Thus New York state, the great Mecca of boxers, repealed in 1900 the Horton law which permitted twenty-five-round contests, and for ten years professional boxing was outlawed within its limits.

In like manner the reformers of the period turned against horse racing, a sport carried on by the wealthy, but supported chiefly by the gambling fraternity. Anti-betting laws, of course, existed in many states, but they were either not enforced on race tracks or exceptions were made to horse racing. In the opening years of the century this was notably true in New York state; but, following the lead of Missouri and Illinois, which legislated against race-track betting in 1905, Governor Hughes, after a strenuous fight, succeeded in getting the Agnew-Hart bill enacted in 1908 and in strengthening the law in 1910.[3] Black pessimism seized racing enthusiasts; some sold their horses and others transferred their activities to Europe.[4] The seasons of 1908-1911 were disastrous, but gradually ways were found to evade the laws. It was reported in 1912 that nearly sixteen hun-

[1] Alexander Johnston, *Ten—and Out* (N. Y., 1927), 187-192; Jack Johnson, *Jack Johnson in the Ring—and Out* (Chicago, 1927), 169 ff.

[2] *N. Y. Tribune,* March 18, 1897, and July 5, 1910.

[3] *Outlook,* LXXXIX, 48, 354 (May 9, June 20, 1908); *New International Year Book for 1911,* 595.

[4] S. C. Hildreth and J. R. Crowell, *The Spell of the Turf* (Phila., 1926), 186.

dred meetings were held in the United States in which about fifteen thousand horses participated and six million dollars in purses and stakes were distributed. By 1914 the race tracks in New York state had reopened. Meantime increasing interest, as well as the recent legislative opposition, had led to the building of courses at Havana, Cuba, Tia Juana, Mexico, and Montreal, Canada, the popularity of which was to be greatly increased within a few years by the adoption of the Eighteenth Amendment.

Professional baseball and boxing provided amusement for the masses, but they did not meet the needs of the wealthy and middle classes who in increasing numbers were finding leisure for sport. The gap was filled by the game of golf. Although country clubs with golf links had steadily increased since the introduction of the game in the late 1870's, it was well past the turn of the century before golf took its place as a sport for the people. The early years were the "dude era" when the wealthy, responding to a new fad or sensing the physical benefits for the middle-aged man, expended large sums in constructing excellent courses.[1] At first laid out in wealthy commuting towns near the great cities, like Brookline, Massachusetts, and Morristown, New Jersey, and in fashionable summer resorts, golf links began presently to appear near every good-sized town and city. Large centers like New York and Boston built public courses, and lesser communities in time imitated them. Hundreds were in existence in 1914 when it was believed that more adults participated in golf than in any other outdoor sport, and yet it was only on the threshold of its great popularity. The newspapers, which in the early years had hardly deigned to notice the game, now gave

[1] J. D. Travis and J. R. Crowell, *The Fifth Estate* (N. Y., 1926), chap. i.

large space to its interests, and followed in detail the matches for the open-golf championship won by J. J. McDermott (1911, 1912), Francis Ouimet (1913) and W. C. Hagen (1914), and the amateur championship won by Jerome D. Travis (1907, 1908, 1912, 1913) and Francis Ouimet (1914). The development of golf between 1898 and 1914 was perhaps the unique feature in the history of American sport during these years.

Tennis, eclipsed during the preceding decade by the popularity of bicycling, experienced a temporary revival as a spectators' game for a few years after 1900 as a result of the American victories of 1900 and 1902 in the international Davis Cup contests.[1] Though appealing to the same general classes as golf, another decade passed before tennis regained anything like its earlier favor with amateur players. By 1911 record-breaking crowds witnessed William A. Larned win the single championship for the fifth consecutive year and the seventh time. In 1912 and 1913 Maurice E. McLoughlin won first honors and in the latter year, with his team mates Harold H. Hackett and R. N. Williams, regained the Davis Cup which since 1903 had been in England and Australia.

Of collegiate sports football occupied in 1898 the leading position, but critical years lay ahead. Loosely supervised by a rules committee representing a few Eastern universities, college football was endangered in the early years of the century by professionalism and by the development of close-formation mass plays which rendered it unnecessarily dangerous. Educators and reformers of various types took pains to point out the exaggerated influence of the game in college life and the increasing toll of fatalities which each season recorded.[2]

[1] *International Year Book for 1898*, 772; *for 1899*, 768.
[2] *Literary Digest*, XXXI, 566, 861 (Oct. 21, Dec. 9, 1905).

The death roll in 1903 reached a total of forty-four, and, though it dropped to fourteen and twenty-four in the two succeeding years, the improvement was partly offset by the serious injuries incurred by those who lived. While ardent followers of the sport had little sympathy with the fond parents who "objected to having their sons maimed or killed for the greater glory of the college" or with the old-fashioned college president who complained that it took ten weeks out of the student's school year, the public at large took a different attitude.[1] The climax came in 1905 when the condemnation of the press was well-nigh universal and Columbia University abolished the game (restored in 1915). President Roosevelt invited football leaders to a White House luncheon to discuss the situation and Chancellor Henry M. McCracken of New York University issued a call to all colleges to join in a conference on the sport.

The result was the formation in 1906 of a new National Collegiate Athletic Association with a revision of the rules. The most important features introduced were the forward pass, the on-side kick, the separation of the rush lines and the necessity of making ten yards rather than five in three downs. The "new football" was denounced by critics on the ground that the game would be spoiled for the spectators, but this effort to open up the game actually made it more interesting. It is doubtful, however, if the new rules greatly decreased fatalities.[2] Some of the most dangerous mass plays known to the game followed the new rules, notably the "Minnesota shift" devised by Dr. Henry Williams of Minnesota, and it was necessary to change them yearly until a second radical revision was effected in 1910.

[1] *Independent*, LIX, 1184, 1294 (Nov. 16, 30, 1905).

[2] See *World Almanac for 1915*, 865, for records; also A. B. Reeve, "Football Safe and Sane," *Independent*, LXI, 1220-1224 (Nov. 22, 1906).

Some of the big games were being attended in 1914 by crowds of fifty thousand, and the leading universities were making plans to build monster stadiums to accommodate larger numbers. Football had not only become the king of college games but the support of the lesser ones. In these years the chief figure was Walter Camp, a man who had been intimately connected with Yale athletics from 1880 to 1910 and who had exercised great influence in the development of the American type of football. Critical of the new game, he yet was able to master its strategy, and many of his pupils carried "Camp football" throughout the country.[1] His retirement ended, for the time being, Yale's premier football position, and Percy D. Haughton, Harvard coach from 1908 to 1916, took his place as the leading authority. Equally important in the Middle West were A. A. Stagg of Chicago and F. H. ("Hurry-up") Yost of Michigan.

To bridge the long winter gap between football and the summer sports, basketball assumed the leadership among America's indoor athletics during the first decade of the century. Widely popular in Y. M. C. A. and athletic-club circles, it achieved its greatest development among the colleges.[2] Before the coming of basketball there were few large gymnasiums, and the influence of this sport seems to have been paramount in the growth of the huge building with its high ceiling and large arena now found on every college campus. Although the older position of track athletics was challenged by football and basketball, it continued to attract a large following. This was due in part to the constant bettering of existing records and in part to the development of international

[1] Hartford Powell, jr., has written an authorized biography: *Walter Camp, the Father of American Football* (Boston, 1926).

[2] J. C. Riley, *How to Coach and Play Basketball* (Champaign, Ill., 1926), 2; E. J. Mather and E. D. Mitchell, *Basketball* (Ann Arbor, Mich., 1922).

contests. All amateur and many professional world records were improved after 1898. Especially stimulating was the revival in 1896 of the Olympic contests. The Olympics at Athens in 1896, Paris in 1900 and St. Louis in 1904 were won by the American team; but notwithstanding American preëminence in track and field sports the London games of 1908 were captured by Great Britain and those at Stockholm in 1912 by Sweden.

The astonishing success of the American athletes at the Olympics was a fresh confirmation to ardent nationalists of the superiority of the American way of life, a theory which was also fortified by the results of the great international yacht races. By their nature exclusive and limited in actual participation to the wealthy, interest in these contests was widespread and reached a climax at the turn of the century. In 1898 Sir Thomas Lipton, a wealthy British tea merchant, challenged the New York Yacht Club, holder of the *America's* cup, and races were arranged for the following year. When the *Shamrock I* appeared to give race it was met and conquered by the *Columbia,* designed and built by N. G. Herreshoff. In 1901 came the *Shamrock II* and in 1903 the *Shamrock III,* but the Herreshoff boats repeated their victories—the *Columbia* in the earlier year and the *Reliance* in the latter. Not until 1913 did Lipton challenge again, but the outbreak of the World War a year later, while his new yacht *Shamrock IV* was crossing the ocean, brought a postponement until 1920.

Gratifying as these victories were, there was much in American sport to disturb the thoughtful student. Wherever there appeared the possibility of making a dollar's profit, professionalism seemed to creep in. The most skillful exhibitions of baseball and boxing were almost wholly professional, and professional leagues of basketball, hockey and other sports were organized. A prejudice against playing for money still persisted in tennis, golf and other games participated in by the more affluent classes, where strong efforts were made to differentiate the amateur from the professional, but the line between the two in many cases was so attenuated as to be almost indiscernible. College athletics, especially football, was so buttressed by professional coaches and dominated by huge gate receipts that it was coming to be more of a business than a recreation even to the players. "Spring practice and autumn practice, the enlistment of an army of expert coaches, the long blackboard drill in strategy, the despatch of trained watchers to study the peculiarities of rival teams," and the elaborate system of recruiting material from the preparatory schools, said the *Nation,* "have gone far towards removing the silly notion that intercollegiate games are played just for the fun of the thing."[1] Whether professional or amateur, the average American was inclined to take his sport too seriously.

Yet encouraging signs were visible. Educators, in an effort to minimize professionalism, tightened the rules governing participation in intercollegiate games, and sought to attach the coach more closely to the faculty body. To prevent college athletics from assuming the status of gladiatorial combats played by the few and witnessed by the many, intramural sports were encouraged and athletic exercise made a compulsory part of the curriculum. Through high school and Y. M. C. A. sports an increasing number of young men were stimulated to physical activity at the same time that sedentary men of middle age found exercise on the golf course. The intense interest in sport amounted almost to an athletic renaissance. Though bringing in its wake the finished spectacles provided by high-priced professionals, it

[1] *Nation*, XCIV, 482 (May 16, 1912).

also stimulated a wide participation by people of all ages and classes.

If golf and motoring represented the most notable additions to outdoor recreational life, the moving picture occupied an even more distinctive place within doors. Although animated picture films were projected on screens as early as 1894 and 1895 in the United States, these first attempts were crude, hard on the eyes of spectators, and interesting mainly as a curiosity.[1] Usually the early exhibition rooms were simply stores fitted with seats and a ticket booth, and the transition from these unpretentious places to the more elaborate theaters especially designed for showing pictures was slow until about 1910.[2] The usual admission price was five cents, a charge which was quite compatible with profits in a period when the hall could be run at a total cost of from $150 to $250 a week, a conventional comedy could be produced for $250, actors received from $15 to $40 a week and authors of good scenarios from $5 to $30. Before moving-picture houses were regularly established, traveling exhibitions introduced the new amusement, and the annual appearance of such exhibitions as "Howe's Moving Pictures" was one of the thrilling events of the small-town season.

It was not until 1905 that Edison set up "Black Maria," the first studio for indoor production, a flimsy structure made of black tar paper and mounted on a circular track so that it might swing with the sun; but so rapid was the advance that within five years not only had the Edison Company built elaborate studios, but the Vitagraph Company of Brooklyn, the Lubin Company

[1] New York City saw its first motion-picture show at Koster and Bial's Theater on Twenty-Third Street on April 27, 1896. Homer Croy, *How Motion Pictures Are Made* (N. Y., 1917), 55.

[2] B. J. Lubschez, *The Story of the Motion Picture 65 B. C. to 1920 A. D.* (N. Y., 1920), 43; P. W. Slosson, *The Great Crusade and After* (*A History of American Life*, XII), 394.

of Philadelphia and the Essanay and Selig firms of Chicago were producing films with an unheard-of dispatch. According to the *Independent* early in 1908, within the previous two years "moving picture theatres or exhibition halls have opened in nearly every town and village in the country and every city from the Klondike to Florida and from Maine to California supports from two or three to several hundred," patronized each day by an average of from two to three million people.[1] Before the end of the decade there were few Americans out of reach of a movie.

The first pictures widely shown were outdoor scenes, especially travel pictures, but slapstick farce, with the comic chase and the inevitable custard pie used as a missile, was quick in making its appearance.[2] There was little to commend these early pictures, produced as they were by second-rate artists and often "made up on the lot" in the most casual fashion, but crude as was the technique, it gave an opportunity for John Bunny and other unforgettable figures to impress themselves upon picture history. Producers, eager to please the multitude, took a page from the book of the dime-novel writers until the "western" became a part of the stock-in-trade of the business. Here the swift-riding cowboy hero, the gambling-house villain with his Mexican henchmen, the pretty school teacher or ranchman's daughter, playing their rôles with infinite variations in a setting of frontier towns and gorgeous mountain scenery, established themselves as part and parcel of American folklore.

While the moving picture was capturing its tens of thousands, musical comedy was enjoying an unprecedented popularity in the cities, but it was a far different

[1] G. E. Walsh, "Moving Picture Drama for the Multitude," *Independent*, LXIV, 306-310 (Feb. 6, 1908).

[2] Lubschez. *The Motion Picture*, 52 ff.

type from the exquisite comic operas composed in the eighties by Gilbert and Sullivan. Much of it was little more than refined burlesque with especially written music and a trained dancing chorus intermixed with vaudeville turns. Perhaps the German-dialect comedians, Joseph Weber and Lewis M. Fields, did this sort of thing as well as any, and their imitators were legion.[1] Higher in the scale was the exceedingly popular musical show which aspired to a more sustained musical score and to a touch of romance, achieved perhaps by placing the scenes in some far-off land. The finest of these, "The Merry Widow" by Franz Lehar, first played in New York in 1907, and "The Chocolate Soldier" by Oscar Strauss, produced there in 1909, were Austrian importations,[2] but the prolific Irish American, Victor Herbert, in such productions as "Babes in Toyland" (1903) and "The Red Mill" (1906) also set a high standard.

The success of the musical show provided opportunity for a host of newcomers whose popularity, founded on the uncertain qualities of personal magnetism and physical beauty rather than long training, was likely to be brief. Such old favorites as Francis Wilson and James T. Powers continued to draw, but few of the musical-comedy stars of 1898 were important ten or fifteen years later.[3] Exceptions are to be found in De Wolf Hopper, Weber and Fields, Sam Bernard, Richard Carle, Lillian Russell and Marie Dressler, while Fred Stone, "Al" Jolson, Elsie Janis and other new stars of more than passing ability continued year after year to delight thousands.

With such avidity did the amusement public respond to the musical show that variations were soon attempted, the most successful being the annual "Revues" or "Fol-

[1] L. C. Strang, *Celebrated Comedians* (Boston, 1901), 102-107.
[2] *The Theatre,* X (1909), no. 105, xiii.
[3] L. C. Strang, *Prima Donnas and Soubrettes* (Boston, 1900), x.

lies" which found their *raison d'être* in the features or foibles of the passing scene. These musical novelties were dealing a deathblow to the old-fashioned minstrel show, for "the fact that actual females appeared in the musical shows created a competition that was fatal to the 'all man' performances of the minstrels."[1] A number of minstrel shows, it is true, still toured the country in the early years of the century, notably the one headed by George Primrose and Lew Dockstader. As late as 1908 Cohan and Harris launched an elaborate show on Broadway—"Forty, Count 'em! Forty!"—but the day of minstrels was done.[2] The older generation of black-face comedians, Primrose, Dockstader, McIntyre and Heath, were turning to vaudeville or contributing their talents to the success of musical comedy, while the newcomers, George ("Honey Boy") Evans, "Al" Jolson and others, presented their "charcoal sketches" before a background of white chorus girls. Theatrical entertainment by Negroes themselves was still largely in the future.

Not content with the regular season, theatrical managers offered their musical shows to the summer visitor on "roof gardens," a theatrical feature which had some vogue during 1908 and for a few years after. Other variations were the spectacular productions of the New York Hippodrome, and finally "that latest importation from the slums of Europe," the cabaret, which by 1912 was an established feature of metropolitan restaurant life. "From the Café Boulevard on the South," wailed Nathan, "to the Campus restaurant on the North, from the 'Morgue' on the West to Joe Blaney's river-front café on the East, the cabaret is the rage." [3] The alleged free entertainment of the cabaret boded ill for the theater, but fortunately

[1] Dailey Paskman and Sigmund Spaeth, *Gentlemen, Be Seated!* (N. Y. 1926), 159.

[2] G. M. Cohan, *Twenty Years on Broadway* (N. Y., 1925), 215.

[3] G. J. Nathan, "The Deadly Cabaret," *Theatre*, XVI (1912), 183.

cabaret entertainment never reached a level high enough to afford real competition. In the hectic atmosphere of these cabarets and dance halls the two-step and waltz seemed too tame, and in their place came the Argentine tango and the less difficult one-step, turkeytrot and fox trot. From the city the new dances spread throughout the country until the one-step became the leading American dance. If the one-step and fox trot did not usher in the "jazz age," their amazing popularity at least shows that the American public welcomed an increasing tempo in its amusements.

In spite of a tendency toward standardization American vaudeville, like almost every other form of light amusement, enjoyed unprecedented popularity. Israel Zangwill in 1905 urged that the variety stage provide a medium for that neglected form of art, the one-act play, but he was far from hopeful as to the future of vaudeville, believing that in all probability "the artlessness of the public and the artfulness of the manager will long keep the present pabulum unaltered, save in increasing staleness." [1] His pessimism was more than justified. The one-act play, it is true, became a part of regular programs, but it lacked both seriousness and art. The only important innovation was the introduction of a "moving-picture news reel" to start the program and perhaps a photoplay to end it.[2] The lowly picture, however, which had crept in as a supplement to the vaudeville show only to take complete possession of many houses, was exercising by 1914 a distinct impetus to vaudeville as the movie theaters found it advisable to vary their programs by introducing vaudeville turns.

With such competition from moving pictures, musical

[1] Israel Zangwill, "The Future of Vaudeville in America," *Cosmopolitan*, XXXVIII (1905), 639-646.

[2] The term "photoplay" came as the result of prize competitions conducted by the Essanay Company in 1910.

shows and cabarets, it is not surprising that the legitimate drama was on the decline. The veteran critic, William Winter, however, laid the chief blame upon "the prevalence of materialism infecting all branches of thought, and of commercialism infecting all branches of action" —upon the theatrical audience "largely composed of vulgarians, . . . who care for nothing but the solace of their common tastes and animal appetites" and upon the "sordid, money grubbing tradesmen" who "have captured the industry that they call 'the Amusement Business' and have made 'a corner in theatricals.'"[1] Winter's indictment was none too severe. Not alone was the control of the drama escaping from the actors to the producers, but the latter were attempting to consolidate their business in the manner of the steel, oil and packing barons. This process had commenced in 1896 when Klaw and Erlanger, the Frohmans and others had established a central booking office with the hope of controlling both the "time" of the theaters throughout the country and the artists who played in them. The better elements among the profession were at first defiant, but few could afford like Mrs. Minnie Maddern Fiske to hold out for the independence of the actor. The breaking of the theatrical trust awaited the advent of the Shuberts (Sam, Lee and Jacob), who began their New York career in 1900 and eventually built a string of playhouses from coast to coast. Their progress was so rapid that in 1910 twelve hundred theaters throughout the country joined with them in defying the trust.

The downfall of the trust in that year distinctly contributed to the salvation of the American theater, but did not necessarily weaken the grip of materialism upon it. Believing that a great endowed theater with a permanent repertory company would improve the situation, Hein-

[1] William Winter, *Other Days* (N. Y., 1908), 306-308.

rich Conried, manager of the Metropolitan Opera House, persuaded some thirty wealthy New Yorkers to contribute thirty-five thousand dollars each for such a project. An enormous playhouse, the New Theater, later the Century, was built on Central Park West at a great expenditure, but being poorly located and ill fitted for the purpose, the plan was relinquished after two seasons (1909-1911).[1] The failure of the New Theater indicated that the immediate future of the American drama was not likely to lie in the endowed or municipal theater. At least one municipal playhouse, the Academy of Music at Northampton, Massachusetts, did, however, have a temporary success, operating for several years after 1912 with its own stock company under the capable management of Jessie Bonstelle.

The real revival of the American drama may be attributed chiefly to the "little-theater movement," which reached America from Europe in the years 1911-1912. Beginning in that season with Maurice Browne's Little Theater in Chicago, Mrs. Lyman Gales's Toy Theater in Boston and Winthrop Ames's Little Theater in New York, these tiny playhouses spread rapidly until within five years fifty were successfully operating. Anxious to divorce the drama from commercialism, the little theater aimed to give plays which had great artistic merit but little appeal to the commercial producer, including the one-act play which Zangwill had visioned as a development in vaudeville. It emphasized the repertory idea and, by appealing to amateurs, hoped to develop a popular appreciation of the best in theatrical art.[2]

In the wake of Maurice Browne's famous Chicago ex-

[1] *The New Theatre* (N. Y., 1909); W. P. Eaton, *At the New Theatre and Others* (Boston, 1910); Arthur Hornblow, *A History of the Theatre in America* (Phila., 1919), II, chap. xxx.

[2] Constance D'Arcy Mackaye, *The Little Theatre in the United States* (N. Y., 1917), chap. i.

periment came the Provincetown Players (1915), the Washington Square Players (1915) and other groups whose interest in the redemption of the theater was important. At the same time the Drama League, organized at Evanston, Illinois, in 1910, sought, through educational effort and the encouragement of the writing and production of creditable plays, to contribute its mite to the cause. The great development of the amateur little theater, however, came in the years which followed. A salutary influence was also exerted by Percy Mackaye and others, who with their large-scale pageants hoped to revive some of the lost dignity of classic grandeur. Impetus likewise came from academic circles, particularly at Harvard, where Professor George P. Baker established in 1912 his "47 Workshop," and at the Carnegie Institute of Technology in Pittsburgh where a four-year course in theater arts was established in 1914.

The subject matter of the drama followed, in general, the public taste. The rococo romanticism which produced the historical novel dominated the theater from 1899 to 1904 when *The Prisoner of Zenda, Janice Meredith, Richard Carvel, When Knighthood Was in Flower* and many other historical novels were rewritten for the stage. Clyde Fitch, the most facile and brilliant playwright of the early years of the century, wrote "Barbara Frietchie" (1899) for Julia Marlowe and "Nathan Hale" (1899) in which Nat Goodwin appeared; while David Belasco, the most powerful and ablest producer of the period, brought out "Madame Butterfly" (1900), "The Darling of the Gods" (1902) and "The Girl of the Golden West" (1905), distinguished for realistic settings as well as perfection in stage detail.

As literature became more realistic and the social conscience somewhat stirred, the public accorded patronage to the "problem play" and the drama dealing with social questions. Charles Klein, after reading Ida M. Tarbell's *History of the Standard Oil Company,* wrote "The Lion and the Mouse" (1906); Edward Sheldon in "The Boss" (1911) dealt with the struggle between capital and labor; Charles Rann Kennedy in "The Servant in the House" (1908) and "The Terrible Meek" (1911) showed how far organized religion might be from the teachings of Christ; and Charles Kenyon in "Kindling" (1911) laid open the life of the slums. Others, as Augustus Thomas in "The Witching Hour" (1907) and David Belasco in "The Return of Peter Grimm" (1911), played with the theme of psychic phenomena.

In spite of the crudity of public taste, of producers who kept both eyes on box-office receipts and of mediocre playwrights anxious to please the public, the acting remained on a high level. Mrs. Fiske, John Drew, the Barrymores, David Warfield, Mrs. Leslie Carter, Otis Skinner, Leo Dietrichstein, Henrietta Crosman and many others make up a roster of stars whose work was worthy of better vehicles. Maude Adams was able for years to pack her houses with the fantasies of Barrie and Rostand, while Richard Mansfield, Robert Mantell, Julia Marlowe and E. H. Sothern continued to find a public to support their Shakespearean productions.

The serious drama, interesting as it was and indicative of the trend of the times, was not so much for the multitude as for that more cultivated class which was in tune with the restless humanitarian strivings of the times. The masses demanded something quite different. The great era of swashbuckling was over, but escape could be found in the mystery or detective play, in the rapid-fire comedy or in plays of thickly coated sentimentality. Of all the actors who achieved Broadway stardom none so typified the traditional American spirit as George M. Cohan. Born of a theatrical family in Providence, Rhode Island, in 1878, he was on the stage at the age of nine, playing the title rôle of "Peck's Bad Boy" at twelve. After years of vaudeville trouping with his father, mother and sister, he found himself at the age of eighteen a variety-house star and the author of successful comedy skits and song hits. With incredible rapidity he wrote, produced and starred himself during these years in one musical comedy after another, at the same time allying himself with Sam Harris in the presentation of scores of plays. His critics, sneering at his free use of the American flag, dubbed him the "Yankee-Doodle comedian" and called his plays "entirely inconsequential,"[1] but no one was more adept in pleasing the multitudes by the aged formula of a judicious mixture of tears, laughs and thrills. Far below the Cohan shows was the burlesque, a type of slapstick musical comedy in which vulgarity was stretched to the limit of the law. Most cities of any size supported a burlesque house and in these "Dave" Marion, the lanky coachman, "Sliding Billy" Watson, the quarrelsome Irishman of Krausemeyer's Alley, and the like, could count on uproarious applause from the less fastidious playgoers. Traveling shows featuring melodrama still toured the smaller towns, while Barnum and Bailey's and other circuses had long since become established institutions.

The pleasures of the theater were obviously limited to dwellers in urban communities. The majority of the people, who still lived in small towns and rural districts, continued to find recreation in church festivals, Sunday-school picnics, clambakes and neighborhood parties, enlivened by singing and the usual guessing and kissing games. The Saturday night band concert was a regular feature of many small towns and was as great an attraction to the near-by farmers on their weekly trip to town as the barroom of the hotel.

[1] Hornblow, *Theatre in America*, II, 345-347.

A species of club life for artisans and the smaller professional men was provided in the numerous secret fraternities which flourished mightily during these years. Whether it was the desire for a romantic escape from the drabness of life, an opportunity for relaxation, the ambition of little men to play big rôles in a small organization, the childish desire to parade in fancy uniforms or the hope of business or professional advancement—whatever the causes, fraternal organizations continued to occupy a large place in the everyday life of many Americans, claiming at the close of 1914 over 15,600,000 members in fifty-seven "principal" organizations.[1] The insatiable desire to join something was responsible for the establishment of a new type of social organization during these years: the civic and luncheon clubs. The first Rotary Club, consisting of one representative of each business, profession and institution in the city, was founded in Chicago in 1905, but further development was not rapid until 1912. When the idea caught hold, it found imitators in the Kiwanis (founded 1915), the Lions and other clubs.

No diversion was more popular in America during the first decade of the century than attending expositions. So successful had been the World's Columbian Exposition held in Chicago in 1893 and so great the impression made upon the nation that a succession of similar enterprises resulted. The Trans-Mississippi Exposition, exhibiting the products, industries and life of the states west of the Mississippi, was held in Omaha, Nebraska, in

[1] The Freemasons and Odd Fellows boasted over 1,600,000 members in the United States and Canada, while ten others claimed over 400,000—the Modern Woodmen of America, Knights of Pythias, Independent Order of Rechabites, Order of the Eastern Star, Woodmen of the World, International Order of Good Templars, Red Men and the famous "animal orders" of Moose, Elks, Owls and Eagles. In the case of the Rechabites and Templars the membership was not entirely in the United States. *World Almanac for 1915*, 563.

the summer of 1898. Encouraged by its success and aided by federal and state governments, the citizens of Buffalo organized a Pan-American Exposition to demonstrate the progress of civilization on both continents and launched it in May, 1901. Hardly had it closed its gates in November before the South Carolina Interstate and West Indian Exposition was opened to the public, projected primarily to demonstrate the new industries and commerce of the advancing South. Already ground had been broken for the Louisiana Purchase Exposition to be held at St. Louis to celebrate the hundredth anniversary of the acquisition of Louisiana (opened in 1904); and plans were under way for the Lewis and Clark Exposition at Portland in 1905, the Jamestown Tercentenary Exposition at Hampton Roads in 1907, the Alaska-Yukon-Pacific Exposition at Seattle in 1909, and finally, as a climax, the two expositions at San Francisco and at San Diego in 1915. Nothing comparable was to come for many years.

The motives behind the organization of these expositions were varied. Sectional rivalry played its part, while local pride and desire for profits seized upon the anniversary of some historical event as an excuse. Manufacturers eager to show their wares, localities to exhibit their products, governments or private organizations to carry on education or propaganda, all coöperated to make possible these monster fairs. Each had its special feature —the Indian exhibits of the Trans-Mississippi Exposition, the great electric tower of the Pan-American symbolic of the remarkable electrical advance of America, the Congress of Arts and Sciences at the Louisiana Purchase Exposition and the marine display at Jamestown. In their essentials, however, they were the same; the Chicago fair of 1893 had set the style and the succeeding expositions followed it. "He sees the same general scheme of department buildings," said Robert Grant in comparing the Pan-American with the great earlier exposition, "a brilliant imposing city towering . . . as by the touch of a necromancer's wand; a kindred profusion of boldly imagined and freely executed groups of statuary; an analogous system of waterways; the same old Midway with a few novel features." [1]

Henry Adams, impressed at St. Louis by the fact that a "third rate town of half a million people without history, education, unity or art and with little capital" could do "what London or New York would have shrunk from attempting" and amazed at the gorgeous electrical spectacle, saw the new American as "the servant of the power house as the European of the twelfth century was the servant of the Church." [2] To the average citizen these expositions were not so much a subject for philosophizing as an excuse to take a trip or go on a vacation. Although the migration may have been chiefly for pleasure, the journeyings of millions of people to new sections of the country and their exposure to unusual sights undoubtedly had an important educational influence upon the generation. It symbolized on a grand scale the new America, a nation with leisure to play and with a material culture as yet unmatched in human history.

[1] "Notes on the Pan-American Exposition," *Cosmopolitan*, XXXI (1901), 451. In the same number (476-482) F. P. Dunne, "Mr. Dooley on the Midway," is an excellent example of current humor.

[2] Henry Adams, *The Education of Henry Adams* (Boston, 1918), 466-467.

CHAPTER XIII

THE NEW FRONTIER

THE conclusion of the Spanish-American War put the question of imperialism definitely before the American people. The navy of Spain annihilated, her colonial forces crushed, the terms of peace remained to be written by the American government. That Cuba was to be separated from Spain was a foregone conclusion, but the disposal of her other possessions must still be decided. The protocol of August 12, 1898, which concluded hostilities, provided that Spain should relinquish all claim to the sovereignty of Cuba and, in lieu of pecuniary indemnity, cede Porto Rico and an island in the Ladrones to the United States.[1] The real issue of imperialism, however, rested on the disposal of the Philippines, a group of islands with a combined area of 115,000 square miles and a total population of more than seven and one-half millions. The decision was not long in doubt; imperialistic pressure soon won over the vacillating McKinley, and on November 13 the commissioners were given instructions to demand the cession of the whole of the Philippines.[2]

Primarily a politician, McKinley was undoubtedly correct in assuming that the majority of the voters were

[1] *U. S. Foreign Relations for 1898*, 828-830.

[2] Secretary of State John Hay was an ardent expansionist, and but one of the commissioners, Senator George Gray, was opposed to annexation. McKinley himself became convinced that it was God's will. C. S. Olcott, *Life of William McKinley* (Boston, 1916), II, 109-111. For the instructions, see *U. S. Foreign Relations for 1898*, 937-949.

in favor of territorial expansion, even when it involved the subjection of an alien race in a remote tropical clime, but he also underestimated the opposition. An anti-imperialist agitation of large proportions developed, cradled at a Faneuil Hall meeting in Boston held almost two months before the peace protocol was signed. From the Faneuil Hall meeting emanated the Anti-Imperialist League, which numbered among its active workers prominent citizens of all political persuasions and which for many months carried on an aggressive agitation.[1] Establishing their headquarters in Washington, they circulated petitions against Philippine annexation, which were presented by the thousands to Congress through their senatorial spokesman, George F. Hoar of Massachusetts.[2] So scathing were their denunciations of imperialism that in May, 1899, the postmaster-general ordered three pamphlets written by Edward Atkinson, one of the League's vice-presidents, to be debarred from mails destined for Manila.

The great debate, which ran through the newspapers and magazines for two years, cut into every religious, economic and political group. Though some church leaders ranged themselves against annexation, others, particularly missionaries, felt with McKinley that it was our duty to take the islands, "to educate the Filipinos, and uplift and civilize and Christianize them as our fellow-

[1] The first president, elected on November 19, 1898, was George S. Boutwell, former governor of Massachusetts, ex-secretary of the treasury and ex-senator of the United States. The vice-presidents were Grover Cleveland, George F. Edmunds, John Sherman, Henry Codman Potter, H. S. Pingree, Samuel Gompers, John G. Carlisle, Andrew Carnegie, Charles Francis Adams, Carl Schurz, Reverdy Johnson, Samuel Bowles, Edward Atkinson, James C. Carter, John C. Bullett, Patrick A. Collins, Herbert Myrick and Theodore L. Cuyler. Irving Winslow, "The Anti-Imperialist League," *Independent*, LI, 1347-1350 (May 18, 1899).

[2] G. F. Hoar, *Autobiography of Seventy Years* (N. Y., 1903), II, 304-329.

men for whom Christ also died." [1] On the one hand, representatives of the tobacco, beet-sugar and other agricultural interests fearful of competition, and labor leaders, like Gompers, who feared the menace of cheap Oriental labor, opposed annexation; on the other hand, big business sensed new fields for economic conquest and saw in the Philippines the key to the Far East.[2] While Republican politicians and the powerful Republican newspapers were inclined to follow the administration and the Democrats to oppose, there were no fixed lines. The Hearst papers, which had supported Bryan in 1896, were rampantly imperialistic, as was also the *Louisville Courier-Journal* under the editorship of Henry W. Watterson. The brains of the anti-imperialist agitation were to be found chiefly in the Northeast, but the votes of the twenty-nine senators who opposed the treaty represented many sections.[3]

Bryan, firmly on the anti-imperialist side, had seen the issue as one upon which he might win the next election and had urged Democratic senators to confirm the treaty, thus allowing the question to be fought out in the coming campaign; but he was doomed to disappointment. However doubtfully the intellectuals may have looked upon the establishment of an overseas empire, the masses, if the vote of 1900 is of any significance, felt differently. Flushed with the easy victory over Spain, inflamed by the vision of a colonial empire, many were

[1] Olcott, *Life of McKinley*, II, 109. The pious McKinley apparently overlooked the fact that the Filipinos were already Christians, Roman Catholics, with the exception of a small number of Mohammedan tribesmen.

[2] *Congressional Record*, XXXIII (1900), pt. i, 704.

[3] Anti-imperialism was strong among the intellectuals, including such men as Felix Adler, President David Starr Jordan of the University of California, Professors L. W. Bacon of Yale, L. J. McGinity of Cornell, Hermann von Holst of Chicago, Charles Eliot Norton of Harvard and W. G. Sumner of Yale. "The Anti-Imperialist Position." *Independent*, LXI, 699 (March 25, 1899).

caught by the propaganda for naval power urged by A. T. Mahan and his followers, or were influenced by the call to take up the "white man's burden," or beguiled by the prospect of figuring more prominently among the empires of the world, or else merely followed a habit of adding land which had characterized our entire national existence.[1]

So nicely did this decision meet the needs of American industrial expansion that it is impossible to disregard its economic implications. Until the twentieth century the economic development of the United States had been in part dependent upon European capital. American securities held abroad, which were estimated at one hundred and fifty million dollars in 1840, four hundred million in 1860 and two thousand million in 1880, had grown to three thousand three hundred million by the end of the century, leaving the United States still overwhelmingly in debt.[2] This situation, however, changed rapidly after 1898. With America already producing an economic surplus, the five hundred millions of American foreign investments in 1900 grew to between two and one-half and three billions by 1914.[3] As with Europe, the export of capital from the United States flowed to the more backward nations. The fifty millions of American capital invested in Cuban sugar and tobacco plantations in 1898 was an influence in bringing on the war,[4] and the heavy investments in Mexico and other Latin-

[1] J. B. Moore, *Four Phases of American Development* (Balt., 1912), 147-148.

[2] R. W. Dunn, *American Foreign Investments* (N. Y., 1926), 2; N. T. Bacon, "American International Indebtedness," *Yale Rev.*, IX (1900), 276.

[3] H. E. Fiske, *The Inter-Ally Debts* (N. Y., 1924), 306. Sir George Paish puts the foreign investments in the United States in 1910 at 6000 million in his article in National Monetary Commission, *The Credit of Nations and Trade Balance of the United States* (Wash., 1910), 175.

[4] 55 Cong., 2 sess., *Sen. Rep.*, no. 885, xxi; P. T. Moon, *Imperialism and World Politics* (N .Y., 1926), 416 ff.

American countries in the succeeding years deeply colored American diplomatic policy.[1]

Although America had at last followed the nations of western Europe in embarking upon overseas expansion the first steps were taken cautiously. Pressure for the annexation of Hawaii had been strong for some years before it was finally consummated in 1898. In spite of American investments in Cuba, the United States had entered the war disclaiming any "intention to exercise sovereignty, jurisdiction or control over said Island except for pacification thereof" and asserting "its determination, when that is accomplished, to leave the government and control of the Island to its people." [2] Having once embarked, however, on the path of imperialism it was not easy to turn aside. United States troops were not withdrawn until Cuba had agreed to the Platt amendment by which she consented, among other things, to sell or lease to the United States necessary coaling or naval stations and conceded "the right to intervene for the preservation of Cuban independence, the maintenance of a government adequate for the protection of life, property and individual liberty, and for discharging the obligations" of the treaty of peace with Spain.[3]

Under this sanction the United States, recalling her troops in 1902, returned them again in 1906, 1912 and 1917, in each case at the instigation of American interests for the purpose of protecting American property

[1] Dunn estimates that in 1899 American investments abroad were distributed as follows: 150 million in Canada, 185 million in Mexico, 50 million in Cuba, 10 million in Europe, 55 million in other Latin-American countries, 5 million in China and Japan and 45 million in life-insurance guarantee investments in Russia and elsewhere. Dunn, *American Foreign Investments,* 12.

[2] Teller Resolution of April 19, 1898. *U. S. Foreign Relations for 1898,* liv.

[3] W. M. Malloy, comp., *Treaties, Conventions, etc.* (Wash., 1910), I, 362 ff.

from revolutionary activities.[1] And with each intervention American economic interests tightened their grip. Frank M. Steinhart, once an army sergeant and American consul general at Havana from 1903 to 1907, became the leading financial figure in Cuba, while the resources of the island were rapidly brought under the domination of the National City Bank of New York, which controlled the General Sugar Company, the Consolidated Railways, the Cuba Company and many other corporations and, through its twenty-four branch banks, financed the native sugar growers. Critics of this aggressive policy did not hesitate to assert that "Cuba is no more independent than Long Island." [2]

The annexation of Porto Rico, the establishment of a protectorate over Cuba and the southward movement of American capital again revived the project of a transoceanic canal. Having gained the consent of Great Britain and purchased the rights of the New Panama Canal Company,[3] there remained only the negotiations with the Republic of Colombia, through whose territory the canal was to be cut. Irritated by the failure of Colombia to ratify the Hay-Herran treaty, the American government in November, 1903, took advantage of a revolution in Panama, dispatched American warships to prevent the landing of Colombian troops, and, within fifteen days of the outbreak of the revolt, recognized the Republic of Panama, signed a treaty which gave the desired permission, and obtained a protectorate over Panama. Without American warships there could have been no successful

[1] *U. S. Foreign Relations for 1906*, 473 ff.; *for 1912*, 242 ff.; *for 1917*, 414 ff.; Scott Nearing and Joseph Freeman, *Dollar Diplomacy* (N. Y., 1925), chap. vi; L. H. Jenks, *Our Cuban Colony* (N. Y., 1928), 58-166; C. E. Chapman, *A History of the Cuban Republic* (N. Y., 1927), chap. ix.

[2] A. B. Hart, "The Caribbean Question," Acad. of Polit. Sci., *Proceeds.*, VII, 423.

[3] *U. S. Statutes at Large*, XXXI, pt. i, 481 ff.

revolution and without American guarantee the Republic of Panama could hardly have existed. "From the morning of the 2nd November," says that archconspirator, Philippe Bunau-Varilla, whose influence can be seen throughout, "all of the inhabitants of Colon were looking toward Kingston, hoping for the appearance of the ship symbolizing American protection," and when it actually came, "without one word having been uttered the revolution was accomplished in the hearts of all." [1]

Some eight years later Roosevelt is reported to have said in a speech at Berkeley, California, that he "took the Canal Zone," [2] a phrase which typifies the determined, if not truculent, attitude of the government as it set about to safeguard the routes leading to the Panama Canal and, by establishing a *Pax-Americana,* to allow unhampered exploitation by American economic interests. Typical of the new imperialism were the methods which were adopted toward the Dominican Republic and Haiti, two diminutive nations which share between them the richest and most populous of the West Indian islands and at the same time occupy a strategic position on the trade routes leading to Panama.

From its first independence in 1844 until the definite assumption of an American protectorate in 1907 the career of the Dominican Republic had been one of almost perpetual disturbance, and in this kaleidoscope of revolutions foreign debts had inevitably accumulated. In 1892 an American concern, the San Domingo Improvement

[1] Philippe Bunau-Varilla, *Panama, Its Creation, Destruction and Resurrection* (London, 1913), 247. See also Herbert Croly, *Marcus Alonzo Hanna* (N. Y., 1912), 379; Theodore Roosevelt, *Autobiography* (N. Y., 1913), 567; J. F. Rhodes, *The McKinley and Roosevelt Administrations* (N. Y., 1922), 264; H. C. Hill, *Roosevelt and the Caribbean* (Chicago, 1927), 54; *U. S. Foreign Relations for 1903*, 231.

[2] "Mr. Roosevelt and Panama," *Independent*, LXXI, 828 (Oct. 12, 1911); Theodore Roosevelt, "How the United States Acquired the Right to Dig the Panama Canal," *Outlook*, XCIX, 314-318 (Oct. 7, 1911).

Company, by buying the debt of £170,000 sterling from a Dutch company got its hands on a portion of the obligation with the understanding that it was to be allowed to collect the customs and turn a portion of them over to the Dominican government. This arrangement the island government repudiated in 1901, whereupon the company appealed to the United States. In the resulting negotiations the Dominican government offered to purchase the claim of the American company for $4,500,000, the payments to be secured by customs receipts, and to allow the United States to send a financial agent in case of failure. A protocol to this effect was signed in 1903,[1] and within a year an American financial agent took over the customhouse. Fearing interference by European nations, Roosevelt forced the Dominican government in 1905 to agree to a refunding of the foreign debt and its payment through a receiver of customs appointed by the United States. A treaty incorporating these provisions passed the Senate in 1907, and the refunding was handled by Kuhn, Loeb and Company of New York.[2] Interference in the political life commenced in 1912 when Taft forced the resignation of a president, and culminated with the invasion of the marines in 1916 and an American military dictatorship, 1916-1924.[3]

The other end of the island, occupied by the Negro republic of Haiti, had a political history quite as stormy as that of its neighbor, but it took care to pay its debts, and no American citizen appears to have been injured in life or property up to the time of occupation. The National Bank of Haiti, founded by French capital, had in 1881 been intrusted with the administration of the Hai-

[1] Malloy, *Treaties, Conventions, etc.*, I, 414-418.

[2] Malloy, *Treaties, Conventions, etc.*, I, 418-420.

[3] M. M. Knight, *The Americans in Santo Domingo*, (N. Y., 1928). 40 ff

tian treasury, but upon its reorganization in 1910 Secretary of State Philander C. Knox insisted upon the injection of American capital, and four New York banks became subscribers. In 1914, because of political disturbances, the United States government suggested several times the establishment of a relationship after the manner of the Dominican treaty of 1907, but was repeatedly refused. Weary of waiting for a voluntary surrender of independence, the United States landed marines on December 10, 1914, who removed five hundred thousand dollars from the National Bank of Haiti, and on July 28, 1915, definitely inaugurated military occupation. After thorough intimidation a puppet president and puppet legislators ratified in November a treaty by which American supervision of Haitian finances was provided for, a native constabulary commanded by American officers established, and the United States empowered to intervene for the preservation of Haitian independence or to insure an orderly government.[1] To enforce this treaty military occupation was continued. In a somewhat similar manner was American capitalism in the Republic of Nicaragua safeguarded and the control over the northern canal route secured by a treaty of 1914.[2]

It was comparatively easy to ride roughshod over the tiny republics of Central America and the Caribbean, but the problem of dealing with Mexico was more complicated. Endowed with great mineral and agricultural riches and cheap labor to exploit them, Mexico offered a rich prize for concession hunters. As early as 1902 American investors, it was estimated, had placed five

[1] U. S. Senate Select Committee, *Inquiry into Occupation and Administration of Haiti and Santo Domingo* (67 Cong., 1922), I, 204-207. See also Carl Kelsey, "American Intervention in Haiti and Santo Domingo," Am. Acad. of Polit. and Social Sci., *Annals*, C, 109-202.

[2] Americans remained in Nicaragua from 1912 to 1925. See I. J. Cox, "Nicaragua and the United States, 1909-1927," World Peace Found., *Pamphlets*, X, 710-782.

hundred million dollars in Mexican railroads, plantations, mines and other industries, an investment which more than doubled in the next ten years owing chiefly to the rapid development of the Mexican oil fields under the leadership of Edward L. Doheny. By 1910 approximately eighty per cent of investments in Mexican railroads were American and close to seventy per cent of the Mexican oil was being taken out by American firms.[1] This rapid economic penetration had been encouraged by Porfirio Diaz, Mexico's strong man, who by the most ruthless methods had retained power for more than a quarter of a century, during which time he had maintained domestic peace and granted concessions with a lavish hand.

The revolution of 1910, which ended the despotism of the aged Diaz, was primarily an uprising of an exploited peasantry, but the conflict of foreign economic interests can be traced throughout. Diaz in his later years, regretting the too rapid development of American oil investments, sought to neutralize it by aiding the English under Lord Cowdray and, as a consequence, it was believed that the rebel leader Madero was encouraged, if not in part financed, by American oil men.[2] At all events, Madero was quickly recognized by the American government, and on March 14, 1912, President Taft prohibited the purchase of arms and munitions in the United States by factions opposing the Madero government. In spite of this aid Victoriano Huerta, a counter-revolutionist, overthrew Madero, had him assassinated and assumed power. Although Huerta gave evidence of ability to maintain himself and of becoming a business man's president, American oil men believed him to be a tool of

[1] Dunn, *American Foreign Investments,* 90 ff.
[2] U. S. Senate Committee on Foreign Relations, *Revolutions in Mexico* (62 Cong., 2 sess., 1913), 750.

the English interests, and supported a revolution headed by Carranza to oust him. At the same time President Wilson, shocked by Huerta's harsh methods, bent every effort to eliminate him. England's desertion of Huerta was facilitated by a promise to repeal discriminatory canal tolls,[1] the embargo on arms was lifted in February, 1914, to aid the revolutionists,[2] and finally on April 21, 1914, Wilson ordered the occupation of Vera Cruz.

The capture of Vera Cruz cost the lives of seventeen American marines and bluejackets and of two hundred Mexican men, women and children, but it ended the political power of Huerta. It did not, however, end the troubles of the United States. A second armed expedition into Mexico was undertaken in 1916 to punish Villa, who was conducting a revolution against Carranza, and finally, when Mexico was relatively pacified, Carranza was ungrateful enough to support the Constitution of 1917 with its clauses aiming to safeguard Mexican mineral rights in the future.

Although the "dollar diplomacy" of Secretary Knox may seem more ruthless than the "moral diplomacy" of Wilson and Bryan, American policy in Latin America was essentially the same under Roosevelt, Taft and Wilson. The conquest of Porto Rico; the acquisition by treaty of the Great Corn and Little Çorn islands, the naval stations at Guantanamo, Cuba, at Mole St. Nicholas, Haiti, at Samana Bay, Santo Domingo, and in the Gulf of Fonseca; and the erection of protectorates over Cuba, Panama, the Dominican Republic, Nicaragua and Haiti—all this, along with wholesale economic penetration, made the Caribbean an "American

[1] Charles Seymour, ed., *The Intimate Papers of Colonel House* (Boston, 1926-1928), I, 192-201.

[2] *U. S. Foreign Relations for 1914*, 447-448.

lake." By the opening of the World War America's first "sphere of influence" had been achieved.

While American imperialism was making rapid strides in the Caribbean a new economic frontier was being established in the Far East. American interests in the Orient had existed since the voyages of the Salem merchantmen in the early days of the republic, but it was the acquisition of the Philippines that made us an active participator in the spoils of the Far East. Although the United States was forced not only to conquer the Philippines from Spain but to put down a costly native rebellion lasting three years, she did not hesitate. Roseate dreams of "the fabulous trade of the twentieth century" [1] and of "China's illimitable markets" [2] may not have been the determining factor in the decision to retain the Philippines, but they richly supplemented the moral considerations of the imperialists.[3] The Philippines were but a stepping-stone to the greatest economic prize of the Orient, the resources and trade of China. For decades European nations had been hacking away at Chinese territory, a business in which Japan had joined after her war with China in 1894-1895, and as the century drew to a close the partition of China was taken up with renewed zeal. In this territorial disintegration the United States had no desire to participate if her interests could be otherwise protected. While of necessity she must recognize spheres of influence and special interests already existing, it was possible to insist upon an equal opportunity to trade and this John Hay did (1899) in his formal declaration of the "open-door" policy.[4]

[1] Whitelaw Reid, *Problems of Expansion* (N. Y., 1900), 142.

[2] Speech of Senator Beveridge in *Congressional Record,* XXXIII (1900), pt. i, 704.

[3] See McKinley's speech in Boston, Feb. 16, 1899. *Boston Herald,* Feb. 17, 1899.

[4] *U. S. Foreign Relations for 1899,* 128 ff.

Hardly had the principle been enunciated before it was tested. In 1900 an antiforeign and reactionary group of Chinese, popularly known as the Boxers, started a movement to rid China of foreigners, an uprising which necessitated an allied expeditionary force consisting of Japanese, Russian, German, French, British and American troops, and involved the inevitable question of punishment and indemnities. Hay seized the opportunity to reaffirm his open-door policy, urging the great powers to coöperate in bringing about permanent safety and peace to China and in preserving Chinese territorial and administrative entity.[1] America's interests coincided with those of the Chinese, and this country was looked upon by many as the savior of China. Friendship between the two nations was further promoted by the remission on the part of the American government of a portion of the so-called "Boxer Indemnity," which was devoted to sending Chinese students to American colleges.[2]

Behind these diplomatic gestures economic penetration proceeded. Already (1898-1900) the American China Development Company had obtained the contract for building the southern section of a railroad from Peking to Canton, and other American firms were engaged in trade or exploitation.[3] American financial concerns were particularly interested in Manchuria, for here it was that Harriman was anxious to extend his railroad operations and here he and powerful American bankers negotiated for the creation of a great bank to foster railroad and industrial development. These negotiations failed only because of the death in 1908 of the emperor and the fall of the party in power, but earlier and later efforts in

[1] *U. S. Foreign Relations for 1901*, app., 12.

[2] L. F. Abbott, *Impressions of Theodore Roosevelt* (Garden City, 1919), 433 ff.; *U. S. Foreign Relations for 1908*, 68.

[3] J. V. A. MacMurray, ed., *Treaties and Agreements with and concerning China, 1894-1919* (N. Y., 1921), I, 519-522.

Manchuria were invariably checkmated by other nations.[1] When in May, 1909, the Chinese government made the agreement with German, French and British bankers for a loan to build the Hukuang railroad, it was only the insistence of the American state department and a personal message from Taft to the Chinese regent which opened the way for American participation.[2] In the same year the Morgan bankers through their agent, Willard Straight, agreed with the Manchurian authorities to finance a railroad to be built by an English firm.[3]

The American state department, believing the opportunity was present to break the Russian and Japanese monopoly of Manchuria, suggested that the interested nations—Great Britain, Germany, Japan and Russia—join with the United States in advancing a great international loan to China to bring the Manchurian railroads under an impartial administration with Chinese ownership.[4] Japan and Russia objected, Great Britain and France backed up their respective allies, and the project failed, the chief result being a *rapprochement* between Japan and Russia and an effort in the face of a common foe to iron out their differences. Even this did not discourage American bankers who, in conjunction with Great Britain, Germany, Russia and Japan, offered China a loan of fifty million dollars upon the security of certain taxes. "Dollar diplomacy is justified at last," wrote Straight, who had been the guiding hand in the negotiations.[5] But the six-power loan was never consummated. However enthusiastic Taft and Knox may have

[1] H. D. Croly, *Willard Straight* (N. Y., 1924), 239 ff.; J. O. P. Bland, *Recent Events and Present Policies in China* (Phila., 1912), 306 ff.

[2] *U. S. Foreign Relations for 1909*, 178.

[3] MacMurray, *Treaties and Agreements*, 800-802.

[4] *U. S. Foreign Relations for 1910*, 234.

[5] Croly, *Willard Straight*, 402.

been for "dollar diplomacy," President Wilson declined to aid in putting China in the same position as Nicaragua, asserting that "the responsibility on the part of our government implied in the encouragement of a loan thus secured and administered is plain enough and is obnoxious to the principles upon which the government of our people rests." [1]

The United States embarked upon imperialism boldly but at the same time in a serious frame of mind. While she did not hesitate to crush the Philippine insurrection and transfer a subject people from one alien jurisdiction to another, she made a sincere effort to improve the welfare of the insular population, an effort undoubtedly stimulated by criticism of the anti-imperialist minority at home. To the Philippines a distinguished commission under the chairmanship of Jacob G. Schurman was sent in 1899 to investigate conditions and adopt a policy which would lead to self-government, and in 1900 a second commission led by William H. Taft was sent to organize a civil government. By an act of July 1, 1902, Congress provided that two years after the taking of a census a government should be set up in which the lower house of the legislature should be elective. Such a legislature was finally established in 1907, and in 1916 by the Jones act the Philippines were given the power to elect the upper as well as the lower house as preliminary to eventual freedom.[2] In a similar manner the Porto Ricans were allowed by an act of Congress in 1900 to elect the lower house of their legislature and in 1917 their upper house.[3]

Prosperity such as these islands had never known came to them as a result of American occupation. In spite

[1] *American Journal of International Law,* VII (1913), 338.
[2] *U. S. Statutes at Large,* XXXIX, 545 ff.
[3] *U. S. Statutes at Large,* XXXIX, 951 ff.

of the fact that the typical governor of Porto Rico was a political henchman who had little interest in problems of colonial government and who rarely held office for more than a year or so,[1] remarkable progress was made.[2] Transportation facilities were improved by the building of roads, railroads and telegraph lines, and a radical program to promote health and sanitation was embarked upon. Simultaneously an aggressive educational program was launched. Only a handful of the children in Porto Rico attended school at the time of the American conquest, but a public-school system was soon established which by 1920 had an enrollment of nearly half the total population of school age, as Americans would regard it, and nine tenths of those of compulsory school age, an achievement which was in large measure due to pioneer efforts of the sociologist, Samuel McCune Lindsay, commissioner of education in Porto Rico, 1902-1904.[3]

In the Philippines the immensity of the task challenged the home government and a succession of able administrators were dispatched to cope with the problem. The first commissions under Schurman and Taft viewed the situation in a statesmanlike way, and the civil governors, Taft, Luke E. Wright, W. C. Forbes and Francis B. Harrison, labored strenuously for the best interests of the subject people. It was as governor-general of the Philippines, in the opinion of many, that Taft made his greatest contribution. Physical and sanitary reconstruction bulked large in the American efforts as did also the attention given to popular education. In Porto Rico instruction was offered in both English and Spanish, but in the Philippines it was decided that English

[1] Arthur Yager, governor from 1913 to 1921, was a notable exception.
[2] Governor of Porto Rico, *Report for 1919*, 53.
[3] J. J. Osuna, "Education in Porto Rico," I. L. Kandel, ed., *Twenty-Five Years of American Education* (N. Y., 1924), 439.

was the best medium through which the speakers of various dialects might be united. The establishment in the short span of a quarter of a century of a modern school system in a country of three thousand islands and of ten million people speaking many diverse dialects, and in the face of unfavorable social, political and economic conditions, was an effort toward the civilization of a backward people probably unprecedented.[1]

Nor were these civilizing efforts limited to American colonies. In some form or other they were also extended to the protectorates. The work of Reed and Gorgas in Cuba and of Gorgas in Panama [2] foreshadowed similar measures to improve living conditions in Haiti and the Dominican Republic. Sanitary improvements of all sorts, including the draining of mosquito-breeding places, were accomplished; waterworks and distributing systems were overhauled and repaired; good roads connecting the chief centers were constructed; telegraph and telephone lines were set up; the postal system was improved, scientific agriculture encouraged and assistance and support given to modernize the school system.[3] The improvement of sanitary conditions and transportation facilities was, of course, necessary to imperialistic exploitation, but the extension of educational facilities involved an almost certain danger that these backward peoples would resent American paternalism. In reality, the whole program of colonial improvement was in no small degree the result of an idealistic sense of responsibility toward less civilized peoples resembling in part the missionary impulse

[1] Gildo Masso, "Education in the Philippine Islands," Kandel, *Twenty-Five Years of American Education*, 447-457. The Bureau of Insular Affairs estimated the population in 1918 at 10,314,000. See also W. C. Forbes, *The Philippine Islands* (Boston, 1928), I, 61-512.

[2] See earlier, 230-232.

[3] U. S. Senate Select Committee, *Haiti and Santo Domingo*, II, 1749-1752.

which actuated the various Protestant denominations a century before.[1]

Imperialism could not fail to leave its imprint upon American civilization. The spectacle of American troops crushing a Philippine movement for independence was repugnant to liberty-loving citizens, while the denial to subject peoples of civil and political rights which were enjoyed at home could not in the long run fail to blunt that eternal vigilance which is the price of liberty. Nor was the ease with which the Constitution was made to subserve the interests of annexation in the insular cases conducive to heightening respect for the judiciary.[2] Furthermore, this adventure in imperialism necessitated heavy financial expenditures and committed the nation for an indefinite period to larger military and naval establishments.

Along with these disadvantages, however, came the usual fruits of imperialism. Trade with Latin America, with the Far East and with our colonial possessions and protectorates increased. As the American sphere of influence widened in the Caribbean, Latin America was inclined to turn her eyes from Europe toward her northern neighbor and to send her sons in increasing numbers to American schools and colleges. In the United States the new interest in Latin America gave great stimulus to the study of Spanish, especially in the high schools of commerce. The country both gained and contributed through the new discoveries in tropical medicine.[3]

In the midst of the ardor and worry of imperialism it

[1] Gustavus Myers, *The History of American Idealism* (N. Y., 1925), chaps. xv-xvi; D. R. Fox, *The Completion of Independence* (*A History of American Life*, V).

[2] The most important of these cases were De Lima *v.* Bidwell, 182 U. S., 1, and Downes *v.* Bidwell, 182 U. S., 244. These and other insular cases are collected in *The Insular Cases* (56 Cong., 2 sess., *House Doc.*, no. 509).

[3] See earlier, chap. x

was interesting to see a strong revival of the American peace movement. The demand for world peace, of course, was not limited to this country, being international in its scope. It had been strengthened by the rapid growth of international socialism, by the rising tide of humanitarianism, by the economic arguments of such men as the Englishman Norman Angell, by the tightening web of international business and finance, and by the inevitable development of a better understanding among various peoples as science and invention lessened the obstacles of intercourse. Peace organizations multiplied rapidly after 1898, the old American Peace Society again forging to the fore; and chiefly through its impetus national peace congresses were held in New York in 1907, in Chicago in 1909, in Baltimore in 1911 and in St. Louis in 1913.

For the first time such efforts had the approval and support not only of derided idealists but also of practical men of affairs. In 1910 Edwin Ginn, head of a well-known textbook publishing house and a lifelong believer in peace through education, established the World Peace Foundation with Edwin D. Mead as secretary and an endowment of one million dollars; and later in the same year Andrew Carnegie donated ten million dollars, the revenue of which was to be administered "to hasten the abolition of international war, the foulest blot upon our civilization." [1] Carnegie went a step farther in 1914 when he created an endowment of two million dollars to finance a Church Peace Union to carry on propaganda for "world organization, justice, and peace," [2] an institution warmly supported by the Federal Council of the Churches of Christ in America which

[1] Carnegie Endowment for International Peace, *Year Book for 1911*, 1.
[2] S. L. Gulick and C. S. Macfarland, *The Church and International Relations* (N. Y., 1917), II, 7.

since 1911 had maintained its own Commission on Peace and Arbitration. To reach the younger generation the American School Peace League was founded by Mrs. Fannie Fern Andrews in 1908.[1] By 1913, eighty peace societies operated in this country,[2] while other forces, such as the famous Lake Mohonk conferences, founded in 1895, were also contributing to the cause. Elaborate plans were under way for the celebration in 1915 of a hundred years of peace between the two English-speaking peoples when the catastrophe of the World War came as a tragic dénouement.

The work of the peace societies, of course, did not go unchecked. In particular they had to meet the propaganda of the Navy League, organized in 1903 by retired navy officers, armor-plate manufacturers and others, and closely interlocked through its board of directors with New York banking houses interested in foreign loans.[3] Its demand for a big navy was ably forwarded by such Spanish War heroes as Robley D. Evans and Richmond P. Hobson, who carried the gospel of greater armament to audiences throughout the country. The work of the Navy League bore much fruit, for its friends were powerful and its principles popular. The Spanish War and the writings of Mahan had paved the way; both political parties advocated an adequate navy, while Roosevelt, friendly as he might be to the peace movement, was a thorough believer in the theory that armaments promote peace.

In spite of the propaganda of the big-navy group, the agitation of the peace societies in the end had its effect upon the politicians. It was the Interparliamentary Union, composed of members of various national legis-

[1] American School Peace League, *First Annual Report* (1909), 11.

[2] W. B. Stevens, ed., *Book of the Fourth American Peace Congress* (St. Louis, 1913), 12.

[3] C. H. Tavenner, *The Navy League Exposed* (Wash., 1906).

latures, which first backed the project of a Hague Conference in 1899, although it was the Czar of Russia who issued the invitation. The initiative for the conference of 1907 came from President Roosevelt and the invitation again from the Czar of Russia. Declining at both conferences to join with the other civilized nations in declaring against dumdum bullets and asphyxiating gases, the United States in all other respects entered with enthusiasm into the work for peace. Especially strong was the American attitude in favor of arbitration,[1] and the first case presented to the Hague Tribunal was the dispute between the United States and Mexico over the Pious Funds of California (1902).

Between 1908 and 1910 America signed no less than twenty-five arbitration treaties, of which twenty-two became effective, providing over a five-year period for the arbitration of matters of a purely legal nature or those involving the interpretation of treaties if they did not affect the honor, independence or vital interests of the parties or a third party. Though the treaties were hardly more than expressions in favor of arbitration, they were a step in the right direction. When Taft, however, in 1911 negotiated treaties for unlimited arbitration with Great Britain and France, they were so emasculated by the Senate that he refused to send them to Europe for ratification.[2]

A new impetus for arbitration came from Wilson's secretary of state, Bryan, who urged that all questions which had failed of diplomatic settlement should be referred to an international commission for investigation and report, the nations in dispute refraining meanwhile from hostilities. Given permission by Wilson to go ahead

[1] J. B. Scott, ed., *Instructions to the American Delegates to the Hague Peace Conferences and Their Official Reports* (N. Y., 1916).

[2] "Arbitration and the United States," World Peace Found., *Pamphlets*, IX, 513-533.

with his "cooling-off" treaties, Bryan effected arrangements embodying this principle with thirty-five countries by the end of 1914.[1] While the Roosevelt, Taft and Wilson administrations, especially the first two, were not averse to playing the game of "dollar diplomacy," all three were anxious to promote international amity. Wilson, in fact, had some presentiment of the impending World War and made an effort to ward it off.[2] But forces over which American peace propagandists and American presidents unfortunately had slight control brought on the disaster of 1914.

America's entrance upon the path of imperialism marked her arrival at economic maturity. But there were other indications pointing to the fact that America had come of age. The older theories of *laissez faire*, so beloved by the classical economists, no longer fitted the more intricate civilization of the new age, and unrestricted individualism was breaking down in every phase of human activity. It had failed in the economic world and the great wave of industrial consolidation which ushered in the new century was in part a recognition by private business of the disasters of untrammeled competition. While big business thus sought to save itself, the nation as a whole demanded protection from these great aggregations of wealth and, through state and federal legislation, endeavored to extend some measure of effective public control over economic life. At the same time the government itself, through the parcels post and the postal-savings bank, extended its own business operations, and through its various bureaus offered agriculture and industry a service of ever increasing value.

[1] Thirty actually signed the treaties. W. F. Johnson, *America's Foreign Relations* (N. Y., 1916), II, chap. xxxvi.

[2] B. J. Hendrick, *Life and Letters of Walter H. Page* (Garden City, 1922), I, 270-300.

Its willingness to employ experts and to partake in the conservation movement was not only a reflection of the spirit of the time, but an object lesson to the nation. Investigations and surveys—official and private—of labor, immigration, trusts, banking, internal waterways and other problems were an indication that leaders of public opinion valued the scientific approach and were finally in a mood to take sober stock of the nation's resources. And in this greater appreciation of the value of science, private business was at the forefront.

Not since the decade of the thirties and forties had America experienced such a wave of reform as flowed over the country in the early years of the century. Even among leaders of large enterprises a new spirit appeared. The bitter attacks of the Muckrakers and the drive for social control made many business leaders see a new light. A sense of responsibility to the community was developing far different from the economic brigandage which had ushered in the century. America had become too big and life had become too complicated for the old freedom and the old independence.

In politics reform no longer concerned itself merely with the uprooting of personal dishonesty, the elimination of an Ames or a Ruef; it presented model charters and advocated commission government. It was no longer satisfied with turning out the villains, but sought to exercise future control through the initiative, the referendum and the recall. The new social consciousness not merely reacted to the exposures of the Muckrakers, but it revealed a humanitarianism committed to intelligent institutional reconstruction. The drive against the slums, against the ruthless exploitation of the labor of women and children, against the waste of life in industry, against the liquor evil and adulterated foods, resulted in legislative codes which did much to improve conditions. Specific measures were often far from perfect, and reform at times overreached itself, but the progress was one of which any generation might be proud.

The willingness soberly to take stock of American civilization and the desire of large elements to improve it also implied an intellectual maturity which introduced a refreshing realism into many institutions. While new sects and strange dogmas continued to find adherents, the older churches turned from theological controversy to contemplate the existing social order, and prospered only as they caught the new spirit. As a whole, the church was less inclined to dwell upon the glories of a future life and more upon the possibility of making this one endurable. Forward-looking educators, eyeing critically the whole educational system, no longer went into ecstasies over the little red schoolhouse, but with the aid of experimental schools and the new psychology tried to improve conditions. Meantime teachers and students in the higher institutions were approaching the whole range of social studies with a new realism. Surcharging the whole intellectual atmosphere were the discoveries of science and their practical application and, unconscious as many scientists may have been of the social implications of their work, the generation in which they lived was alert to turn the new knowledge to human betterment.

The quest for social justice was not wholly indigenous either in its conception or in its execution. The transit of civilization so evident in our earlier history continued unabated into the twentieth century. While foreign leadership in the fine arts had always been acknowledged, we now turned to western Europe as a schoolmaster in the field of human relations and as a leader in the development of new governmental institutions. Scientific city government, the initiative, the referendum. woman suffrage and other forms of the new democracy had already been tried abroad. Western Europe had preceded us with the income tax, the parcels post, scientific banking methods, workingmen's compensation, social legislation, and with government control of business. It preceded us with university settlements and Red Cross stamps just as it did with gasoline engines and modernistic art. It speaks volumes for the intelligence and broad patriotism of this generation that it recognized the worth of foreign innovations and so readily adapted them. Probably never since the time of the early colonial period had the importation of European methods been more conscious or so widely approved.

While the spirit of the time was critical, it was not one of morbid probing into the sores of the body politic; nor was it one of discouragement. Like France during her revolution, America set herself to the task of reform with buoyancy and enthusiasm, and the men of this generation applied themselves to the work of reconstruction with the same confidence that their forefathers had shown in the building of railroads and the conquest of the frontier. But sympathetic as were the masses to a better America their chief energies were concentrated upon the task of carrying on the economic life, and with an ever increasing tempo raw materials were being exploited and wealth created. The distribution of this wealth may have been as unequal in 1914 as in 1898, but there was relatively more of it per capita, and the constant effort at reform had made the nation a better place to live in for the common man.

CHAPTER XIV

Critical Essay on Authorities

PHYSICAL SURVIVALS

THOUGH not yet far removed in time, an increasing amount of nondocumentary material of the period from 1898 to 1914 is finding its way into such repositories as the United States National Museum under the direction of the Smithsonian Institution in Washington, where the Langley airplane is on exhibit, and the Ford Museum at Dearborn, Michigan, which is rich in exhibits of transportation. Industrial museums maintained by such concerns as the American Steel and Wire Company at Worcester, Massachusetts, the Bethlehem Steel Company, the New York Central Railroad and the Baltimore and Ohio are also valuable for tracing the history of invention.

Structural remains appear on every hand and, as many public buildings are dated, it is easy to place them chronologically. By comparing the Singer Building, the Woolworth Building and the Metropolitan Tower in New York City, constructed at the end of the first decade, with the Flatiron Building, completed in 1902, it is possible to note the development in skyscraper architecture over a brief period. The Grand Central and Pennsylvania terminals in New York and the Union Station in Washington represent the new mode in railway stations. The new factories of reënforced concrete with large wall space of glass can be seen in any industrial center, a good example being the plant of the Naumkeag Mills at Salem, Massachusetts. Of government buildings the state capitols of Minnesota and Pennsylvania may serve as illustrations. A brilliant example of municipal bridge building is the Manhattan Bridge in New York, which was opened in

1909, and of industrial bridge building the Tunkhannock Viaduct of the Delaware, Lackawanna and Western Railroad. The revamped Erie Canal, known as the Barge Canal, is almost entirely the work of this period, as is also the Cape Cod Ship Canal, completed in 1914. The San Pedro, Los Angeles and Salt Lake Railroad was built during these years, as were the earlier units of the New York subway. Near the larger cities may be found suburban developments, perhaps the most famous of which is Shaker Heights at Cleveland, which were laid out and built since 1898, and where illustrations of all types of small dwelling houses abound.

Examples of the work of painters and other exponents of the graphic arts are preserved in the Metropolitan Museum of Art in New York, the Museum of Fine Arts in Boston, the Corcoran Art Gallery in Washington, the Art Institute of Chicago, the Detroit Institute of Arts, the City Art Museum of St. Louis and other galleries. The work of the sculptors Ward, Saint Gaudens, French, MacMonnies and others may be seen either in the same museums or in the places suggested earlier in chapter xi. For pictorial source material the years after the turn of the century are particularly rich. Mechanical processes had so cheapened the reproduction of photographs and other pictures that most of the popular magazines were lavishly illustrated, a condition which was to be changed during the World War owing to the high cost of labor and materials. For pictures illustrating almost all phases of civilization, see R. H. Gabriel, ed., *The Pageant of America* (15 vols., New Haven, 1926-1929).

GENERAL BIBLIOGRAPHY

F. J. Turner and Frederick Merk, eds., *List of References on the History of the West* (Cambridge, 1922), and L. B. Schmidt, *Topical Studies and References on the Economic History of American Agriculture* (rev. edn., Phila., 1923), are rich in references to the literature of recent years. An exhaustive bibliography of labor is appended to J. R. Commons and others, *History of Labour in the United States* (2 vols.,

N. Y., 1918). A detailed bibliography of the Negro has been compiled by M. N. Work, ed., *Bibliography of the Negro in Africa and America* (N. Y., 1928). The Library of Congress has sponsored a number of bibliographies including A. P. C. Griffin, ed., *Selected List of Books on Municipal Affairs with Special Reference to Municipal Ownership* (Wash., 1906). Volumes XXV and XXVII of the *American Nation: a History* (28 vols., N. Y., 1904-1917)—J. H. Latané, *America as a World Power, 1897-1907,* and F. A. Ogg, *National Progress, 1907-1917*—issued under the editorship of A. B. Hart, note the main sources. The bibliographies in the volumes of the *Chronicles of America Series* (50 vols., N. Y., 1918-1921), edited by Allen Johnson, are briefer, but suggest some of the later books. The *Dictionary of American Biography* (20 vols., N. Y., 1928-), edited by Allen Johnson and Dumas Malone, includes bibliographical material.

PERIODICAL LITERATURE

In no period of American history is the periodical literature more important to the historian. Of the weeklies the *Nation* (N. Y., 1865-) under the editorship of Paul Elmer More (1909-1914) continued to give independent and discriminating, though rather conservative, editorial comment on current events. More popular was the *Independent* (N. Y., 1848-1928, when it was combined with the *Outlook*), whose interests became less religious and more political, and which was mildly progressive in tone. The *Outlook* (N. Y., 1893-), under the editorship of Lyman Abbott, with Roosevelt added as associate editor after he retired from the presidency, was both theologically and politically progressive. The *Literary Digest* (N. Y., 1890-) is invaluable to the historian for its summaries of contemporary editorial opinion. The *New Republic* (N. Y., 1914-), with a brilliant staff of editors headed by Herbert Croly, quickly took its place as the ablest progressive weekly. *Harper's Weekly* (N. Y., 1857-1916) is useful for its editorial comment and pictures, as are *Life* (N. Y., 1883-), *Puck* (N. Y., 1877-

1918) and *Judge* (N. Y., 1881-) for the light they throw on the foibles of the time.

Of the monthly magazines the *North American Review*, edited after 1899 by George Harvey, ran to rather heavy articles on contemporary politics. The *Atlantic Monthly* (Boston, 1857-), under the editorship of Bliss Perry, 1899-1909, and then under Ellery Sedgwick, was literary rather than political, but contained many articles on contemporary problems. The *Century* (N. Y., 1881-), edited from 1881 to 1909 by Richard Watson Gilder, *Harper's* (N. Y., 1850-), edited by Henry M. Alden, and *Scribner's* (N. Y., 1887-) were all high-class illustrated literary magazines. Perhaps *Scribner's*, which contained monthly comment for many years on contemporary art, is the most rewarding to the historian. On the other hand, the muckraking magazines, including *McClure's* (N. Y., 1893-), under the direction of S. S. McClure; the *Cosmopolitan* (N. Y., 1886-), edited by John Brisben Walker; *Munsey's* (N. Y., 1889-); *Collier's* (N. Y., 1877-); and the *American* (combined with *Frank Leslie's* in Sept., 1905, and edited by a group of seceders from the McClure staff) are invaluable for their articles on contemporary problems. Magazines devoted to special interests should be consulted also, particularly the *Theatre* (N. Y., 1901-); *American Architect* (N. Y., 1876-); *Architectural Review* (N. Y., 1891-); *Architectural Record* (N. Y., 1891-); and *House Beautiful* (Boston, 1891-).

The *New York Times* (1851-), which in 1896 came under the control of Adolph S. Ochs, had become by 1914 the leading American newspaper, though its chief value was in its voluminous news service rather than in its editorial comment, which was generally conservative. The *New York Tribune* (1841-1924), under the direction of Whitelaw Reid, 1872-1905, was as rabidly partisan as under Horace Greeley, but its influence was declining. The *New York Herald* (1835; since 1924 the *Herald-Tribune*), still dominated by the Bennetts, had lost its influence, appealing chiefly to the sporting element. The *New York World* (N. Y.,

1860-), under the control of the Pulitzers and edited by Frank I. Cobb, took the leadership among the liberal newspapers. Other papers of strength, independence and wide influence were the *Louisville Courier-Journal* under Henry W. Watterson, the *Springfield Republican* under the third Samuel Bowles and Solomon B. Griffin, the *Kansas City Star* under William Rockhill Nelson and the *San Francisco Bulletin* under Fremont Older. These newspapers, great because of their editors, were, however, exceptions. The average paper was little more than a party organ or an advertising medium for personal gain, newspapers of which the widely read *Chicago Tribune* (1847-) is perhaps the outstanding example.

General histories include J. M. Lee, *History of American Journalism* (rev. edn., Boston, 1923), and W. G. Bleyer, *Main Currents in the History of American Journalism* (Boston, 1927), informative but not critical. See also D. F. Wilcox, "The American Newspaper: a Study in Social Psychology," Am. Acad. of Polit. and Soc. Sci., *Annals*, XVI, 56-92, and for the darker side Upton Sinclair, *The Brass Check* (Chicago, 1920). Algernon Tassin, *The Magazine in America* (N. Y., 1916), contains material on the period since 1898. O. G. Villard, *Some Newspapers and Newspaper Men* (N. Y., 1923), is a keen appraisal by a newspaper man of some of his contemporaries. For particular newspapers or magazines, see F. M. O'Brien, *The Story of the Sun* (rev. edn., N. Y., 1928); Elmer Davis, *History of the New York Times* (N. Y., 1921); Allan Nevins, *The Evening Post: a Century of Journalism* (N. Y., 1922); Providence Journal Company, *Half a Century with the Providence Journal* (Providence, 1904); Richard Hooker, *The Story of an Independent Newspaper* (N. Y., 1924), a history of the *Springfield Republican;* and M. A. DeWolfe Howe, *The Atlantic Monthly and Its Makers* (Boston, 1909).

DOCUMENTARY SOURCES

The documentary source material for recent years becomes so enormous that it is only possible to list a few collections.

In I. G. Mudge, ed., *Guide to Reference Books* (5th edn., Chicago, 1929), 270-278, there is a list of catalogues and indexes of government documents. Besides the *Congressional Record,* necessary in following legislative progress, and the publications of the Bureau of the Census, essential for statistical data, nearly every department has issued reports and bulletins which are important in a study of social history. Of particular value are the *Bulletins* of the Bureau of Labor, which include some of the more scholarly work done on the labor problem during the period. Indispensable also are the reports of other departments and special commissions, many of which are noted in later sections of this chapter.

The number of usable source books is rapidly increasing. On labor, see P. H. Douglas, C. N. Hitchcock and W. E. Atkins, eds., *The Worker in Modern Economic Society* (Chicago, 1923), and D. J. Saposs, ed., *Readings in Trade Unionism* (N. Y., 1925), the latter dealing primarily with the philosophy and policy of trade unionism. A valuable source book on immigration is that by Edith Abbott, ed., *Immigration: Select Documents and Case Records* (Chicago, 1924). On general economic history, material on these years is incorporated in E. L. Bogart and C. M. Thompson, eds., *Readings on the Economic History of the United States* (N. Y., 1916); Felix Flügel and H. U. Faulkner, eds., *Readings in the Social and Economic History of the United States* (N. Y., 1929), containing also a general bibliography of American economic history; and L. C. Marshall, ed., *Readings in Industrial Society* (Chicago, 1923). Brief but generally accurate contemporary reviews of current history are given in the *International Year Book* (N. Y., 1898-1901), continued as the *New International Year Book* (N. Y., 1907-). The *American Year Book* (N. Y., 1910-1919; 1928-) also contains summaries of contemporary developments in many fields.

TRAVELERS' ACCOUNTS

Foreign visitors, particularly those from Great Britain, continued to publish in large numbers volumes of their impressions of the United States. One of the most serviceable is that by the Frenchman, P. H. B. d'Estournelles de Constant, *America and Her Problems* (N. Y., 1915). The book of the British journalist William Archer, *America Today* (London, 1900), is discriminating, as is that of G. A. Birmingham, *From Dublin to Chicago* (N. Y., 1914). Sir Philip Burne-Jones, *Dollars and Democracy* (N. Y., 1904), is interesting as the impressions of a well-known artist who came over for a short time to paint pictures. Arnold Bennett, *Your United States* (N. Y., 1912), and W. L. George, *Hail Columbia* (N. Y., 1921), are impressionistic but useful. While most of the European travelers mingled chiefly with the well-to-do, Stephen Graham, *With Poor Immigrants to America* (N. Y., 1914), is the account of an Englishman who came over in the steerage and mingled with the poor. Mrs. Desmond Humphries, *America—through English Eyes* (London, 1910), is a bitter attack by a strongly biased observer. In Abbé Felix Klein, *America of Tomorrow* (Chicago, 1911), are the impressions of a scholarly French priest. H. P. Robinson, *The Twentieth Century American* (N. Y., 1908), presents a scholarly comparison between the people of Great Britain and the United States, and H. G. Wells, *The Future in America* (N. Y., 1906), the comments of a great English socialist. Allan Nevins, ed., *American Social History as Recorded by British Travellers* (N. Y., 1923), gives extracts from several British travel books of the period and an exhaustive bibliography of books on America written by Englishmen.

GENERAL SECONDARY WORKS

Less objective than his earlier volumes, but interesting because of the author's personal acquaintance with many of the leading figures, is J. F. Rhodes, *The McKinley and Roosevelt Administrations, 1897-1909* (N. Y., 1922). F. A. Ogg, *National Progress, 1907-1917*, cited earlier, is a skillful summary of political history. On the political phase, consult also Edward Stanwood, *A History of the Presidency* (2 vols., new edn., Boston, 1928). Of the various brief surveys that of C. A. Beard, *Contemporary American History, 1877-1913* (N. Y., 1914), is the best for interpretation. The most brilliant synthesis yet made of these years appears in C. A. and Mary R. Beard, *The Rise of American Civilization* (2 vols., N. Y., 1927), in which social, economic and political factors are skillfully interwoven. An interesting but somewhat diffuse narrative, stressing social history but with eccentric emphases, is presented in the volumes of the journalist Mark Sullivan, *Our Times, the United States, 1900-1925* (4 vols., N. Y., 1926-), of which three volumes have appeared to date.

Several appraisals of the South interpret tendencies since 1898: Edwin Mims, *The Advancing South* (N. Y., 1926), and his *The Southern Woman Past and Present* (Lynchburg, 1915); J. M. Moore, *The South Today* (N. Y., 1916); and W. J. Robertson, *The Changing South* (N. Y., 1927). Some of the worst aspects of Southern civilization are pictured in Frank Tannenbaum, *Darker Phases of the South* (N. Y., 1924). In Katherine G. Busbey, *Home Life in America* (N. Y., 1910), and P. L. Haworth, *America in Ferment* (Indianapolis, 1915), American writers of the time attempt to summarize the whole contemporary scene. R. M. La Follette, ed., *The Making of America* (10 vols., Chicago, 1906), is a symposium by specialists on many phases of American civilization.

On the public lands B. H. Hibbard, *History of the Public Land Policies* (N. Y., 1924), is reasonably full on the recent years. On conservation, see C. R. Van Hise, *The Conservation of Natural Resources in the United States* (N. Y., 1910); G. W. James, *Reclaiming the Arid West* (N. Y., 1917); and R. P. Teele, *Irrigation in the United States* (N. Y., 1915). In Roy Gittinger, *The Formation of the State of Oklahoma* (Univ. of Calif., *Publs.*, VI, 1917), a detailed history of the achievement of statehood by one of the new states is given. For the farmers' movements Edward Wiest, *Agricultural Organizations in the United States* (Univ. of Kentucky, *Studies*, II, 1923), is useful. Books which concern rural life in general but are of especial interest for the West are M. C. Burrett, *The County Agent and the Farm Bureau* (N. Y., 1922); O. M. Kile, *The Farm Bureau Movement* (N. Y., 1921); and the *Report* of the Commission on Country Life (N. Y., 1911).

For specific subjects D. R. Dewey, *Financial History of the United States* (10th edn., N. Y., 1928), has long been considered standard; and for the tariff F. W. Taussig, *Tariff History of the United States* (7th edn., 1923), is the most useful, though written from the antiprotectionist point of view. Of the many economic histories which have recently appeared, H. U. Faulkner, *American Economic History* (N. Y., 1924), and W. W. Jennings, *A History of Economic Progress in the United States* (N. Y., 1926), are fullest on this period. Among the secondary works which cover various aspects of these years should be noted the popular but suggestive volumes in the *Chronicles of America Series*, cited earlier. Among those touching on the social history of the period since 1898 are S. P. Orth, *The Armies of Labor* (XL), his *Our Foreigners* (XXXV), and his *The Boss and the Machine* (XLIII); Holland Thompson, *The New South* (XLII), and his *The Age of Invention* (XXXVII); John Moody, *The Railroad Builders* (XXXVIII), and his *Masters of Capital* (XLI); and B. J. Hendrick, *The Age of Big Business* (XXXIX).

PERSONAL MATERIAL

In the field of political history the most important memoirs are Theodore Roosevelt, *Autobiography* (N. Y., 1913), R. M. La Follette, *Autobiography* (Madison, Wis., 1913), and W. J. Bryan and Mary B. Bryan, *The Memoirs of William Jennings Bryan* (Phila., 1925). No unbiased biography of Roosevelt has yet appeared. Of the books dealing with him, the most valuable are J. B. Bishop, *Theodore Roosevelt and His Time* (2 vols., N. Y., 1920), and *Selections from the Correspondence of Theodore Roosevelt and Henry Cabot Lodge, 1884-1918* (2 vols., N. Y., 1925). The biographies of Hanna, those by Herbert Croly, *Marcus*

Alonzo Hanna (N. Y., 1912), and Thomas Beer, *Hanna* (N. Y., 1929), are objective and critical, and Hanna thereby emerges a greater man. The volumes on Wilson are of varying value. The official biography, based on the family papers, is that of Ray Stannard Baker, *Woodrow Wilson, Life and Letters* (N. Y., 1927-), two volumes of which have been published. Others include W. E. Dodd, *Woodrow Wilson and His Work* (Garden City, 1920), laudatory; H. J. Ford, *Woodrow Wilson the Man and His Work* (N. Y., 1916), popular and favorable; W. A. White, *Woodrow Wilson* (Boston, 1924), interesting with an attempt at interpretation; J. P. Tumulty, *Woodrow Wilson as I Knew Him* (Garden City, 1921), by his secretary; and James Kerney, *The Political Education of Woodrow Wilson* (N. Y., 1926), perhaps the best sketch of his political career. Two suggestive and interpretative lives of Bryan are M. R. Werner, *Bryan* (N. Y., 1929), and Paxton Hibben, *The Peerless Leader, William Jennings Bryan* (N. Y., 1929). On the progressive movement in city and state intensely interesting pictures are given in Brand Whitlock, *Forty Years of It* (N. Y., 1913), F. C. Howe, *Confessions of a Reformer* (N. Y., 1925), and Tom Johnson, *My Story* (N. Y., 1911). N. W. Stephenson, *Nelson W. Aldrich* (N. Y., 1930), gives an excellent picture of one of the important conservative leaders. Less critical, but valuable, is H. S. Duffy, *William Howard Taft* (N. Y., 1930).

Among editors and publishers who have written their reminiscences are R. U. Johnson, *Remembered Yesterdays* (Boston, 1923); G. H. Putnam, *Memoirs of a Publisher* (N. Y., 1916); E. P. Mitchell, *Memoirs of an Editor* (N. Y., 1924); Poultney Bigelow, *Seventy Summers* (2 vols., London, 1925); H. W. Watterson, *"Marse Henry"* (2 vols., N. Y., 1919); L. F. Tooker, *The Joys and Tribulations of an Editor* (N. Y., 1923); M. A. McRae, *Fifty Years in Newspaperdom* (N. Y., 1924); S. S. McClure, *My Autobiography* (N. Y., 1914); and E. W. Bok, *The Americanization of Edward Bok* (N. Y., 1920). The memories of two journalists who were also prominent clergymen are given in Lyman Abbott, *Reminiscences* (Boston, 1915), and Washington Gladden, *Recollections* (Boston, 1909). William Lawrence in *Memories of a Happy Life* (Boston, 1926) not only tells the story of Massachusetts Episcopalianism, but talks pleasantly of the Boston aristocracy. Charles Stelzle, *A Son of the Bowery* (N. Y., 1926), is the story of an active leader in the movement for a socialized gospel. Essential for Catholicism are James Cardinal Gibbons, *A Retrospect of Fifty Years* (Balt., 1916), and A. S. Will, *Life of Cardinal Gibbons* (2 vols., N. Y., 1922). Three of the ablest college administrators have left books dealing with educational problems: W. R. Harper, *The Trend in Higher Education* (Chicago, 1905); C. W. Eliot, *University Administration* (Boston, 1908); and G. S. Hall, *Life and Confessions of a Psychologist* (N. Y., 1923). Important in the pure-food movement is Harvey W. Wiley, *An Autobiography* (Indianapolis, 1930).

Numerous but of varying value are the reminiscences of actors, managers and playwrights. They include George Arliss, *Up the Years from Bloomsbury: an Autobiography* (Boston, 1928); John Barrymore, *Confessions of an Actor* (Indianapolis, 1926); George M. Cohan, *Twenty Years on Broadway and the Years It Took to Get There* (N. Y., 1925); Eddie Foy and A. F. Harlow, *Clowning through Life* (N. Y., 1928); N. C. Goodwin, *Nat Goodwin's Book* (Boston, 1914); DeWolfe Hopper, *Once a Clown, Always a Clown* (Boston, 1927); Otis Skinner, *Footlights and Spotlights* (Indianapolis, 1924); Augustus Thomas, *The Print of My Remembrance* (N. Y., 1922); and Francis Wilson, *Francis Wilson's Life of Himself* (Boston, 1924). Rudolph Aronson in *Theatrical and Musical Memoirs* (N. Y., 1913) tells something of the activities of a manager, and John Philip Sousa, *Marching Along* (Boston, 1928), the story of the foremost bandmaster of the period. The memoirs and writings of athletes are dealt with later under Sports and Recreations.

Many biographies of business leaders have appeared in recent years, but since they are usually written at the instigation of their families, they should be used with caution. Among these should be noted Ida M. Tarbell, *The Life of Elbert H. Gary* (N. Y., 1925); George Harvey, *Henry Clay Frick, the Man* (N. Y., 1928); Anna R. Burr, *The Portrait of a Banker: James Stillman, 1850-1918* (N. Y., 1927); J. W. Jenkins, *James B. Duke, Master Builder* (N. Y., 1927); Carl Hovey, *Life Story of J. P. Morgan* (N. Y., 1911); J. G. Pyle, *Life of J. J. Hill* (N. Y., 1917); and George Kennan, *E. H. Harriman* (2 vols., N. Y., 1922).

BUSINESS AND FINANCE

In the third volume of V. S. Clark, *History of Manufactures in the United States, 1607-1928* (Carnegie Inst., *Contribs. to Am. Econ. History*, 3 vols., N. Y., 1929), there is a scholarly summary of the manufacturing development of recent years; the same story is more popularly told in Malcolm Keir, *Manufacturing* (N. Y., 1928). Detailed statistical material is obtainable in the following publications of the Bureau of the Census: *Twelfth Census of the United States* (1900), VII-VIII; *Thirteenth Census* (1910), IX; and *Reports on Manufactures* for 1905 and 1914. The *Report* of the Industrial Commission (19 vols., Wash., 1902) is a mine of information; see particularly vols. i and xix.

Histories of specific industries which cover some of the period after 1898 include Ida M. Tarbell, *The History of the Standard Oil Company* (2 vols., N. Y., 1904), scholarly and impartial; C. H. Montague, *Rise and Progress of the Standard Oil Company* (N. Y., 1903); J. H. Bridge, *The History of the Carnegie Steel Company* (N. Y., 1903); H. L. Wilgus, *A Study of the United States Steel Corporation* (Chicago, 1901); Arundel Cotter, *The Authentic History of the United States Steel Corporation* (N. Y., 1916); and Abraham Berglund, *The United States Steel Corporation* (Columbia Univ., *Studies*, XXVII, no. 2, 1907). On coal, see Scott Nearing, *Anthracite: an Instance of Natural Resource Monopoly* (Phila., 1915); Eliot Jones, *The Anthracite Coal Combination in the United States* (*Harvard Econ. Studies*

XI, 1914); H. R. Mussey, *Combination in the Mining Industry* (Columbia Univ., *Studies*, XXIII, no. 3, 1905); and *What the Coal Commission Found* (Balt., 1925), an authoritative summary by the staff of the coal commission appointed in 1922 by President Harding. On textiles the following are useful: T. M. Young, *The American Cotton Industry* (N. Y., 1902); M. T. Copeland, *The Cotton Manufacturing Industry in the United States* (*Harvard Econ. Studies*, VIII, 1912); H. B. Brown, *Cotton* (N. Y., 1917); A. H. Cole, *The American Wool Manufacture* (2 vols., Cambridge, 1926); and P. T. Cherington, *The Wool Industry* (Chicago, 1916). On the shoe manufacture, see F. J. Allen, *The Shoe Industry* (N. Y., 1916); and on the preparation of two foodstuffs, R. G. Blakey, *The United States Beet Sugar Industry* (Columbia Univ., *Studies*, XLVII, no. 2, 1912), and C. B. Kuhlman, *Development of the Flour Milling Industry in the United States* (Boston, 1929). For biographies of leading business men and financiers, see under Personal Material.

Many studies were made during the years when consolidation went on rapidly, including R. T. Ely, *Monopolies and Trusts* (N. Y., 1900); W. M. Collier, *The Trusts* (N. Y., 1900); and C. R. Van Hise, *Concentration and Control* (rev. edn., N. Y., 1914), all adversely critical; and J. H. Bridge, ed., *The Trust: Its Book* (N. Y., 1902), a defense. Perhaps the best single volume is that of J. W. Jenks and W. E. Clark, *The Trust Problem* (rev. edn., Garden City, 1917), originally written by Professor Jenks who made a lifelong study of business consolidation. Useful are two later books: Eliot Jones, *The Trust Problem in the United States* (N. Y., 1921), and H. R. Seager and C. A. Gulick, *Trust and Corporation Problems* (N. Y., 1929). John Moody, *The Truth about the Trusts* (N. Y., 1904), is statistical and especially valuable in showing the interrelations of financial power. On financial concentration a decade later the Committee on Banking and Currency of the House of Representatives, *Money Trust Investigation* (3 vols., Wash., 1913), is illuminating. The reports of the Federal Trade Commission on the United States Steel Corporation, on the International Harvester Company, on the meat-packing combination and other industries are also invaluable.

Besides the standard work by Dewey, cited earlier, general summaries of finance and banking are available in A. B. Hepburn, *A History of Currency in the United States* (N. Y., 1915); and in A. D. Noyes, *Forty Years of American Finance, 1865-1907* (N. Y., 1909), and his *The War Period of American Finance, 1908-1925* (N. Y., 1926). See also W. O. Scroggs, *A Century of Banking Progress* (N. Y., 1924); H. W. Lanier, *A Century of Banking in New York* (N. Y., 1922); and E. T. B. Perine, *The Story of the Trust Companies* (N. Y., 1916). Henry Clews, *Fifty Years in Wall Street* (N. Y., 1908), is interesting as the story of an eyewitness.

TRANSPORTATION AND COMMUNICATION

RAILWAYS: Two popular books which deal with later phases of railway history are John Moody, *The Railway Builders,* already cited, and Agnes C. Laut, *Romance of the Rails* (2 vols., N. Y., 1929). Much recent history is given in Slason Thompson, *Short History of American Railways* (N. Y., 1925), and Edward Hungerford, *The Modern Railroad* (Chicago, 1911). R. E. Riegel summarizes for one section of the country in *The Story of the Western Railroads* (N. Y., 1926), while the story of the last great railroad line built is told by Montgomery Schuyler, *Westward the Course of Empire* (N. Y., 1906). Among the more valuable accounts of particular railways are Stuart Daggett, *Chapters on the History of the Southern Pacific* (N. Y., 1922); Nelson Trottman, *History of the Union Pacific* (N. Y., 1923); Edward Hungerford, *The Story of the Baltimore and Ohio Railroad, 1827-1928* (2 vols., N. Y., 1928); and anon., *A Century of Progress: History of the Delaware and Hudson Company* (Albany, 1925). On the many problems which confronted the railroads and the public, the *Annual Reports* of the Interstate Commerce Commission, and the Industrial

Commission, *Report* (cited earlier), IV, on transportation, provide a wealth of information. The case against the railroads is well presented in Frank Parsons, *The Heart of the Railroad Problem* (Boston, 1906), and the whole question of government regulation in F. H. Dixon, *Railroads and Government* (N. Y., 1922). Important in understanding the problem are the two books by W. Z. Ripley: *Railroads; Rates and Regulations* (N. Y., 1915), and *Railroads; Finance and Organization* (N. Y., 1915).

RAPID TRANSIT: The history of electric-trolley transportation has not yet been written. One phase of the story of transportation, in New York City, can be found in J. B. Walker, *Fifty Years of Rapid Transit* (N. Y., 1918), and in G. H. Gilbert, L. I. Wightman and W. L. Saunders, *The Subways and Tunnels of New York* (N. Y., 1912). D. F. Wilcox, *Analysis of the Electric Railway Problem* (N. Y., 1921), develops in detail the causes for the decline of the electric railways.

WATERWAYS: The revival of interest in waterways brought the *Preliminary Report* of the Inland Waterways Commission (Wash., 1908), and the *Final Report* (Wash., 1912), which surveys the existing situation with respect to inland water transportation. The papers published in the *Annals* of the American Academy of Political and Social Science, XXXI, will be found illuminating. A. F. Harlow, *Old Towpaths* (N. Y., 1926), gives a popular account of the decline of canal transportation, and Herbert Quick, *American Inland Waterways* (N. Y., 1909), dwells on the possibility of resuscitation. On the New York state project, consult N. E. Whitford, *History of the Barge Canal of New York State* (Albany, 1922); *History of the Canal System of the State of New York* (Albany, 1906), a supplement to the *Annual Report* of the state engineer and surveyor; and H. W. Hill, *Waterways and Canal Construction in New York State* (Buffalo, 1908). On other canals, see *Intercoastal Waterways* (62 Cong., 2 sess., *House Doc.*, 391). For the Panama Canal the *Annual Reports* of the Isthmian Canal Commission (1904-1914) are important. Good secondary accounts are

J. B. Bishop, *The Panama Gateway* (N. Y., 1913); G. S. Mills, *The Panama Canal* (London, 1913); W. J. Abbott, *Panama and the Canal* (N. Y., 1914); and D. H. Smith, *The Panama Canal: Its History, Activities and Organization* (Balt., 1927). The standard study of the relationship between railroads and waterways is H. G. Moulton, *Waterways vs. Railways* (Boston, 1912).

AUTOMOBILES AND HIGHWAYS: The best summary of early automobile history is in R. C. Epstein, *The Automobile Industry* (Chicago, 1928), although excellent short accounts can be found in Waldemar Kaempffert, ed., *Popular History of American Invention* (2 vols., N. Y., 1924), and Mark Sullivan, *Our Times,* mentioned before. Of the many books on Ford perhaps H. L. Arnold and F. L. Fourote, *Ford Methods and the Ford Shops* (N. Y., 1915), and J. G. de R. Hamilton, *Henry Ford* (N. Y., 1927), are as useful as any. On the influence of automobiles on road building, consult the *Official Good Roads Year Book of the United States* (Wash., 1912-); L. W. Page, *Roads, Paths and Bridges* (N. Y., 1912); C. E. Foote, *Practical Road Building* (Phila., 1917); H. E. Howe, *The New Stone Age* (N. Y., 1921); H. P. Willis and J. R. B. Byers, *Portland Cement Prices* (N. Y., 1924); and the following textbooks: H. B. Drowne and A. H. Blanchard, *Text Book on Highway Engineering* (N. Y., 1914); W. K. Holt and W. C. Voss, *Concrete Work* (2 vols., N. Y., 1921); and H. G. Tyrrell, *History of Bridge Building* (Chicago, 1911), and his *Concrete Bridges and Culverts* (Chicago, 1909).

AIR NAVIGATION: The history of aviation is popularly told in R. S. Holland, *Historic Airships* (Phila., 1928); in A. L. Roth, *The Conquest of the Air* (N. Y., 1909); and in detail in Victor Lougheed, *Vehicles of the Air* (Chicago, 1919). The book edited by the Aero Club of America, *Navigating the Air: a Scientific Statement of the Progress of Aeronautical Science up to the Present Time* (N. Y., 1907), contains twenty-three chapters by experts.

COMMUNICATION: On electrical communication the pamphlets published by the Information Department of the

American Telephone and Telegraph Company are useful. Also consult J. J. Fahie, *A History of Wireless Telegraphy, 1838-1899* (N. Y., 1899); J. V. L. Hogan, *The Outline of Radio* (2d edn., Boston, 1925); O. E. Dunlap, jr., *The Story of Radio* (N. Y., 1927); and T. T. Baker, *The Telegraphic Transmission of Photographs* (London, 1910). Recent developments in the postal system are noted in D. C. Roper, *The United States Post Office* (N. Y., 1917).

THE PROGRESSIVE MOVEMENT

No adequate political history of the early years of the century has yet been written. Certain phases are dealt with in F. E. Haynes, *Third Party Movements since the Civil War* (Iowa City, 1916), and his *Social Politics in the United States* (Boston, 1924); and B. P. DeWitt, *The Progressive Movement* (N. Y., 1915). For the philosophical basis Herbert Croly, *The Promise of American Life* (N. Y., 1909); W. E. Weyl, *The New Democracy* (N. Y., 1912); and C. E. Merriam, *American Political Ideas, 1865-1917* (N. Y., 1920), are valuable. Leading personalities are dealt with in the volumes listed under Personal Material.

On state politics, see A. O. Barton, *La Follette's Winning of Wisconsin, 1894-1904* (Madison, Wis., 1922); Hester E. Hosford, *Woodrow Wilson and New Jersey Made Over* (N. Y., 1912), a campaign document; and, for a picture of the "system" in New York, S. B. Thomas, *The Boss or the Governor* (N. Y., 1914), or J. W. Forrest and James Malcolm, *Tammany's Treason* (N. Y., 1913), both telling the story of the Sulzer impeachment trial. Some of the new governmental devices are discussed in W. B. Munro, *The Initiative, Referendum and Recall* (N. Y., 1912); J. D. Barnett, *The Operation of the Initiative, Referendum and Recall in Oregon* (N. Y., 1915); A. H. Eaton, *The Oregon System* (Chicago, 1912); and, for sources, C. A. Beard and B. E. Shultz, *Documents on the Initiative, Referendum and Recall* (N. Y., 1912).

Classic in their descriptions of graft and of efforts at reform are the books of Lincoln Steffens, *The Shame of the Cities* (N. Y., 1904), and *Upbuilders* (N. Y., 1909). For San Francisco a detailed story is given in Franklin Hichborn, *"The System" as Uncovered by the San Francisco Graft Prosecution* (San Francisco, 1915), which should be supplemented by Fremont Older, *My Own Story* (San Francisco, 1919). For Ohio the memoirs of Whitlock, Johnson and Howe, listed under Personal Material, are essential. Introductions to the problems of city government, containing suggestions for reform, are C. A. Beard, *American City Government* (N. Y., 1912); D. W. Bartlett, *The Better City* (Los Angeles, 1907), a story of social welfare in Los Angeles; Charles Zueblin, *American Municipal Progress* (N. Y., 1902); F. C. Howe, *The City the Hope of Democracy* (N. Y., 1905); and D. F. Wilcox, *The American City: a Problem in Democracy* (N. Y., 1900). On the new types of city government the following are important: J. J. Hamilton, *The Dethronement of the City Boss* (N. Y., 1910), a study of the Galveston and Des Moines plans; E. S. Bradford, *Commission Government in American Cities* (N. Y., 1911); Henry Bruère, *The New City Government* (N. Y., 1912); F. H. MacGregor, *City Government by Commission* (Madison, Wis., 1911); and Tso-Shuen Chang, *History and Analysis of the Commission and City-Manager Plans of Municipal Government in the United States* (Iowa City, 1918). For the ownership or control of public utilities, see *Municipal and Private Operation of Public Utilities* (3 vols., N. Y., 1907), a report to the National Civic Federation of its Committee on Public Ownership and Operation; *State Regulation of Public Utilities* (Am. Acad. of Polit. and Social Sci., *Annals*, LIII, no. 142); C. L. King, *Regulation of Municipal Utilities* (N. Y., 1912), excellent to that date; and C. D. Thompson, *Public Ownership* (N. Y., 1925), the most complete summary.

LABOR

The sources for the labor movement include the numerous labor journals, notably the *American Federationist* and the annual reports of the American Federation of Labor and its constituent units. Of the utmost value are the *Bulletins* of the Department of Labor (1896-1912), followed by the *Bulletins* of the United States Bureau of Labor Statistics (1913-), comprising several hundred carefully written pamphlets on various aspects of the labor problem. After 1898 many states, through their departments of labor, also published reports and studies. Of the general histories covering the recent period Selig Perlman, *A History of Trade Unionism in the United States* (N. Y., 1922), is perhaps the most satisfactory, though brief résumés appear in J. R. Commons and others, *History of Labour in the United States,* already cited; Mary R. Beard, *A Short History of the American Labor Movement* (rev. edn., N. Y., 1924); S. P. Orth, *The Armies of Labor,* mentioned earlier; G. G. Groat, *An Introduction to the Study of Organized Labor in America* (rev. edn., N. Y., 1926); G. S. Watkins, *An Introduction to the Study of Labor Problems* (N. Y., 1922); and, from the radical point of view, Anthony Bimba, *The History of the American Working Class* (N. Y., 1927).

The history of several unions has been written, including Louis Levine, *The Women's Garment Workers* (N. Y., 1924); Harry Best, *The Men's Garment Industry of New York and the Strike of 1913* (N. Y., 1914); and Andrew Roy, *A History of the Coal Miners of the United States* (Columbus, Ohio, 1907). On particular strikes, see B. M. Rastall, *The Labor History of the Cripple Creek District* (Univ. of Wis., Econ. and Polit. Sci. Ser., *Bull.,* III, 1908); *Report to the President on the Anthracite Coal Strike of May-October, 1902,* by the Anthracite Coal Strike Commission (Wash., 1903); C. P. Neill, *Report on the Strike of Textile Workers in Lawrence, Mass., in 1912* (62 Cong., 2 sess., *Sen. Doc.,* no. 870, 1912); Bureau of Statistics, Commonwealth of Mass., *Twenty-Third Annual Report of Strikes and Lockouts for the Year 1912* (Boston, 1913); and Subcommittee of the Committee on Mines and Mining, *Conditions in the Coal Mines of Colorado* (63 Cong., 2 sess., 2 vols., Wash., 1914).

Among the books which make an effort to interpret the labor movement are W. B. Catlin, *Labor Problems in the United States and Great Britain* (N. Y., 1926); F. T. Carlton, *History and Problems of Organized Labor* (N. Y., 1920); W. E. Walling, *American Labor and American Democracy* (N. Y., 1926); John Mitchell, *Organized Labor* (Phila., 1903); and Helen Marot, *American Labor Unions* (N. Y., 1914). Samuel Gompers, *Seventy Years of Life and Labor* (N. Y., 1925), is not only an autobiography and a history of the American Federation of Labor, but also an interpretation of the movement. On the more radical developments, see D. J. Saposs, *Left Wing Unionism* (N. Y., 1926); J. G. Brooks, *American Syndicalism: the I. W. W.* (N. Y., 1913); P. F. Brissenden, *The I. W. W., a Study of American Syndicalism* (Columbia Univ., *Studies,* LXXXIII, 1919); C. H. Parker, *The Casual Laborer and Other Essays* (N. Y., 1920); and J. M. Budish and George Soule, *The New Unionism in the Clothing Industry* (N. Y., 1920). J. A. Fitch, *The Causes of Industrial Unrest* (N. Y., 1924), is valuable for the psychological background, as is Bruce Smith, *The State Police* (N. Y., 1925), for the history of one *bête noire* of labor.

A general picture of conditions at the turn of the century can be gleaned from the section on labor in the *Final Report* of the Industrial Commission (Wash., 1902), and of the situation fifteen years later from the *Final Report* of the Commission on Industrial Relations (Wash., 1915). On wages, consult Robert Hunter, *Poverty* (N. Y., 1904); John Ryan, *A Living Wage* (N. Y., 1906); R. C. Chapin, *The Standard of Living among Workingmen's Families in New York City* (N. Y., 1909); F. H. Streightoff, *The Standard of Living among the Industrial People of America* (Boston, 1911); and Whitney Coombs, *The Wages of Unskilled Labor in the Manufacturing Industries in the United States, 1890-1920* (N. Y., 1926). On aspects of labor and social legislation the following provide an excellent introduction: J. R. Commons and J. B. Andrews, *Principles of Labor Legislation* (rev. edn., N. Y., 1927); G. G. Groat, *Attitude of American*

Courts in Labor Cases (Columbia Univ., *Studies,* XLII, no. 108, 1911); H. W. Laidler, *Boycotts and the Labor Struggle* (N. Y., 1913); H. R. Seager, *Social Insurance* (N. Y., 1910); and I. M. Rubinow, *Social Insurance* (N. Y., 1913), the most complete survey up to that time. On workingmen's compensation consult, in addition to *Bulletins,* nos. 45, 57, 203 and 240, of the U. S. Bureau of Labor Statistics, the books by C. R. Henderson, *Industrial Insurance in the United States* (Chicago, 1904); D. H. Van Doren, *Workmen's Compensation and Insurance* (N. Y., 1918); E. H. Downey, *Workmen's Compensation* (N. Y., 1924); and G. F. Michelbacker and T. M. Niel, *Workmen's Compensation Insurance* (N. Y., 1925). Valuable also is *Workmen's Insurance and Benefit Funds in the United States* (U. S. Commissioner of Labor, *Twenty-Third Annual Report,* 1908).

RACE RELATIONS

For the Negro, the *Negro Year Book* (1912-), published annually by the Tuskegee Institute, and the *Annual Reports* of the National Association for the Advancement of the Colored People (Wash., 1911-), are helpful. Two recent histories of the race contain material in the period since 1898: Benjamin Brawley, *A Social History of the American Negro* (N. Y., 1921), and C. G. Woodson, *The Negro in Our History* (3d edn., Wash., 1924). On conditions in the first decade of the century, read R. S. Baker, *Following the Color Line* (N. Y., 1908), a reprint of articles first appearing in the *American Magazine,* and B. T. Washington and W. E. B. Du Bois, *The Negro in the South* (Phila., 1907). The death of Washington brought forth B. F. Riley, *The Life and Times of Booker T. Washington* (N. Y., 1916), and E. J. Scott and L. B. Stowe, *Booker T. Washington* (Garden City, 1916). On Negro education, consult *Bulls.,* nos. 38 and 39, of the U. S. Bureau of Education (Wash., 1916), and, on migration, T. J. Woofter, *Negro Migration* (N. Y., 1920). One of the most interesting phases is studied in E. B. Reuter, *The Mulatto in the United States* (Boston,

1918). The ablest study of lynching is Walter White, *Rope and Faggot* (N. Y., 1929), and of colored labor C. H. Wesley, *Negro Labor in the United States* (N. Y., 1927).

The conditions of the Indian and the present problem of that race are surveyed by the Institute for Government Research, *The Problem of Indian Administration* (Balt., 1928). More valuable for this period are F. E. Leupp, *The Indian and His Problem* (N. Y., 1910), and G. E. E. Lindquist, ed., *The Red Man in the United States* (N. Y., 1923), the latter presenting the results of an inquiry by the Interchurch World Movement. For other race relations, see Immigration.

IMMIGRATION

The most complete study of immigration ever made is the forty-one-volume *Report* of the Immigration Commission (Wash., 1911), which is summarized in J. W. Jenks and W. J. Lauck, *The Immigration Problem* (6th edn., N. Y., 1926). An excellent state document is the Massachusetts Commission on Immigration, *Report on the Problem of Immigration* (Boston, 1914). General studies which are scientifically written and suggestive include P. F. Hall, *Immigration* (N. Y., 1906); J. R. Commons, *Races and Immigrants in America* (N. Y., 1908); H. P. Fairchild, *Immigration* (N. Y., 1911); E. A. Ross, *The Old World in the New* (N. Y., 1914); G. M. Stephenson, *A History of American Immigration, 1820-1924* (Boston, 1926); R. L. Garis, *Immigration Restriction* (N. Y., 1927); and D. C. Brewer, *The Conquest of New England by the Immigrant* (N. Y., 1926).

Some studies of a high order have been done on special races in America, notably S. C. Johnson, *A History of Emigration from the United Kingdom to North America, 1763-1912* (N. Y., 1914); K. C. Babcock, *The Scandinavian Element in the United States* (Univ. of Ill., *Studies in the Social Sciences,* III, no. 3, 1914); Thomas Burgess, *Greeks in America* (Boston, 1913); R. F. Foerster, *The Italian Immigration of Our Times* (*Harvard Econ. Studies,* XX,

1919); and A. B. Faust, *The German Element in the United States* (2 vols., Boston, 1909). The question of Japanese immigration is handled dispassionately by H. A. Millis, *The Japanese Problem in the United States* (N. Y., 1915), a report to the Federal Council of the Churches of Christ in America, and by S. L. Gulick, *The Japanese Problem* (N. Y., 1914), both of whom tend to deflate the Japanese menace. They are answered by Montaville Flowers, *The Japanese Conquest of American Opinion* (N. Y., 1917).

WOMEN AND CHILDREN

Perhaps the most usable book on the history of woman suffrage in this country is Carrie Chapman Catt and Nettie R. Shuler, *Woman Suffrage and Politics* (N. Y., 1926), but more complete is Elizabeth C. Stanton, Susan B. Anthony, Matilda J. Gage and Ida H. Harper, eds., *The History of Woman Suffrage* (6 vols., N. Y., 1881-1922). Popularly written but giving some insight into the objectives of the new woman is Rheta C. Dorr, *What Eight Million Women Want* (Boston, 1910), and one phase of what they actually did is described in Mary R. Beard, *Women's Work in Municipalities* (N. Y., 1915). Other books of a general nature or interpretation are Elizabeth McCracken, *The Women of America* (N. Y., 1904); T. S. McMahon, *Women and Economic Revolution* (Madison, Wis., 1912); and Jessie Taft, *The Woman Movement from the Point of View of Social Consciousness* (Chicago, 1915). The story of women's clubs is told by Mary I. Wood, *The History of the General Federation of Women's Clubs* (N. Y., 1912). For other special phases, see Thomas Woody, *A History of Woman's Education in the United States* (2 vols., N. Y., 1929); Alice Henry, *The Trade Union Woman* (N. Y., 1915); and A. S. Duniway, *Path Breaking* (Portland, Ore., 1914), which tells of suffrage victories in the Far West. No study would be complete without reading Ida H. Harper, *Life of Susan B. Anthony* (3 vols., Indianapolis, 1908).

Both political and civil rights are considered in A. E.

Hecker, *A Short History of Woman's Rights* (2d edn., N. Y., 1914). On divorce the following will be found useful: W. E. Carson, *The Marriage Revolt* (N. Y., 1915); F. S. Hall and E. W. Brooke, *American Marriage Laws in Their Social Aspect* (N. Y., 1919); the *Proceedings* of the National Congress on Uniform Divorce Laws held at Washington, D. C., February 17, 1906; and the *Proceedings* of the Adjourned National Congress on Uniform Divorce Laws held at Philadelphia, Pa., November 13, 1906. For statistics, see the *Reports* of the United States Bureau of the Census: *Marriage and Divorce, 1887-1906* (Wash., 1908), and *Marriage and Divorce, 1916* (Wash., 1918) for the decade after 1906.

The best summary of measures to conserve child life is G. B. Mangold, *Problems of Child Welfare* (N. Y., 1914). For earlier efforts, which were bearing fruit after 1898, see J. A. Riis, *A Ten Years' War* (N. Y., 1900), and his *The Battle with the Slums* (N. Y., 1902); and Homer Folks, *The Care of Destitute, Neglected and Delinquent Children* (N. Y., 1902). For later developments, see H. H. Hart, ed., *Preventive Treatment of Neglected Children* (N. Y., 1915). L. H. Gulick and L. P. Ayres, *Medical Inspection of Schools* (N. Y., 1913), is a scholarly study made for the Russell Sage Foundation.

Of the many federal and state studies made of children's and women's wages the most complete and valuable is the *Summary of the Report on Conditions of Women and Child Wage Earners in the United States* (U. S. Bur. of Labor Statistics, *Bull.*, no. 5, 1916), further summarized in W. J. Lauck and Edgar Sydenstricker, *Conditions of Labor in American Industries* (N. Y., 1917). In John Spargo, *The Bitter Cry of the Children* (N. Y., 1906), there is an amazing picture of child-labor conditions in the first decade of the century, and some idea of the situation as it existed in 1914 can be gleaned from the *Summary of the Report on Conditions of Women and Child Wage Earners in the United States* (U. S. Dept. of Labor, *Bull.*, no. 175, 1915), and from Helen L. Sumner and Ella A. Merritt, *Child Labor Legisla-*

tion in the United States (U. S. Dept. of Labor, Children's Bur., *Industrial Series,* no. 1, 1915). On the work of the government, see also J. A. Tobey, *The Children's Bureau* (Balt., 1925). An excellent historical sketch of the juvenile-court movement is H. H. Lou, *Juvenile Courts in the United States* (Chapel Hill, N. C., 1927).

The history of the birth-control movement in America is told by Mary W. Dennett, *Birth Control Laws* (N. Y., 1926), and the student is also directed to Theodore Schroeder, ed., *List of References on Birth Control* (N. Y., 1918), and J. E. Johnson, ed., *Selected Articles on Birth Control* (N. Y., 1925). For sterilization, see H. H. Laughlin, *Eugenical Sterilization, 1926. Historical, Legal and Statistical Review of Eugenical Sterilization in the United States* (New Haven, 1926). On the size of families, consult the pertinent publications of the Bureau of Census, in particular Niles Carpenter, *Immigrants and Their Children, 1920* (*Census Monographs,* VII, 1927). Significant is the study of R. E. Baber and E. A. Ross, *Changes in the Size of American Families in One Generation* (Univ. of Wis., *Studies,* no. 10, 1924), showing the decline of American families in the Middle West.

RELIGIOUS TRENDS

Formal church histories covering the period since 1898 are practically nonexistent. A brief but suggestive review, however, is found in the little book by H. K. Rowe, *The History of Religion in the United States* (N. Y., 1924), and much material, chiefly statistical, is in H. K. Carroll, *The Religious Forces of the United States* (rev. edn., N. Y., 1912). Gilbert Seldes, *The Stammering Century* (N. Y., 1928), gives a sophisticated picture of recent tendencies. For important source material the student must scan the *Minutes* of the General Assembly of the Presbyterian Church; the *Minutes* of the National Council of the Congregational Churches; and the *Journals* of the Delegated General Conference of the Methodist Episcopal Church (North), and similar records.

Other material can be found in the lives and memoirs of churchmen noted under Personal Material.

Elizabeth R. Hooker, *United Churches* (N. Y., 1926), is a study of the trend toward church consolidation. In E. B. Sanford, *Origin and History of the Federal Council of the Churches of Christ in America* (Hartford, 1916); and C. S. Macfarland, *The Churches of the Federal Council* (N. Y., 1916), and his *The Progress of Church Federation* (N. Y., 1917), are accounts of the founding and early years of the Federation by leaders in the movement. On the Sunday school, see E. W. Rice, *The Sunday School Movement, 1780-1917, and the American Sunday School Union, 1817-1917* (Phila., 1917); and *Organized Sunday School Work in America, 1905-1908* (Twelfth International Sunday School Convention, *Official Report*), and also the report of the fourteenth convention covering the years 1911-1914.

Those pioneers of the social gospel, Josiah Strong and Washington Gladden, had done the bulk of their writing before 1898, but Strong's *Religious Movements for Social Betterment* (N. Y., 1900) and Gladden's *The Christian Pastor and the Workingman* (N. Y., 1898) are important. Consult W. D. P. Bliss, ed., *The New Encyclopedia of Social Reform* (N. Y., 1907), for specific topics. For a picture of actual work done by a socialized church, read W. M. Tippy, *The Church a Community Force* (N. Y., 1914), a description of the activities of the Epworth Memorial Church, Cleveland; and H. F. Ward, *A Year Book of the Church and Social Service in the United States* (N. Y., 1915). A brief review of the rise of the social gospel is that by Shailer Mathews, "The Development of Social Christianity in America," G. B. Smith, ed., *Religious Thought in the Last Quarter Century* (Chicago, 1927). The relationship between labor and the churches was enlarged upon in Charles Stelzle, *The Workingman and Social Problems* (N. Y., 1903), and in C. B. Thompson, *The Churches and the Wage Earners* (N. Y., 1909). The books which more than all others influenced perhaps the younger clergy of the day were those by Walter Rauschenbusch, *Christianity and the Social Crisis*

(N. Y., 1907), and *Christianizing the Social Order* (N. Y., 1912), but they were only the most notable of many efforts to interpret the social ethics of Jesus. The sketch by Mathews, cited above, should be supplemented by H. U. Faulkner, "American Christianity and the World of Everyday," in *Essays in Intellectual History,* dedicated to J. H. Robinson (N. Y., 1929), chap. viii.

On Christian Science, which developed rapidly after 1898, Sibyl Wilbur, *The Life of Mary Baker Eddy* (rev. edn., Boston, 1913), is an official biography, while Georgine Milmine, *Mary Baker G. Eddy: the Story of Her Life and the History of Christian Science* (N. Y., 1909), was bitterly resented by members of that church and every effort was made to suppress it. The church was equally hostile to E. F. Dakin, *Mrs. Eddy: the Biography of a Virginal Mind* (N. Y., 1929). On faith healing, see Elwood Worcester, Samuel McComb and C. H. Coriat, *Religion and Medicine* (N. Y., 1908); Elwood Worcester and Samuel McComb, *The Christian Religion as a Healing Power* (N. Y., 1909); R. C. Cabot, *Psychotherapy and Its Relation to Religion* (Boston, 1908); and W. S. Sadler, *The Truth about Mind Cure* (Chicago, 1928). On one practitioner of faith healing, read, besides Seldes, Rolvix Harlan, *John Alexander Dowie and the Christian Catholic Apostolic Church in Zion* (Evansville, Wis., 1906). For New Thought, H. W. Dresser, *A History of the New Thought Movement* (N. Y., 1919), is suggestive, but for its philosophy it is essential to look into the volumes of Ralph Waldo Trine, Orison Swett Marden and Elbert Hubbard.

HUMANITARIAN REFORM

TEMPERANCE: Essential for the temperance movement is *The Anti-Saloon League Yearbook* and the *Yearbook* of the United States Brewers' Association as well as other material printed by the rival organizations. The most intelligent writing on the liquor problem in the early years of the century was sponsored by the Committee of Fifty, and included

Raymond Calkins, *Substitutes for the Saloon* (Boston, 1901); W. O. Atwater and others, *Physiological Aspects of the Liquor Problem* (2 vols., Boston, 1903); and *The Liquor Problem* (Boston, 1905), a summary of a ten-year investigation. An able presentation of the connection between the church and prohibition is P. H. Odegard, *Pressure Politics* (N. Y., 1928), which should be supplemented by Justin Steuart, *Wayne Wheeler, Dry Boss* (N. Y., 1928), chaps. i-iv being on this period. A more general treatment is E. H. Cherrington, *The Evolution of Prohibition in the United States* (Westerville, Ohio, 1920).

THE SOCIAL EVIL: The interest in prostitution brought a number of investigations, the most important of which were *The Social Evil* (Committee of Fifteen, *Report*, N. Y., 1902; 2d edn., 1912), dealing particularly with New York City; and the Vice Commission of Chicago, *The Social Evil in Chicago* (Chicago, 1911). In the *Report* of the Minneapolis Vice Commission (Minneapolis, 1911); the *Report* of the Portland Vice Commission (Portland, Ore., 1913); and the *Report* of the Hartford Vice Commission (Hartford, 1913), it is possible to glean information in regard to conditions in typical cities as well as to projects for reform. Information on the white-slave traffic is available in C. G. Roe, *Panders and Their White Slaves* (N. Y., 1910), and in the *Report* of the Commission for the Investigation of the White Slave Traffic, So Called (*Mass. House Doc.*, no. 2281, 1914).

HOUSING AND SOCIAL WORK: The most complete account of the crusade for better tenement-house laws is that by R. W. De Forest and Lawrence Veiller, *The Tenement House Problem* (2 vols., N. Y., 1903), which contains the report of the New York State Tenement House Commission of 1900. This should be supplemented by E. E. Wood, *The Housing of the Unskilled Wage Earner* (N. Y., 1919). R. A. Woods and A. J. Kennedy, *The Settlement Horizon* (N. Y., 1922), sketches the development of social settlements historically. For other humanitarian enterprises, see the sections entitled Religious Trends, and Women and Children.

EDUCATION

Essential in a study of American education are the *Annual Reports* of the Commissioner of Education, the *Biennial Surveys of Education,* published by the Bureau of Education, and the *Bulletins* of that Bureau. E. P. Cubberley, *Public Education in the United States* (Boston, 1919), is less full and useful than for earlier periods. It should be supplemented by I. L. Kandel, ed., *Twenty-Five Years of American Education* (N. Y., 1924), the most valuable survey of recent trends. On the newer philosophy of education, see John Dewey, *The School and Society* (Chicago, 1899), and his *Democracy and Education* (N. Y., 1916); John and Evelyn Dewey, *Schools of Tomorrow* (N. Y., 1915); and Irving King, *Education for Social Efficiency* (N. Y., 1913). Of rural schools J. D. Eggleston and R. W. Bruère, *The Work of the Rural Schools* (N. Y., 1913), gives a good picture, and for financial problems Mabel Newcomer, *Financial Statistics of Public Education in the United States, 1910-1920* (N. Y., 1924), is an excellent compilation.

Some interesting work has been done on various phases of college education. Besides the biographies of leading university administrators listed under Personal Material, C. F. Thwing, himself a college president, has given thumb-nail sketches of his contemporaries in *Guides, Philosophers and Friends* (N. Y., 1927). E. E. Slosson, *Great American Universities* (N. Y., 1910), is a popular book giving a brief sketch of several of the leading universities, while Abraham Flexner, *The American College* (N. Y., 1908), is a detailed and scientific study. Another thorough study is that by L. V. Koos, *The Junior College* (2 vols., Minneapolis, 1924). The question of academic freedom has been brilliantly handled in Thorstein Veblen, *The Higher Learning in America* (N. Y., 1918). Upton Sinclair, *The Goose Step* (Pasadena, 1923), specifies many breaches. Reports on special cases can be found in the *Bulletins* of the American Association of University Professors. For certain phases of adult education, see L. E. Reber, *University Extension in the United States*

(U. S. Bur. of Educ., *Bull. for 1914,* no. 19); A. J. Klein, *Correspondence Study in Universities and Colleges* (Bur. of Educ., *Bull. for 1920,* no. 10); and Reuben L. Lurie, *The Challenge of the Forum* (Boston, 1930), which recounts the spread of the open forum. On the Chautauqua movement, see J. L. Hurlbut. *The Story of Chautauqua* (N. Y., 1921), and H. A. Orchard, *Fifty Years of Chautauqua* (Cedar Rapids, 1923).

SCIENCE AND SCHOLARSHIP

A popular summary of general scientific advance is in Joseph Meyer, *The Seven Keys of Science* (N. Y., 1927), while good résumés of recent years are to be found in F. H. Hooper, ed., *These Eventful Years* (2 vols., London, 1924). E. S. Dana and others, *A Century of Science in America* (New Haven, 1913), has five chapters on geology and eight covering other sciences. Rather scanty on the period since 1898 are R. T. Young, *Biology in America* (Boston, 1922); G. P. Merrill, *The First One Hundred Years of American Geology* (New Haven, 1924); and E. F. Smith, *Chemistry in America* (N. Y., 1914). On the last-named science there has been fortunately some effort to inform the general public as to its progress in such books as E. E. Slosson, *Creative Chemistry* (N. Y., 1919); E. E. Slosson and O. W. Caldwell, eds., *Science Remaking the World* (Garden City, 1924); R. K. Duncan, *The Chemistry of Commerce* (N. Y., 1907); Hale Harrison, *American Chemistry* (N. Y., 1921); H. E. Howe, *Chemistry in the World's Work* (N. Y., 1926); Pauline G. Beery, *Chemistry Applied to Home and Community* (Phila., 1923); E. F. Armstrong, ed., *Chemistry in the Twentieth Century* (London, 1925); and above all in H. E. Howe, ed., *Chemistry in Industry* (2 vols., N. Y., 1924).

The marvelous contributions of chemistry to medicine are recounted in Julius Stieglitz, *Chemistry and Recent Progress in Medicine* (Balt., 1924), and by a group of experts, many of whom have themselves made history, in Julius Stieglitz, ed., *Chemistry in Medicine* (N. Y., 1928). On medical history the most complete study is F. H. Garrison, *An Introduction to the History of Medicine* (3d edn., Phila., 1924), although there are smaller histories such as J. G. Mumford, *A Narrative of Medicine in America* (Phila., 1903). Special phases are treated in S. A. Knopf, *A History of the National Tuberculosis Association* (N. Y., 1922), which should be supplemented by E. L. Trudeau, *An Autobiography* (Garden City, 1916); Benjamin Harrow, *Vitamines* (N. Y., 1921); George Dock and C. C. Bass, *Hookworm Disease* (St. Louis, 1900); and S. B. Wolback, J. L. Todd and F. W. Palfrey, *The Etiology and Pathology of Typhus* (Cambridge, 1922).

The advance in the profession of nursing is narrated in Lavinia L. Dock, *A History of Nursing* (4 vols., N. Y., 1912). For public health and its administration the following are important: M. J. Rosenau, *Preventive Medicine and Hygiene* (N. Y., 1917); H. H. Moore, *Public Health in the United States* (N. Y., 1923); R. D. Leigh, *Federal Health Administration in the United States* (N. Y., 1927); J. A. Tobey, *The National Government and Public Health* (Balt., 1926); and M. P. Ravenel, ed. *A Half Century of Public Health* (N. Y., 1921). The discovery of the cause of yellow fever is popularly told in Paul De Kruif, *Microbe Hunters* (N. Y., 1920). The cleaning up of Panama is recounted officially in the *Annual Reports* of the Isthmian Canal Commission and informally in W. C. Gorgas, *Sanitation in Panama* (N. Y., 1915).

No social science has been surveyed with the same thoroughness as has history in H. E. Barnes, *The New History and the Social Studies* (N. Y., 1925), but the others have been sketched in brief but scholarly fashion by various experts in H. E. Barnes, ed., *The History and Prospects of the Social Sciences* (N. Y., 1925), and in E. C. Hayes, ed., *Recent Developments in the Social Sciences* (Phila., 1927). The newer tendencies are emphasized in W. F. Ogburn and A. A. Goldenweiser, *The Social Sciences and Their Interrelations* (Boston, 1927), and Wilson Gee, ed., *Research in the Social Sciences* (N. Y., 1929). On some of the great figures of the period, read H. W. Odum, ed., *Masters of Social Science* (N. Y., 1927).

LITERATURE AND THE FINE ARTS

LITERATURE: Historical treatment of recent American literature is as yet somewhat scanty; but F. L. Pattee, *The Development of the American Short Story* (N. Y., 1923), and his *The New American Literature* [1890-1930] (N. Y., 1930) are reasonably full, and much that is useful may be found in W. P. Trent and others, eds., *The Cambridge History of American Literature* (4 vols., N. Y., 1917-1921). Surveys have also been written by J. L. Haney, *The Story of Our Literature* (N. Y., 1923), and by Carl and Mark Van Doren, *American and British Literature since 1890* (N. Y., 1925). For poetry Louis Untermeyer, *American Poetry since 1900* (N. Y., 1923), and his *Modern American Poetry* (rev. edn., N. Y., 1925) are valuable. For statistics on the classes of books published, see F. E. Woodward, *A Graphic Survey of Book Publication, 1890-1916* (U. S. Bur. of Educ., *Bull. for 1917*, no. 14). Brilliantly executed books of literary criticism covering the work of recent years include P. H. Boynton, *Some Contemporary Americans* (Chicago, 1924), and his *More Contemporary Americans* (Chicago, 1927); S. P. Sherman, *On Contemporary Literature* (N. Y., 1917); and H. L. Mencken, *Book of Prefaces* (Garden City, 1927). Longer appraisals of modern American authors are in the *Modern American Writers* series, which includes B. R. Redman, *Edwin Arlington Robinson* (N. Y., 1926); Burton Rascoe, *Theodore Dreiser* (N. Y., 1925); and R. M. Lovett, *Edith Wharton* (N. Y., 1925). O. W. Firkins, *William Dean Howells* (Cambridge, 1924), is a scholarly study.

MUSIC: Recent musical history in America is traced by Arthur Elson in the last chapter of L. C. Elson, *The National Music of America and Its Sources* (rev. edn., Boston, 1924). A good summary is given in Arthur Farwell and W. D. Dailey, eds., *Music in America* (D. G. Mason, ed., *The Art of Music,* 14 vols., 1915-1917, IV). H. C. Lahee, *Annals of Music in America* (Boston, 1922), is also useful. The interest in Negro music can be traced in such works as Dorothy Scarborough, *On the Trail of Negro Folk Songs* (Cambridge, 1925); H. E. Krehbiel, *Afro-American Folksongs* (N. Y., 1914); J. W. Johnson, *Book of American Negro Spirituals* (N. Y., 1925); and R. N. Deft, *Religious Folk Songs of the Negro as Sung at Hampton Institute* (Hampton, Va., 1927). The story of the more famous symphony orchestras in America is told by M. A. DeWolfe Howe, *The Boston Symphony Orchestra* (Boston, 1914); F. A. Wister, *Twenty-Five Years of the Philadelphia Orchestra, 1900-1925* (Phila., 1925); and C. E. Russell, *The American Orchestra and Theodore Thomas* (Garden City, 1927). The life of the great leader has also been told by his wife, Rose F. Thomas, in *Memoirs of Theodore Thomas* (N. Y., 1911), and by a lifelong friend, G. P. Upton, in *Theodore Thomas* (Chicago, 1905). For American opera, see H. E. Krehbiel, *Chapters of Opera* (N. Y., 1908), and his *More Chapters of Opera* (N. Y., 1919); H. C. Lahee, *The Grand Opera of Today* (Boston, 1912), containing accounts of the Boston and Philadelphia enterprises; and E. E. Hipsher, *American Opera and Its Composers* (Phila., 1927). Much historical material is in John Philip Sousa, *Marching Along,* and Rudolph Aronson, *Theatrical and Musical Memoirs,* both mentioned earlier. For popular songs, see C. K. Harris, *After the Ball* (N. Y., 1926); Sigmund Spaeth, *Read 'Em and Weep* (Garden City, 1926), and his *Weep Some More, My Lady* (Garden City, 1927).

GRAPHIC ART: Samuel Isham, *The History of American Painting* (N. Y., 1905), has been brought down to date in a new edition completed by Royal Cortissoz (N. Y., 1927). Unfortunately C. H. Caffin, *The Story of American Painting* (N. Y., 1907), closes too early for the newer developments. E. H. Blashfield, *Mural Painting in America* (N. Y., 1913), is a critical survey by a successful exponent, and Frank Weitenkampf, *American Graphic Art* (N. Y., 1912), contains a history of the various forms of illustrative art. Of the many books treating American painters and illustrators of the period the following are among the best: J. C. Van Dyke, *American Painting* (N. Y., 1919); A. E. Gallatin, *Certain Contemporaries* (N. Y., 1926); J. W. McSpadden, *Famous Painters of America* (N. Y., 1916); and Royal Cortissoz, *American Artists* (N. Y., 1923).

SCULPTURE AND ARCHITECTURE: For American sculpture Lorado Taft, *History of American Sculpture* (rev. edn., 1924), written by a great teacher and sculptor, and C. H. Caffin, *American Masters of Sculpture* (N. Y., 1903), are standard works. The volume by Joseph Hudnut, *American Sculpture* (N. Y., 1929), is notable not only for its competent criticism but also for its literary style, while J. W. McSpadden, *Famous Sculptors of America* (N. Y., 1924), is founded largely on personal acquaintance. Three recent histories bring out clearly the trends in architecture during the period: T. E. Tallmadge, *The Story of Architecture in America* (N. Y., 1927); Fiske Kimball, *American Architecture* (Indianapolis, 1928); and G. H. Edgell, *The American Architecture of To-day* (N. Y., 1928). For skyscrapers these should be supplemented by W. A. Starrett, *Skyscrapers and the Men Who Build Them* (N. Y., 1928).

SPORTS AND RECREATIONS

PARKS AND PLAYGROUNDS: An excellent introduction to the problem of urban recreation is C. M. Robinson, *The Improvement of Towns and Cities* (4th edn., N. Y., 1913). The revived interest in parks brought out a number of studies and reports, including George Burnap, *Parks, Their Design, Equipment and Use* (Phila., 1916); L. F. Hanmer, *Public Recreation: a Study of Parks, Playgrounds and Other Outdoor Recreation Facilities* (N. Y., 1928); and, most valuable of all, L. H. Weir, ed., *Parks, a Manual of Municipal and County Parks* (2 vols., N. Y., 1928). See also articles on "Recreational Facilities" in the *Annals* of the American Academy of Political and Social Science, XXXV, no. 2. Important for city playgrounds are C. E. Rainwater, *The Play*

Movement in the United States (Chicago, 1922); H. S. Curtis, *The Play Movement and Its Significance* (N. Y., 1917); and the *Proceedings* of the Annual Playground Congresses (N. Y., 1908-), published by the Playground Association of America.

SPORTS: A summary of much recent development is in E. A. Rice, *A Brief History of Physical Education* (N. Y., 1924). Most of the information in regard to golf is to be found in the personal memoirs of leading players: J. D. Travers and J. R. Crowell, *The Fifth Estate, Thirty Years of Golf* (N. Y., 1926), by a champion whose career included almost the whole history of American golf; J. D. Travers, *Travers' Golf Book* (N. Y., 1913); Charles Evans, jr., *Chick Evans' Golf Book* (Chicago, 1921); and Andra Kirkaldy, *Fifty Years of Golf: My Memories* (London, 1921). For tennis, see A. W. Myers, ed., *Lawn Tennis at Home and Abroad* (London, 1903), and A. F. Wilding, *On the Court and Off* (N. Y., 1913). In football, as in golf, one is largely dependent upon biographical material. The life of the greatest of the football figures is given in Harford Powel, jr., *Walter Camp, the Father of American Football* (Boston, 1926), an authorized biography. Also to be noted are W. H. Edwards, *Football Days* (N. Y., 1916); A. A. Stagg and W. W. Stout, *Touchdown* (N. Y., 1927), giving the reminiscences of Stagg; and P. D. Haughton, *Football and How to Watch It* (Boston, 1922). P. H. Davis, *Football* (N. Y., 1911), and A. M. Weyand, *American Football* (N. Y., 1926), are both historical.

Yacht racing is treated in W. P. Stephens, *American Yachting* (N. Y., 1904); H. L. Stone, *The "America's" Cup Races* (London, n.d.); W. D. Bowman, *Yachting and Yachtsmen* (N. Y., 1927); and W. M. Thompson, W. P. Stephens and W. U. Swan, *The Yacht "America"* (Boston, 1925). For the Olympic games, consult T. A. Cook, *International Sport* (London, 1910), a short history of the movement from 1896 to 1908 with valuable appendices. A popular but comprehensive story of professional boxing in America is Alexander Johnston, *Ten—and Out* (N. Y., 1927), which should be supplemented by J. J. Corbett, *The Roar of the Crowd* (N. Y., 1927), and Jack Johnson, *Jack Johnson in the Ring—and Out* (Chicago, 1927). On baseball, chiefly professional, A. G. Spalding, *America's National Game* (N. Y., 1911); F. C. Richter, *Richter's History and Records of Baseball* (Phila., 1914); and E. J. Lannigan, *Baseball Cyclopedia* (N. Y., 1922), contain historical data, but these should likewise be supplemented by J. J. McGraw, *My Thirty Years in Baseball* (N. Y., 1923), and J. J. Evers and H. S. Fullerton, *Touching Second* (Chicago, 1910).

THE MOTION PICTURE: The most thorough description of the early years of the moving picture is F. A. Talbot, *Moving Pictures* (Phila., 1912), and perhaps the best brief résumé is B. J. Lubschez, *The Story of the Motion Picture* (N. Y., 1920). For the business aspect, see W. M. Seabury, *The Public and the Motion Picture Industry* (N. Y., 1926), and for a psychological approach, Hugo Münsterberg, *The Photoplay, a Psychological Study* (N. Y., 1916). The reminiscences of picture players are beginning to appear, *e.g.*, W. S. Hart, *My Life East and West* (Boston, 1929).

THE STAGE: For the legitimate drama Arthur Hornblow, *A History of the Theatre in America* (2 vols., Phila., 1919), covers the recent years briefly, and A. H. Quinn, *A History of the American Drama* (2 vols., N. Y., 1927), more fully. A good picture of the American theater at the opening of the century is given in Norman Hapgood, *The Stage in America, 1897-1900* (N. Y., 1901), and much interest attaches to the reminiscences of the veteran critic, William Winter, in *Other Days* (N. Y., 1928), and *The Wallet of Time* (2 vols., N. Y., 1913). Interpretations of new tendencies are W. L. Phelps, *The Twentieth Century Theatre* (N. Y., 1918); Archibald Henderson, *The Changing Drama* (N. Y., 1914); and O. M. Sayles, *Our American Theatre* (N. Y., 1913). Several have told the story of the little-theater movement: Constance D'Arcy Mackay, *The Little Theatre in the United States* (N. Y., 1917); Sheldon Cheney, *The New Movement in the Theatre* (N. Y., 1914);

and Louise Burleigh, *The Community Theatre* (Boston, 1917). M. J. Moses, *The American Dramatist* (rev. edn., Boston, 1925), has chapters on Belasco, Fitch and other dramatists of the day. Entertaining but of varying historical value are the reminiscences of Broadway stars, some of which are listed in the section on Personal Material. American vaudeville and its stars are pleasantly discussed by Caroline Coffin in *Vaudeville* (N. Y., 1914); and the declining minstrel show in Dailey Paskman and Sigmund Spaeth, *"Gentlemen, Be Seated!"* (Garden City, 1928), and Carl Wittke, *Tambo and Bones: a History of the American Minstrel Stage* (Durham, N. C., 1930). An excellent résumé of American pageantry with descriptions of several pageants held during these years is in Robert Withington, *English Pageantry* (2 vols., Cambridge, Mass., 1918-1920), II, chap. ix.

INDEX

From the Depths

At the beginning of the twentieth century America was stirred by many cries for social reform.

They See the Promised Land

The invasion of Europe by American trusts.

From the office of J. Pierpont Morgan lines of influence ran around the world.

Big Business at Home and Abroad

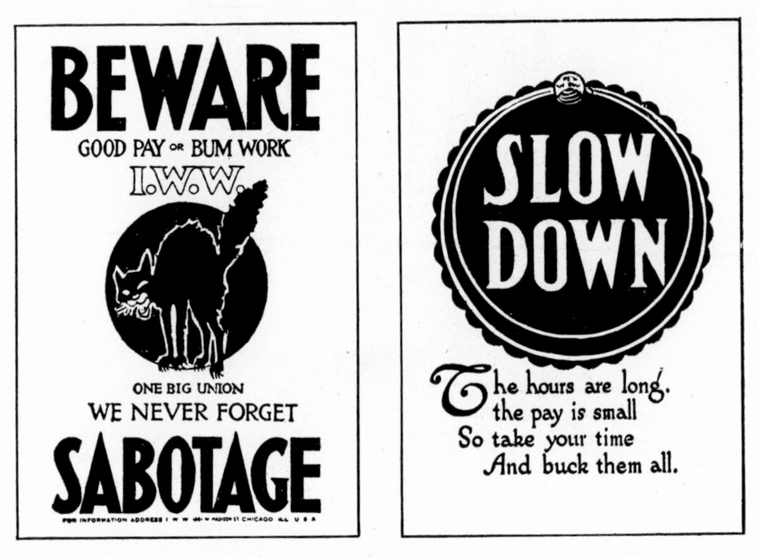

Propaganda stickers of the I. W. W.

Eviction during the coal strike of 1902.

The Wars of Labor

Debs and Bryan thought Roosevelt's Progressivism scarcely original.

Tom L. Johnson preaching reform in Cleveland.

Social Politics

Ida M. Tarbell,
author of
The History of
the Standard Oil
Company,
etc.
*
*

Lincoln Steffens,
author of
The Shame
of the
Cities,
etc.
*
*
*

Orville and Wilbur Wright at Kitty Hawk, North Carolina, December, 1903.

Man Flies

Old-law shaft before 1901.

New-law court after 1901.

Legislation brought light and air to the poor in New York.

A neat simplicity supplanted stuffiness in the homes of the "middle class."

Homes

The ideal American girl in the first years of the twentieth century was both active and statuesque.

The Queen

Child labor, as in this Pennsylvania glassworks, was roundly condemned.

Municipal playgrounds were established as a substitute for the country child's open fields and woodlands.

Children

John Dewey

The burning evangelism of "Billy" Sunday contrasted with

the cool serenity of Christian Science symbolized in the Mother Church.

Religious Forces

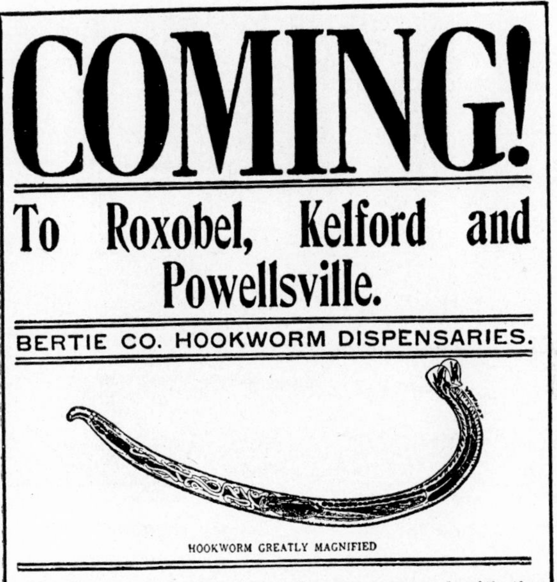

COMING!

To Roxobel, Kelford and Powellsville.

BERTIE CO. HOOKWORM DISPENSARIES.

HOOKWORM GREATLY MAGNIFIED

The County Commissioners have so arranged with the North Carolina Board of Health that the towns of Roxobel, Kelford and Powellsville will secure the services of The State and County Free Hookworm Dispensaries.

Dr. Covington, a state specialist on these diseases, and Mr. Conner, an expert microscopist, will be in attendance at these dispensaries on the days and dates printed below.

Everybody should visit these dispensaries on the dates given below, be examined and see if they have any of these diseases. If you have, medicine will be given that will change you from a tired, indolent, despondent kind of a man to one who goes about his work with a vim and a rush, always finding pleasure in everything. Ask any of the thousands who have already been treated in this county. They know. All this without any cost to you whatever. All is paid for by the state and county. Come, bring your wife and children with you, let them see the different varieties of worms that often infect people. See the hookworm eggs under the microscope and hear talks on this disease.

Remember the dates as this will be your last opportunity to be examined and treated free of all cost.

In visiting the dispensaries do not neglect to bring with you a very small box on which you have written your name and age containing a small specimen of your bowel movement as only in this way can an examination be made. In making this examination, if present, any of the worms are found, whether it be the tape worm, round worm, or any of the other various varieties.

A Poster Used in the Anti-Hookworm Campaign in North Carolina

Sargent's portrait of Chase.

Gutzon Borglum's "Mares of Diomedes."

Vigorous Romanticism in Art

"Put up your swords or draw them on Mary Tudor, the sister of your King!"
A scene from When Knighthood Was In Flower.

Historical Romance on the Stage

© Life

A cartoonist's view of the Philippines. Liberty: "Stop this bloody work, Sam. He is the one who is fighting for me."

The J. Fenimore Cooper School at Sabana Grande, Porto Rico, typical of the new American régime.

Two Aspects of Imperialism